Óscar Romero's Theological Vision

EDGARDO COLÓN-EMERIC

Óscar Romero's Theological Vision

Liberation and the Transfiguration of the Poor

UNIVERSITY OF NOTRE DAME PRESS

NOTRE DAME, INDIANA

University of Notre Dame Press
Notre Dame, Indiana 46556
undpress.nd.edu

Published in the United States of America

Library of Congress Cataloging-in-Publication Data

Names: Colon-Emeric, Edgardo Antonio, 1968– author.
Title: Oscar Romero's theological vision : liberation and the transfiguration
of the poor / Edgardo Antonio Colon-Emeric.
Description: Notre Dame : University of Notre Dame Press, 2018. |
Includes bibliographical references and index. |
Identifiers: LCCN 2018043823 (print) | LCCN 2018044729 (ebook) |
ISBN 9780268104757 (pdf) | ISBN 9780268104764 (epub) | ISBN
9780268104733 (hardback : alk. paper) | ISBN 0268104735 (hardback :
alk. paper)
Subjects: LCSH: Romero, Óscar A. (Oscar Arnulfo), 1917–1980. |
El Salvador—Church history—20th century. | Liberation theology.
Classification: LCC BX4705.R669 (ebook) | LCC BX4705.R669 C65 2018
(print) | DDC 230/.2092—dc23
LC record available at https://lccn.loc.gov/2018043823

To Cathleen, Lito, y Benben

And to my *hermanas y hermanos* in Central America

Cristo vive. De verdad vive.

CONTENTS

ACKNOWLEDGMENTS

For the past few years, Romero has been a constant companion. I have had his image before me as I read scripture and pray. The downloaded audio files of his homilies have been playing in my ears as I have gone running on trails. The altar on which he was killed has time and again been a place where I have recommitted my life and scholarship to Jesus. And yet, a Puerto Rican, Methodist clergyperson like myself writing a book about a Salvadoran Catholic martyred bishop is not an obvious combination. An acknowledgment of the oddity of this occurrence is in order by way of testimony and thanksgiving.

I first heard of Óscar Romero when I attended a Jesuit high school in Puerto Rico. The priests who taught there were very attuned to the situation in Central America, and they shared with us news about what was happening in these countries during the late 1970s and early '80s. When the Paulist film *Romero* hit the screens in 1989, I went to see it. The actor who played the role of Romero, Raul Julia, had actually graduated from my high school. The release of this film was followed by the tragic news of the assassination of the Jesuit priests at the University of Central America. The convergence of these events marked me and contributed to my eventual abandonment of engineering studies in favor of the study of theology.

When I joined the theology faculty at Duke Divinity School in 2007, I decided to organize a Spanish reading group. I was not sure what we would read until I ran into one of the prospective members for this group in the library. There, while I was talking amid the stacks of books, my eyes fell upon a collection of Romero's homilies. The idea was born for a Romero Reading Group. We met every Wednesday to read and discuss in Spanish (and Spanglish) Romero's homily for the lectionary texts of the week. The hours that we spent with these homilies made a very strong impression on all of us. My students and I were struck by the paradoxes of this prelate's teaching and way of life: a patriotic prophet, a lover of the poor and the popes, a plain priest and a powerful preacher. The more we read, the more we were humbled and inspired by the transparency of Romero's witness to Christ. The only constant in seminary is change. Students come and students go, and the Romero Reading Group would peter out after a few years, but Romero's words found fertile ground in many of us. In some of my students those seeds sprouted into essays, lectures, and even dissertations on Romero. In my case, those seeds eventually became this book, but for that to happen they needed to dig root in Salvadoran soil.

I traveled to El Salvador in the winter of 2007 to lay the groundwork for future seminary student pilgrimages in Central America. It was then that I visited the *Hospitalito* where Romero lived as archbishop and died as a martyr. Little did I know that this pilgrimage site would become such a central part of my professional and spiritual pilgrimage. Through a peculiar chain of events in 2010 I became the director of a program for forming Methodist pastors for churches in Central America. Since then, Romero's theology and the pilgrimage sites associated with his story (the *Hospitalito*, the UCA, the cathedral, and El Paisnal, to name a few) have become integrated into the curriculum of the program, the spiritual formation of teachers and students, and my research questions. Romero's episcopal motto of *Sentir con la iglesia* (To sense with the church) became the motto for the graduates of our Central American program and one of the pillars of my vision for theological education. More than that, the witness of the Methodists in Central America convinced me that the legacy of Romero is so rich that it overflows the Catholic Church itself.

In December 2015, the students of the Methodist Course of Study in Central America visited the town of Juayúa in El Salvador. The central plaza had been the site of a mass execution of persons of indigenous ancestry in 1932. The church on the western side of the plaza is known as the Church of the Black Christ on account of the larger-than-life black-skinned crucified Jesus that hangs behind and above the altar. The locals say that the statue was carved out of dark wood by Franciscan missionaries in the sixteenth century in their effort to decolonialize the gospel by making Christ look more like the people who lived in the region. However, more recent studies have punctured holes in the missionary story. The wood for Jesus was at first a light wood. Centuries of chemical interaction between the wood and the smoke from burning candles have darkened the color of the crucified Jesus. In the church, the Central American students engaged in an exercise of *lectio divina*. At the foot of the *Cristo Negro*, they read the story of the transfiguration several times and reflected on questions like: *Is it good for us to be here? What do you see when you look at this Christ transfigured into black? Do you think that the Father is well pleased in this representation of his son? What do you feel? Fear? Confusion? How does Jesus tell you to respond? Do you see the glory of Christ in this face? Do you find liberation in this image? The appearance of Jesus changed while he was praying. How has the appearance of Jesus's face changed in response to your prayers? What would you tell people about what you have seen in this place?* Later we had a time to reflect on what we had felt. Some of my students interpreted this representation as misguided. Jesus was not black. And why do we look for him on the cross? He is not dead; he is risen. Others interpreted it as good news. Jesus clothes himself in dark skin because dark-skinned people have suffered for centuries in this part of the world. In effect, the piety of the people decolonialized Jesus. The more they prayed, the more his skin darkened. The encounter in Juayúa sparked my thinking on the theme of this book. Whether in dusky black or dazzling white, the transfiguration of Christ upsets our expectations regarding the identity of the Son of God. This is the reason why Óscar Romero's theological vision could not help but be a scandal to some even as it was good news to many.

After Juayúa, I developed the themes of transfiguration further through presentations at the Festival of Homiletics in Atlanta (spring 2016), the Glory of God Conference in Durham University (summer 2016), and the Romero Days Conference at the University of Notre Dame (2017). As I worked on these papers and presentations, I began to understand the way in which the study of this Central American Catholic priest confirmed the vocation of a Puerto Rican Methodist theologian. Everything is received according to the mode of the

Intercessor

receiver, says Thomas Aquinas, and the clearer my vision of Romero became, the more evident the parallels with John Wesley. Both are exemplars of what in Methodist academic circles is referred to as practical divinity. Both are interested in a theological vision that is popular, pastoral, and prophetic. The more I understood Romero's theological vision and sought to live in accordance to it, the more authentically Methodist my witness to Christ became.

The narration of how this book came to be shows that it is not my work alone. The journey from watching a Romero movie to writing a Romero book has been long, but it has been good because I have enjoyed good companionship along the way. I am grateful to the editorial staff at the University of Notre Dame Press for their special attention and support from the initial proposal in the fall of 2016 to the editing, formatting, and printing of 2018.

I am grateful to the members of the Romero Reading Group, in particular to Ismael Ruiz-Millan, who lives and leads in the spirit of Romero, and Matthew Whelan, whose courageous dissertation on Romero and agrarian reform convinced me of the importance and viability of a monograph focused on the teaching of Romero. I am also grateful to the research assistants who have supported my work on this project: Justin Ashworth, Katie Benjamin, Mandy Rodgers-Gates, and Alberto La Rosa for their help with gathering materials, talking through arguments, and reading drafts.

I am grateful to the Salvadoran Methodists, especially to Juan de Dios, Marta Landaverde, Emerson Castillo, Ana Cristina Perez, and Adela Samayoa for their friendship and their example of Christian discipleship. In a mysterious way, they are among the fruits that have grown from the grain of wheat that was Romero.

I am especially grateful to my wife, Cathleen, and to my children Nate and Ben. They have had to put up with the many days and nights spent away from home in Central America and with my long talks about Romero. Without their patience, love, and, of course, gentle ribbing, this book would not have been possible. More than that, they always help me to recalibrate my priorities and rediscover the joy and value of my vocation as husband and father.

Finally, I am grateful to God. Scripture says that "every perfect gift, is from above, coming down from the Father of lights" (James 1:17). Romero was such a gift, an exemplar of what John Wesley referred to as Christian perfection, the perfect love of God and neighbor. By the time you read this book, Óscar Romero will have been canonized. Blessed Óscar Romero will be San Óscar. The fact that a saint grew up in the land of El Salvador gives the lie to those who think that the only thing that this country offers the world is gangs. Sadly, the raising of the archbishop to the altars takes place in a context as polarized, unjust, and violent as it ever has been. Yet although the canonization will not bring peace, the declaration of Romero as a saint is an affirmation of faith: God is not finished with Romero yet. The gift of Monseñor Romero keeps on giving. For those who are willing to receive this gift, Romero still has power to speak and move. My hope is that more of us will be moved to work for a prophetic peace and a liberating reconciliation in our land and around the world. God willing. *Primero Dios.*

March 24, 2018
Feast of Óscar Romero

Diario	Óscar Romero, *Mons. Óscar A. Romero: Su diario* (San Salvador: Imprenta Criterio, 2000).
Evangelii Nuntiandi	Pope Paul VI, *Evangelii Nuntiandi*, December 8, 1975, http://w2.vatican.va/content/paul-vi /en/apost_exhortations/documents/hf_p-vi _exh_19751208_evangelii-nuntiandi.html.
Gaudium et Spes	Second Vatican Council, *Gaudium et Spes*, December 7, 1965, www.vatican.va/archive /hist_councils/ii_vatican_council/documents /vat-ii_const_19651207_gaudium-et-spes_en.html.
Homilías	Óscar Romero, *Homilías: Monseñor Óscar A. Romero*, ed. Miguel Cavada Diez, 6 vols. (San Salvador: UCA Editores, 2005–9).
Lumen Gentium	Pope Paul VI, *Lumen Gentium*, November 21, 1964, www.vatican.va/archive/hist_councils /ii_vatican_council/documents/vat-ii_const _19641121_lumen-gentium_en.html.
Medellín	Conferencia II, Medellin, in *Las Cinco Conferencias Generales del Episcopado Latinoamericano*, ed. Consejo Episcopal Latinoamericano (Bogotá: Ediciones Paulinas, 2014).
Populorum Progressio	Pope Paul VI, *Populorum Progressio: Encyclical on the Development of Peoples*, March 26, 1967, http:// w2.vatican.va/content/paul-vi/en/encyclicals /documents/hf_p-vi_enc_26031967_populorum .html.

Puebla	Conferencia III, Puebla, in *Las Cinco Conferencias Generales del Episcopado Latinoamericano*, ed. Consejo Episcopal Latinoamericano (Bogotá: Ediciones Paulinas, 2014).
Sacrosanctum Concilium	Second Vatican Council, *Sacrosanctum Concilium*, December 4, 1963, www.vatican.va/archive /hist_councils/ii_vatican_council/documents /vat-ii_const_19631204_sacrosanctum-concilium _en.html.
ST	Thomas Aquinas, *The Summa Theologica of St. Thomas Aquinas*, trans. Fathers of the English Dominican Province (Allen, TX: Christian Classics, 1948).
Voz	Óscar Romero, *La voz de los sin voz: La palabra viva de Monseñor Romero*, ed. Rodolfo Cardenal, Ignacio Martín-Baro, and Jon Sobrino (San Salvador: UCA Editores, 1980).

INTRODUCTION
TO A SCANDAL

While studying theology in Rome, Óscar Romero frequented the streets in the vicinity of St. Peter's Basilica where poor people were to be found. After one such visit, on Christmas Eve 1941, Romero wrote in his journal, "The poor are the incarnation of Christ. Through their rags, . . . the loving soul discovers and worships Christ." Not everyone can see this image. Privilege, ideology, and prejudice have become something like a second nature: a thick veil that prevents our seeing the light of Christ shining from the lives of social outcasts. Saint Paul is right that the "the god of this world has blinded the minds of unbelievers" (2 Cor. 4:5) and, one must add, of believers too! Humanity needs to learn again to see, and for this reason, Romero believes, the world needs the church. It is on the mountain that is the church that the veil of shame that shrouds peoples in darkness is torn off.[2] But a blind church is of no use to a blind world. The church too needs to learn to see again. It needs to learn to see Christ's glory in the "faces of *campesinos* without land . . . the faces of workers fired without cause, without enough wages to maintain their homes; the faces of the elderly; the faces of the marginalized; the faces of people dwelling in slums; the faces of children who are poor and who from their childhood begin to feel the cruel bite of social injustice" (*Homilías* 6:346).³ For Monseñor Romero, a privileged place of encounter with the glory of Christ is on the mountain that tradition knows as Tabor, the Mount of Transfiguration. The light of the transfigured Christ has the power to transform the flesh of the poor into an icon of glory and to open the eyes of the blind to behold this glory and be changed.

Seeing the glory of God in the face of the poor of Jesus Christ can be costly. In his final Sunday homily on March 23, 1980, Romero offered his congregation a narration of the most noteworthy events in the life of the archdiocese. There was nothing unusual about this. It was his custom to weave church announcements in with the proclamation of the gospel. On that particular Sunday, he gave them a sneak preview of a hymn recently composed by Guillermo Cuéllar in honor of the Divine Savior of the World, the patron of El Salvador (*Homilías*, 6:445). The hymn would be sung as the *Gloria* for the *Misa salvadoreña.*

> Vibran los cantos explosivos de alegría,
> Voy a reunirme con mi pueblo en catedral.
> Miles de voces nos unimos este día
> Para cantar en nuestra fiesta patronal.
>
> ———
>
> The songs resound full of joy,
> I am gathering with my people at the cathedral.
> Thousands of voices join together on this day
> To sing on this our patron feast.

The lyrics describe the people of God gathering in San Salvador to celebrate the Feast of the Transfiguration on August 6. Romero says that he particularly likes the final stanza.

> Pero los dioses del poder y del dinero
> Se oponen a que haya transfiguración.
> Por eso ahora vos, Señor, sos el primero
> En levantar tu brazo contra la opresión.
>
> ———

> But the gods of power and of money
> Are opposed to there being transfiguration.
> This is why you, oh Lord, are the first one
> To raise your arm against oppression.

The following afternoon the servants of the gods named by Cuéllar assassinated the archbishop. Why? Preaching at the death of other martyrs, Romero himself offered an explanation: "Why are they killed? They are killed because they are obstacles." (*Homilías*, 5:354). He got in the way of those who saw El Salvador as their hacienda and worked hard to keep its citizens as their peons. To put it another way, Romero's message was a scandal. The Greek word *skandalon* refers to a stumbling block, something that gets in the way. One can be scandalized when seeing someone fall or when stumbling oneself. The reaction to the fall may be infantile, or pharisaical, or just.[4] The term *scandal* can be used to name not only the taking of offense but the giving of it, the cause of the stumbling. The scandal can come from an enemy who sets traps that impede another's progress in life. Poverty is a scandal in this sense. Poverty is the stumbling block along the way of life for the majority of people in El Salvador. From the country's conquest in the sixteenth century to the genocides of the twentieth, poverty has been one of the distinctive marks of El Salvador. Years of misguided rule by a powerful oligarchy who saw themselves as the owners of El Salvador led to a massively unequal and unjust distribution of land and goods in the country. In the time of Romero, 60 percent of the rural population owned no land and 90 percent lacked the means for daily sustenance. "Land hunger" and food hunger were the lot of the people of El Salvador.[5] The scandal of poverty gave rise to the scandal of violence as the oligarchy colluded with the government to block all attempts at agrarian reform. In the infamous *Matanza* of 1932, the government ordered the military to repress an insurrectionist movement demanding land reform in the western part of the country. The result was the slaughter (*matanza*) of roughly 2 percent of the national population. Since most of those killed were of indigenous descent, the *Matanza* was in effect an act of genocide. It is because of the *Matanza* that El Salvador lacks a sizable indigenous population today. In El Salvador, obstacles to the progress of the people seem to always be popping up. Like the mythical hydra, the enemy who set these obstacles has many heads (the Salvadoran oligarchy, the US military, the multinationals, the powers and principalities, etc.) but has caused one scandalous result—the death of Salvadorans.

The scandal can also come from God, whose landmarks on the way to salvation can trip up those walking on the way that perishes. The means that God employs to turn humanity from death to life can give offense. Like Paul, Romero knows that the cross cannot fail to provoke a crisis (*Homilías*, 3:215). The Transfiguration is a scandal in this sense. Mount Tabor shocks the sensibilities of the wayfarer. It presents a vision of glory that can be attained only through the Passion. As it points forward to the cross, the vision of the transfigured humanity of Jesus issues an imperative to all human beings. Do not be conformed to this world. Do not settle for mediocrities. Be transformed. The Transfiguration is a scandal for the pusillanimous who dismiss its promises as pie in the sky. It is also a scandal for the pharisaical. Tabor threatens to upset an order in which many have a vested interest. The scandal of the Transfiguration has political dimensions. It sheds light on a world where glory comes from humility and not from power and privilege. From the heights of Mount Tabor, the glory of God shines forth more from the sore-covered flesh of Lazarus than from the sumptuous lifestyle of the rich man. In brief, the scandal of the Transfiguration is succinctly stated in Romero's aphorism *Gloria Dei, vivens pauper,* "The glory of God is the living poor."

ÓSCAR ROMERO, A FATHER
OF THE LATIN AMERICAN CHURCH

Who was Óscar Romero? Many excellent biographies have been written about him.[7] Indeed, it may seem that stories of his life, especially of his time as archbishop, are about all that has been written about him. In a way, this is quite understandable. The 1970s and '80s marked a dramatic time for people in Central America. Vast income inequality, failed attempts at land reform, and rumors of a Cuban-style revolution contributed to a shifting social landscape. Some expected the church to serve as a bastion of national stability, while others dreamed of a Christian guerrilla movement. In this context, the choice of Romero for the country's premier ecclesial post was greeted with dismay by some and relief by others. However, both reactions misread the man and the moment. Days after his installation, on March 12, 1977, his friend Father Rutilio Grande and two companions (Manuel Solórzano and Nelson Lemus) were murdered while driving to El Paisnal. Some of Romero's biographers refer to this moment as his conversion. The road to El Paisnal was Romero's road to Damascus. The sight of those three corpses turned the conservative, timid, bookish bishop into a flaming prophet. Romero himself preferred to speak of the transformation caused by the sight of these bodies not as a conversion but as a growing awareness of what the Lord required of an archbishop in the current context.[8] Be that as it may, the death of Rutilio Grande left a deep impression on Romero's ministry as archbishop. It placed Romero's service as archbishop under the sign of martyrdom. There was now no doubt about it; he was the pastor of a persecuted church. The murder of Grande was followed by the murders of Alfonso Navarro (May 11, 1977), Ernesto Barrera (November 28, 1977), Octavio Ortíz (January 20, 1979), Rafael Palacios (July 20, 1979), and Alirio Macías (August 4, 1979), to name only the priests. In lieu of another biography of his life, I offer here titles collated from the tradition responsible for his memory *Romerismo*. The plaque that hangs on the wall of the house where he lived during his time as archbishop features titles like "prophet," "martyr," and "saint." But the tradition of Romero has also included other lesser-known titles like "son of the church" and "father of the church."[9] Before we examine these, it may be helpful to say a few words about how the tradition of Romero grew.

Romerismo began during the years when Romero served as archbishop.[10] Its main sources were the pulpit, the road, and the office. In life, most people encountered Romero through his homilies. The overflowing crowds at the cathedral and the unprecedented radio audience projected his voice far beyond that of the typical priest or even archbishop. The tradition of Romero grew not only from the memory of his word but from the personal encounters that many had with him. Romero visited the cantons and poor communities of his archdiocese with greater frequency than what was canonically required or customary. There Romero experienced firsthand the conditions of his people, and the people saw their archbishop walking in their midst. The archbishopric also contributed to development of *Romerismo*. During his tenure in San Salvador, the thresholds to the archdiocesan offices were crossed by people looking for help in finding relatives who had disappeared or in seeking justice for someone who had been abused or killed. They found in Romero a compassionate shepherd and a fierce defender of his flock. In sum, even before he was murdered people had a rich collection of memories and experiences of Romero. Immediately after his death, the pieces of *Romerismo* began to be assembled in a mosaic. In the homily at the funeral mass of March 25, 1980, Ricardo Urioste, vicar general for the archbishop, cried in lament, "They killed our father; they killed our pastor; they killed our guide."[11] Urioste went on to speak of Romero as "a man of deep faith, deep prayer, and constant communion with God."[12] He might have been "accused of being a blasphemer, a disturber of the public order, an agitator of the masses," and derided as "Marxnulfo Romero" (Arnulfo was his middle name), but to the clergy and religious of his archdiocese his martyrdom was the capstone on "the life of a prophet, a pastor, a father of all Salvadorans, especially the neediest."[13] A biographical sketch published a week after his death describes him in the following manner: "He was truly a pastor, a prophet, a friend, a brother, and a father to the entire Salvadoran people, especially to the poorest, weakest, and most marginalized among them. He was the voice of the voiceless . . . . He was a man of prayer; only in this way can his strength in the face of so much adversity be understood. . . . A man of great human quality; he knew how to receive people; how to discover their worth."[14] The rich heritage glimpsed in these descriptions went underground at his burial.[15] For the next three years after Romero's death, the church hierarchy kept silent about its martyred leader. Remembrances of the anniversary of his death at the *Hospitalito*, the cancer hospice center where he lived and died, were low-key affairs. The name of Romero was not spoken in public. His memory survived in family homes and clandestine organizations. Things began to change in 1983 with the visit of John Paul II to El Salvador. The image of the Polish pontiff kneeling before the tomb of the Salvadoran prelate fixed the eyes of the world and El Salvador on a tradition that had been suppressed but not broken. The plaques adorning the grave gave testimony to the ongoing devotion of the people and their gratitude for his intercession on their behalf in life, death, and life beyond death. The pope's unscheduled visit to the cathedral where Romero was buried encouraged *Romerismo* to leave the catacombs and go public. The archdiocesan paper, *Orientación*, published excerpts from Romero's homilies. The University of Central America "José Simeón Cañas" (better known as the UCA) built a chapel in honor of his memory. T-shirts were printed with Romero's face. For most of the 1980s, the most energetic transmitters of *Romerismo* were leftist political organizations. Naturally, the Romero that they transmitted was painted in populist and revolutionary colors. Indeed, concerns about leftist exploitation of the martyred archbishop's memory proved to be one of the main obstacles to the canonization of Romero. → Nothing wrong with that. Though I am

A new stage in *Romerismo* was inaugurated with the signing of the ~ leftist peace accords in 1992. The collapse of the Soviet Union and the end by of the civil war opened the door to a wider diffusion of his memory. Massive celebrations were organized for the anniversaries of his birth (August 15) and death (March 24). These dates became holy days in the calendar of *Romerismo*. Interestingly, the Feast of the Transfiguration (the national feast day when Romero published his pastoral letters) has never been included in this calendar. The growing public acceptance of these celebrations contributed to the consolidation of a geography of *Romerismo*. The *Hospitalito* and the cathedral (and to a far lesser extent his birth home) became places of pilgrimage that drew Catholics and non-Catholics from all over the world. The people who knew Romero became star witnesses in the transmission of this tradition, and formal organizations were constituted for this very purpose.

The latest stage in *Romerismo* was made possible by the official processes of beatification and canonization. In the apostolic proclamation of his beatification, Pope Francis calls Romero a "bishop and martyr, shepherd after the heart of Christ, evangelizer and father of the poor, heroic witness of the kingdom of God, a kingdom of justice, fraternity, and peace."[16] Archbishop Paglia, the biographer for the ceremony, speaks of Romero as a defender of the poor, *defensor pauperum,* like the ancient church fathers."[17] The scholarship that supported the processes and the ceremonies surrounding his beatification gave official sanction to the inherited traditions at the same time that it transformed them by incorporating them into the cult of the church universal.

There are tensions within *Romerismo* that the beatification exposed. Rodolfo Cardenal points to three dueling versions of Romero: the nationalist, the spiritualist, and the liberationist.[18] The Vatican's declaration of the archbishop as martyr forced the government to craft their own version of Romero as national hero. Indeed, all travelers by the departure gates of the Monseñor Óscar Arnulfo Romero International Airport walk past a mural displaying the archbishop in service to the poor. Next to the mural is a plaque with an apology from the government for its complicity in the civil war. Romero in this version of the story is a patriot whose memory promotes national unity in a factious society. By claiming to be inspired by Romero, the government seeks to have some of Romero's aura rub off and lend credibility to its political agenda. Even the news media have seized on Romero's hagiological coattails and promoted his figure widely without accounting for their own role in besmirching his image or explaining the reasons behind their change of attitude. The nationalist version of Romero places him on the high altar of public opinion usually reserved for the founding fathers of El Salvador and the national soccer team. Within the Catholic Church, the process of beatification promoted an image of Romero that in Cardenal's view is overly spiritualized. This version presented a bishop who was pious, compassionate, traditional, and loyal to the magisterium. These features belong to Romero, but a full portrait cannot be painted from them alone. The promoter of the spiritualist version that Cardenal focuses on is Roberto Morozzo della Rocca. For Cardenal, Morozzo's biography of Romero, *Primero Dios,* is defective on many grounds: tendencies to spiritualize Romero, to downplay his conversion, to highlight

[margin note: Much like Dr. King in America]

So a conservative like Morozzo

tensions with liberation theologians and leftist groups, and more. In all, Cardenal charges Morozzo not with poor historiography but with bad ideology. The spiritualist reading of Romero rules out a priori vital aspects of Romero's life in order to make him more palatable to a sector of the church that will never tolerate even this watered-down version of Romero. *Sadly so.*

Finally, there is the liberationist version. For Cardenal, there is no doubt that this is the most authentic version. *Yes!!* "While the institutional church washed its hands of Monseñor Romero, other ecclesial sectors kept his memory alive and cultivated his tradition. The obstinacy of the communities, lay groups, especially, of the women, of several priests, male and female religious, and, in general, of the poor kept alive the memory of the martyred archbishop."[19] Even as Romero belongs to the church universal and to the world, the chief responsibility for safeguarding his memory falls to the Salvadoran Church and in particular to the poor. El Salvador has a long way to go before the jubilant titles attributed to Romero can be spoken without blushing. Romero will be "the saint of all of El Salvador" and a "symbol of peace" when justice is done, forgiveness is asked for, and embrace is offered. "Only then will Monseñor cease being a stone of stumbling and scandal, because he will have become the stone on which is raised an El Salvador that is reconciled with its past and present and opened to the future of the kingdom of God."[20]

This survey of *Romerismo* depicts a living tradition that cannot be reduced to a few slogans or captions. In addition to Romero's written works (homilies, diaries, letters, and newspaper columns) and the testimony of those who knew him, there is a vast production of cultural artifacts that reach a much larger audience than the first two media.[21] Romero's face is visible all over El Salvador in murals, portraits, posters, and T-shirts. His story is told through music of diverse genres, from the classical "Elegía Violeta para Monseñor Romero" to the popular "Corrido a Monseñor Romero." Novels have been written and films have been made about him. It is important to note, in transmitting the story of Romero, that his story is not his alone but also that of the people whom he served and for whom he died. The density and diversity of *Romerismo* are signs of vitality, not incoherence, and do not preclude us from identifying recurring themes. Óscar Romero is a prophet. This is one of the most common and enduring images of him. The song "El profeta," by the musical group Yolocamba-Ita (the same group that wrote the music to the Salvadoran *Gloria* mentioned earlier), paints a vivid picture.[22]

Por esta tierra del hambre
Yo vi pasar a un viajero
Humilde, manso y sincero,
Valientemente profeta,
Que se enfrentó a los tiranos
Para acusarles el crimen
De asesinar a su hermano,
Pa' defender a los ricos.

Throughout this land of hunger
I saw a pilgrim pass by
Humble, meek, and sincere,
Courageously prophetic,
Who confronted the tyrants
To accuse them of the crime
Of murdering their brother
To defend the rich. ⟩ → Yes: Trump and COVID ⟩

In the popular imagination, the act of raising one's voice against the status quo is considered prophetic. A prophet is someone who speaks truth to power. Romero fits the popular mold, but he overflows it because he is also a prophet in the biblical sense. In scripture, a prophet is a herald of God for the people of God. Prophets are not simply pious social critics; they are also dreamers who dare to imagine a world where God is king, and for this reason they are persecuted. Romero's homilies strongly denounce the injustices in Salvadoran society but even more strongly announce the good news of Jesus Christ. The best witnesses to Romero's prophetic vocation are his enemies; by assassinating his character and his body they ironically confessed through gritted teeth that he is a prophet.

Óscar Romero is a martyr. In El Salvador, the numerous stories of abuse, disappearances, and deaths revolve around one single story, that of Óscar Romero.[23] There are other heroic witnesses and many more unjust deaths. But the story of Romero crystallizes the relationship between the heroism of the martyrs and the suffering of the people. The narratives of martyrdom in El Salvador are gathered in a kind of hierarchical order: Romero, Grande, the martyrs of the UCA, the Maryknoll sisters, the massacres of El Mozote, and so on. The order was seen in Romero's preaching at funerals where the role of the priests was particularly highlighted. The order is also seen in the popular traditions about local martyrs, whose stories are always connected in some way with Romero's story. In Romero's story two things are eminently manifest: "both the identification with the fate of the poor people and the unconditional surrender for the cause of their salvation at all levels from the most immediate and urgent, the bare fact of being alive, to the fullness of participation in the life of God."[24] In other words, it is not that Romero's life and death are more important than those of the many thousands of Salvadorans who lived and died in those decades but rather that Romero's life and death throw light on those other lives and deaths.

Óscar Romero is a son of the church. By this I mean that he grew up within the fold of the church. He loved the church as a mother, and the pope as a father. His adoption of the Ignatian motto *Sentir con la iglesia* in 1970 was a fitting expression of his filial adherence to the church in its rich complexity. As a son, Romero was willing to work wherever his ecclesial parents needed him. In his case, this meant being a pastor. It is important to remember that his three years as archbishop represent a small fraction of Romero's life of ministry. By the time he assumed this leadership role in 1977, Romero had already spent twenty-five years in priestly service in the parish of San Miguel and eight years of episcopal service split between San Salvador and Santiago de María. These thirty-three years are not to be brushed aside as irrelevant to his story in the mistaken belief that they represent the old, conservative, traditionalist Romero. On the contrary, I believe that these years are crucial for understanding the man who became known simply as Monseñor. However much he changed throughout his life and whatever transformation he experienced on the night that he stood before the corpse of his friend Father Rutilio, the archbishop of San Salvador always was and remained a son of the church.

Óscar Romero is a father of the Latin American church. What is a church father? In the New Testament, the figure of Paul presents an important precedent for this postbiblical title. Paul calls the Christians in Corinth his "beloved children. For though you might have ten thousand guardians in Christ, you do not have many fathers. Indeed, in Christ Jesus I became your father through the gospel" (1 Cor. 4:15). Paul calls the Galatians "little children, for whom I am again in the pain of childbirth until Christ is formed in you" (Gal. 4:19). Traditionally, the term *church father* has been reserved for the exemplary bishops who led the church through the political and theological controversies of the first six centuries. While there is no official list, certain common traits characterize the church fathers. José Comblin identifies four: a holy life, an orthodox faith, an understanding of the signs of the times, and popular recognition.[25] The church fathers were not academic theologians but pastors (or monks) dedicated to edifying the church.

The title *church father* is a useful way of remembering Romero. In the patristic era, the bishops of Asia Minor who attended the Councils of Nicaea were called fathers because their teaching was received as apostolic by the universal church. In the contemporary era, Elmar Klinger argues, "Bishops from Latin America helped to set the future course of the Church at the Second Vatican Council, said by Paul VI to share the same status as the Council of Nicaea."[26] In particular, the bishops of Latin America have helped the universal church claim the great commission of opting for the poor and recognizing the centrality of liberation to the message of the gospel. The bishops of the patristic era often paid a price for their orthodoxy. Many of them experienced persecution, torture, and even assassination for their defense of church dogma. These stories are so far removed from today's pluralist sensibilities that they seem like ideological fantasies. They are easy prey for revisionist histories that downplay any theological significance to their persecution and reduce them to political ploys for power. The persecution of bishops like Romero for preaching that God loves the poor but hates poverty, and the religiously charged manner in which he was murdered, point to the ongoing vitality of the patristic tree. Through seasons of neglect and abuse that it has endured, the old tree has become weathered, but it has not withered.

It must be acknowledged that the category of church father is not without its problems. For one thing, few women fit in this type.[27] In antiquity their voices were seldom recorded, and throughout history they have not been welcomed to the kind of institutional posts that allowed church fathers to speak with official authority.[28] Second, the patristic mold privileges individual voices over communal movements and theological texts over church ministry and daily life. Speaking of Romero as a Latin American church father does not break the limitations of this mold. However, Romero's life and teaching help us to resituate the patristic tradition. Church fathers do not spring up like Melchizedek, "without father, without mother, without genealogy" (Heb. 7:3). Romero can be a father of the church only because he was first a son of the church. The exceptional character of his teaching is not the product of a solitary genius (which he was not) but the good fruit that testifies to the health and vitality of the Latin American church whose branches bore him up.

THE EMERGENCE OF A LATIN AMERICAN SOURCE-CHURCH

Until recently, the church in Latin America had yielded few if any theologians who were comparable in stature to the church fathers of old.[29] The reasons for this sterility are to be found in the history of the church in Latin America. Throughout most of the five hundred years of Christian presence on the continent, ecclesiastical leaders were chiefly concerned with the accurate transplantation of European Christianity to American soil. The heroic and holy deeds of early missionaries like Antonio de Montesinos, Pedro de Córboba, and Bartolomé de las Casas in proclaiming the gospel and defending the indigenous were choked under the colonial regimes' desire for European control. The time of independence did not fundamentally alter this dynamic. The churches of the newly liberated republics reacted to the shifting political winds with an aggressive strategy of Romanization. The result was what Henrique de Lima Vaz referred to as a reflection-church (*igreja-reflexo*) rather than a source-church (*igreja-fonte*).[30] The reflection-church is characterized by dependency on the source-church. Latin American elites, whether in the social sphere or in the ecclesial one, looked to Europe for the orientation of all projects and the answers to all problems. There was a marked tendency to depend on Europe for ecclesial personnel, spiritualities, theologies, and finances. Imitation rather than creativity was the most apt descriptor for the acts of the church throughout the long years of the colony, and these were not overcome by independence.[31] It was not until the period after the Second World War that the first sprouts of an authentically Latin American church began to crack the colonial streets and blossom. The foundation of the Council of Latin American Bishops played a pivotal role in cultivating these sprouts.

With the gathering of bishops at Medellín in 1968, a source-church begins to emerge, at least among the episcopacy. Medellín itself needs to be understood as nourished by two developments—the winds of change blowing from Vatican II and the social upheavals shaking Latin America. The first can be described as an *aggiornamento*, a pastoral adaptation based on a contemporary reading of the signs of the times. The second can be expressed as *concientización*, an awakening from a centuries-long colonial slumber to realize that one has a role to play in historical events besides that of spectator. Previously, Latin America was considered a satellite that revolved around a European center. The periphery was its standard orbit. At Medellín, the church in Latin America experienced a Copernican revolution. As the church looked squarely in the face at the social realities of the Americas, it became less anxious about its European features; it spent less time in front of a mirror and more time in front of the window. When it did so, the Latin American church discovered that it did not need to feel inferior to the churches across the Atlantic.[32] The result was an increase in the church's generative capacity. It ceased being an echo of Spain and found its own voice. It became a source-church.

Latin American theologies are often regarded as synonymous with Catholic liberation theologies. The identification is understandable but exaggerated. Not all Latin American theologians are Catholic, and not all Latin American theologies are liberation theologies. However, Catholic liberation theologies do represent the most substantive theological development in the Latin American church, and these will be focus of our study. These theologies had a number of doctrinal sources.[33] First, the discussions on secularity that took place in Europe after World War II repositioned the church in an attitude of dialogue with the world. The ensuing reflection on earthly realities and the signs of the times found its outlet in Vatican II's "Pastoral Constitution on the Church in the Modern World," *Gaudium et Spes*. The second tributary was the encyclical *Populorum Progressio* of 1967. With an eye to the peoples of Africa and Latin America, Paul VI denounced the growing economic gap between nations, which led to fundamentally unjust and unstable social situations. Behind this encyclical lay the influence of two French Thomists: Jacques Maritaine's philosophy of integral humanism and Marie-Dominique Chenu's theology of work. Chenu convened a dialogue between Marx and Christianity analogous to the Scholastic conversation between Aristotle and Christianity. The French Dominican argued that just as the non-Christian Aristotle had helped Aquinas discover the natural human (*homo naturalis*), a dialogue with the non-Christian Marx could help Christians discover the economic human (*homo oeconomicus*). It is important to remember that Chenu was the teacher of one of the founders of Latin American liberation theology, Gustavo Gutiérrez. The third doctrinal source for Latin American theology was the Second General Conference of Latin American Catholic Bishops, which took place in Medellín, Colombia, in 1968. The documents produced by this conference united the language of the "signs of the times" (*signa temporum*) of Vatican II with the social reality of poverty that marked Latin America. Latin American theology was also fed by new thinking from gatherings of theologians occurring between 1964 and 1968. At these gatherings, theologians like Juan Luis Segundo, Lucio Gera, and Gustavo Gutiérrez presented papers on Latin American theology that expressed and stimulated the theological reflection of a growing Latin American Christian audience. Also important during these years were the gathering of Jesuits in Rome for their thirty-first general congregation and the installation of the Basque priest Pedro Arrupe as general of the order.

The Latin American theology that resulted from the confluence of these tributaries was not a narrow brook but a rushing river with various branches. It is more accurate to speak of Latin American theologies or liberation theologies than a singular liberation theology. Juan Carlos Scannone identifies four currents of liberation theology.[34] All four are united in the importance accorded to action or praxis; they start not from ancient texts but from the contemporary presence of God in the poor and in historical realities. What comes first is the theologal dimension of the faith, which hears in the cry of the poor the voice of Christ. What distinguishes the various streams of these theologies is the manner in which they understand the relation between the act of faith, the reading of scripture, the signs of the times, and the poor. All four streams spring from praxis, but whose praxis? First, the liberating praxis could be focused on the pastoral praxis of the church. This version is characterized by its accentuation of the integral and evangelical content of liberation. It is the theology that was promoted by Medellín and ratified by Puebla. Scannone mentions Eduardo Pironio as one of the exponents of this position.[35] I note this because, as we will see, Pironio is one of the most important sources for Romero's understanding of liberation theology. Second, liberation theology can be done from the praxis of revolutionary groups. This version draws heavily on Marxist analysis, and its theological reflection is from and for radicalized groups that are intent on promoting a social revolution. The reflection of this group, though theological, may keep the term *liberation theology* at arm's length out of concern for the manner in which practitioners of the first version have "spiritualized" it. Scannone mentions the name of Hugo Assmann and the group of Christians for Socialism as paradigmatic of this version. The third version works from historical praxis. Its agenda calls for profound changes in the social arena. At the same time, it remains committed to the church and to the Christian tradition. The unity of salvation history and secular history is affirmed by this theology against all reductive accounts that collapse one into the other. Like the second version but with more caution, it draws on Marxist analysis as a tool for understanding and shaping social reality. Gustavo Gutiérrez, at least in his earlier decades, swam in this stream. The fourth version works from the praxis of Latin American peoples. This version is commonly referred to as *teología del pueblo*. It springs from the appropriation of the teachings of Medellín for the Argentine context. Lucio Gera is usually considered the chief founder of this theology.[36] It differs from the previous streams not only in its geographic provenance but in how it understands the place of the people in Latin American theological reflection. For this version of theology, the people are understood from a historical-cultural perspective rather than from a social-structural perspective; the people are a nation before they are a class. "The people" includes a diverse community of social classes and even cultures, but it is the poor, as privileged bearers of national culture, who are the special focus of this theology.[37]

Óscar Romero is a prophet and martyr, son and father of a Latin American source-church that includes all these powerful theological currents. He would have felt most comfortable in the first, but his primary identification was not with a theological stream but with a concrete church: the church in El Salvador, which was struggling to emerge from the shadows of history in order to let its light shine. The first 1,500 years of the Common Era saw a succession of churches around the Mediterranean basin serving as guiding lights for the church universal: Jerusalem, Alexandria, Antioch, Rome, and Constantinople. In the sixteenth century, the church in Spain was a source for Reformation debates and for disputes in the Indies. The Franco-German churches were sources for the Second Vatican Council.[38] Liberation theology can be understood within this framework. In attempting to rethink theology from a Latin American context, the Latin American church took a giant step from being a "reflection-church" to being a "source-Church."[39] Reflection-churches belong to the Greek chorus that at best interprets or explains the actions of the former. For four centuries, this was the only role for Latin American churches. Even in the chorus, the church in El Salvador was assigned the role of understudy. In the late twentieth century, through the company of actors that formed around Óscar Romero, the Salvadoran church became a source-church. With courage and humility, it offered Latin American evangelical responses to Latin American situations while at the same time deepening communion with the universal church. Romero's leadership in this emergence received strong encouragement from Rome.

> It is wonderful to see how the pope, from his universal magisterium, when he addresses himself to a region, it is as if he were only thinking of that region. And he speaks of "the specific identity of Latin America," as if to say, you have a very Latin American way of being, you are very special, your church has a mode of being that is not the same as that of the church in Europe, Africa, or any other place. Try to discover better your Latin American church identity, and live it out with its problems, needs, and challenges. (*Homilías*, 4:319–20)

A caveat is in order. A source-church cannot survive if it loses its connection to its source.[40] Without returning to its springs, without *ressourcement*, the fountain dries and the well becomes stagnant. Óscar Romero can be called a father of the Latin American church precisely on account of the transparency of his pastoral praxis to Jesus Christ. This wise father knew how to draw from the wellsprings of the gospel and tradition to slake the thirst for justice of the Salvadoran people: he practiced *ressourcement* for the sake of *aggiornamento*.

RESSOURCEMENT FROM THE PERIPHERY

The term *ressourcement* is credited to Charles Pegúy. It represents a call to turn from "a less profound to a more profound tradition."[41] This turn was embraced by Dominicans at Salchoir like Ives Congar and Marie-Dominique Chenu and the Jesuits at Fourvière like Henri Bouillard and Henri de Lubac. This return from the less profound tradition of neo-Scholasticism to the more profound tradition of the church fathers was vigorously rejected by influential theologians like

Réginald Garrigou-Lagrange, for whom this *nouvelle théologie* was simply a new strain of the virus of modernism against which the church needed to be inoculated. The "new theology" eschewed the overly deductive, closed systems of what was called Denzinger theology and drank instead from the threefold fountains of theology: the scriptures, the liturgy, and the fathers. The *ressourcement* theologians were characterized by combining this return to the sources of Christian doctrine with a committed engagement with the contemporary world. This engagement was displayed in the courageous response of many of these theologians to the Nazi threat in Europe.[42] In their unification of theology and life, the work of these *ressourcement* theologians set the stage for many of the "new" directions that the church took at Vatican II.

In this study of Romero's theological vision, we will practice what Latino/a theologians call *ressourcement* from the margins.[43] It entails a return to the wellsprings of theology (sacred scripture, the divine liturgy, and the church fathers) but from the periphery. The Christian sources are approached, not with European questions like secularization or the death of God, but with Latin American questions like exploitation and the death of the poor. *Ressourcement* from the margins is not limited to approaching the traditional Christian sources with questions from a different social location; it also taps new wells. Latino/a *ressourcement* theologians must learn (in the words of Bernard of Clairvaux) to "drink from their own wells."[44] The Holy Spirit gushes life in Latin America too. The church in Latin America can be a source-church because the Spirit has fed a well in its soil. Gustavo Gutiérrez states, "The water that rises out of it continually purifies us and smoothes away any wrinkles in our manner of being Christians, at the same time supplying the vital element needed for making new ground fruitful."[45] The wells of the church fathers are life-giving; they offer fresh water and are also examples of where and how to dig (or not) a well. But one cannot live off someone else's spirituality or theology. One's thirst will not be slaked by someone else's drink. We need to drink for ourselves. A Latino/a *ressourcement* from the margins looks for springs in the lands, histories, and cultures of Latin America. Michelle Gonzalez adds that "while European theologians struggled to *rediscover* traditional Christian sources, liberation theologians struggled to *discover* the voices of forgotten and marginalized people in Christian history. Theirs was not merely a return to established historical sources, but an active rewriting of Christian history and theology."[46] This active rewriting is precisely what Óscar Romero does in a speech that he delivered at the University of Louvain on February 2, 1980. There, at the ceremony where he was receiving his second doctorate *honoris causae*, Romero spoke about the relationship of faith to politics from the perspective of the poor. He concluded his speech with an explicit example of *ressourcement* from the margins. "The early Christians used to say, *Gloria Dei, vivens homo*. We can make this concrete by saying, *Gloria Dei, vivens pauper*."[47]

Gloria Dei, vivens pauper: "The glory of God is the living poor." This saying is an adaptation of Irenaeus of Lyons's saying, *Gloria Dei, vivens homo*, "The glory of God is the living human." A turn to Romero is an act of *ressourcement* from the margins. It is a turn in the spirit of Peguy from the "less profound" theology of Latin American neo-Scholasticism to the more profound "new theology" of Medellín. It is also a return to the fountains of scripture, liturgy, and the fathers motivated by a desire to engage the contemporary world, which in Latin America means the world of the poor. Finally, this *ressourcement* has a revisionist component to it. It is not that the patristic wells are deficient but rather that the Spirit that filled them is still active, replenishing old aquifers and creating new ones. Romero is not only a good subject for *ressourcement* from the margins; his retrieval of Irenaeus proves him to be an exemplary practitioner.

The intent behind introducing Irenaeus is twofold. First, it places Romero's *Gloria Dei, vivens pauper* within a diachronic Christian conversation. Irenaeus's dictum has a history, and understanding this history helps us understand Romero's version. Second, and more important, it adds credence to the maturity of the Latin American church in its development from reflection to source. The archbishop of San Salvador is not simply repeating the words of the bishop of Lyons. He rewrites them for El Salvador. Romero's theology is evidence that the same Spirit that moved Irenaeus to act against the heresies in Lyons is at work in El Salvador preaching the apostolic message of life.

AN IRENAEAN VISION OF GOD AND HUMANITY

The popularity of Irenaeus's formula is a relatively recent phenomenon.[48] The phrase does not appear in the manuals of theology in circulation during the first half of the twentieth century. Hans Urs von Balthasar is among the first theologians to use the phrase. In *The Glory of the Lord*, von Balthasar interprets the phrase as a succinct synthesis of the theology of Irenaeus.[49] In the years immediately preceding the Second Vatican Council the phrase is used as theological shorthand for the doctrine of creation (human fulfillment and divine glory converge), salvation history (the fulfillment of the human is achieved by the Son and the Spirit), ecclesiology (all Christians are priests who are called to glorify God by living for God), and moral theology (the virtuous life glorifies God). In none of the writings of this period is the Irenaean formula studied within its original context. It is always applied, not analyzed. There is no mention of the Irenaean aphorism in the final versions of the documents of Vatican II, yet it was present in the process of redaction of these same documents. For instance, the phrase appears in drafts of *Gaudium et Spes*. The dictum supported the development of a Christian humanism that was Christocentric. The first part of the phrase (*Gloria enim Dei vivens homo*) undergirds the church's concern for human affairs because the glory of God is related to human fulfillment and by extension social development. The second part of the phrase (*Vitam autem hominis visio Dei*) keeps the humanism Christian by underlining the novelty of the Incarnation, which makes the vision of God possible. Following Vatican II, the phrase is picked up by Paul VI, John Paul II, the Liturgy of the Hours, and the Catholic Catechism. Turning to Latin America, the 1968 "Letter to the Jesuits of Latin America" cites the first part of the statement as a theological warrant for the defense of human dignity and rights.[50] The documents from the conferences of the Latin American Council of Bishops (CELAM) also draw on Irenaeus with a similar goal in mind. There are oblique references to it at the conferences in Medellín (1968) and Puebla (1979),[51] and there are direct references at Santo Domingo (1992) and Aparecida (2007).[52] In some cases, the *homo* is underlined in order to emphasize human dignity; in others the *vivens* is highlighted to connect faith and life. The Irenaean aphorism also appears in the writings of Latin American liberation theologians. For instance, Pablo Richard uses it to link human flourishing with divine glory.[53] The phrase also shows up among Latino/a theologians. Alejandro García-Rivera appeals to the Irenaean motto as the linchpin for his theological aesthetics.[54] Miguel Díaz uses it to lend theological weight to the struggle (*la lucha*) of Latinos and Latinas for basic dignity.[55] Nancy Pineda-Madrid makes a similar case for Chicanas.[56] It is worth noting that none of these writers refers to Romero's version of the Irenaean saying.

THE SCANDAL OF THE TRANSFIGURATION

Irenaeus was the first church father to reflect on the mystery of the Transfiguration.[57] According to the bishop of Lyons, on Mount Tabor Christ reveals the glory of God and the glory of the human. The manifestation of God on the mountain to the confused disciples affirms the dignity of human beings, who though the humblest of intellectual creatures have received the highest of possible callings, namely, to become beloved children of God the Father. Irenaeus's vision of human flourishing and final fulfillment is deeply theocentric. This is clear in the full version of the famous saying that Romero cites only in abridged form: "The glory of God is the living human, but the life of the human is the vision of God."[58] The light of the Transfiguration gives life because it makes the Father known in the face of Jesus Christ. Hans Urs von Balthasar titled his book on Irenaeus *The Scandal of the Incarnation*. The bishop of Lyons preached the scandal of the Incarnation against those who believed in the hierarchical categorization of humanity and condemned life in the flesh as not worth saving. The theological vision of the archbishop of San Salvador is focused on the scandal of the Transfiguration. This may seem odd. The Transfiguration is not a major feast in Western Christianity or a significant topic in Latin American theology. However, El Salvador is a country dedicated to the transfigured Christ, *El Divino Salvador del Mundo*, and the Transfiguration is therefore not only a liturgical feast but also a celebration of national identity. Throughout most of its history, this celebration was patriotic. It became a scandal only when Romero translated it from the world of the poor. It became a stumbling block for the oligarchs who condemned the life of the poor as not worth living, and for all who were invested in the opaque and disfigured status quo. For Romero, the Transfiguration, like the Incarnation, is partial and preferential. The glory of God first illumines the faces of the landless campesino, the market woman, and the hungry child. As these faces behold their God, they become transparent to his glory and shine from the church to the world. Romero's theological vision may be called a doxology of the cross. The voice of the Father glorifies the Son and all human flesh, beginning with weak, malnourished flesh. In his final homily on the Transfiguration, preached three weeks before his death, Romero asks, "By what right have we catalogued people into first-class humans and second-class humans, when in the theology of the human there is only one class, that of children of God?" (*Homilías*, 6:346). God makes himself known through the flesh of Jesus, the long-expected suffering servant, and his cross-bound friends. This is the scandal of the Transfiguration. The *gloria Dei* of Tabor is most luminous in the *vivens pauper* of El Salvador, and the life and hope for these poor ones and for all humanity is the vision of the God who became poor for their sake.

What does Lyons have to do with El Salvador? There are suggestive parallels between the second century and the twenty-first. According to John Behr, "Irenaeus is *par excellence* the theologian of the flesh."[59] Irenaeus is a good ally for those who want to argue against the extrinsicism of grace. Salvation for Irenaeus is something that occurs *in* history, even as its end transcends history. Irenaeus is also a foe of racial and class-based ideologies. It is for this reason that J. Kameron Carter turns to the bishop of Lyons. In Irenaeus, Carter finds an anti-Gnostic theologian whose struggle against the heresy of supersessionism illumines the path for antirace intellectuals.[60] "In Irenaeus," Eric Osborn said, "Athens and Jerusalem meet at Patmos."[61] Analogously, we might say that in Romero, Tabor and Rome meet in El Salvador.

The fruitfulness of the encounter between Romero and the church fathers has been suggested before. Thomas Greenan Mulheron compares Romero to John Chrysostom.[62] Claudia Marlene Rivera Navarrete also finds in Romero echoes of the prophetic teachings of Gregory of Nyssa and Basil the Great on wealth.[63] Margaret Pfeil considers it in her writings on Romero's theology of Transfiguration.[64] Damian Zynda offers a creative reading of Romero's life from the perspective of Irenaean spirituality.[65] The current book extends their trajectory. Here I suggest that Romero is like Irenaeus, not because he repeats the old Christian apologist and defender of human dignity, but because the springs of Christianity that watered Lyons bubbled afresh in San Salvador. In other words, the relation between the two is not so much genealogical as analogical and indeed theologal. Both drank of the same Spirit. Irenaeus was one of the first Greek fathers. Romero was one of the first Latin American church fathers. His theological vision is a fresh sign of the emergence of the Christianity of the Global South from being a reflection-church to being a source-church. Romero is not just an inspirational figure; he is a teacher from El Salvador for the universal church. He is the *doctor transfigurado*, the *doctor de los pobres*. The hope for this study is that its readers (and author) will be captivated by the doctrine of this humble pastor and inspired to think more clearly and act more decisively in solidarity with the poor.

THE OUTLINE OF THE ARGUMENT

The Feast of the Transfiguration lies at the heart of Salvadoran civic and religious life. It is surprising, then, that it has received scant attention from scholarship on Romero or Central American works on Christology. Margaret Pfeil's treatment of the subject is the most conspicuous and significant exception.[66] In this book I seek to fill in this gap, at least in part, by studying Romero's theological vision from the perspective of Mount Tabor and the Irenaean saying that serves as theological shorthand for its chiaroscuro mystery—*Gloria Dei, vivens pauper*. Most writing on Romero treats his version of the Irenaean saying as a pithy saying. By contrast, I argue that the phrase *Gloria Dei, vivens pauper* is the interpretive key to his theology. The formula synthesizes Romero's understanding of the gospel, salvation, Christ, the church, and eschatology. In this book I propose to examine each of these theological topics in light of the scandal of the Transfiguration.

In chapter 2, "Microphones of Christ," we will study Romero's homiletical theology and practice. He was first and foremost a pastor. Attending to his theology and theological method requires consideration of his preaching. The chapter begins by pointing out the ambiguity of the plans to inscribe on the facade of the Cathedral of San Salvador the words *Ipsum audite*—Listen to Christ. The cathedral pulpit has historically been a sign of both liberation and domination. From the ambiguities and contradictions of the Salvadoran Tabor, I trace the contours of Romero's preaching life. I color in these lines with a presentation of his most important homily on preaching, which he delivered on January 27, 1980. The picture that emerges from this exercise resembles a diptych with one panel devoted to the scriptures and the other to the signs of the times. The task of preachers is to invite the congregation to join in a Spirit-led contemplation of events in the life of the church and the country in the light of the Word. When this contemplation is fruitful, the church becomes the microphone of Christ, who is the microphone of God. As a microphone of Christ, Romero has been known as "the voice of the voiceless."[67] Does this mean that the poor have no voice but Romero's? The final part of this chapter considers some of the problems inherent to social advocacy through privileged speakers like Romero. By examining his use of the Augustinian distinction between the voice and the word, I show that Romero's advocacy through preaching was indeed empowering and that from his practice we can name criteria for testing the authenticity of preaching on behalf of the poor. Illumined by the study of Romero's homily, chapter 3, "The Transfiguration of El Salvador," leads us to consider Romero's theological vision of salvation. The history of Latin America has been written in blood. Latin American theologians heard the question of salvation in the voice of blood and responded with a theology of liberation. In this chapter, I consider the possible contribution of Romero's vision of liberation as transfiguration to the problem of violence in El Salvador addressed in the pastoral letter *I See Violence and Discord in the City*, written by the Archbishop José Luis Escobar Alas in 2016. This letter speaks of a pedagogy of death that has been transmitted from the time of the conquest to the present gang warfare. In fact, the designation of the Transfiguration as the titular feast of San Salvador has its origins in Pedro de Alvarado's victory over the indigenous *cuscatlecos* in 1524. Romero's vision of salvation as transfiguration inherits this problematic and offers a solution. The main part of the chapter studies nine homilies that Romero preached on the Transfiguration from 1946 to 1980. The theological image that emerges from this study can be likened to an icon written from a rich palette of sources: scripture, the doctors of the church, the magisterial tradition, and the liturgical practices of the Salvadoran church. The result is a distinctively Catholic, orthodox, Salvadoran icon that invites contemplation and empowers action. Perhaps the most distinctive feature of this icon of the Transfiguration is its representation of the witnesses that Jesus gathered on Mount Tabor as people with a history of violence. Joining them in listening to Christ is a way to unlearn the pedagogy of death at work in El Salvador and reorient the natural aggressiveness of human beings toward a pedagogy of life. For Romero, the Transfiguration has the power to energize the violence of love, which can build a civilization of peace and reconciliation in the bloodied soil of Central America.

From the work of salvation, we turn our attention to the person of the Savior. The chapter "The Face of the *Divino Salvador*" considers Romero's Christology. We begin by returning to the founding ambiguity of the proclamation of the gospel in the Americas as represented by the multiplicity of images of Christ in the Cathedral of San Salvador. The Spanish-looking Christ allegedly donated by Charles V and the *Colocho* Christ paraded by the people on August 5 raise many questions; I focus on who Christ is and whose images are his. I begin to answer by studying Romero's 1979 sermon series on the Divine Savior. In these Romero places the transfiguration of Christ within the narrative framework of the "bread of life" discourses in John 6. I fill out the picture that emerges from these sermons by adding the color that comes from the ritual celebration of the *Divino Salvador*. By following the movement of the *Colocho* Christ in the processional known as the *Bajada*, we will explore Romero's teaching on Christ's humiliation. We will then consider the glorification of Christ within the ritual framework of the *Descubrimiento*, the unveiling of the transfigured Christ. Along the way we will also study the music that accompanied the descent and ascent of the *Divino Salvador*. The liturgical context for Latin American theology has been overlooked by many theologians, yet it is critical because orthodoxy, orthopraxis, and doxology are tied together. Within this parabolic movement we will examine the questions of Christ's incarnation among the poor as the "God who sweats on the street," his kenosis and cry of dereliction on the cross, Romero's appropriation of the Ignatian motto of living *Ad majorem Dei gloriam* (For the greater glory of God), and the epiphanies of this glory in the history of Central America. The chapter ends with a meditation on *el Cristo roto* (the broken Christ), a popular devotional story that Romero presents as a parable for what the beautiful face of the *Divino Salvador* looks like in the context of suffering in Latin America.

From Christology we turn to Romero's ecclesiology in chapter 5, "The Transfigured People of God." In the chapel at the University of Central America in San Salvador there is a collection of Stations of the Cross whose gruesome images of broken, naked bodies show the final consequence of poverty, namely death. This introduction to the connection of poverty and death leads to an examination of the place of the poor in the thinking of the church. From Vatican II through Medellín to Puebla, a distinct theological trajectory can be traced and expressed concisely as "the preferential option for the poor." The poor are a sign of the times, a missiological imperative, and an ecclesiological criterion. With the church of the poor, poverty becomes a theological locus. Romero approaches the question of the poor with these teachings in mind but with his own unique perspective, a perspective succinctly stated in his episcopal motto, *Sentir con la iglesia*. We will consider the origins of this motto in Ignatius of Loyola before examining Romero's *ressourcement* from the margins of this tradition in his experience with the Ignatian exercises. Every year that he was archbishop, Romero published a pastoral letter on the Feast of the Transfiguration. A study of the Transfiguration epistles of 1977, 1978, and 1979 reveals the heart of Romero's adaption of the Ignatian motto. *Sentir con la iglesia* means *sentir* with the hierarchy and holding in union the church of the Beatitudes and the church of the sacraments. *Sentir con la iglesia* means *sentir* with the church militant in El Salvador. This means adopting a radical Christian monotheism that fights against all kinds of idols (national security, profits, sensuality). In this fight Romero finds allies among historic Protestant churches and enemies within the Catholic Church itself. Most of all s*entir con la iglesia* means *sentir* with the poor. The church's life and mission must be oriented toward the life of the poor. Indeed, the church is called to be the church of the poor. For Romero, the paradigmatic exemplar in this *sentir* is Mary. In Mary's Magnificat, true happiness and justice combine. When the poor become Marian, they become sacraments of hope.

For the last chapter of this work we turn to eschatology. Chapter 6, "The Vision of God," begins with Romero's visit to Mount Tabor in 1956. From this mountain Romero described seeing the history of salvation unfold before his eyes, but it was a limited vision because only in the light of glory is seeing complete. I return in this chapter to Romero's version of the Irenaean aphorism *Gloria Dei, vivens homo.* The first substantive Romero text that will be treated in this chapter is his address at Louvain on February 2, 1980. It was for that occasion that he rewrote Irenaeus. For Irenaeus of Lyons, the saying was a check against the heresies of Gnosticism and Docetism. For Romero of El Salvador, the dictum emerged as a defense of a humanity threatened not just by atheistic secularism but by economic barbarism. *Gloria Dei, vivens pauper* establishes not only the minimum conditions for justice and life but orients all humanity toward its goal—seeing God in the light of glory. The study of this text will allow us to see aspects of Romero's theological vision that would otherwise be easily overlooked: his account of divinization, his theological aesthetics, and his Irenaean understanding of martyrdom. The study of these topics casts doubt on the authenticity of the famous saying attributed to Romero "If they kill me, I will resurrect in the Salvadoran people." Not only is this statement suspect because of its dubious provenance, but its theology is at odds with Romero's broader eschatological vision. The final part of the chapter is devoted to the study of Romero's final homily preached on March 24, 1980, the first anniversary of Sara Meardi de Pinto's death. In this homily,

Romero speaks of the grain of wheat that falls to the ground and connects this saying of Jesus with the death of Sara Meardi de Pinto. From this unlikely diptych, Romero offers a theology of hope. This theology distinguishes without separating temporal progress and the coming of the kingdom. It unites working for historical ends with the reward of eschatological ones. The vision seen on this diptych confirms Romero's *ressourcement* of Irenaeus from San Salvador. Paradoxically, the martyrs are the epitome of the human being fully alive. Herein lies the deepest scandal of the Transfiguration. In Romero's theological vision, the martyrs are prophetic provocateurs; they see the God who became poor and truly become alive.

CHAPTER 2

MICROPHONES
OF CHRIST

On the Mount of Transfiguration, the voice of the Father issues an imperative to the disciples: Listen to him! Listening to Christ in his glory and in his humility is not an option but a command that includes an implicit promise. If the disciples "listen to him," they will enjoy communion with the Father and the Spirit. The plan for the Cathedral of San Salvador called for carving in stone the Latin version of the Father's command: *Ipsum audite.* The transfiguration of Christ is a mystery of light and word. It was not simply a passing event, a mountaintop experience, but an invitation to see and hear and be transfigured.

When one reads the gospel accounts of the Transfiguration, it is easy to empathize with Peter and not know what to say. The event is shrouded in the mysterious language of the Old Testament epiphanies: clouds, night, dazzling light, angelic beings. The optic stimulation may overwhelm input from other sensory channels and stupefy our mind to the auditory dimensions of the event: the voice of the Father. The Father reveals the Son to his disciples and commands them to listen to him. On Mount Tabor, the capacity of the human to see and hear God's revelation in Christ is affirmed. The celebration of this event as a feast of the church becomes in turn a celebration of the divine origins of the Christian message. In the words of one of its early witnesses: "You will do well to be attentive to this as to a lamp shining in a dark place, until the day dawns and the morning star rises in your hearts" (2 Pet. 1:19). Mount Tabor is not only the stage for a glorious theophany but the pulpit for the preaching of a luminous Word.

In this chapter we will consider Óscar Romero's theology and practice of preaching. As we saw in the previous chapter, like most of the church fathers, Romero was above all a pastor. His homilies are his chief theological texts, so catching a glimpse of his theological vision requires attending to his preaching. If it seems that these considerations belong more in a book on homiletics than in a book of theology, that may be symptomatic of a problem to which Romero is an answer—the academic captivity of much modern theology. That Romero's theology must be gleaned chiefly from sermons instead of systematic works is a reminder that the homily has been one of the chief carriers of theological reflection throughout history. Listening to these sermons, one can hear the heart of Romero's faith and also of the people who first listened to him.

The chapter is structured as follows. First, I will offer a general sketch of Romero as a preacher by painting him against the background of preaching in the Americas. The luminous Word had a difficult journey from Tabor to the Americas. Some preachers indeed were attentive to the light of the gospel "as to a lamp shining in a dark place." Others were lured by will-o'-the-wisps and the stranger fires of silver and gold. It is from the chiaroscuro of the history of the church in the Americas that Romero steps into the pulpit. The second part of the chapter is devoted to an examination of a homily preached on January 27, 1980, titled "The Homily, Actualization of the Word of God." In this sermon, Romero leads us on a mystagogical catechesis of preaching, helping us to see that the preacher is the microphone of Christ, who is the microphone of God. As we will see, this microphone needs to be used to give voice to the voiceless, which raises a question that will be addressed in the third part of the chapter. Can someone be the voice of the voiceless without being a part of the

Great question

problem? Romero's theology and practice of preaching offer guiding criteria for keeping the church's witness authentic to those for and with whom it speaks.

PREACHING IN THE AMERICAS

Herman Melville speaks of the world as a ship on a journey with the pulpit as its prow.[4] In its passage through Latin American history that brow has plunged straight to the abyss of genocide time and time again. And yet from the belly of the big fish of empire, a chorus of voices has always preached a different word.

On the fourth Sunday of Advent, December 21, 1511, Father Antonio de Montesinos took to the pulpit of the church in Santo Domingo.[5] He was the voice crying in the wilderness to a congregation of conquistadors: "You are living and dying in sin on account of the cruelty with which you use these innocent peoples." He questioned the entire colonial enterprise of Indian enslavement with a series of loaded questions. "By what right and justice do you hold these Indians in such horrible and cruel bondage? By what authority have you waged such detestable wars on these people who dwelt in their peaceful gentle lands, whose infinite number you have consumed with untold deaths and violations? . . . Are these not human beings? Do they not have rational souls? Are you not required to love them as you love yourself? Do you not understand? Do you not feel? Are you asleep?"[6] Montesinos was not an isolated case. In the pastoral letter presented on the Feast of the Transfiguration of 1978, *The Church and Political Organizations*, Romero writes that in the Americas the prophetic mission of Christ on behalf of the poor also counted with apostles like "Fray Bartolome de las Casas, Bishop Juan del Valle, and Bishop Valdivieso, who was murdered in Nicaragua for his opposition to the landowner and governor Contreras" (*Voz*, 94).[7] There is a line connecting the luminous gospel of Tabor to preaching in Central America. However, this line is not bright and solid but dashed, dotted, and broken.

From the beginning, the Church in the Americas had two faces, two voices: the dominant one, represented by soldiers and clerics who justified violence on behalf of evangelization and colonization, and another largely represented by religious who protested these abuses. The two faces are not simply a sign of hypocrisy:[8] not all mistaken people are hypocrites, nor are all sincere people good. Rather, they are a sign of the drama of redemption that plays out in the church, which journeys through history as a mixed body (*corpus per mixtum*) of people who are both saints and sinners (*simul justus et peccator*), wheat and tares.

The two faces of the church have been present throughout the history of Latin America from the wars of conquest in the sixteenth century to the wars of independence of the nineteenth, to the civil wars of the twentieth. In one aspect, the church published *Inter caetera* (1493), a papal bull that divided the world between the Spanish and the Portuguese so that the Christian religion might be enlarged "and the barbarous nations be subdued and brought to the faith."[9] And in another aspect, the church published *Sublimis Deus* (1537), an encyclical declaring that "said Indians and all other people who may later be discovered by Christians, are by no means to be deprived of their liberty or the possession of their property, even though they be outside the faith of Jesus Christ."[10] One aspect of the church is shown in Pedro de Córdoba, who in 1510 preached the earliest known sermon to the indigenous, and another is shown in Pedro de Alvarado, who on the Feast of the Transfiguration in 1526 conquered the people of Cuscatlán in what would become San Salvador.[11] These are two faces of the same church, and it was on this precariously poised pulpit that Romero preached and called people to "listen to him!"

By disposition a quiet man, Romero was transfigured when he preached.[12] His words flowed with a confidence and beauty that still have power to captivate the ear, illumine the mind, and captivate the heart. He had natural gifts for rhetoric that were obvious from early in his years as a priest. In fact, it was at least partly in recognition of these gifts that Romero was chosen from among his seminary classmates to continue his theological studies at the Gregorian University in Rome.[13] These gifts grew during his time as archbishop. He often preached for hours on Sundays and many times throughout the week.[14]

Romero usually dedicated Saturdays to preparing his sermons.[15] Beginning in August 1977, he includes a section of news of ecclesial and national events that serve to frame the homily. On a few occasions he refers to these by a specific title ("The gazette of the life of our church," "My diary of this week"), but most frequently the events are presented simply as the reality that the word of God needs to illumine. I refer to this as the diptych character of Romero's preaching, which we will consider further in what follows. He insists that the exposition of the word of God is the most important part of the homily.[16] But it is the narration of weekly events that is most distinctive and has elicited the strongest (positive or negative) reactions.

On Saturday mornings, he met with colleagues to discuss both the lectionary texts and the events of the week.[17] In the afternoons, Romero continued his sermon preparation by reading biblical and other theological texts. The signs of wear on the books in Romero's small personal library show his appreciation for the Jerome *Biblical Commentary* and also for a three-volume *Theology of Scripture* written by Maximiliano García Cordero.[18] Above these, Romero relies on the magisterial tradition. Anybody reading or listening to Romero's sermons will be struck by how often and at what length he cites from the official documents of the Catholic Church. There are more references to the teachings of the councils and the popes than to all the church fathers, Scholastics, and liberationists combined. Most of Saturday night and early Sunday morning were spent in prayer.

During his years as archbishop, Romero lived on the grounds of the Hospital de la Divina Providencia, a cancer hospice center run by Carmelite nuns. *El Hospitalito*, as it is commonly known, is a necessary context for understanding Romero as a homiletician.[19]

When preaching at the cathedral, Romero declared, *Ipsum audite* (Listen to him! Listen to Christ!). When praying at the *Hospitalito* he heard God saying, *Ipsos audite* (Listen to them! Listen to the cry of the sick!). The *Hospitalito* was another place where Romero encountered suffering. In the cancer-ridden bodies of the patients he saw the agony of the mothers of the disappeared and the hope of an entire nation. It was both home and Gethsemane, a lonely place where he met God. All his homilies were prepared at the *Hospitalito*, where he is said to have remained awake in prayer late into the night. It was there that his final homily was preached. "In the *Hospitalito*, one finds the roots of Romero. In the cathedral, one can see its fruits. In both places, Romero lived with God and with the people. But one can say that, in the *Hospitalito*, he lived more intimately with God and, in the cathedral, more publicly with his people."[20]

It was not his custom to write full sermon manuscripts, and he usually stepped up to the microphone with a mere handful of notes. Miguel Cavada Diez, the general editor of the critical edition of Romero's homilies, underlines the oral character of Romero's preaching.[21] When stepping to the pulpit, the archbishop "did not bring his homilies previously written. He relied only on an outline and some documents that he read at the opportune moment."[22] An examination of his sermon outlines, many of which are preserved, shows the serious care with which Romero prepared his homilies. There is nothing rushed or canned about his sermon development.[23]

The two thematic poles of Romero's sermons were God and the people, and these two were related through the church, which was the most constant and common topic of his preaching. Fifty of the 193 homilies in the critical edition have the word *church* in the sermon title.[24] Many more have the word *church* or similar terms (*people, communion*) in the sermon subheadings. Through his preaching, Romero sought to console the afflicted, denounce the criminal, support the just claims of the people, give hope, and declare God's transcendence over human plans.[25] The themes of Romero's preaching were interpreted through and arose from the intersection of the liturgical calendar and the events of the day.

It is difficult to overstate the importance of the liturgical calendar in the preaching of Romero. For Romero, the liturgical year is a school of Christian theology and spirituality.[26] He likens the beginning of a liturgical year to the beginning of a new school year with disciples graduating to a new gospel and set of biblical lessons (*Homilías*, 4:25). The celebration of the liturgical year is not an act of remembrance like the celebration of El Salvador's independence on September 15. Through the liturgy parishioners participate in the mysteries of Christ. "This is the mass each Sunday. And the liturgical feasts of the year, the feast of August 6 in our cathedral, are presences of the mystery of Christ" (*Homilías*, 2:26).[27] The three lessons assigned by the lectionary guide the encounter with the word of God and also give form to the sermon. It is Romero's custom to preach sermons that have three points. Romero assigns titles to each of these headings, hoping to give his listeners anchor points that they can grasp and hold. The three points tend to be related to each other in a logical fashion.[28]

Romero treats the liturgical year not as an artificial imposition on the history of El Salvador but as a Christological lens for rightly reading the signs of the times in the country. The mysteries unfolded by the liturgical calendar and the national holidays of the secular calendar overlap, but they are not to be confused. Jesus's reply to the question of the disciples regarding the time for the renewal of the kingdom of Israel (cf. Acts 1:6–8) evokes this distinction. There is a sacred history and a secular history. "In spite of the dark shadows of our history, God has his history, and he shines his glory on the history of our homeland" (*Homilías*, 2:475). God intends to transform the secular history of each nation by energizing it with the history of salvation. Reading the events of the day in conjunction with the liturgical year makes the Gospels of Matthew, Mark, Luke, and John become more Central American and Salvadoran history in turn more like salvation history.[30]

Jon Sobrino is not exaggerating when he writes that "the homilies of Monseñor Romero were and continue to be an unprecedented ecclesial and social phenomenon."[31] The novelty of the homilies stemmed from the forceful manner in which the truth of the word of God was proclaimed for the particular situation of El Salvador as well as by the unique homiletical method that he developed. Romero's sermons correlate biblical characters and events with contemporary ones. When preaching on the effects of life lived in a flesh without Christ, Romero presents the example of Jezebel, "an evil woman who, when she saw that Elijah fought for God's rights against the false prophets, sent him a note like those sent by the UGB today: Tomorrow, you will be with the false prophets too, dead" (*Homilías*, 5:207). The UGB was the Unión Guerrera Blanca, a right-wing death squad. "And Elijah was afraid. Who is not afraid before a death threat? And

Elijah fled because the UGB had threatened him, Jezebel, the wicked wife of Ahab" (*Homilías*, 5:207). The burst of applause that met the uttering of these lines is clear evidence that the congregation understood the layers of meaning in Romero's words. Applause became an increasingly noticeable response to Romero's preaching, so much so that Romero was at times moved to comment on this.[32] He rejected the charges of those who claimed that his preaching was aimed at garnering applause. He did not silence his congregation's applause. He appreciated it as an expression of solidarity and as a positive response to the pastoral direction of the ministry of the church. By the end of his life, Romero realized that his homilies were the most important aspect of his episcopal ministry.[33] It was through his spoken word that he touched most people in El Salvador. It was in the pulpit that he became a microphone of Christ.

THE MICROPHONES OF CHRIST

On January 23, 1980, a bomb blew up the transmission equipment of the YSAX, the radio station known as the Voz Panamericana, the Pan-American voice. The bomb was placed by a right-wing paramilitary group trying to silence the message of the church. Technicians worked hard to make repairs and were able to finish just in time for Monseñor Romero's Sunday homily on January 27. As Romero's voice rode the airwaves that morning thanks to YSAX, he was not preaching from the cathedral. Members of labor unions had occupied the cathedral to protest the closing down of their factories. While negotiations with the union and the factory owners were going on, the archbishop moved his Sunday masses to the Basilica of the Sacred Heart. If some were to see this relocation as tucking tail and running, they would be mistaken. The Basilica was no mighty fortress shielding Romero from trouble. On March 9, a bomb set to detonate during mass was set next to the altar of the Basilica. For unknown reasons, the bomb did not explode. Whenever Romero stood to preach, he was placing his life at risk. It was no different on the morning of January 27, when he preached "The Homily, Actualization of the word of

God" (*Homilías*, 6:223–46). The gospel lesson assigned by the lectionary came from Luke 4:14–21. This is the story of Jesus's sermon in Nazareth when he preached to his home congregation, "The Spirit of the Lord is upon me."

Romero understood that some expected him to speak only on politics and economics. He was accused of being a partisan polemicist. However, Romero always insisted that he was first and foremost a preacher of the gospel. His main purpose in preaching was not to call the government to account for its failed and fatal policies (important a goal as this was) but to unfold the paschal mystery of Christ's passion, death, and resurrection.[34] In this sense, Romero's preaching may well be described as mystagogical catechesis.[35] In the case of the January 27 sermon, the lectionary readings for the day are Nehemiah 8, 1 Corinthians 12, and Luke 4. The Old Testament and gospel readings each contain a sermon within the text. This happy convergence affords Romero the opportunity for leading the congregation in a catechesis on the mystery of preaching. The elucidation of the mystery is divided into three sections.

First, Jesus is the Father's living sermon. Romero opens with a Christology of preaching. In Jesus, the revelation of God reaches its culmination: God's plan of salvation literally puts on flesh. The Incarnation is the Father's most eloquent sermon. Romero cites a paragraph from one of the documents of Vatican II, the Constitution on Divine Revelation, *Dei Verbum* 4: "Jesus perfected revelation by fulfilling it through his whole work of making himself present and manifesting himself."[36] Romero models a homiletical appropriation of magisterial tradition.[37] Listeners are encouraged to savor these words. What they say leads us to thanksgiving because in Jesus we have the privilege of becoming intimate with God. Jesus preaches when he sits to speak at the synagogue in Jerusalem. Romero refers to this as the most sublime sermon ever preached. But Jesus preaches through his miracles, his deeds, and his death. Jesus preaches when he casts out demons and when he heals the sick. The multiplication of the bread is a sermon. The resurrection is a homily. He preaches in life and in death, and in life beyond death he sends the Spirit, another sermon. Not only does Christ preach sermons, he himself is a sermon.

The best microphone of God is Christ, and the best microphone of Christ is the church, and you are the church; each one of you from your place, from your own vocation: the religious, the married, the bishop, the priest, the kindergartener, the college student, the day laborer, the construction worker, the woman selling in the market. Each one of you, wherever you are, needs to live the life of faith fiercely because you are a true microphone of God our Lord in your context. Thus the church will always have preaching. The church will always be a homily even if we lack the happy opportunity that I have every Sunday of entering into communion with so many communities that during this week have made known to me their longing to hear again this radio station, which has become as basic as bread for our people. But on the day that the forces of evil deprive us of this wondrous means of communication that they have in abundance, and the church is reduced to nothing, know that they have done us no real harm. On the contrary, then even more will we be living microphones of the Lord declaring his word everywhere. (*Homilías*, 6:231–22)

The expression is arresting. Christ is God's best microphone. The metaphor of the microphone is widely used throughout Romero's preaching.[38] The metaphor was based on a practice. Romero used microphones to extend the reach of his preaching voice. From this practice arises his reflection on the instrumentality of the preacher. The microphone becomes a symbol of the relation and distinction between the preacher and the preached, or, as we will see later, between the voice and the Word. The instrumentality of the humanity of Christ carries the word of God across the creator-creature distinction. His human flesh modulates the eternal will to the audible range. Christ is God's best microphone because the God that seemed far off becomes intimately near in him, as if he were speaking right next to one's ear. Jesus is anointed by the Spirit, or, in Romero's colloquialism, Jesus is soaked in the Spirit, and by the Spirit his microphones continue to make him present to all.

The homily facilitates an encounter with Christ from scripture. "The whole Bible and all preaching revolves around the great saving mystery of Christ that culminated in his passion and resurrection"

(*Homilías*, 6:224). The lectionary is an orderly way of guiding the church into this mystery. It does not guarantee good preaching, but it is an aid that helps preachers hear what the Spirit is telling the church universal as it is gathered in a particular locale. The encounter with Jesus facilitated by preaching is not an end to itself. "The main thing," Romero says, "is not the preaching, this is only the path, the main thing is the moment when, illumined by this word, we adore Christ and our faith surrenders itself to him. And from there, we go to the world to make this word real" (*Homilías*, 6:225).

Second, the church is the living prolongation of Jesus's sermon. From the Christology of preaching, Romero turns to offer a homiletical ecclesiology. "The truth of the church depends on the truth of Christ" (*Homilías*, 6:228). The sermon is more (though not less) than a human word. This is what a sermon does. "It says that the word of God is not a reading of past times but a living word, a Spirit word that is being accomplished here today" (*Homilías*, 6:224). The church can say, "The Spirit of the Lord is upon me" because it is the microphone of Christ. It can say, "This is fulfilled here today" all the time, even on Sunday, January 27, 1980, in the Basilica of the Sacred Heart, at 8:00 a.m. The time may be one of national crisis; the cathedral is now occupied by Marxists guerrillas, and the church radio stations are being bombed by government security forces, yet even so now is the day of salvation. Again and again, the pastor reminds his flock that "the word of God is present here, because you are the church, I am the church, we are the continuation of the living sermon that is Christ, our Lord" (*Homilías*, 6:226). The church is both the who and the what of preaching. "The church," Romero announces, "is the prolongation of the homily that Christ began over in Nazareth" (*Homilías*, 6:226).

The microphone of Christ that is the church is a shared mic. Preaching is a communal act. Romero reflects on how each of the four gospels was composed for and in community. He can imagine Luke, a disciple who never knew Christ, becoming convinced of the fidelity of the eyewitness who told him of the events of Jesus. The stories of Luke's sources became the bricks for the evangelist's orderly account of the deeds of Jesus. The gospels of Matthew, Mark, Luke, and John are not conceived in the inspired imagination of brilliant writers but in the heart of congregations. No one should be astonished by the differences between the various gospel accounts. The particularities of the Gospel of Luke, the manner in which it highlights the mercy and forgiveness of God, God's love for the poor and his call to absolute self-denial, and the centrality of prayer and the Holy Spirit in the life of Jesus and his followers, are no cause for skepticism regarding its authenticity. The gospels are not personal biographies; they are communal sermons and as such deeply contextual.

Third, the effects of preaching are various; some accept Christ and some reject him. As microphone of Christ, the church preaches the good news to all, but especially to those who hear only bad news, the poor. The homiletical priority of the poor is what the council of Latin American bishops referred to as the preferential option for the poor. The roots of this posture are deeper than church councils, the tradition of the Catholic social teaching, or even the Gospel of Luke. The roots grow from the soil of the faith of Israel, whose people learned through hard experience to hope for the year of the Lord's favor, the year of jubilee. El Salvador too hopes for the favor of the Lord, not only in terms of debt forgiveness but in terms of a social restructuring that is the consequence of the Lord's declaration of the good news: new societies, new seasons. In this connection Romero addresses himself to the hopes of young people in particular. Romero admires their social and political sensitivity, but he worries that many of them are looking for liberation along false paths. Only in Christ can true freedom and justice be found. The focus on the young seems surprising until we remember that the bishops that met at Puebla yoked the preferential option for the poor to a preferential option for young people.[41]

The homiletical priority of the poor and the young is not exclusivist. The gospel offers good news to all. The archbishop elucidates this last point by turning from the gospel lesson to the first lesson from the Old Testament, which comes from the book of Nehemiah, chapter 8. In this lesson, the people of El Salvador learn of how the people of Israel responded to Ezra's reading of the Law with a hearty amen. According to Romero, this is what every preacher wants to hear. Every sermon has as its goal eliciting an amen from the congregation.

However, it is to attain this goal while forsaking rhetorical aspirations. The sermon is not an oratorical piece of art but a vehicle for bringing people and God together. A preacher soaked in the Spirit announces the love of God, and the people of God, also soaked in the Spirit, respond with an amen of repentance, an amen of thanksgiving, an amen of wonder, an amen of compassion.

The amen to the sermon is still not the full congregational response. Romero reminds his listeners that after the people heard the Law being read the priests instructed them to "go your way, eat the fat and drink sweet wine and send portions of them to those for whom nothing is prepared, for this day is holy to our LORD" (Neh. 8:10). This is the kind of amen that Romero longs to hear from the people of El Salvador. "How beautiful the day when a new society, instead of selfishly storing and hoarding, shares, gives and provides and all rejoice together because we feel ourselves children of the same God! What else does the word of God want, in this Salvadoran context, but the conversion of all so that we feel like family!" (*Homilías*, 6:235). Still, Romero is experienced enough to know that this desire is not always fulfilled. The people of Nazareth rejoiced when they heard Jesus preaching until he started denouncing their incredulity and false piety. At that point, the mood of the congregation became bitter and hostile. "This is the lot of prophets," Romero states. "They will always have to say good things, and also for the sake of the happiness of the people, they will also point out their sins so that they convert. The humble listen and are saved. The rest become hardened and are lost" (*Homilías*, 6:235).

At this point, one might expect Romero to wrap up the sermon. He has fulfilled his promise of offering a short catechesis on preaching. He has been preaching for about forty-five minutes, and yet Romero is only about halfway done. "It is now time to see if the church of the archdiocese, our communities, and our ecclesial work is truly a microphone of God," he says and then preaches for another forty minutes (*Homilías*, 5:236). The archbishop turns his attention to two tasks. First, he surveys the life of the church in El Salvador during the previous week. Second, he considers the situation in El Salvador as a whole during the same week. In both cases, he seeks to illumine the contemporary situation with the light of the gospel. What follows is one part church announcements, one part newscast, one part prophetic reading of the signs of the times. As I said, this was a genuinely novel homiletical practice for Catholic preaching in El Salvador, and one that was far from universally appreciated.[42]

On that Third Sunday after Epiphany in 1980, Romero preaches about the ecclesial celebrations of the week: a one-year anniversary mass for a priest and four children, the election of a new leader for a religious community, and ceremonies marking the week of prayer for Christian unity. Romero sees the Holy Spirit that soaked Jesus at work in a school for adult vocations to the priesthood and in a parish where young women are making religious vows while committing themselves to living within the wider community. "Happy are they," Romero says, "if they let themselves be invaded by the Holy Spirit" (*Homilías*, 6:236). These events might seem trivial until one remembers that one of the slogans of the militant Right was "Be a patriot, kill a priest" (*Homilías*, 1:82). ⁊ Wow)

Romero reads from letters that he received during the week. He reads one from a nun offering words of encouragement, hope, and prophecy to Romero: "God loves us. We must not doubt this, and he expects something from all this, something great. It is inconceivable that so much pain and blood will not one day blossom into a good harvest" (*Homilías*, 6:237). He reads from John Paul II's catechesis on Christian unity and from his address to the diplomatic corps. He hears in the pope's words a sermon of God encouraging all Christians in El Salvador to pick up the microphone and speak on behalf of the common good for all rather than seeking the approval of a privileged few. Romero also reads a letter from campesinos who are being threatened with death if they fail to join a Christian farmers' union. Since the campesinos could not even write their names, they signed the letter with their thumbprints.

One of the most striking aspects of Romero's narration of the life of the church and the events of the week is his attention to people's names. He calls for justice for José María Murillo, Aníbal Corado Tejada, Emilio Estrada Alegría, Santos Rivas Lemus, Antonio Alas Pocasangre, Fidel Américo González, Efraín Ernesto González, Juan

Umaña, and an unidentified young man, all nine campesinos who were dragged out of their houses, tortured, killed, and dumped outdoors by government forces in reprisal for the death of two national guardsmen. The government also listened carefully to these parts of the sermons because their campaign of lies and disinformation was so effective that even they did not really know what was happening in the country.

Romero reaches out in solidarity to those who are experiencing pressure from right- and left-wing forces. He calls for the release of Mr. Dunn, a former ambassador from South Africa, kidnapped presumably by Marxist guerrillas. Knowing that it is possible that the kidnappers are listening to the sermon, he says, "This is the orientation of the church, human rights. You must not crave for impossible things, but must subordinate all demands and strategies to the dignity of the human, no matter who they are because they are children of God" (*Homilías*, 6:241). For Romero, human rights are not an abstraction; they have names and faces.

Turning to the events of the week in Salvadoran society, Romero focuses his attention on a massacre that occurred on the previous Tuesday, January 22. On that same day in 1932, General Martínez initiated a campaign of repression against a largely indigenous group of people who were advocating for land reform. Under the banner of suppressing communists, the general effectively eliminated the indigenous population from El Salvador. Forty-eight years later, in 1980, various leftist organizations staged the largest march that the country had ever seen. They started from the monument to *El Divino Salvador del Mundo* and walked toward the center of the city. As they drew near the national palace, the marchers were met with machine-gun fire. Some were killed, more were wounded. The crowd dispersed and sought shelter where they could. Around three hundred found refuge in the cathedral. Romero worked to evacuate the refugees to the offices of the archdiocese, where they received food and care. The government sought to control the story by taking over all radio broadcasts, bombing YSAX, and publishing a version of events that placed responsibility for the violence squarely on the shoulders of the marchers. The archbishop quickly appointed a special commission to investigate the events.

Romero reads ten points from the report of his fact-finding commission. In brief, the government version of events is false. The protestors were marching peacefully, and the military opened fire without any prior provocation. Romero's recitation of the facts is frequently punctuated by massive bursts of applause from the congregation. In the words of one his interpreters, "Romero's preaching was timely, not just because he meticulously recounted the sorry tragedies and outrageous injustices of the past week, but because in the face of those events he had come to a carefully discerned and courageously articulated response which his hearers almost instantly recognized as the voice of the One Who is just and compassionate."[43]

Following the reading of the report, Romero offers his pastoral judgment. First, he turns to the victims and their relatives. He offers to them the hope of the gospel, the prayers of the church, and his pastoral solidarity.[44] Second, he addresses the government. He asks them to cease the repression and rein in its security forces.[45] Finally, he speaks to the popular organizations. He praises them for their restraint in the face of the government's provocative actions and exhorts them to deliberately turn away from violence.[46]

Romero concludes by affirming his conviction that the homily has done its work: it has illumined the reality of the times in light of the word of God. He invites his listeners to join themselves to Christ's Eucharistic sacrifice and to cry to God from the depths of their soul for their country and its people, so that all might find the paths that God wants rather than those marked by blood and suffering. He ends by asking the congregation to stand and profess the creed.

The preaching of "The Homily, Actualization of the Word of God" is Romero's most developed and sustained reflection on the homiletical task.[47] On that Sunday in January 1980, Romero led his congregation into the mystery of preaching. Romero's sermons are like diptychs. On one panel is Christ as the word of the Father, the Word that gives life to the church. On the other panel are the events in the life of the church and the Salvadoran society that are illumined by this luminous Word. The panels need to be seen together. John Drury offers an interpretation of how diptychs work.[48] "Unlike a triptych ... a diptych does not have a central panel. Its centre is a hinge—in a sense, nothing at all. So the eye cannot rest. With no center to return to after roving, it must shuttle from one panel across the divide to another across the divide, travelling back and forth between the two worlds as angels do."[49]

The spiritual dynamism required for the contemplation of the diptych is an apt analogy for Romero's homiletical approach. His proclamation moves back and forth between the interpretation of the scriptures and of the signs of the times. The light always comes from the scripture panel. The events panel reflects back the light and also teaches one where and how to stand in order to better see this light. Preachers are tasked with contemplating these two panels together. They are to read the "signs of the times" in the light of the Christ and then communicate what has been contemplated by letting themselves serves as microphones of Christ. The hinge is not "nothing," as Drury calls it, but the Holy Spirit who unites the word of God encountered in scripture with the body of the Word in history, the church. The movement between the panels is then not a haphazard, distracted, roving eye but a Spirit-led discernment. In his preaching, Romero is not only transmitting to the congregation what he has contemplated but modeling for them a practice of contemplation that they can use to illumine their own daily lives.[50]

Preaching, then, has sacramental and evangelical dimensions. It is mystery because the Word that is preached is Christ. It is sacrament because for those who welcome the message it bears grace. It is liturgy because the Word is proclaimed within the context of worship and leads to Eucharistic worship. It is mission because the response of the people to the sermon on January 27 was not only their applause but the profession of the creed with its implied anathemas to all other gods and idols. The ancient "Credo" of the apostles lives again in a hearty Salvadoran "Creo."[51]

THE VOICE OF THE VOICELESS

Romero's sermons were broadcast throughout the nation several times a week. It is estimated that 73 percent of the rural population and 47 percent of the urban population heard his sermons. During his years as archbishop one could walk down the street and catch every single word of his Sunday homily because every radio was tuned to YSAX.[52] The blowing up of the radio station reminded Romero of the fragility of his preaching ministry. Without a doubt, the radio station YSAX was Romero's microphone. But "The church is Christ's best microphone," and all Christians are called to be bearers of Christ's message. The more the government blows up radio stations, the more each believer must become a "living microphone" declaring Christ everywhere. This is more than a metaphor. When YSAX was destroyed by another, bigger bomb on February 17, many showed up to the Basilica the following Sunday carrying tape recorders so that they could rebroadcast the sermon when they returned to their communities (*Homilías*, 6:305). The community, not YSAX, was Romero's best microphone, and Romero used this microphone to transmit the word of God and the voice of the voiceless.

The voiceless are those who in fact do have a voice but whose words are discounted. They may be physically alive but they are socially dead. Most of Romero's flock had experienced social death because of unjust policies that robbed them of their dignity and rendered them socially irrelevant and invisible. The invisibility and inaudibility of the campesinos is the consequence of a long history of exclusion. From El Salvador's conquest in the sixteenth century to the genocides of the twentieth, the vast majority of the Salvadoran people have been relegated to the role of extras in their own story. In the time of Romero, the wealth of the country was concentrated in the hands of fourteen families who saw themselves as the sole and rightful beneficiaries of the economic boom of the 1960s. At a time when the gross national product grew by 6 percent, the share of campesinos who were landless grew from 12 to 40 percent.[53] Not only did the oligarchy not think that this group of people had anything to contribute to the future of their country, they feared that if these masses entered the political process a revolution like that of Cuba would soon follow. For them, keeping the poor voiceless was vital to the stability of El Salvador.

Speaking for the voiceless is an urgent imperative for the church. Confronted with the violent muting of the people, Romero avers that "the voice of the church makes its own the voice of those who can no longer speak, those who were murdered so cruelly, so wickedly, so immorally in order to cry out to God" (*Homilías*, 2:157). In its ministry of prayer, the church amplifies the desires of its people before God. As pastor, Romero listened to the petitions of his congregation, saying that "the voice of the poor always finds an echo when it is heard" (*Homilías*, 4:61). A microphone transmits to the amplifier what it first picks up. If the voiceless are to be heard, the microphone of Christ needs to be held close to their lips.

Speaking for the voiceless is a risky endeavor. Romero's sermons were resisted precisely because they gave voice to the cries of those who were seen as obstacles to the government's plans for El Salvador. "These sermons," preaches Romero, "want to be the voice of those who have no voice. This is the reason why they irritate those who have too much voice" (*Homilías*, 5:155). The irritation was expressed in the form of bullets, bombs, propaganda, and the occasional jamming of radio frequencies.[54] In addition to these dangers, speaking for the voiceless entails the risk of contributing to their continuing marginalization. The first of these risks was certainly the most pressing in Romero's time, but the second of these is one that has beset even the church as liberator in the Americas since the time of Montesinos.

In an essay on the future of the poor in academic scholarship, Mark Lewis Taylor poses a First World question that must be answered by advocates for the "Third World." Briefly stated, "How is it possible to hear and acknowledge the voice and speech of the subaltern without engaging in controlling exercises that reinforce their speechlessness?"[55] The difficulties in assuming a representative role are daunting. At times, the subaltern becomes a podium on which the privileged advocate stands in order to garner personal attention and accolades. Even when the advocacy is not so openly cynical, the eloquence of an advocate can have the unintended consequence of silencing the subaltern, who lacks the education and social standing to be heard. Indeed, something like this happened during the colonial period.[56] It seems that when it comes to the "voiceless," the choices for those in positions of privilege are constricted to either paternalism or silence. Advocacy has reached an impasse.[57]

Romero's situation was far removed from the social location that is the chief target of Taylor's critique. Romero was not a "benevolent Western intellectual." He was a Salvadoran pastor who was not theorizing about the representative role of the church vis-à-vis the poor but enacting this role. He was aware of the danger of speaking for others. In speaking for the voiceless, he and the church faced the same fate as the voiceless—marginalization and death. Moreover, he was critical of those who wore the representative mantle too easily. "It is presumptuous for human groups to pass themselves as speakers of the people. The people are very autonomous, very varied, very multifaceted. No one can claim to be 'the voice of the people'" (*Homilías*, 5:8). Does not this admission undercut Romero's claim to be the voice of the voiceless? No, and here is why.

First, Romero's representative role was based on the prior initiative of God who calls, anoints, and sends prophets to speak to and for the people of God.[58] It is because "the Spirit of the Lord is upon him" and upon the people of God in El Salvador that Romero listened and preached good news to the poor.[59] Romero did not claim to be unique in his role as voice of the voiceless. It is highly significant that Romero never arrogated this title for himself personally. He had not received a special charism. He spoke of this vocation as ecclesial.[60] It was the church that had been called to speak for the poor. All the baptized, from the campesino to the archbishop, shared in this responsibility.

Second, Romero affirmed that the church had taken up the microphone on behalf of the voiceless only for a season. "The church has played an auxiliary role, it has been the voice of the voiceless. But when you are able to speak, and you are the ones that must speak, the church is silent" (*Homilías*, 5:542). He rejoices when the voiceless find their voice.[61] Indeed, he looked forward to the time when the church could direct its energies more to evangelism than to the defense of human rights because the latter was well taken care of by society (*Homilías*, 6:43). The manner in which Romero's homiletical diptych modeled a dynamic, prayerful conversation between scripture and the events of the week was intended to hasten that day.

Third, Romero acknowledged that as archbishop he had a privileged voice, but he did not monopolize his access to microphones.

Even in the context of the mass he shared the microphones with his people. A beautiful example of this sharing is found in his sermon for Baptism of the Lord Sunday, January 13, 1980. When Romero turned from the reading and interpretation of scripture to the reading and interpretation of the people in light of the gospel, he passed the microphone to Beatriz, a sister from a religious community in Arcatao. She read a statement from the community on behalf of José Elías Torres Quintanilla, a police officer who had been kidnapped by a leftist group. Sister Beatriz and her companions had been kidnapped too but later had been released, and Beatriz was sent to Monseñor Romero to bear the news. Beatriz spoke boldly, asking for the release of the officer while denouncing acts of violence and revenge on both sides. At the same time, Beatriz saw that the root of the problems was found in the oppression of the campesinos, for which the government bore most of the responsibility. In any case, Beatriz insisted that her community was not partisan. They did not need to be pressured into carrying out their Christian mission, which included "interceding for the life of every human being" (*Homilías*, 6:183).

There is a fourth way in which Romero broke through the advocacy impasse. It was based on the distinction between the voice and the Word. In the third sermon in a series on the Advent spirit, Romero preaches from the fourth gospel on the relationship between John the Baptist and Jesus (*Homilías*, 4:63–83). Jesus is the "I am," John is the "I am not." Jesus is the light; John is not. Jesus is the Word; John is the voice crying in the wilderness. "The voice is a noise that reaches into the ear, but in this voice goes the Word, the Verb, an idea" (*Homilías*, 4:65). In developing this relationship, the archbishop of San Salvador draws on a sermon preached by Augustine for the feast day of John the Baptist. There the bishop of Hippo states: "A word; if it hasn't got a significant meaning, it isn't called a word. A voice, on the other hand, even if it's just a sound, and makes a meaningless noise, like the sound of someone yelling, can be called a voice, it can't be called a word."[62] Augustine illumines the relation between the representative and the represented. A word while remaining in the mind can be voiced in many ways. The Bishop of Hippo uses the example of the word *God*. The syllables that make up the word are not the

mental word; they are not the concept, not what the mind has conceived. When the mind voices the word, it takes on a certain sound,
definite syllables. From the one mental word, a multilingual person
can speak in many external words: *Adonai, Kyrios, Dominus, Herr, Lord,
Señor,* and so on. Turning the analogy to Jesus, the one Word could be
expressed in many different voices: Moses, Elijah, Deborah, Miriam.
When all these voices speak into the same microphone, as it were, we
have John the Baptist. He is "the sign and sacrament of all voices."[63]

The representative, John the Baptist, is the Voice made flesh. The
represented, Jesus, is the Word made flesh. In the Augustinian distinction between voice and Word, Romero finds a theological rationale for the radio broadcasts of his Sunday sermons. The Word is
carried by the sound of the voice and the waves of the radio. It is
the presence of the Word in his words that makes these broadcasts
more than a speech. As preachers embrace the instrumentality rather
than the protagonism of their voice, the Word is heard more clearly
and the power of the sermon increases.[64] In this same distinction,
one can find a theological rationale for the representative ministry
of the church on behalf of the poor. Romero reminds his listeners of
how the term *concept* is derived from the verb "to conceive" (*Homilías,*
4:66). All words are first conceived in the depths of the person before
they are pronounced out loud. Analogously, when people welcome
the Word, they conceive it anew in their hearts.

When they listen to Christ, the voiceless find their true voice; their
words are strengthened with the power of the luminous life-giving
Word of Tabor. Romero presents Ezekiel and Paul as witnesses. Every
Salvadoran who listens to the Word can say with Ezekiel, "The Spirit
entered into me and set me on my feet" and sent me to the people of
El Salvador (cf. Ezek. 2:2). As Romero explains, "If God calls a child
of the earth to open his or her capacity to receive the Spirit of God,
the first thing this clay feels is that it is now standing up, that it is elevated, that there is a vertical dimension which unites it with a God, in
whose name it must speak" (*Homilías,* 5:83). The Word humanizes the
voice. At the same time, listening to Christ is a humbling experience.
Paul's example is eloquent in this regard. He has a vision of the third
heaven and then receives a thorn in the flesh to keep him from falling

through pride. And yet even while pierced, Paul continues to preach. Romero sees in this incident a very hopeful sign. God uses even the weak, people with aches and pains, as his instruments.

Microphones amplify weak voices. The voice of the preacher as microphone of Christ serves as an instrument of the risen Christ who still speaks through the scriptures and who identifies himself with the poor, the least, the people treated as disposable, the voiceless. Can the voiceless speak? Romero's answer to this question is an emphatic yes. To be human is to be *capax verbi*. All "the religious, the married, the bishop, the priest, the kindergartener, the college student, the day laborer, the construction worker, the woman selling in the market" are called to be little YSAXs transmitting the love of God to their communities. This is the lesson of John the Baptist, the paradigm of human personhood (*Homilías*, 6:232). Taylor bases the hope of avoiding the pitfalls of paternalism and silence on a mysticism of delirium.[65] Romero grounds his hope and practice on the incarnation of the Word that ennobles all voices. What does the voice of the voiceless sound like? A few criteria of authenticity can be found in Romero's homiletical practice.

First, the voice of the voiceless sounds like the voice crying in the wilderness. Moses's desire that all of God's people should be prophets (cf. Num. 11:39) begins to be fulfilled in baptism. "A holy matrimony is John the Baptist in the home. A holy lawyer, a holy professional, a holy engineer, a holy wage worker, a holy woman is John the Baptist whom God uses to announce that the kingdom of God is already near" (*Homilías*, 5:41). As these people answer God's call they find their voice. Some are known for their powerful sermons and signs, others for their quiet, serene, patient devotion to God. Some are fiery like Elijah, others are quiet like Anna.[66] Barbara Reid rightly asserts that in Romero there is something of both. "His fasting and prayer, night and day, shaped his spirit, so that, like Anna, he could speak of God's grace to all who were looking for redemption, and, like Elijah, he could become fiery in his denunciation of the forces that impeded God's action."[67] Prophets do not only condemn sin but also see visions. Isaiah preaches oracles of judgment against Israel and also speaks of a peaceable kingdom. When reviewing the events of 1979, a year of murders and shattered hopes for reform, Romero boldly invites his congregation to be grateful. "Not everything is evil. The optimistic vision of the Christian always finds more good things than bad" (*Homilías*, 6:137). The voice crying in the wilderness is the voice of a dreamer who believes and hopes that the Lord is coming.

All Christians have a role in preparing the way of the Lord. "All of us are called to life. All of us are called to grace. All are called to happiness. All are a project of God" (*Homilías*, 5:38). Consequently, the taking of a human life is a sin against God and a national disgrace. When a person is killed, one of God's projects is scrapped, and Romero wonders how many John the Baptists, how many Pauls, how many servants of the Lord, have been lost in El Salvador not only to state oppression but to abortion. Indeed, one of the purposes of preaching is precisely to encourage the voiceless to cry out for other voiceless like the unborn. The injustice and violence in El Salvador can be attributed in large part to the cowardice of the baptized. In failing to heed the voice of the victim, the Salvadoran Christians have betrayed their baptismal vocation. The prevalence of this contradiction leads Romero to exclaim: "What are baptized people doing in the realm of politics? Where is their baptism? Baptized in the political parties and in grassroots popular movements, where is your baptism? Baptized professionals, baptized workers, baptized shopkeepers. . . . Wherever there is a baptized person, there is the church, there is a prophet" (*Homilías*, 5:87). This is why even if all the radio stations are blown up, and all the priests and bishops are killed, as long as one baptized believer in El Salvador remains true to his or her prophetic vocation, God will not lack living microphones of his word of truth and justice (cf. Luke 19:20).

Second, the voice of the voiceless sounds like many voices. The voice crying in the wilderness is always part of an ecclesial chorus. It takes a church to raise prophets. Latino/a theologians refer to this as *teología en conjunto*.[68] In this case, it may be more accurate to call it preaching *en conjunto*. All Christian prophecy is but a participation in the prophetic office of Christ, a kind of Christian karaoke, so to speak. The "I" is always ecclesial. This was true in the time of Montesinos.[69] It was true in the time of Romero. The bishops gathered at Medellín heard "a deafening clamor bursting from millions of people, asking their pastors for a liberation that does not come to them from anywhere" (*Medellín* 14.2). The words of Paul VI to the bishops in Latin America could have been said by the bishops of Central America in the sixteenth century: "You are now hearing us in silence, but we hear the cry rising from your suffering."[70] Romero did not hear only the cry of the poor; he heard their faith. The voiceless were not perpetual disciples; they were his teachers, his prophets.[71] To be sure, Romero does not discount the existence of prophets outside the church, nor is he unaware that his listening audience includes people who are not Christian.[72] But it is the people of God that live in El Salvador who are his prophets. They point the way forward through the morass of conflicting political and economic interests tearing the nation. They comfort him and when necessary call him to repentance and conversion. On numerous occasions Romero insists that the church that preaches for the poor must first be a church that listens to the poor. "Everyone who raises his or her voice to denounce another must be willing to be denounced themselves. If the church denounces injustices, it must be willing to also listen when it is being denounced. The church too is required to convert. And the poor are the constant cry that denounces not only the injustices of society but also the lack of generosity from our own church" (*Homilías*, 6:280).

The poor lead the church's public speech; they are the church's voice coach.[73] The church must listen to the poor because the crucified Christ speaks through his crucified people. Romero would say a loud amen to the words of Francis in the apostolic exhortation *Evangelii Gaudium* (The joy of the gospel) regarding the importance of the poor: "We are called to find Christ in them, to lend our voice to their causes, but also to be their friends, to listen to them, to speak for them, and to embrace the mysterious wisdom that God wishes to share with us through them."[74]

Third, the voice of the voiceless sounds like the voice of the good shepherd. It is a voice that calls people by name. The naming stories read on the feast day of the birth of John the Baptist speak to how God uniquely calls people for service. Romero sees, in the saintly cast and miraculous wonders revolving around the naming of the child that is to prepare the way, a paradigm of human personhood. On the one hand, the role of John the Baptist is unique. He is a bridge between the Old Testament and the New. He is the sum of all the prophets. He is the forerunner of Christ. This is his identity and vocation. On the other hand, his vocation is universal because by baptism all Christians are consecrated for a prophetic mission similar to that of the forerunner. His divine call while still in the womb of Elizabeth is a paradigm for the call of all human beings. God does not call all people in the same way, but God calls all people to the same end—holiness. It is not only the great saints and the king of saints that are called by God. It is the voiceless, the invisible, the disposable; they too have a vocation, and they are called by name because God cares for each one of them as his own child. In them too, he is well pleased, even as he is calling them to conversion. This is why when Romero looks at his congregation full to overflowing with people who are counted as nothing in the eyes of the world, he says: "Those of us who are here, none are anonymous, each, from the humblest, to the smallest who has come to this mass, to the poorest and most ill person who is listening to this message through the radio and of whom no one will ever speak in history, has a history, has his own history, and God has loved him in particular. Each one is an unrepeatable phenomenon. God has not made humans in molds; he has made us with a history particular to each one of us" (*Homilías*, 5:36). To be human is to be a vocation.[75] The care Romero takes in calling the victims of violence by name is a way of giving voice to the voiceless. The act of naming the voiceless is an empowering act. It restores dignity to those often dismissed into the anonymity of the poor or the marginalized. They are subjects, persons with voices, faces, and names.

The voice of the shepherd transcends the polarities common in human affairs. It comes not from the Right or from the Left but from above. The divine origin of the words riding on the human voice is also the reason why the voice should not sound like the voices of the world. It is pastoral and prophetic. In his *Pages from the Notebook of a Tamed Cynic*, Reinhold Niebuhr remarks on how it is difficult to be prophetic with a congregation once you get to love them. Romero did not experience this tension between the priestly and prophetic offices. Romero's approach was direct. At the same time he was pastoral. A clear example of this is Romero's words to the killers of Rutilio Grande, the Salvadoran proto-martyr, who Romero imagines may well be listening to the radio broadcast of the sermon: "Brother criminals, we want to tell you that we love you, and that we are praying to God for your heartfelt repentance because the church is incapable of hating" (*Homilías*, 1:35). The perpetrators of violence are criminals who need to repent, and they are also brothers whom the church loves.

THE LUMINOUS WORD

On the day of his death, Romero addressed a letter to Pedro Casaldáliga, bishop of São Paolo, Brazil. The message was typed but unsigned and unsent. In the letter, Romero thanks Casaldáliga for his show of solidarity in response to the destruction of the radio station YSAX, La Voz Panamericana, and commits himself to "keep on with our mission of expressing the hopes and the anguish of the poor, in a spirit of joy at being accorded the privilege of running the same risks as they, as Jesus did by identifying with the causes of the dispossessed."[76] Romero concludes his brief letter stating his confidence in the triumph of resurrection. After his death, Casaldáliga wrote a poem in reply:

> Saint Romero of the Americas,
> our shepherd and our martyr,
> no one shall ever silence
> your last homily.[77]

Romero's life and death constituted a coherent and compelling homily.[78] This homily does not end, for at the end of the day Romero is only an instrument. He is a microphone that picked up the Word crying out from tortured bodies and transmitted it with the hope that an entire nation would listen to him, meaning Christ, and be transfigured (*Homilías*, 1:97). Those who had too much voice hated hearing the Word that came from this microphone and did everything in their power to silence it. Most tuned in to the Voz Panamericana radio station and heard with joy the truth spoken by Romero. José Antonio, a displaced campesino, testified, "I cried for that man. My great wish was to know him, but I was able to see him only when he lay dead. I knew only the voice. I loved that voice."[79] José Antonio laments, but not like those without hope, for in Romero's own words is the consolation: "All who preach Christ are voice, but the voice passes away, preachers die, John the Baptist is gone, only the Word remains. The Word remains, and this is the great consolation of preachers. My voice will disappear, but my Word who is Christ remains in the hearts of those who have wanted to receive him" (*Homilías*, 4:65).

Even at its strongest, the pan-American voice of the church has been fragile and small. Until recently, all who preached the luminous Word that is Christ were male voices, and even these were too few given the power of the dominating voices inside and outside the church. Prophetic speech, speaking for or before someone (*pro-phetes*), is a delicate thing. The throat becomes inflamed; the mouth dries; the tongue slips; the voice breaks. Preachers die. Montesinos is gone. Las Casas is gone. Romero is gone. Generations of people speaking and longing for liberation and transfiguration are gone. And yet this is the great consolation. The voiceless still speak because the Word remains. Listen to them. *Ipsos audite!* Listen to him. *Ipsum audite!*

CHAPTER 3

THE TRANSFIGURATION OF EL SALVADOR

I met Herbert on a Thursday night, December 6, 2007, at Bethel Methodist Church in Zacamil. This church is in the heart of gang territory. The bullet holes on the church building spoke for themselves, but Herbert's witness was more eloquent still. He had once been a gang leader with the Mara Salvatrucha. Feared by his community, he was known as *El Diablo*. He harassed people going to the local Methodist church, Bethel, and on one occasion assaulted the pastor, beating him, kicking him, leaving him for dead. After years of this dance macabre, the bill came due. Herbert was hospitalized after a shootout with the rival M18 gang. Herbert was in need of a blood transfusion, but for this to happen he needed a blood donor. No one could be found to donate. Not his gang brothers for fear. Not his family for shame. The only person willing to step up was Wilfredo, the local Methodist pastor. When Herbert left the hospital he visited the Methodist church in Zacamil. In the middle of the worship service he walked down the aisle to the pulpit and interrupted the pastor to ask "Why? Why did you do it?" The pastor's answer was simple: Christ did the same for me. The answer may sound cliché to cultured ears, but it sounded like gospel to Herbert, who at that moment gave his heart to Jesus and became a Christian. Herbert went on to lead the youth group and was also given responsibility for a rehabilitation house next door to the church. Through Herbert's ministry three of his fellow gang members were converted and eventually became pastors. Two years after I met Herbert he was dead. A gang member gunned him down in front of his son while he was selling newspapers. The blood-washed sidewalk was a testament to the inexorable "morgue" rule common in gangs.[1]

From its origins in a violent encounter, blood runs freely throughout the story of the Americas. In the words of a hymn by Justo González, "From all four of earth's faraway corners flows together the blood of all races . . . hardy blood that was brought by the Spanish, noble blood of the suffering Indian, blood of slaves that stood heavy oppression, all the blood that was bought on the cross."[2] How all the blood that was spilt in the Americas is related to the blood of Calvary poses the question of salvation that will occupy our attention in this chapter.

Since the topic for this chapter is salvation, it is appropriate to start with a brief history of the name of this country of "The Savior." The tiniest country in Central America bears a name densely packed with contradictions, possibilities, and ironies. It has been lauded by its prelates and people as a privileged name. At the same time, the mystery of sin at work in conquistadors, dictators, death squads, and *maras* (gangs) make the name a prayer petition: "*Salva, Salvator, Salvatorem*" (Savior, save the Salvadoran!).[3] From the beginning of its contact with Europeans who named it, the people of the land of the Savior stand in desperate need of salvation.

From the history of the name of El Salvador, we turn to the question of violence and salvation in the Americas. We will briefly consider how Latin American theologians attempt to hear and respond to the voice of blood crying from the continent. The responses of these theologians set the context for Romero's own response, namely, the transfiguration of Christ. At the heart of this chapter is an examination of Romero's homilies on the theophany of Mount Tabor. What emerges from these homilies is an icon-like representation of the transfigured Christ and the transfigured people drawn from a rich palate of sources: scripture, the doctors of the church, the magisterial tradition, and the liturgy of the Salvadoran church. The study of Romero's homilies, collected over many years, on the Transfiguration reveals a number of consistent features as well as theological development. The most singular feature that emerges over time is the presentation of the Transfiguration as an ecclesial vocation that reorients natural human aggressiveness in a constructive direction.

In the final part of the chapter, I consider the possible contribution of Romero's vision of liberation as transfiguration to the recent pastoral letter *I See Violence and Discord in the City*, written by Archbishop José Luis Escobar Alas. This letter speaks of a pedagogy of death that has been transmitted from the time of the conquest to the present gang warfare. Romero's vision of salvation complements the work of this letter. The Transfiguration energizes the violence of love informing a pedagogy of life that can lead to peace and reconciliation.

THE NAME OF EL SALVADOR

What's in a name? In this case a synopsis of the problems and hopes of a people. According to Jesús Delgado Acevedo, author of the definitive history on the subject, "Most modern authors like to link the name of San Salvador to the liturgical celebration of the transfiguration of our Lord Jesus Christ."[4] The historical link is forged from different sources. Some historians follow the chronicles of the Franciscan friar Francisco Vázquez and assert that the name was given in honor of a Spanish victory over the indigenous on August 6, 1526. Others follow the Dominican friar Francisco Ximénez, who attributes the naming to Pedro de Alvarado. The difficulty with these seventeenth-century sources is that even as they give a rationale for the date of the patronal feast they do not explain the name itself, since the title of "Divine Savior" is not one that is typically associated with the Transfiguration. Attempts to look for a textual basis for this association in the Roman missals of the day have proven in vain.[5] The missals then and now associate the Feast of the Transfiguration with Christ's kingship. Christ as savior is the focus of the Christmas season.[6]

Delgado proposes a couple of alternative genealogies for the name of El Salvador. He suggests that the name originates from the arrival of an expedition led by Diego de Holguín, one of Alvarado's lieutenants, during the Christmas season of 1524. Additionally, Delgado draws a tantalizing though in the end unverifiable parallel between Alvarado and Columbus as a further explanation. It is well known that when Columbus reached dry land on October 12, 1492, he named it San Salvador because he interpreted the landing as a saving deliverance from a storm that had beset his ships and crew. Like Moses, Columbus was rescued from the waters. The name of San Salvador for the city in Cuscatlán may have a similar provenance. Pedro de Alvarado endured many hardships during the conquests of these lands. He or others after him may have interpreted the victory over the indigenous as a saving deliverance and named the place San Salvador for this reason, even if the most significant battle was won on the Feast of the Transfiguration.[7]

However the historical questions regarding the name and the date of the feast of the Divine Savior are settled, it is clear that from very early on a strong association was made between naming and conquering.

A HISTORY OF VIOLENCE

El Salvador is born out of a history of violence. From the colonial era onwards, chroniclers see a similitude between the Spanish victory over the Cuscatlecos on August 6, 1526, and the victory of Christian crusaders over Muslim forces on August 6, 1456, to which the Feast of the Transfiguration is dedicated. In both cases a decisive blow had been struck against the foes of the church. Throughout its history, the celebration of the Divine Savior blazed with ecclesial and patriotic overtones, even as the actual content conveyed by these tones varied. During colonial times, the celebration ratified allegiance to the crown. After independence, the celebration expressed the political aspirations and concerns of the new republic. An 1864 flier announcing the *Fiesta del Dios Salvador* is explicit in its hopes. "Why should the august religion of the savior of humanity not be wed to the holy interests of the homeland [*patria*]? Why should the happiness and future of human beings on earth not be entrusted to the decrees of heaven and the law of religion? The Salvadoran people have felt this truth instinctively and are perhaps the first American people to have united perfectly the cult of religion and of the homeland in a single thought."[8]

In brief, the feast of the *Divino Salvador del Mundo* became a reference point for a national identity born from the violent conquest of the indigenous. A mid-twentieth-century diocesan yearbook states matters boldly: "From this historic date in which the Cuscatleco warriors laid down their arms and accepted Spanish dominion, the Catholic Church began its civilizing work of channeling those new intelligences by paths of eternal life, leading them away from their primitive, backwards customs that made of them a people of low moral caliber."[9]

Without a doubt the most significant endorsement of the fittingness of the name of El Salvador to the small Central American republic was that given by Pope Pius XII in his address to the first Salvadoran Eucharistic Congress in 1942.

> In order to distinguish humans and peoples from each other, Divine Providence wanted to dispose each a name, "a brief word—if we are to define it with the exact terms used by one of the princes of your beautiful tongue—that takes the place of that of whom it is said and is taken for the very thing itself"; and among those that could have been given to your land, the most beautiful name imaginable was chosen. This name was not taken from recent history, nor from that of antiquity, nor from among the natural gifts with which God has enriched you: bountiful soil, clear skies, unsurpassable beauty in the height of your mountains, in the serenity of your transparent lakes, in the greatness of your waterfalls, your volcanos, your immense sea. God allowed that this would be called with a name that is proper to his divine Son: the republic of San Salvador; the republic of El Salvador. It was not only—we would want to think it thus—the burning piety of Pedro Alvarado that in the dawn

of the American conquest baptized you so highly; it was nothing less than the very Providence of God.[10]

In his sermons on the Transfiguration, Romero allows his interpretation of the naming of El Salvador to be guided by Pius XII's message to the Salvadoran Eucharistic Congress. Romero speaks approvingly of what the pope called "the piety of Pedro Alvarado" without examining the dark side of the conquest. This omission is regrettable. It limits the scope of Romero's study of the question of violence by muting questions of colonialism. Romero's analysis of the structures of sin in need of transfiguration is not invalidated by his omission, but it needs to be extended. This is precisely what Archbishop José Luis Escobar Alas does in his 2016 pastoral letter on the problem of violence, *Veo en la ciudad violencia y discordia* (I see violence and discord in the city). To be sure, Romero is deeply concerned with the problem of violence in El Salvador. Indeed, a good portion of his third pastoral letter, *The Church and the Popular Political Organizations*, is dedicated to this question and even offers a typology of violence.[11] We will look at this letter in the fifth chapter of the book.

In Escobar's judgment Pedro de Alvarado cannot be presented as a paragon of piety when he was in fact a pedagogue of death. Escobar writes, "The process of conquest and colonization that Pedro de Alvarado and his men accomplished on arriving to the Cuscatlecan lands can be labeled hard and most cruel."[12] To substantiate this claim, Escobar appeals to Bartolomé de las Casas's *Short Account of the Destruction of the Indies*, which details the hunger for gold that drove Alvarado to commit all kinds of atrocities throughout what is now Central America. Far from extolling the piety of Alvarado, Las Casas paints the portrait of a tyrannical butcher.

> Oh, if one were to catalog all those orphaned by him, all those whose children he stole, all those whose wives he took, all the women he widowed, and all the adultery, violence, and rape that could be laid at his door, as well as all those he deprived of liberty, and all the torment and calamity countless people suffered because of him! If one could calculate how many tears were shed and how many sighs and anguished

groans were caused by his actions, how much grief he occasioned in this life, and how many souls he consigned to eternal damnation in the life hereafter—not only the countless hordes of natives, but also the Christian wretches whose association with him led them to commit vile atrocities, mortal sins and inhuman barbarity. May God have mercy on him, and may he be satisfied with the terrible death that visited him.[13]

Alvarado's legacy was not only the beautiful name of El Salvador but "a pedagogy of death that explained, modeled, and indicated how to kill, whom to kill, by what means and for which reasons to kill."[14] The curriculum for this pedagogy has been developing since the violent encounter between Europeans and Amerindians in the sixteenth century.

Escobar begins this tragic tale in 1524 with Pedro de Alvarado's conquest of Cuscatlán. The social exclusion of the indigenous population inducted conqueror and conquered alike in a pedagogy of death that justified the use of violence as an instrument for social reform. Escobar terms this colonial period as the incubator of violence. After independence from Spain in 1821, there was hope for an improved social situation, but criollo promises of a more just society for all Salvadorans were fleeting. For the indigenous and for not a few mestizos, the constitution of the republic institutionalized and legitimated the unjust colonial situation. In 1832, Anastasio Aquino led a large number of indigenous and ladinos in an uprising with the aim of ending the concentration of land in the hands of a small criollo elite. They were, however, defeated by government forces constituted of a larger number of indigenous and ladinos. As Escobar described, "Brothers were killing each other and bleeding each other for the defense of interests that were unfavorable to their own."[15] What he called the "first explosion of violence" fueled an already accelerating spiral of violence. Institutionalized violence provoked insurrectional violence, which in turn gave rise to repressive violence. In 1932, this violent spiral exploded again in a massive uprising of campesinos and indigenous people. Escobar passes over the details of the role of Farabundo Martí and Marxist ideology in the uprising and the excesses of General Maximiliano. Instead, he draws attention to the warnings delivered by his predecessor Monseñor José Alfonso Belloso y Sánchez, who in a pastoral letter written in 1930 spoke of the unjust conditions that needed to be transformed if El Salvador was to enjoy peace. The letter was unheeded, and the result of the uprising was more death, the virtual extinction of indigenous people from El Salvador, and hardening of the structures of social exclusion. The powder keg of social injustice that exploded in the 1930s blew up again in the civil war of the 1980s. From his reading of this history of violence, Escobar identifies four root causes that contribute to its perpetuation: social exclusion, the idolatry of wealth, radical individualism, and a culture of impunity.

The oldest and deepest root of the problem of violence in El Salvador is social exclusion. Unemployment and underemployment contribute to a sense of social exclusion, but even more problematic is the way in which people feel disempowered. Not only is their work undervalued, but they themselves are undervalued.[16] Of course, this problem is not new. It dates back at least to the time of the conquest. However, the original violent act of exclusion has now become integrated into what Francis calls an "economy of exclusion."[17] In this economy some turn to violence as a way of finding a measure of recognition and inclusion that is otherwise denied to them. The second root of the problem of violence in El Salvador is the idolatry of money. Money has become the ticket to inclusion in an economy that does not serve humans but enslaves them to squandering and consumption. The logic of the market compels the acquisition of the newest trifles; these in turn dull consciences to the plight of those who lack the basic necessities of life. Violence is also enabled by individualism. The loosening of social bonds has formed individuals whose ideal of self-realization is completely disconnected from or even at odds with the common good. The individual good has become the highest good, one that must be attained as soon as possible without undue consideration to matters of legality, let alone morality. Finally, violence in El Salvador is abetted by a culture of impunity. The signing of the Peace Accords in 1991 led to a cessation in hostilities and little else. There was no national reconciliation. The offers of amnesty created a climate where the most heinous crimes apparently carried no real consequences. This culture of impunity robbed the older generations of any moral capital that could be invested in the guidance of the younger generations. It is incorrect to lay the blame for this situation at the feet of the crafters of the Peace Accords. The roots of this problem are much older. The history of violence in El Salvador from the time of the conquest to the present could be described as the reign of impunity. Conquistadors were not punished for killing Indians. Criollos were not punished for parceling and selling Indian common lands. Not even the assassins of Óscar Romero were brought to justice. Escobar writes: "Peace is the fruit of justice and justice is the fruit of truth. No one can legislate on a lie; thus no one can build justice on a lie springing from this matter of impunity."[18]

The history of violence has manifested itself with many faces. There is the dominating violence of the period of the conquest that subjugated the indigenous; the usurping violence of the period of independence that privatized communal lands; the social violence of the first half of the twentieth century; the ideologized violence of the second half; and the criminal violence of the twenty-first century. An initial outburst of violence becomes institutionalized and generates a second outburst of insurrectional violence, which generates in turn a third outburst of repressive violence. The cycle repeats over and over again, in an ever-faster, bigger spiral. "The pedagogy of death taught the people torture, repression, dismemberment, kidnapping, violence, massacres, and multiple methods for murder, which were comprehended and apprehended by the people who, lacking a pedagogy of life and a quality education, were not able to decode such macabre teachings."[19] When the church rejected this pedagogy in favor of the gospel of life, it faced persecution and even death, as was the case with Antonio de Valdivieso, the first martyred bishop of the Americas, and Óscar Romero, its recently beatified archbishop.

SALVATION AND VIOLENCE

From the beginning of its contact with the Europeans who named it, the land of the Savior has stood in desperate need of salvation.

Humans need God for their being, well-being, and eternal being. At the heart of creaturely existence is the constant awareness of one's dependency on God. However, Nancy Pineda-Madrid is right when she states that "our awareness is never more acute than in the battle with evil."[20] It is at that time that we too lift up our eyes to the hills and ask: From where shall my help come? One need only look to the Psalmist's cry for deliverance: How long, O Lord? Why have you forsaken me? From where shall my help come? For Romero, his help comes from Mount Tabor, where the Divine Savior of the World revealed the glory of God and humanity. In short, salvation means transfiguration. Before delving into Romero's theology of the Transfiguration, we would do well to consider briefly the account of salvation that has dominated the Latin American landscape for most of its history, Anselm's teaching on satisfaction.

Salvation understood as satisfaction is one classic answer to the mystery of sin and evil. Indeed, Anselm's work *Cur Deus homo* answered this question with such cogency and penetration that it became (at least informally) *the* answer. Briefly stated (and that it can be briefly stated is both one of the strengths and liabilities of this answer), by sinning, humanity offended God and needs to render satisfaction for this offense. The debt that humanity owes to God in order to make amends is infinite. Only God can pay it. Only humanity owes the debt. Hence, the God-man, Jesus, is needed. By laying down a life of sinless obedience, this person who is divine can satisfy the debt owed by the humanity that he has made his own. To put it crassly, an innocent divine victim suffers the punishment due to a sinful humanity and in this way makes possible a fresh start for all. Putting it crassly is important because it is in the form of penal substitution theories that Anselm's account has become widely disseminated.

Western soteriology during the last millennium can be read as commentary on Anselm's work. However, Pineda-Madrid is one of a chorus of contemporary theological voices that have raised concerns about the adequacy of Anselm's answer.[21] First, there is concern that his account is too focused on the cross. It critiques the present age but does not announce the coming kingdom. It glorifies suffering with Christ without attending to the new life his resurrection makes possible. The focus on suffering is particularly troubling for women, who have been taught that the way of salvation is paved by their personal sacrifice. Second, there are concerns that Anselm's account is ahistorical. Salvation occurs over our heads in a transcendent transaction between the Father and the incarnate Son. The result is the relaxing of any tension between the church and the world, a tacit acceptance of the unjust status quo. To put it another way, one can preach Anselm's soteriology from the rooftops without disturbing any social structures. One can question whether Pineda-Madrid's reading of Anselm is fair to Anselm. What is beyond doubt is that the concerns she names (glorification of suffering, futurist eschatology) are real and have malformed Christian theology and life in Latin America and beyond. The reduction of Christ's saving work to the death on the cross to the exclusion of other aspects of life (especially his public ministry) supports a separation of faith and life that leaves theology particularly susceptible to ideological manipulation.

Dissatisfaction with Anselmian answers to Latin American questions has alternative formulations. If the problem is oppression, then Gustavo Gutiérrez is right, salvation means liberation.[22] If the problem is pervasive injustice, then Elsa Tamez is right, salvation means justification.[23] If the problem is exclusion, then Jon Sobrino is right, salvation means solidarity.[24] If the problem is a history of violence, then Romero is right, salvation means the transfiguration of this history. These are not mutually exclusive questions or answers. Each is looking for language to interpret the scandal of the blood that was shed in the Americas in light of the scandal of the cross. In doing so, they practice a *ressourcement* from the margins. Gutiérrez translates the *nouvelle théologie*. Tamez translates the Protestant perspectives on Paul.[25] Sobrino translates the prophetic ecclesiology of Cyprian. Romero translates the anthropology of Irenaeus. Their works are original. The act of translation results in the transplantation of the living tradition of Christianity into Latin American soil. In the case of Romero, the transplantation is fertilized by the local history and practices revolving around the celebration of the Transfiguration. The result is an understanding of the transfigured human that is Irenaean and Salvadoran.

THE TRANSFIGURATION
OF THE *DIVINO SALVADOR*

The Feast of the Transfiguration is celebrated on August 6. On August 6, 1456, news of the Christian victory over the Turks at Belgrade on July 22, 1456, reached Pope Callixtus III.[26] The Orthodox churches already celebrated the Transfiguration on August 6, but the traditional day of observance in the West was the second Sunday of Lent.[27] The popes responded to the news of the victory by adding the Eastern date to the Western calendar. For El Salvador, whose name is dedicated to the transfigured Christ, the savior of the world, the Transfiguration is not only a liturgical feast but a national holiday. It is preceded on August 5 by the *Bajada*, an outdoor procession and service with a statue of the transfigured Christ. On August 6, the archbishop preaches sermons that weave together national, liturgical, and biblical threads. The scripture lessons for the day are almost identical. Only the version of the Transfiguration story that is read varies in accordance with the liturgical year.[28]

In this section I take a diachronic view of Romero's preaching on the Transfiguration spanning from his early days as a parish priest to the final weeks of his life. The sampling of sermons will not be exhaustive. Too few of the sermons that Romero preached before he became archbishop are available. However, the Transfiguration sermons that I consider here cover a sufficiently broad time span to allow a wide-angle view of Romero's theology of transfiguration.

Eternity Contemplates You (1946)

Óscar Romero preached on the Transfiguration on August 6, 1946, at an outdoor mass for the troops stationed in San Miguel.[29] This was his first parish. Romero was only twenty-nine years old at the time. As the text reads, it is a very short homily, perhaps five to seven minutes in length. It is steeped in military, patriotic, and transfiguration imagery. It begins with a story about how Napoleon prodded the fighting vigor of his troops as they passed by the pyramids of

Egypt with a declaration that their valor was being contemplated by the near eternity of forty centuries of history. The San Miguel troops have an even greater honor. From the altar where the Eucharist will be celebrated, true eternity will contemplate them. The patron of El Salvador, the Divine Savior of the World, is the Lord of hosts. He has made the small Central American republic his Salvadoran Tabor. From this summit, Romero blesses his troops with "the strength of your arms, the manliness of your uniforms, and the sacrifice of your military life."[30] For this reason, the soldiers can say with the apostles, "Lord, it is good to be here." It is good to be a Salvadoran. For the pastor of San Miguel, the greatest patriot is the one who eagerly bends the knee before the Divine Savior and serves the country dedicated to his name. The greatest traitor is the one who draws the country away from its glorious religious inheritance in search of other lights. Romero reminds his congregation about the soldiers who fought for democracy during the Second World War. By faith, "even their cannons and tanks became altars."[31] The soldier is a priest. From the altar of the mass, the transfigured Christ contemplates the soldiers and their altars.

The Feast of the Transfiguration (1963)

In 1963 Father Romero had the honor of preaching at the Cathedral of San Salvador for the Feast of the Transfiguration.[32] In panegyric terms, Romero refers to the Transfiguration account as the Salvadoran gospel. Even the silence in scripture regarding the name of the "monte excelsum" in which Christ appeared in glory is interpreted as an invitation for the Salvadorans to read their own geography into the account. The rugged Central American landscape has been prepared by divine providence to evoke Mount Tabor. Pope Pius XII himself saw this resemblance in "the unsurpassable beauty of its mountain heights, in the serenity of its clear lakes, in the greatness of its cascades, its volcanoes and immense sea."[33] Not only was the land geographically suited to become an American Tabor, but its history was guided by providence as well. The land was the stage for a drama that had its prologue in the mythic history of "Votán and Quetzalcoatl," but its first act began with Pedro de Alvarado's arrival.[34] As I noted earlier, Romero follows Pius XII in glossing over the dark side of conquest to call attention to the piety of the conqueror who entrusted the protection of the lands of Cuscatlán to the Holy Trinity and bestowed on the city of San Salvador its noble name.[35]

Romero's patriotic rhetoric interprets the Feast of the Transfiguration as a civilizing and Christianizing act. Its celebration marks the triumph of Christianity over pagan forces in Belgrade and Cuscatlán. For Father Óscar, "The sixth of August comes to be like the vocation of our homeland."[36] A long line of national leaders have pledged their service to church and state before the image of the Divine Savior given to El Salvador by none other than Charles V. The Transfiguration and the history of El Salvador are now tied together. The gospel account of Jesus's revelation of his glory on Mount Tabor is "like the national sacred hymn that exalts the beauty of our soil, interprets the sense of our history, and inspires the civic and religious hopes of our peoples."[37] The Transfiguration is not a one-time event in the life of Jesus. Its light continues to shine on the church, the nation, and history. Events in the life of the church like the second Eucharistic Congress about to be convened in El Salvador are like a new Tabor.[38] Romero sees in the Transfiguration a synthesis of the scriptural story and the world's destiny, and he plumbs three dimensions of this synthesis.

First, the theophany of Tabor reveals Christ as the Divine Savior of humanity. The presence of Old and New Testament witnesses, the luminous cloud, the glorious face, and the heavenly voice all point to the divine identity of Jesus. In interpreting the lectionary texts for the day, Romero engages the assistance of two theological luminaries: Thomas Aquinas and Leo the Great. With the aid of Aquinas, he draws the attention of the faithful to the splendor of Christ: "The clarity of the face of Christ was not a clarity that came from the outside, but an emanation of the divine person and the glory of the soul that Jesus bore hidden in order to suffer the mysteries of redemption."[39] At Tabor, Jesus invited his disciples to see him with *claritas* so as to steady their journey to Jerusalem and Calvary.[40] Thus the Transfiguration was Jesus's response to Peter's rejection of the Passion. By the scandal of the Transfiguration Jesus prepared his disciples for the scandal of the cross. Integral to this preparation was attentive listening to the voice of the Father. Leo the Great helped Romero articulate what a careful listener should expect to hear from this voice.[41] At the Transfiguration, it is the Father who makes the Son known and calls disciples. The voice speaks of the unity of essence and equality of power between Father and Son and on the basis of the identity of Christ charges humanity to listen to him.[42] For Romero, preaching of the divinity of Christ must precede any talk of him as savior of humanity. Before the apostles are shown the all-too-human agony of Christ in Gethsemane, they are shown his glorification. Tabor precedes Calvary not only chronologically but also theologically and pedagogically. Tabor prepares the way for Calvary by already anticipating the cross. "In a word, the manifestation of Jesus as God on Tabor is also the manifestation of Jesus as suffering victim of humanity. The same credentials that on Tabor certified him as Son of God serve to certify him as 'man of sorrows' whose sufferings will have enough merit to save humanity because he is God."[43]

The second dimension of the Transfiguration that Romero considers is the ecclesiological. Moses and Elijah represent the people of God who preceded Christ. Peter, James, and John stand in as representatives of the people of God who followed Christ. The rays of Jesus's radiance reach back to the creation of humanity and forward to its consummation. The contemplation of this mystery turns the soberest doctors of the church into poets. Romero remarks in amazement that "the theology of Aquinas becomes sublime poetry when he compares these two portions of humanity to a Palm Sunday procession that becomes cosmic so as to include all human beings, those who walk before and behind the Divine Savior, crying 'Hosanna,' as if imploring salvation from him."[44] The church prolongs and perfects the mission that God began in Israel.

The third dimension of the Transfiguration that Romero considers is the anthropological. On Mount Tabor, humanity catches a glimpse of its destiny in Christ and of the role of the church in attaining this destiny. Peter speaks for all humankind when, seeing a preview of the glorious promised end, he cries, "Lord, it is good for us to be here." The transfiguration of Christ should kindle desire for the transfiguration of humanity. Humans were made for joy and light. The longings for truth, greatness, and happiness that all humans have express an implicit desire for transfiguration and impart an obligation for the country whose origins are tied to this feast. The closer the harmony between the president and the pope, the better the longing of the nation to live under the glory of the Transfiguration is satisfied. When the government draws closer to Rome, as when it established diplomatic relations with the Holy See in 1862, the people progress in their transfiguration. When the government forgets its solemn duty, the specters of Masonry and Marxism haunt the population and threaten to lure them away from the church, who alone can satisfy the hungers of Salvadoran hearts.[45]

Romero ends the homily with three goals abstracted from Pius XII's message to the Salvadoran ambassador at the Roman See. First, there should be ever-improving relations between the church and the state. This means that the laws and structures that the state implements to secure the provision of temporal goods for the common good of all need to be in harmony with the church's provision of spiritual goods for the redemption of all. Second, the government needs to understand and operate according to the social teaching of the church. The "clarity of Tabor" that shines in Catholic social doctrine "illumines the true fraternity among human beings, the true hierarchy of temporal and eternal goods, and the vigorous yet gentle principles of justice."[46] Third, the government must respect the church's freedom as it carries out its educational mission. These three goals shine with the light of Tabor, and their attainment would greatly advance the transfiguration of El Salvador.

The contrast between this sermon and the one from 1946 is stark in terms of the length of the text and its theological richness. Of course, the context too is very different. The first sermon was preached at an outdoor mass; the second was preached at the cathedral in San Salvador.

Bishop Romero returned to the archdiocesan pulpit in 1976.[47] He begins by likening the reading of the gospel account of the Transfiguration to hearing an old nursery song; listeners are transported back to their childhood. Again, Romero reminds his congregation of how the name of the country was bestowed on it by its Spanish conquistador Pedro Alvarado. He does not remark on the violent ambiguities of that baptism by blood. Instead, he makes his own the message sent by Pius XII to mark the celebration of the First National Eucharistic Congress in El Salvador in 1942. As we saw in the previous sermon, Romero has great appreciation for this papal endorsement. Continuing the celebratory nature of his sermon, Romero again reminds his listeners of the historical origins of the Feast of the Transfiguration from its celebration in the East in the fifth century to its adoption by the West in the fifteenth to its transatlantic transmission in the sixteenth. By the providence of God, the "most luminous theophany in the gospel" has become the national feast for a country.[48]

The light of Tabor illumines the three pillars on which the reality of El Salvador in its full spiritual, historical, and social density is built: Christ, his salvation, and the church. These are the three themes of the 1963 sermon. In comparison with that homily, the Christological section is relatively short. Romero contents himself with reflecting on the identity of the Christ of El Salvador as the *Divino Salvador del Mundo*. Only a divine person could be the redeemer of humanity. In Jesus, God's good signs and design are made known. "By a strange paradox," Romero says, "the luminous vision of Tabor has been a tragic announcement of the transfiguration of Calvary."[49] The brevity of this section may be explained by the fact that in this homily, unlike that of 1963, Romero is not painting Jesus against the backdrop of Chalcedon but against the backdrop of Medellín.

From the Christology of Tabor, Romero turns to soteriology. The true liberation of humanity is found in the Christ who identifies himself with the history and spirituality of El Salvador. Christians do not have to turn to atheistic wells to quench their thirst for justice. Salvadorans do not need to beg for a cup of water from foreigners. The solution for the problems of El Salvador is not far off. The fountains of salvation are found in Christ's body, the church in El Salvador.[50] For its part, the church must recommit itself to listening to the cries of the oppressed and responding with the liberation that was announced and attained in Jesus Christ. Negatively, the liberation proclaimed by the church cannot be reduced to historical projects that work for liberation only in the realms of culture, economics, and politics. Moreover, the liberation proclaimed by the church resolutely rejects the use of violence. Positively, the liberation proclaimed by the church seeks to free the human being for fulfillment in all dimensions, horizontal and vertical. At the heart of the church's message of liberation is the proclamation of salvation in Christ and the summons to conversion. Romero tells his congregation that social structures must be changed and humanized but that these changes will be in vain unless the persons who lead or are subject to them are changed and humanized. As corroborating evidence, Romero offers the judgment of Paul VI that "the best structures and the most idealized systems soon become inhuman if the inhuman inclinations of the human heart are not made wholesome."[51]

The church prolongs the mystery of the incarnation of Christ and his transfiguration. Romero makes his own the words of the Dogmatic Constitution on the Church. The church has a mission: "to bring the light of Christ to all men, a light brightly visible on the countenance of the church."[52] At the heart of this mission is the encounter with Christ the *Divino Salvador*, the same Christ that orients the history of the nation and all creation. "Any other Christ and any other liberation that announces a Christ and liberation different from that preached by the faith will always be an imaginary Christ and a fictive liberation regardless of how 'historically' these are presented."[53] Romero charges his listeners to make this mission concrete by shining the light of the church on the realities of the country. He calls on the church and the state to work together under the guidance of the Divine Savior of the World, the national patron, to transform the country. He ends as he began with a flowery encomium to the Transfiguration as a national feast that "seems like a pleasant return to the venerable homestead, like someone leaning over the cradle of infancy or the baptismal font to press on it a kiss of faith, thanksgiving, and commitment."[54]

"The Church, Body of Christ in History" (1977)

The man who stepped to the pulpit of the Cathedral of San Salvador for the Feast of the Transfiguration in 1977 stood in a very different place than in 1976. Romero was now archbishop of San Salvador, and the church that he served was being persecuted. The celebration of this feast became the occasion for the release of Romero's second pastoral letter to the archdiocese, which he presented as an offering to the Divine Savior.[55] To be more precise, he presented the people of God, Christ's transfigured body, whose faith was represented by this letter, to the Father. The bulk of the homily is devoted with summarizing the content of the letter. Hence, the exposition of the biblical texts is muted. He makes no mention of the assigned scripture lessons beyond the gospel narrative.[56]

The sermon repeats the patriotic motifs of the earlier homilies. Again, Peter's amazed cry of "It is good to be here" is interpreted in a plain, not ironic, way. Romero identifies himself with the honest-hearted apostle. When he looks at the congregation gathered to celebrate the patron feast of El Salvador, the archbishop too is moved to exclaim, "It is good to be here." How can he not be moved? He has a word of God for the people of God: "This is my Son, the beloved, listen to him." On that morning, Romero believes that the word of the Father is confirmed in his church. Once more he praises the faith brought from Spain by Pedro de Alvarado. The church must continue to listen carefully to Christ as it seeks to live the faith in its own history.

In addition to these well-known national tunes, Romero sounds some interesting if short new notes from the Transfiguration story. In this homily he challenges the separation of salvation history from secular history. One might say that this is not new. In fact, in El Salvador the story of the Transfiguration and the story of the conquest are, if anything, too closely tied together. However, what has changed is the basis for their unity. The founding act of Pedro de Alvarado is still seen in positive light, but it is no longer decisive. What truly matters is the cultivation of a keener awareness of how God works within (and not only beyond) history to save his people, the church.

"We have to be saved with our proper history, but a history that is thoroughly penetrated by the light of salvation and Christian hope. And the entire history of El Salvador, its politics, its economy, and all that constitutes the concrete life of Salvadorans, has to be illumined by faith" (*Homilías*, 1:232).

The other new note heard in this homily is the attention to the problem of violence. No longer does Romero dismiss it cavalierly as a threat, mostly from the Left. He addresses it directly by rejecting appeals to violence.

> The church never preaches hatred. The church always preaches love. Even when the church protests what the episcopal gathering at Medellin called "institutionalized violence," it must cry out violently like the prophets when they violently cried out against the unjust order of their time. It is not that the church preaches violence, but others have provoked violence, hatred, torture, pain, and social inequality. The church has to use forceful language because it is the language of Christ, who without hatred or violence wants to uproot souls from the reign of sin to plant them in the reign of God. (*Homilías*, 1:232)

"The Son of Man, Light of the Pilgrim People on Earth" (1978)

The title for the sermon that Romero preached for the national patron feast signals a shift from the preaching of the previous year. Although he released a new pastoral letter on August 6, 1978, "The Church and Popular Political Organizations," he did not settle for summarizing its content as he did in 1977. Instead he framed the letter more clearly within the context of the lectionary readings for the day, which proclaimed the coming of the Son of Man.

The term *the Son of Man* appears in the gospel lesson. The disciples who witnessed the Transfiguration are charged to be silent about the vision on Mount Tabor "until the Son of Man has been risen from the dead" (Matt. 17:9). The Old Testament lesson from Daniel also makes reference to this mysterious character "like a Son of Man coming with the clouds of heaven" (Dan. 7:13). In his homily, Romero uses the Hebrew original behind the expression—*ben ha'adam*. It is characteristic of his preaching that he teaches. Even though his congregation is made of people who are largely uneducated, he refuses to dumb things down. In fact, it is because the bulk of his people have few opportunities for education that he turns the homily into an academy, and the object of the lesson for that morning is the Son of Man. In a way, it is a generic term applicable to anyone. Everyone is a child of Adam, everyone is human. This assertion may seem banal, but its daily contradiction in El Salvador proves that it is not universally shared. In the history of Israel, *the Son of Man* developed a unique sense that can be applied either to figures like the prophets or to the people as a whole. In its generic use, *ben ha'adam* is a human one. In its distinctively prophetic use, it is *the* human one. It is in this latter sense that it is being used in the scripture lessons for the Feast of the Transfiguration. "Christ is the head, paradigm, and exemplar of a redeemed human race" (*Homilías*, 3:147). The paradigm is a dramatic one. On the one hand, "The Son of Man must undergo great suffering, and be rejected by the elders, the chief priests, and the scribes, and be killed" (Mark 8:31). On the other hand, "You will see the Son of Man seated at the right hand of the Power, and coming with the clouds of heaven" (Mark 14:62). The dynamism of humiliation and glorification continues to be seen in his historical body, the church. In brief, the title "Son of Man" is "the key to understanding the mystery of Christ, the key to history and nature, the key to our hopes" (*Homilías*, 3:146).

The Son of Man is the key to navigating the political landscape of El Salvador. He does not allow the church to sit as a spectator on the sidelines of history. Neither does he allow the church to marry a particular social structure, project, or party. Instead he calls it to engage the political actors working for the common good. The church can even make alliances with political organizations where those seem prudent. Political activism is a valid way of responding to the injustices in El Salvador. Even so, "There are also other ways of translating the faith into work for justice and the common good" (*Homilías*, 3:149). The roots of the problems in El Salvador are not only political, and hence neither is their solution. If the first danger is political reductionism, the second is the temptation to use violence as a tool for social change.

The Son of Man is also the key to the problem of violence. The community gathered around Jesus was acquainted with violence. At one point in their lives or another, all had been victims and aggressors; they had experienced persecution in their service to God and had defended themselves vigorously against their assailants. Mount Tabor is not a refuge from the troubles of the world but a vantage point from which a new response to violence can be seen: the violence of love. We will return to this theme later in the chapter.

The transfiguration of the Son of Man is the lightning bolt that pierces the gloom of Salvadoran history. The splendor of this light has the power to ignite the faith of the people, which Peter compares to "a lamp shining in a dark place until the day dawns and the morning star rises in your hearts" (2 Pet. 1:19). The glory of Mount Tabor brings all things into the light. "The church, brothers, as a lamp in the night, does not only shed light on the contemporary social problems, she also illumines the moral intimacy of matrimony, the moral intimacy where she has her fountain of life; she is also against abortion; she is also against immoralities, against vices, against all that is darkness and leads humans along the road to perdition. This lamp of the transfigured Christ wants to transfigure our people" (*Homilías*, 3:152).

"The Mission of the Church in a Time of National Crisis" (1979)

The 1979 Transfiguration sermon begins on a solemn note. Two days before the feast, Father Alirio Napoleón Macías had been murdered. Romero assured his congregation that even as the priest's body rested at his parish, his soul was present in the cathedral. This brief, clear affirmation of faith in the communion of saints was enthusiastically approved by the congregation. As in previous festal sermons, Romero recalls Pius XII's comments on Alvarado's act of naming. The name of San Salvador is a gift of divine providence and also a responsibility. Salvadorans must listen to Christ. The pastoral letter *The Mission of the Church in a Time of National Crisis* was written in obedience to this divine call. The homily is devoted to summarizing the content of this letter, which is itself devoted to interpreting the national crisis from the perspective of Puebla. The Latin American bishops gathered there earlier in the year acknowledged the poverty of the church's contribution to the social tremors shaking the nations.

The church contributes its pastoral vision. It is not an expert in economics, sociology, or politics. It lacks the technical expertise for judgments on those matters. Its vision is pastoral, yet this pastoral vision is its contribution. The church is uniquely poised to hear the cry of the suffering people. It sees the deterioration of moral values in the countries of Latin America; it confesses with honesty and sadness that there are fractures within the church. Romero endorsed Puebla's judgment of the church's mixed witness: "Not all of us in the Church in Latin America have sufficiently committed ourselves to the poor" (*Puebla* 1140).

The church contributes its evangelical mission. It has been charged by its Lord to denounce sin; it calls all to conversion. The church does this from the perspective of a theological anthropology that vindicates "the dignity of the human, even if he is the poorest of persons, if he is someone who has been tortured, a prisoner, a murder victim" (*Homilías*, 5:191). Everyone has value because all humans are made in the image of God. The Transfiguration reveals the transcendent dimension of all truly human action. "Christ tells us from his transfiguration: this is the goal, making new human beings who are clothed of God and of whom God can say: 'My beloved Son in whom I am well pleased.' The interpreters say that the man of the first reading that Daniel saw as the figure of a man in the midst of the glory of God is Christ glorified and surrounded by the entire people that is saved" (*Homilías*, 5:195).

The survey of the festal sermons discloses important features of Romero's theology of Transfiguration. Thematic leitmotifs are evident: the church as transfigured body, the transfiguration of history, the centrality of Christ. We will look at these with more detail later in the chapter. For now, I want to highlight the diachronic changes in Romero's preaching. First, in terms of form, the earlier sermons lack the concrete narration of the events in the life of the church and the nation that became standard elements of Romero's preaching.

The liturgical feast is highlighted, and this is one of the hallmarks of Romero's preaching, but this highlighting does not illumine anything in particular. Archbishop Romero's judgment of the papal nuncio's preaching as "very discolored and abstract" could have been applied to his own homilies.[57] Second, in terms of tone, the serenity of the language sharply contrasts with the fraught historical situation. In the 1976 festal homily, Romero acknowledges that there are national crises in need of resolution, but his denunciation lacks bite. Indeed, the only ones mentioned in connection to violence are the agents of the liberation theology that he rejects. The purpose of his appeal to Paul VI's message to the leaders of the nations is vague.[58] The call to conversion hints more of national nostalgia than of hope for the kingdom. The early Transfiguration homilies did have a bright side. The first cathedral sermons were more expository of the biblical text than the latter ones. Returning to the image of the homiletical diptych introduced in the previous chapter, one can see increasing attention being given to the panel of the events of the day in comparison to the scripture panel.

Can the differences between Romero's early festal homilies and his latter ones be attributed to Romero's "conversion" on the road to Paisnal? As I mentioned in the first chapters, there are questions regarding the historical accuracy and also the heuristic utility of the conversion narrative. Perhaps the most important reason for the relatively diminished attention given to the biblical text in the festal homilies is that Romero is using the feast as a time to introduce his latest pastoral letter. The presentation of the pastoral letters on the day of the feast is not a promotional gimmick but an act of dedication. The letter is actually being offered to Christ for his vetting.

Our understanding of Romero's vision of the Transfiguration would be incomplete if written only with colors drawn from the festal sermons. The Western Church has an ancient tradition of preaching on the Transfiguration on the second Sunday of Lent. It is to these sermons that we now turn. The selection comes from Romero's time as archbishop; hence a truly diachronic perspective is not really possible. Nevertheless, the distance from the scripted themes of the titular feast and the absence of a pastoral letter needing introduction allow for different hues to emerge in Romero's theology. For one thing, the Old Testament and Epistle lessons vary significantly more.[59] For another, to state the obvious, these are Lenten homilies.

"The Church, the Spiritual Israel" (1978)

Romero often remarks on the density of the history of El Salvador.[60] On the second Sunday of Lent in 1978, this history must have weighed on him. It had been nearly a year since he had been installed as archbishop of San Salvador. In that time three of his priests had been murdered and countless members of his flock had been harassed, chased, and slaughtered. This crucible tested and refined the church in San Salvador and its pastor. The doctorate *honoris causa* that he had received from Georgetown University five days earlier and many other expressions of solidarity encouraged Romero that he was leading his church in the right direction. The coincidence of the beginning of Lent with the end of a year of service in San Salvador offered Romero the opportunity and obligation to lead his church in a time of self-examination. Lenten self-examination originates not from self-absorption but in response to a saving encounter. "The transfigured Christ, he is the one who always speaks to us because the Father gave us this counsel—listen to him" (*Homilías*, 2:276).

All Christians from the campesina to the pope must consider how they are listening to and translating the heritage of Tabor in their daily lives. The weak and the poor have something to offer too, even if it is only refusing to hate their oppressors. Lenten observance can contribute to the transfiguration of the whole human being. As the church listens to Christ, it becomes "a humble echo of that divine and orienting voice" and gains power "to illumine with it our realities" (*Homilías*, 2:275). As the church listens to Christ in solidarity with Abraham, it can be referred to as the "spiritual Israel." Romero uses the term as the title for the homily and associates it with Paul's exhortation in 2 Timothy 1:9. God calls Christians to lead holy lives. Romero's Lenten Transfiguration homily unfolds in three moves centered on each of the lectionary readings.

First, the Old Testament lesson teaches that God saves humanity by constituting a particular people, the people of Abraham. Romero's sermon offers a brief primer on salvation history. No mention is made in this homily about Pedro de Alvarado. The story of salvation does not begin with the conquest. It begins with Creation. Scripture teaches that human beings were made perfect because they were made by and for God. However, Adam and Eve fell; humanity sinned, that is to say, humans turned away from God (*aversio a Deo*). The consequence of this turn was the tragic history of greed and violence with which El Salvador is all too well acquainted. But there is a plot twist in Genesis 12. God calls Abram. With God's graceful call and Abram's obedient response a new chapter in the history of humanity begins to be written, and a people is created whose entire history is one slow, long turn toward God (*conversio ad Deum*). Abraham is the father of the people of Israel and the father of faith. His descendants by history and faith (Moses, Elijah, Peter, James, and John) are gathered on Mount Tabor at the transfiguration of *the* child of Abraham, the true Isaac, Jesus Christ. God saves humanity by transfiguring a people.

Second, the gospel proclaims the transfigured Christ as the heir of God's saving promises to Abraham and his descendants. The transfiguration of Christ is likened to an anticipation of Easter, an epiphany of "a resurrected one who will no longer be touched by death or the miseries of earth" (*Homilías*, 2:284). Peter is right to say that "it is good to be here," but wrong to want to stay. Christ is the way, and the way goes through the cross. The transformation of the history of humanity from *aversio a Deo* to *conversio ad Deum* includes chapters of passion and death. The movement from Lent to Holy Week to Easter is a liturgical expression of the dynamism underlying the current historical moment in El Salvador. As Romero explains, "This is why, brothers and sisters, we should not be surprised that a church is so marked by the cross, for otherwise it would not be marked by the Resurrection. A compromising church, a church that seeks honors without the agony of the cross, is not the true church of Jesus Christ" (*Homilías*, 2:284).

Third, in the epistle lesson, Paul tells Timothy that "God saved us and called us to a holy life" (2 Tim. 1:9). The transformation seen on Mount Tabor must be experienced in daily life. Transfigured faces must translate into holy lives. The call to holiness echoes and amplifies the call to Abraham. In solidarity with Abraham and Christ, all humans are called by God to love. This call challenges and dignifies the hearer. Against the backdrop of a history that has relegated Latin America to the Third World, to the underdeveloped world, Romero states that "love is what gives humans their true development. Avarice, Paul VI has said, is the clearest sign of moral underdevelopment" (*Homilías*, 2:285). The Lenten self-examination requires considering how we love and encourages to love more and more. In this way, "Lent transfigures us, Lent renews the inward person" (*Homilías*, 2:287).

"Lent, the Transfiguration of God's People" (1979)

Romero preached this Transfiguration sermon on March 11, 1979, against the backdrop of national uncertainty and suspicion. The previous week a power outage had interrupted his homily (*Homilías*, 4:256). The cause of the outage was unclear, but in El Salvador it was hard to avoid seeing malicious intent behind something as ordinary as a blackout (*Homilías*, 4:263). It had been a dense week in the history of the church: a pilgrimage from Aguilares to El Paisnal in commemoration of the second anniversary of Rutilio Grande's assassination, a spiritual retreat for priests, the breakup of a *latifundio* and its distribution among campesinos, and a labor conflict between a union and a bottling company that had left a young man dead on Saturday (*Homilías*, 4:263–64). Like a mother weeping for her lost son, the cathedral had received the body of Rafael Larín into her embrace. Only moments before the Sunday mass began was the body taken to its final resting place in Cojutepeque. These events were signs of the times. The hour of darkness had overtaken El Salvador. The expanding canon of harassed, tortured, disappeared, and murdered ministers of the gospel was a clear if terrible reminder that persecution had always been one of the marks by which the authentic church of Christ could be recognized. Not that suffering and violence were to be accepted as normal. Romero consistently denounced the temptation to *conformismo*, to accepting the status quo as divinely sanctioned. But the church had to be willing to follow Jesus wherever he leads, even if it was to the cross.

The second Sunday of Lent offered the church in San Salvador an anticipation of the jubilation of August 6 and an invitation to listen to the voices of the suffering ones. In their cries of lament and protest, the archbishop heard the Lenten trumpet calling the people of God to transfiguration, as Romero said in his sermon title.

As in his previous Lenten Transfiguration homily, Romero reprises the history of salvation beginning with God's covenants. It bears stating that the Lenten focus on salvation history was promoted by Vatican II as a way of preparing people for baptism and penance.[61] Because of the readings for the day from Genesis 17, Romero focuses on the covenant with Abraham. But Romero also references the covenant with Noah. Following a biblical commentary offered by one of his priests, Father José Luis, Romero speaks of the rainbow as the sign that God is giving humanity a natural world that is purged of sin (*Homilías*, 4:266–67). The covenant with Noah "demands from human beings respect for nature," which Romero sees contradicted in El Salvador. God's covenants are not limited to human beings: the Salvadoran landscape matters too, and caring for it is a religious duty. From the covenant with Noah, Romero turns to the covenant with Abraham. If the first covenant gifted human beings with a universal nature, the second gifted them with a particular history. In its pilgrimage through history, the people of God has its peaks and its valleys. The two peaks that were most readily visible from Mount Tabor were Moses and Elijah, the summits of law and prophecy. Romero depicts these two as Lenten figures; they fasted; they prayed; they suffered, but through it all they had faith like their father, Abraham, who "believed against hope" (Rom. 4:18). The transfiguration on Tabor was not a flash out of the blue; it has a history that Romero's congregation need to know if they are to advance on their journey to that high mountain.

How necessary this is for us here in El Salvador! Believing against hope, even when all the lights appear to be off and all the paths closed. If the faith of Abraham, translated into his people as a believing people, makes it all the way to us, let us imitate him. If the courage of Moses, even when he suffered persecution from his own people, brought him to death in order to be faithful to God's plan for his life; if the fidelity of Elijah led him to rise and keep working, even when he pessimistically contemplated suicide, what hinders us, Salvadoran brothers and sisters, people of God of 1979? Our desert, our Lent, our blood, all this can become liberation, light, consolation, and hope. (*Homilías*, 4:271)

In the present hour of darkness, Salvadorans need to have a faith that is filled with hope, a hope that comes from the transfigured Christ. He is the model and cause of the transfiguration of the people of God. Toward this end, Romero exhorts the church to "open the doors to Christ!" (*Homilías*, 4:272). The doors needing to be opened are not just the doors of the believer's heart but also "the doors of politics, the doors of commerce, the doors of sociology, all the doors that human beings handle, all the fields that human beings cultivate" (*Homilías*, 4:272). All these doors must be opened to Christ so that they may be transfigured. In Christ is to be found the solution to the problems of El Salvador. Echoing the rhetorical questions of Paul in the lectionary lesson from Romans 8:32–34, "What great thing do you desire that God, who has given you the greatest thing there is, Christ his Son, cannot give to you?" (*Homilías*, 4:273). If the beloved Son of Tabor is sacrificed on Calvary for the sake of humanity, the Salvadorans can be certain that there is a way out of the historical cul-de-sac in which they find themselves. "And even if we are always walking in poverty and tribulation, without fatalism, but with an elevated mind, let us make each Salvadoran and the whole Salvadoran society, a great transfiguration" (*Homilías*, 4:284).

From its orientation toward baptism or baptismal renewal, Lent offers a singular opportunity for this transformation. In baptism Christians are incorporated into Christ; the baptized already enjoy a foretaste of the life of the kingdom. Living into one's baptism means that one is committed to "be the unity of those who are divided, be the repentance of those who are in sin, be magnets for those who have lost their way" (*Homilías*, 4:277). The relegating of baptism to a cultural practice or worse to a mechanism for social promotion (through a search for well-positioned godparents) stunts the growth of the people of God and slows their transfiguration. Echoing his episcopal motto, *Sentir con la iglesia*, Romero invites his congregation to feel their unity as a transfigured body with their glorified head. "Ah, if we sensed that the church, a pilgrim on earth, already had its head immersed in heaven! And that following it member by member, the entire body went up until it was constituted the definitive church of glory! The young man who was lying here, dead, if he died faithful to this covenant of the people of God, is already a living member with the church triumphant" (*Homilías*, 4:274).

"Lent, God's Plan for the Transfiguration of All Peoples through Christ" (1980)

On March 2, 1980, Romero began what would be his final Transfiguration homily with an expression of gratitude for the services of Radio Noticias del Continente, whose radio transmitters had filled the void left by the bombing of the diocesan radio station YSAX. The archbishop's declaration that the word he preached sought to illumine the realities of the people was met with a resounding applause.

As in his other Lenten transfiguration homilies, Romero begins with Israel. "The transfigured Christ is like the end and fullness of the history of Israel" *Homilías*, 6:340). He draws attention to the parallels between the "deep sleep" that fell on Abram as the sun was setting (Gen. 15:12) and the sleep that fell on Adam when God drew Eve from his side (Gen. 2:21). It is as if God's covenant with Abram recapitulated and reoriented God's creation of Adam and Eve. These historical parallels are evidence of a divine plan. The history that begins with Abram has a destination that is attained in the transfigured Christ and is prolonged in the transfiguration of the histories of all peoples.

The central text for this homily is the Lukan account of the Transfiguration. Romero observes that, according to the evangelist, the conversation between Jesus, Elijah, and Moses revolved around the exodus: "his departure from this world, a departure in pain, a departure in cross, a departure in humiliation" (*Homilías*, 6:343). The Transfiguration anticipates an unending, glorious Passover (*Pascua*). To announce this hope properly, the disciples must be schooled in the "dolorous language" of the Passion. The conversation on Tabor presented them with masters of its grammar. Lent invites the church to join in this dolorous, glorious conversation. If Lent is God's plan for transfiguring all peoples from Christ, as the sermon title suggests, then El Salvador is well on the way to transfiguration. The three years that Romero has been archbishop have been a time of Lent. "This is what is most important in this moment of our national history. That Christ be the glory of God, the power of God, and that the scandal of the cross and its pain do not make us run away from Christ and cast off suffering but embrace it" (*Homilías*, 6:343).

In countries where prosperity abounds, Lent calls for self-denial and sharing. In countries where unjust denial to bread and life is institutionalized, Lent calls for "giving to our sufferings, our blood, our pain, the same worth that Jesus gave to his situation of poverty, oppression, marginality and injustice" (*Homilías*, 6:339). Lent calls not for a resigned conformity with the status quo but for a bold conformity with Christ's passion, "which redeems the world and the people" (*Homilías*, 6:339). Lent should energize, not enervate social consciousness. The forty days of preparation school the people in God's plan to save all peoples from their iniquities and injustices and to transform them by means of "the beauty and justice and holiness of Christ himself" (*Homilías*, 6:340). Only the revelation of a renewed humanity that from its trust in Christ can embrace suffering and poverty without glorifying them can lead the nation out of its morass into true liberation. The mission of the people of God that is the church is to accompany the people of El Salvador with this hope.

The Transfiguration is God's plan for the integral liberation of El Salvador and the world. It is not, however, a specific blueprint for social transformation. It does not offer specific policy proposals. It is less a road map for restructuring the nation than a compass that one uses to orient the road map. Many political projects lose their bearings because they lack an adequate understanding of the human being. The human being was made for God. Hence, any plan for liberation that ignores human captivity to personal sin and the human vocation to eternal life will end up forging new links to the chains binding humanity. "Christ, standing on the summit of Tabor, is the most beautiful image of liberation. This is how God wants human beings: uprooted from sin and death and hell; living their eternal, immortal, glorious life. This is our destiny. To speak of that heaven is not alienation but motivation for working for the great tasks of the earth with more purchase and pleasure" (*Homilías*, 6:346).

For Romero, the transfigured Christ is the anticipated presence of this definitive liberation. Since the day when he rose from the dead, his eternal light shines in the midst of history and offers human beings the greatest incentive to work for integral transformation—the pledge of eternal life. This may seem a base motive, but it is on the contrary the highest because it was for this reason that humans were made. The country desperately needs people who live what Romero calls the "grand theology of transfiguration" (*Homilías*, 6:349). He offers his own synthesis of this theology: "The theology of transfiguration is saying that the path to redemption goes through the cross and Calvary but that the goal of Christians lies beyond history, not in order to become alienated from history but to give more meaning to history, its definitive meaning" (*Homilías*, 6:348).

A SALVADORAN ICON

The survey of these sermons on the Transfiguration allow us to glimpse Romero's vision of the encounter of Christ with the people of El Salvador. As Margaret Pfeil notes, "In his contemplative attraction to the Transfiguration, Romero found himself in good company."[62] His depiction of the Transfiguration must be interpreted in conversation with the broader Christian tradition. In a classic study on the Transfiguration, Arthur Michael Ramsey states that on Mount Tabor "we perceive that the living and the dead are one in Christ, that the old covenant and the new are inseparable, that the cross and the glory are of one, that the age to come is already here, that our human nature has a destiny of glory, that in Christ the final word is uttered and in him alone the Father is well pleased."[63] Romero has not forgotten this gospel. He knows that when the Transfiguration is downplayed, certain errors creep more easily into the faith. Mount Tabor can serve as a bulwark against the separation of the Old Testament from the New, a bifurcation of the work of creation from that of redemption, and the loss of a proper eschatology. It may be that one can follow Christ and bypass Mount Tabor, but the journey to Jerusalem becomes more intelligible and bearable in its light. The Transfiguration is a window through which the glory of God shines and "a mirror in which the Christian mystery is seen in its unity."[64] Romero's theology of the Transfiguration is faithful to these classical motifs. At the same time, his depiction of the event on Tabor must be understood as belonging within the "Salvadoran school."

Romero's icon of the transfigured Christ weaves patriotic and biblical themes, his comparison of the topography of Tabor and of El Salvador, his repeated remembrance of Pius XII's judgment regarding the naming of El Salvador, and so on. Its colors, forms, and themes clearly locate it within that particular ecclesial and historical tradition. What theological themes can be drawn from these sermons? Is it possible to sketch the contours of a theology of the Transfiguration? Margaret Pfeil identifies three interrelated theological commitments that sustain Romero's teaching on the Transfiguration: "an eschatological understanding of Salvadoran history as part of salvation history, . . . an ecclesiology firmly grounded in a view of the people of God as the Body of Christ in history; and finally, a contemplative awareness of the ethical implications of Jesus' invitation to his disciples to accompany him from Tabor to Calvary."[65]

A word of caution is warranted. These are sermons, and they should not be pressed to adhere to a theological mode of discourse that is alien to their purpose. The homiletical brushstrokes with which Romero paints this icon of the patron of El Salvador do not have the precision of the Scholastic touch, nor should they. Theological discourse occurs in different genres that have their own internal logics by which they are formed and measured. No one would call Monet sloppy for not employing the sharp contrasts of Caravaggio. Neither should Romero's theology be dismissed as "pastoral" because it is not written in the language of the academy. With this caution in mind, let us look at the themes of Romero's theology of the Transfiguration. Though the themes are distinct, there will inevitably be overlap in their exposition.

The Christology of the Salvadoran Tabor

Two Christological titles emerge from Romero's Transfiguration homilies: Divine Savior and Son of Man. The festal homilies proclaim him as the Divine Savior of the World who has the solution for the problems facing El Salvador. The Lenten homilies proclaim the trans-figured Christ as the Son of Man. The Son of Man is the fullness of God's glory. *Son of Man* is a collective term that includes Christ as head and his body. In him, human nature glimpses its high calling. Let us look at each of these in turn.

The Transfiguration reveals the Divine Savior of the world. Romero, like Leo the Great and Aquinas, emphasizes the Trinitar-ian theology of the unity of essence of the Father and the Son. No mention is made of the Spirit's presence as the cloud or of the Spirit acting in any explicit way on Mount Tabor. The voice gives the dis-ciples deeper insight into Christ's identity and also charges them to "listen to him." The Christian paradoxes of humiliation and exalta-tion, shame and glory must be understood not as intellectual puzzles but as manifestations of the mercy of God, whose love will stop at nothing in saving humankind. On Tabor, Christians learn to see that Jesus is divine and that because he is divine he can be the savior of the world. The Chalcedonian notes are certainly more prominent in the earlier sermons, but the reasons for this shift are more contextual than theological. The festal sermons became the occasions for the release of pastoral letters, and the Lenten sermons have a dynamic that is oriented toward cross and baptism. The high Christology of the early sermons reemerges in the Christmas homilies, which in fact are more liturgically and historically linked to the theme of the Divine Savior.

The privileging of the divinity of Christ or the "Christology from above" approach was polemical in Romero's context. Jon Sobrino's heart sank as he heard about Romero's 1976 homily.[66] He saw in this sermon a not-so-subtle critique of his work on Christology from below that emphasized the "historical" Jesus. In that work, Sobrino expressed concerns regarding what he termed "the inoperativeness of traditional christologies."[67] He worried that high Christologies veered toward abstraction. The emphasis on concepts like "nature" and "being" had contributed to a divorce between faith in Christ and the life of Jesus. Alongside the danger of abstraction, Sobrino suspected that classical Christologies were inadequately dialectical. A one-sided Jesus was presented, a Jesus who pronounced blessings without woes, a Jesus who loved the poor without speaking against injustice. Finally, Sobrino worried about a misleading absolutization of Christ. Making of Christ an absolute without attending to the historical and dialectical (conflictual) development of his personality lifted him from the hustle and bustle of daily existence. It presented a transcendent Christ that seemed to soar above the plane of human history. When this happened, it seemed as if only the eschatological mattered and as if pursuing inner historical ends was irrelevant. Sobrino sought to overcome these failures of traditional Christologies by deeply grounding his own in the historical Jesus and in the history of suffering of Latin America.[68] It seemed to him that in the face of the problems of El Salvador, Romero was sounding a retreat to a fortress theology.[69]

It would be interesting to analyze the Christologies of Romero and Sobrino side by side and render judgments regarding their similarities, differences, strengths, and weaknesses. Such an analysis would require studying Sobrino's Christology and its own historical development. This is not possible within the confines of the current project. Instead, I limit myself to a few observations. First, it is unlikely that Romero had read Sobrino's book on Christology.[70] Still, Romero would have been familiar enough with the work of the Basque Jesuit that his Christology might still have been Romero's homiletical target. Second, the size of the target must not be exaggerated. Romero's words of critique are in passing and he devotes far more attention to presenting a high Christology than to opposing a low one. Third, much of what Romero says that is critical of liberation is simply a Salvadoran appropriation of Paul VI's *Evangelii Nuntiandi*, one of Romero's favorite papal texts. Having said all this, Sobrino does have a point. Romero's homily was tone deaf to the reality of El Salvador in 1976. Margaret Pfeil's comments are spot on. "Romero's sanguine portrayal of social transformation failed to account for the deadly disparity of power operative among the various sectors of Salvadoran society at the time. Though acutely attuned to the dangers of transgressing the boundary between pastoral ministry and political involvement, Romero seemed unaware at that point of the extent to which his own acceptance of the status quo was itself fraught with political implications."[71]

The problem with the 1976 homily was not Christological but hermeneutical. Romero was insufficiently aware of the complications with his social location, and he failed to see that his irenic vision of harmony was itself part of the problem. When, as archbishop, he explicitly referenced "Christologies from above" and "Christologies from below," he did not present them in opposition to each other but as two great impulses motivated from the desire of wanting to know Christ better (*Homilías*, 2:181).[72]

The Transfiguration reveals the Son of Man. In him, the dignity of human beings as creatures made in the image of God shines forth. In his Lenten homily on the Transfiguration in 1979, Romero quotes from John Paul II's opening speech at Puebla: "The human being is a wonder of God, unrepeatable" (*Homilías*, 4:275).[73] Humans are creatures made in the image of God who desire communion with their maker. The image longs for its exemplar. This longing begins to be satisfied on Mount Tabor. According to Leo the Great, Peter's proposal to build three tabernacles on Mount Tabor was the result of being "seized with a sort of frenzied craving for things eternal."[74] The church father interprets Jesus's silence as tacit acknowledgment that the proposal was not dishonest (*improbum*) but disordered (*inordinatum*) with respect to how God planned to lead people through suffering to glory.[75] While it is only in his 1963 homily that Romero draws explicitly on Leo the Great's exposition, the theme of Peter's excessive desire is well known in the Salvadoran tradition. For instance, the archbishopric's announcement for the celebration of the Transfiguration in 1947 states that Peter's declaration "Lord, it is good for us to be here" is affirmed by the Salvadoran people's solemn assembly. It is good to gather year after year on this feast, "savoring and tasting these great things that fill the soul with unspeakable and ineffable consolation."[76]

The revelation of the Son of Man on Mount Tabor entails the elevation of human nature, which in turn presupposes and proclaims the goodness of creation. Peter's blurted words are every Christian's confession. It is good for us to be here because it is good to be. The affirmation of the goodness of being is made concrete in Romero's defense of what might be called the right to fiesta. When soldiers confiscated the fireworks that were to be used in celebration of the Feast of Saint Bartholomew, the patron saint of Arcatao, Romero protested. "Oh that they would respect the joy of the people! They even took their fireworks away! In a town, there is no fiesta without fireworks" (*Homilías*, 5:261). Romero was prophetic not only denouncing sin but also in announcing fiesta. In his homilies, the narration of the events that transpired in the life of the church during the previous week could include the lament for murdered campesinos, an announcement of upcoming confirmations, and a happy birthday wish for a fellow cleric. Given the suffering in his church, one might expect the archbishop to speak only of weighty things. It seems incongruous to mix quotidian, prosaic affairs with the serious events of the week. But this kind of festive interruption was common in Romero's preaching. As he explains, "That is what church fiestas are like: with blood of martyrdom, with hope of Christianity" (*Homilías*, 5:47). He would have agreed with Chrysostom: "Where love rejoices, there is a festival."[77] Romero understands well that feasts and parties have their place in the life of the church and the country. Life is characterized by patterns and routines. Feasts are disruptions or interruptions of the quotidian. The celebration of a feast puts daily life in pause, but at the same time feasts affirm and perfect the quotidian. An editorial published in *Orientación* on the eve of the Feast of the Transfiguration in 1978 states: "The feast wants to live life intensely. And within that life the feast presents an anticipation of the future reality. This is why a feast must always have an element of novelty. In each feast one tries to exceed what was done in previous years."[78] There is an element of excess and novelty intrinsic to all feasting, but in liturgical feasts, the excess and novelty come from God. "In the liturgical feast we try to anticipate the future of the fullness of the kingdom of God and to live it in history. This is why liturgy can never be far from history. It will always be inserted in history."[79]

The wounds of sin on human nature and the natural realm obscure but do not altogether destroy the beauty of creaturely existence. Whatever foolish things Peter may have done and said on Tabor, he was not wrong in affirming the goodness of being on Tabor. By the light of Christ, every place becomes Tabor. San Salvador is Tabor. El Paisnal is the *monte excelsum* where Jesus led his disciples. By this same light, the hospice patient at the *Hospitalito* is an icon of the transfigured Christ. The rays of Tabor fall on the just and the unjust and reveal that whatever else persons may be, saints or sinners, rich or poor, they are first and foremost images of God and as such worthy of reverence and respect.

The Ecclesiology of the Salvadoran Tabor

The church prolongs the mystery of the Transfiguration in Salvadoran history. Through the church, the transfigured Christ is the source, cause, and exemplar of the transfiguration of the Salvadoran people. The church is Christ's transfigured body in history. Romero's homily on the Feast of the Transfiguration in 1978 declares that the nature of the church is to shine. "Dear brothers and sisters, this is why the church—which feels itself a lamp of God, a light borrowed from the shining face of Christ to illumine the life of humanity, the life of the peoples, the complications and problems that men and women create in their history—feels the obligation to speak, to shine, like the lamp in the night feels the need to shine in the darkness" (*Homilías*, 3:148).

In spite of Romero's love for the mystics and the wide attestation of transfigurations in church history, he makes no mention of miraculous transfigurations beyond that of Jesus and his people. "God saves by constituting a people" (*Homilías*, 2:281). Divine providence plays a key role in setting the stage for the Transfiguration by sending prophets who prepared the way for Christ. In Aquinas a similar motif appears under the language of *convenientia*.[80] The cast of witnesses, the words of the Father, the event itself are expressed in terms of *convenientia*. For Romero, the fittingness goes beyond what led to Tabor. Following Pius XII, the manner in which Tabor came to what became Central America is to be understood as providential. Romero's appeal to the authority of the bishop of Rome is a constant throughout his preaching ministry. This appeal is not explicit in his brief 1946 homily, but it is clear in all the other Transfiguration sermons. The impact of Pius XII's message to the Eucharistic Congress of 1942 is felt implicitly in all his homilies on the Transfiguration and is explicitly cited in the homilies of 1963, 1976, 1977, and 1979. Given the complex history of the celebration of the Transfiguration in El Salvador, it is somewhat surprising to see Romero continuing to cite this source without qualification. It would have been easy for him to omit any further mention of it, but for the fact that one of the most distinctively Salvadoran themes for the Salvadoran Tabor is centered on the figure of Pedro Alvarado.

How are we to understand Romero's refusal to abandon Alvarado's story? Charles Pinches is right when he states: "Romero clearly held two things together: first, that nation and church were not the same thing, and, second, that the greatest service he could offer to them both was to speak for the suffering ones in El Salvador."[81] The people of El Salvador are not to be confused with the people of God. For Romero, writing off Alvarado amounted to a lack of faith in the transfiguring power of the Divine Savior. The manner in which Romero reflects on the relation of these two peoples might be dismissed by some as unsophisticated and clunky, but it is guided by the biblical revelation of a God who acts in history. "Put stubbornly, Romero is not prepared to relinquish the history of El Salvador to the nation of El Salvador. To do so would be to abandon its people, which the church, and Romero as its chief shepherd, is called to serve."[82] If God is able to weave his history of salvation from the messy history of Israel, can God not do so from the history of El Salvador? That Romero returns to Pius XII tells us that he still regards Salvadoran people capable of transfiguration. "Transfiguration does not strike their names from the familial and national story in which their lives were lived, but it does place those lives into a different story, which extends through Moses, Elijah, Jesus, and beyond."[83]

So even though the founding story of Alvarado's naming is not rejected, it is increasingly qualified. Romero the archbishop does not liken cannons to altars as Romero the priest did. As we saw, already in 1977 Romero contextualizes the foundational act within a broader and more mysterious history of salvation. No local history is to be confused with God's designs. The history of El Salvador cannot simply be read off books. One cannot find pages of good history amid the tomes of bad history. The entire history is marked by violence and in need of transfiguration. It is a Lenten story. A proper understanding of the history of El Salvador begins not with the conquest but with creation and covenant, and it ends not with neocolonialism but with new creation.[84]

The Soteriology of the Salvadoran Tabor

If the church is Christ's transfigured body in history, the transfigured people whose pilgrimage is illumined by the Son of Man, then salvation must not be cordoned off from history. God saves within history, and at the core of this history is the creation of the people of Israel. The Transfiguration is not a lightning flash piercing an otherwise dark night; it has a history. Indeed, the transfigured Christ is the end point and fullness of the history of Israel. On Mount Tabor, Romero teaches his congregation to see a synthesis of the history of salvation and a prefiguration of Calvary.

Romero, like Leo and Aquinas, understands the Transfiguration in connection with the Passion. The voice of Christ teaches the disciples not to fear the manner in which the redemption will be accomplished—the cross. The light of Tabor is not soft-toned mood lighting; it is a spotlight that reveals sharp contrasts between what is in the light and what is still in the shadows. The light of Christ can be polarizing.[85] For some the message of the church will be attractive. They see in the church signs of the happiness for which they long. For others, the message of the church will be repulsive. It will be dismissed as a crutch that a humanity come of age no longer needs or as the ravings of the successors of a poor Galilean fisherman who universalized his mountaintop experience.

As the years passed, Romero came to see that Lenten celebration of the Transfiguration needed to set the tone for the festal celebration of August 6. The state-church coordination characteristic of the celebration of the Transfiguration throughout the centuries was predicated on an implicit compartmentalization of secular and salvation history, a divorce. The divorce resulted in the domestication of the church, which contented itself with speaking solely about the life to come. The celebration of the *Divino Salvador* cannot soar above the problems of the country. It must be adapted to the realities of the people. In the instructions to the priests preparing for the August feasts of 1977, the archdiocese hopes that "these patronal celebrations will constitute a splendid opportunity for the people of God, in the historic context in which we are living, to continue to grow in awareness of what is a true church and become profoundly convinced that the only one teacher whom they must follow because he has the words of eternal life is Jesus of Nazareth, whom the Father presented with those words: *Ipsum audite.*"[86]

One of the most important ways in which Christians hear and respond to these words is through the liturgy. Romero has what Margaret Pfeil calls a "thoroughly liturgical worldview."[87] As she explains, "Through the practice of the liturgical celebration of the Transfiguration, he invited contemplation of the transfigured Jesus as part of the *askesis* of becoming the Body of Christ in Salvadoran history."[88] By *askesis*, Pfeil means a process of repentance and conversion that the liturgy enables and that touches all aspects of daily life.[89] This liturgical asceticism serves to transfigure Christians by unmasking the idols and facilitating an encounter with Christ. The voice of the Father returns the disciples to Christ's not yet glorified humanity through the injunction "Listen to him." The history illumined by the Transfiguration has a downward shape: from Tabor to Gethsemane, from glory to suffering. "Remaining in the beautiful or spectacular that is an experience of God is not an authentic experience of God. History goes on."[90] Romero does not condemn the celebration of the Feast of the Transfiguration, but the celebration must be cognizant of the present reality. "Our country is suffering too much to be thinking of parties. Let us not slap the face of our suffering country with dances, floats, and queens. All this will have its place when peace returns to the country" (*Homilías*, 5:153). The asceticism calls for fasting from some celebrations, as Romero suggests here and as he modeled when he refused to attend the installation ceremony for the president of El Salvador. In the former case, he worried that the party was not affirmation of life but of the status quo. In the latter case, he wanted to starve the government of any claims to religious legitimacy.[91]

When the Feast of the Transfiguration is kept in tune with the times, then the liturgy offers a tremendous service to both church and country. The feast offers a vision of unity that is both Salvadoran and catholic, local and universal. It also strikes a note of transcendence that confirms the importance of working for temporal ends without wholly collapsing the eschatological into history.

The transfiguration of Christ calls humans to embrace their full liberation. The revelation of the Son of Man as the Divine Savior is not only an indicative but an imperative. The transfiguration of Christ impels human action. The link between the Transfiguration and Christian ethics is evident in Romero's interpretation of the Transfiguration as integral liberation. Romero like Thomas Aquinas underlines the eschatological dimensions of the Transfiguration but for an active rather than a contemplative purpose. Pfeil makes this point very clearly. "In his Transfiguration homilies, Romero consistently invites the ecclesial community to train its collective mind's eye and heart's desire on the transfigured Jesus, but he also urges it to extend its contemplative gaze from the eschatological horizon of the transfiguration to the gritty suffering of daily life."[92]

The Transfiguration is how God plans to liberate creation from its bondage to sin and decay. A column in *Orientación*, the archdiocesan journal of San Salvador, states that the Transfiguration promotes a more complete liberation of the human than the French and Russian revolutions.[93] Many contemporary humanisms and liberation theologies falter because of their inadequate understanding of the human being. Romero stands by the anthropology that John Paul II articulated at Puebla, which itself stood on the tradition of Irenaeus: "For the glory of man [is] God, but [His] works [are the glory] of God; and the receptacle of all His wisdom and power [is] man. Just as the physician is proved by his patients, so is God also revealed through men."[94] Without a Christocentric view of the human, we will misunderstand the significance of the sad parade of faces described by Puebla (cf. *Puebla* 31–39): "faces of *campesinos* without land, abused and killed by the military and the powerful; faces of workers fired without cause, without enough wages to maintain their homes; faces of the elderly; faces of the marginalized; faces of people dwelling in slums; faces of children who are poor and who from their childhood begin to feel the cruel bite of social injustice." In these faces, according to Puebla, we should recognize the suffering features of Christ. For Romero, the identification of Christ with these suffering ones is not alienating but dignifying; it fuels the prophet's question: "By what right have we catalogued people into first-class humans and second-class humans when in the theology of the human there is only one class, that of children of God?" (*Homilías*, 6:346). It was this identification that prompted Montesinos's question "Are these not humans?"[95]

The Transfiguration is the truest revolution. In the words of Medellín, "It is useless to change economic, social, and political structure; new structures are pointless without new humans" (*Medellín* 1.3). The Christ of Mount Tabor is the most beautiful image of liberation. He came to free humans for transfiguration. The voice of the Father heard on the mountain dignifies humanity and grounds the church's plan of liberation on revelation. If the human being lies at the center of the church's concern, it is because Jesus has identified himself with all human beings, particularly with those who suffer.

On Mount Tabor, God's saving project is revealed. "The project of God must stand out among human projects if these want to be truly human projects and not antihuman" (*Homilías*, 6:344). Transfiguration is not only an eschatological promise. The transfiguration of God's people begins here and now. The Transfiguration is a challenge that the Divine Savior sets before his people, and everyone must respond from within his or her own vocation. Rich and poor, married and single, professionals and day laborers all can contribute to the transfiguration of their homeland (*Homilías*, 5:195).

THE TRANSFIGURATION
OF THE HISTORY OF VIOLENCE

With these motifs in mind, it is now time to turn to the question of violence with which we opened this chapter and with the quest for an

answer. I briefly sketched some of the answers that have been offered
to the question: liberation, justification, solidarity. Historically, these
answers have been sidelined by Anselm's "substitution." Granted,
this is not the best reading of Anselm's answer to the question, but it
has proved an influential one. For Pineda-Madrid, the problem with
Anselm is not that his theology endorses violence but rather that his
Cur Deus homo does very little, if anything, to resist violence. Pineda-
Madrid longs for an account of salvation that has eschatological significance even in the present age. In particular, she seeks an answer
to the question of salvation that has something helpful to contribute
to the exposure and eradication of feminicide in Juarez. Ultimately, I
think that what Pineda-Madrid longs for is something that cannot be
attained. There is in contemporary scholarship a longing for a kind
of fortress theology that is protected from abuse by methodological
moats, epistemological buttresses, and praxiological sentry boxes. To
be sure, some theological houses are too unguarded and others are
downright dangerous. But as long as finite, fallen human beings are
involved, no theological systems will be foolproof.[96] What Romero
offers is not a safe, soaring *summa* but a theological vision of life in the
light of Tabor. This vision has the power to shed light on the problem
of violence without offering a tamper-proof theology. In this section,
I want to show how the lessons of the Salvadoran Tabor can sustain
hope for the transfiguration of the pedagogy of death that has been at
work throughout Salvadoran history into a pedagogy of life.

The Transfiguration of Aggression

Óscar Romero's icon of the Transfiguration draws attention to an
easily overlooked detail. The five people whom Jesus gathered around
him on Mount Tabor were aggressive in their temperament and
actions. Moses killed the Egyptian who was oppressing the Hebrew
people. Elijah ordered the slaying of the prophets of Baal. Peter drew
his sword against the guards coming to arrest Jesus. James and John,
the sons of thunder, wanted to call fire to rain down from heaven on
the Samaritans who had refused to extend hospitality to Jesus and his
disciples. Romero does not see their gathering as accidental. Moses,

Elijah, Peter, James, and John are stand-ins not only for the people of the Old and New Covenant but for humanity with its history of violence.

On Mount Tabor, the natural aggression that God gave human beings is affirmed as good but in need of transformation. In summoning his aggressive friends to the high mountain, Jesus shows himself willing and able to channel his friends' potential for violence in new directions. Listening to Christ humanizes their natural aggressiveness. Thus the church as the microphone of Christ does not preach passivity in the face of violence and suffering. "There is nothing to fear when the Salvadorans subject all the aggression that God has given them at the service of building the true justice, the order that must truly be defended" (*Homilías*, 3:204).

In a seminal essay entitled "The Cross and Violence," Ignacio Ellacuría explores the complexity and ambiguity of the phenomenon of violence.[97] There is no compelling evidence to suggest that Romero read this essay. However, the impact of Ellacuría's thought on this topic is deep enough and the overlap with Romero's analysis is broad enough as to warrant a brief look at key elements of his argument.[98] First, aggressiveness belongs to humans' animalistic nature. It is natural and necessary from a biological and sociological standpoint. "Without aggressiveness there is no evolution," writes Ellacuría.[99] Theologically, aggressiveness is "a positive force in the human without which one could not be realized in the total human dimension. Not only is aggressiveness something that should not be suppressed, but something whose presence is indispensable so that human life and liberty may be what they should be."[100] However, aggressiveness takes on a diabolical hue when it impels human action without being oriented toward properly human goals. Second, violence is uniquely human. Natural disasters like earthquakes and personal calamities like cancer may have disastrous consequences but are only termed "violent" improperly speaking. For Ellacuría, violence, properly speaking, is a symptom of something gone wrong. In other words, violence itself is not the root of the problem; it is instead a human reaction or epiphenomenon. "Violence emerges as the rationalization of aggression. Rationalization not in the sense that aggressiveness is subjected to reason but in the destructive sense that the destructive power of aggression is increased and worsened by the cold calculus of reason."[101] In his essay, Ellacuría does not diagnose the underlying disease; he focuses instead on distinguishing the different manifestations of violence.[102] Third, not all violence is violent *in sensu stricto*. The imprecatory psalms distinguish the violence of the powerful oppressor from the violence with which God punishes oppression.[103] Both forms of violence are destructive, but the violence of the oppressor is the originating destabilizing violence, and the "violence" of God is punitive and restorative. The fundamental element in violence is not physical force, for this may be found in natural disasters and in just punishment. According to Ellacuría, "The hallmark of violence is not the method that is followed but the injustice committed. And this hallmark becomes most prominent in those structures that make human life impossible, structures that despite being beyond the individual [*supraindividuales*] do not cease being the responsibility of all, especially of the powerful."[104] Fourth, for Ellacuría, the worst form of violence is institutionalized violence. This often faceless form of violence that permeates many levels of society is the maximum expression of the mystery of sin. This violence is "not the consequence of an originating impersonal sin behind which the uneasy conscience of the powerful hides but of a personal sin, of an attitude of sin, for the desire to dominate, of the disdain for person, of envy and pride, in sum, of selfishness that is the direct negation of charity."[105]

Ellacuría's analysis of violence helps us understand better what is at stake in Romero's theology of transfiguration. The potential for a kind of aggression is part of what makes us human. In response to a 1972 earthquake that killed thousands in Managua, Romero distinguishes between what tradition calls natural evil and moral evil.[106] He elucidates the former by way of Teilhard de Chardin and what Romero terms "evil of maturation." There are evils in the world that do not have their origin in human sin but seem to instead be inextricably woven into the fabric of an evolving universe. The recapitulation of all things in Christ is the end point of this evolution, but the process of growing to the full stature of Christ allows and even seems to require pain as the counterpart of growth.[107] For Romero, there is a healthy aggression without which courage is not possible. "The aggression that each human bears can make of him a criminal or a saint" (*Homilías*, 3:255). But just as there is a healthy aggression, there is an unhealthy aggression that the pedagogy of death drilled into the Salvadoran society to the point that it became second nature. If the Transfiguration is to go to the roots of the problem of violence, then its light cannot be the source of individual visions alone. It must also illumine peoples with their histories and institutions. The scene at Mount Tabor is a hopeful sign that the light of the Transfiguration has the power to humanize aggression and build the civilization of love.

The Civilization of Love

The spiral of violence in El Salvador turns so furiously that few probe beyond its surface to study its origins. Violence itself is not the disease but the symptom, the underlying disordered condition. The presence of violence is evidence that something has already gone wrong. Hence, it is not self-explanatory, or even self-sustaining. Criminal acts contribute to the acceleration of the spiral of violence, but they do not generate the cyclical motion. In his pastoral letter, Escobar speaks of the violence in El Salvador as a symptom of a culture marked by social exclusion, the idolatry of wealth, individualism, and impunity. This civilization bears the mark of Cain. In other words, it is not really civilized.

In Romero's judgment El Salvador is not civilized. It is underdeveloped, not on account of its literacy rates and GDP, but because of the institutionalization of intolerance to truth.[108] To be sure, Romero is concerned about the social symptoms of underdevelopment. The fact that more than four thousand Salvadorans died in one year from diarrhea is symptomatic of moral underdevelopment of El Salvador's social structures (*Homilías*, 3:210). The archbishop ardently hopes that the poor masses that make up the bulk of his congregation will move from less human social conditions to more human ones. He wants progress for the civilization that is being built in El Salvador. But progress is not to be pursued in a naive manner as if it were the highest good.[109] The avaricious person, even if highly educated, successful, and respected, is the most uncivilized person. Romero is blunt: "There is no underdevelopment so shameful as avarice, reducing life to having more and more, and not seeing that the true ideal is being, being Christian, being a child of God, and giving things their relative worth" (*Homilías*, 5:522). This shameful underdevelopment is the result of the pedagogy of death. This is the civilization of Cain whose borders Pedro de Alvarado expanded. Romero was a booster of the pedagogy of life, and the civilization that promotes the pedagogy of life is the civilization of love.

Paul VI, in his message for the Celebration of the Day of Peace in January 1977, identified the true civilization as the civilization of love.[110] The phrase clearly resonated with Romero, who used it in a sermon later that year as a way of reordering the language of development that had served as warrant for the oppression of underdeveloped masses by civilized elites. The civilization of love, not of greed, he considered "the strength that will make a better world" (*Homilías*, 1:165). Interestingly, though Romero uses this phrase early in his tenure as archbishop, it is not until after Puebla that it gains prominence in his social vision. In all likelihood, Romero's renewed promotion of the idea owes its vigor to its employment by John Paul II in his address to the peoples of Latin America at the third gathering of CELAM in 1979.

All, from the campesino to the president, are invited to work for the civilization of love. All can work because all can love; therefore, all must work. Passivity is not an option, nor is mere activism. The civilization of love cannot be built by human effort alone. The work of the popular political organizations is important for advancing the common good of this civilization but not definitive. The work of economists and sociologists matters, but it is not decisive. Romero paraphrases Psalm 126:1: "If the Lord does not build our civilization, in vain labor those who build it" (*Homilías*, 6:275).[111] There are no spectators in the drama of God's romance for humanity, but the initiative is all God's. "We do not create love, God creates love. And if a mother is capable of loving her child, it is because God has placed in the heart of the mother a mother's love. And if there are marriages that love each other until death with exemplary fidelity, that love comes from God" (*Homilías*, 4:460).

Love does not seem to be enough. Romero agrees with John Paul II. "At first sight love seems to be an expression that lacks sufficient energy to face the grave problems of our time."[112] Many in their day had lost faith in love and turned away from its language to embrace languages that were foreign to the church, like the cries of hatred and violence or languages that the Church speaks but as a second language, like the language of rights. To be sure, the word *love* can be bandied about in cheap ways. A cheap brand of love is often passed off as a substitute for justice.[113] Even so, there is nothing more powerful than love.

The true greatness of human beings resides not chiefly in their capacity to know but in their capacity to love (*Homilías*, 1:181–82). The human heart has the power to give meaning and direction to the very movements of creation. "Neither the star, nor the flower, nor the bird, nor the dawn, nor the sea, nor the landscape has the power that the human has, the power to love. The human gives sense to the dawn and to the bird and to the flower because he cuts the flower and gives it a sense of love when he gives it to a cherished being" (*Homilías*, 1:182).

The human being is the sanctuary of the cosmos, the heart of creation. The original mandate of subduing the earth and having dominion over all manners of creatures is fulfilled in love. "Love is the only thing that can transform the world" (*Homilías*, 1:183). Romero likens the civilization of love to the agape meal where all freely share of the goods of the common table. Interestingly, although in agreement with venerable church tradition and scripture, Romero places love of self as the spring for love of others. All people are to cultivate a restless desire to enlarge "that capacity of love that bears respect for one's own dignity, and from one's own dignity and love, leads to respecting the dignity of others and loving others" (*Homilías*, 1:182). In actualizing this capacity, human beings attain their maximum development. In other words, they become holy. "One of the most beautiful claims of the essence of the human is the stretched-out hand of the beggar who cries, 'Alms for the love of God.' What an opportunity for sanctity that beggar gives us! When you do things for the love of God that action is holy" (*Homilías*, 1:184).

Love is the rule by which humans are measured. More than once does Romero appeal to Saint John of the Cross's dictum: "At dusk you will be tested on love," or, in Romero's version, "At the sunset of your life, you will be tested on love."[114] The church learns to love in the school of God's love. "God is self-giving. God is self-surrender" (*Homilías*, 4:459). From eternity, the Father gives all that he is to the Son; the Father does not hold anything back but surrenders himself completely. The love that is God is the fountain of all love. The civilization of love grows by the banks of this endless stream. The civilization of love is built by love. To be more precise, it is a civilization built by the violence of love.

The Violence of Love

The Transfiguration energizes the violence of love. The phrase "the violence of love" is among Romero's most well-known statements. No doubt this is due in part to James Brockman's collection of Romero sayings published under that title.[115] The phrase occurs in an Advent sermon from 1977, where it serves as an apologia for the ministry of his archdiocese. The first lesson for that first Sunday of Advent comes from Isaiah 2:1–5. The people to whom Isaiah preached, like Romero's congregation, stood on a precarious political perch. The threat of one political power filled them with doubt of God's covenant faithfulness and tempted them to look for salvation in another political power. Faced with these problems, Isaiah rejected the option that Romero imagines many of his compatriots were urging as the solution to the national crisis, the option that many were pushing on the archbishop—armed violence. It is in this biblical and political context that Romero's slogan appears. "We have never preached violence, only the violence of love; the violence that left Christ nailed to a cross, the violence that one does to oneself to overcome one's selfishness so that there may not be such cruel inequalities among us. That violence is not the violence of the sword or of hatred;

it is the violence of love, of fraternity, that wants to turn weapons into pruning hooks for work" (*Homilías*, 2:36).

The sharp social critique in Romero's preaching earned him all manner of sobriquets (communist, Marxist, demagogue) that he had to constantly fend off. What is striking on this occasion is the manner in which he deflects the charge. The church does preach violence, the violence of love. The phrase is striking in its language and its singularity. This is the only time that the phrase appears among his published sermons, letters, and diaries. However, Romero does pair violence in paradoxical phrases on other occasions.

Romero speaks of the "violence of Christ" that cries forgiveness from the cross (*Homilías*, 4:193). There is a kind of violence that belongs to the cost of discipleship. "It is the violence that one does to one self to never be pleased with the mediocrities of life, to improve oneself, to be better" (*Homilías*, 1:164). The urgent demand to tear oneself away from unhealthy attachments or to set aside goods for the sake of greater goods is not only a personal call but an ecclesial one. Romero also speaks of the "violence of nonviolence" (*Homilías*, 3:255). The one who turns the other cheek or responds to violence with forgiveness and understanding is stronger than the one who strikes. "This is why they said that the martyrs did not lack for courage when they allowed themselves to be killed but that from their situation as victims they were stronger and won the victory over their foes" (*Homilías*, 3:256).

One possible clue to the significance of the language of the "violence of love" lies in its origins. The phrase is common in medieval mystical theology. In a study of love in the Middle Ages, Pierre Rousselot distinguishes between physical love and ecstatic love.[116] The use of the term *physical* seems odd at first, for Rousselot does not mean corporeal or material as such. Instead, he draws on the Greek roots of the word *physis*, nature. Thus, for Rousselot, "Physical here signifies *natural* and serves to designate the doctrine of those who base all real or possible loves on the necessary propensity of natural beings to seek their own good" (78). The great theologian of this conception of love is Thomas Aquinas, so Rousselot refers to it as the Greco-Thomist school.[117] The *ecstatic* conception of love is very different. The more thoroughly love displaces the subject "outside of itself" (*ek-stasis*), the more perfect it is. Love is not something natural that follows some rational order. The title of one Richard of St. Victor's treatises on love sums things up well, *De quatuor gradibus violentiae caritatis* (The four degrees of violent love). Love is something free and violent.[118] For the Thomist school, when you love, you find yourself. For the Victorine school, when you love, you lose yourself. For the former, love perfects; it elevates. For the latter, love wounds; it kills. The paradigm for the *physical* belongs to the realm of nature, the love of a creature for its creator, a child toward a parent, a parent toward a child. The paradigm for the *ecstatic* lies in the realm of romance, the love of a lover for a beloved.[119] In brief, the physical conception is characteristic of the Thomist school. The ecstatic paradigm is characteristic of the Victorine school. Both schools are represented on Mount Tabor.

The company gathered around Jesus on that high place was aggressive. They burnt with zeal, and this is a good thing. There is a healthy aggression without which holiness is not possible. Romero says that "the aggression that each human bears can make of him a criminal or a saint" (*Homilías*, 3:255). The manner in which aggressiveness is cultivated and channeled makes all the difference. On Mount Tabor, Romero says, "Jesus channeled the aggressiveness of those rich temperaments toward a constructive task of building justice and peace in the world" (*Voz*, 119). For Romero, "The Son of Man did not come to kill but to save, so Christ does not mutilate human forces but orients them with Christian forces" (*Homilías*, 3:151). The church has the task of calling Christians to live into the "holy aggressiveness that God has given to all humankind" (*Homilías*, 3:212).

One cannot say that Romero's usage is explicitly dependent on the medieval schools studied by Rousselot. The archbishop might have borrowed the phrase from some other source or even coined it himself. However, given Romero's love for mystical theology, its medieval resonances should not be ignored. The verve of Romero's rhetoric is at home in the Victorine school: the violence of love, holy aggressiveness. The logic of Romero's rhetoric is more at home in the Thomistic school. On Tabor, grace does not destroy nature but perfects it.

Tabor, a School for the Pedagogy of Life

The plan for the civilization of love can be glimpsed on the transfigured mountain. The voice of the Father instructs the disciples to listen to Christ, a Christ who came preaching violence, "the violence of redemption, the violence that made his body the victim of violence so as to pay for the sins of all the crimes and the sins of all the people" (*Homilías*, 3:152). The pedagogy of life calls for cultivating "that capacity of love which bears respect for one's own dignity, and from one's own dignity and love leads to respecting the dignity of others and loving others" (*Homilías*, 1:182). Victorine rhetoric. Thomistic logic. In actualizing this capacity, human beings become holy, civilized after the pattern of the city of God. To promote this civilization, the church must be willing to forgo legitimate rights and privileges. Only as it empties itself into the crowded streets of the *Bajada* does the church discover that "true freedom is that which commits violence against itself and like Christ, who almost forgot that he was a king, becomes a slave to serve others" (*Homilías*, 2:351).

Tabor is a school for the civilization of love. The civilization of love can redeem the civilization of Cain by exposing its crimes and reminding it of its vocation, for Cain too belongs to God. Every year the transfigured Christ encounters his people in San Salvador to ask them, "What have you done with my mystery?" Not that the mystery itself changes, but as the circumstances change, the mystery sheds new light on the situation of the country. The church that is found faithful in its preaching of love shines as united, bloodstained, and hopeful. As the church turns to Christ, it asks him: "Who are you? . . . Who are you so that I may follow, so that I may lend my feet to walk in the paths of the history of my homeland and my mouth to proclaim your message and my hands to go and bring and work for your kingdom?" (*Homilías*, 1:231). At the same time, the church that asks questions of Christ must be open to being interrogated by him: "Who do the Salvadorans say that I am?" The liturgical disciplines that facilitate this encounter with Christ also help the church become his body in Salvadoran history.[120] This is, I think, the significance of the fact that the statue of the Transfigured One displayed on August 6 bears the seal of the Republic of El Salvador. The threads from which this history has been woven are frayed and stained, but they can be mended and washed clean.

Writing from within this tangled history, Archbishop Escobar calls on all Salvadorans "to wait in contemplation and action on the God of life, struggling to attain *the loving challenge of the transfiguration of Christ for all Salvadorans, the transfiguration of our people*, stated by Blessed Monseñor Oscar Arnulfo Romero."[121] The God revealed on Tabor is a God of life who is against violence in every form, a God of justice. This God does not infantilize his creatures but gives them freedom so that they may learn from the divine pedagogue of peace how to channel their aggression in responsible directions.[122] As Escobar says, the Transfiguration occurs "poco a poco."[123] After sharing the Eucharist with his disciples, Jesus invited the three witnesses of the Transfiguration to another hill to pray. There when Judas came to arrest Jesus, Peter drew his sword to defend him. His aggressiveness had not yet been fully reoriented by the light of Christ. The contradiction of Peter serves as a warning and an exhortation. The civilization of love is not built overnight. Forming a pedagogy of life takes time.

POSTLUDE

I end where I began with brother Herbert, Pastor Wilfredo, and Bethel Methodist Church in Zacamil. I do not imagine that either of them knew or know too much about Romero. Yet in their Methodist Church they too were inducted into the academy of Tabor. The encounter with Jesus illumined the darkness in which he walked. He was no longer conformed to this world but transfigured by the renewing of his mind. This renewal did not mean that he became diminished. The conversion of *El Diablo* to Hermano Herbert did not turn the ravenous wolf into a passive lamb but made him a hound of God. The cup of salvation is caffeinated. The baptismal pool is not a warm bath but an ice bucket challenge. Hermano Herbert's energy, his aggressiveness, was not squelched. It was reordered. Zeal for his house consumed him. Only now that house was not the Mara Salvatrucha but Bethel, the House of God. His work with the youth, his evangelism of gang members, his walk with victims of addiction all testify to the violence of love that moved him. Hermano Herbert did not know much of Romero, nor would he have walked in the *Bajada*; but he knew the *Divino Salvador*. He knew the one whose garments are woven from the threads of Salvadoran history. Hermano Herbert's story is part of Romero's story because both, in their own way, belong to the church, Christ's transfigured body in history.

CHAPTER 4

THE FACE OF THE
DIVINO SALVADOR

When the disciples arrived with Jesus at Caesarea Philippi, little did they know that they were about to witness one of the most important confessions of faith in salvation history (Matt. 16:13–20). There by the base of Mount Hermon, Jesus led his disciples closer to the truth of his identity by asking questions. First, he asked a more abstract question: "Who do people say that the Son of Man is?" Then, he asked a more personal one: "Who do you say that I am?" This latter question was what prompted Peter's confession: "You are the Christ, the son of the living God." Peter's answer was divinely inspired and authoritative, but it is not the only answer. Jesus addressed his question with a second-person plural pronoun. Jesus was not just asking Peter. Other disciples have heard Jesus's question and have replied with their own words about Christ, and in this sense each one generated different Christologies. Every year the Feast of the Transfiguration affords Salvadorans the opportunity to join the conversation that began at Caesarea Philippi. Romero imagines the questions that the encounter provokes. The faithful Salvadoran asks: "Who are you so that I may follow, so that I may lend my feet to walk in the paths of the history of my homeland and my mouth to proclaim your message and my hands to go and bring and work for your kingdom?" (*Homilías*, 1:231). The Savior questions his namesake in turn: "Who do the Salvadorans say that I am?" And the inspired Salvadoran answers, "You are the *Divino Salvador del Mundo*."

The Divine Savior of the World is encountered in El Salvador through different images. There is the statue of Christ believed to have been donated by Charles V in the late sixteenth century. This image stands in the cathedral by the chancel area. It is separated from the congregation by a rail. It is too heavy to be carried about in processions. One might say that this image represents the biblical and doctrinal Christ whose spiritual conquest gave birth to El Salvador. Its immovability is a fitting symbol of the firmness of the Catholic faith.[1] There is the Salvadoran Christ carved by Silvestre Antonio García in 1777. Church literature asserts that this *criollo* Christ, "with tinges of *mestizaje*, represents, between anguish and enthusiasm, the uncertain longings of a young people."[2] This image stands in the nave of the cathedral. Votive candles burn in front of it. It is an image close to the people and their problems, so much so that is known by an affectionate nickname—*El Colocho*, a Salvadoran word for loose, frizzy hair. Church literature states that "this is the changing Jesus to whom each soul clings in moments of tribulation, many times wanting to make Christ to the measure of circumstances, the needs of the moment, passions, whims, and ideologies."[3] This image travels the streets of San Salvador. It allows itself to be touched, dressed, and carried.

In the previous chapter we considered the homilies preached on the Feast of the Transfiguration and explored the theology of salvation proclaimed by these. In this chapter, we turn our attention from the work of salvation to the Savior. This chapter studies Romero's Christology in conversation with the popular piety of Christological imagery, hymnody, and spirituality. We begin by returning to the founding ambiguity of the witness to Christ in the Americas. The images of the Divine Savior displayed in the cathedral are an apt statement of the question. Who is Jesus and whose is Jesus?

THE OTHER FACE OF CHRIST

The remarkable coincidence of the name and deeds of the Genovese captain who led Europe to the Americas has been a matter of wonder since the times of the conquest: Christopher Columbus, the Christ bearer who colonizes.[4] Before his sea odyssey, Christ appeared to be a stranger to half of the globe. But who was the Christ who landed with Columbus on Guanahaní? In *The Other Spanish Christ*, John Mackay paints a bleak picture of this savior.[5] The real Christ, the one born in Bethlehem, was thrown into prison in Castile. The other Christ, the one who arrived, was actually an impostor who bore the name of the real Christ and some of his features but little else. This Christ was born from the fusion of Christianity and Islam in the Iberian Peninsula. It was the product of a popular Catholicism steeped in a deep sense of tragedy and an equally deep longing for immortality.

The Spanish Christ was chief and foremost a victim, the word made death.[6] What landed with Columbus on Guanahaní was a docetic Christ, a Christ lacking true humanity. As a child, he is everyone's godson. As an adult, he is a cadaver. This Christ is to be cuddled or pitied; he is not to be obeyed. Like spectators at a bullfight, those who contemplate the Spanish Christ experience catharsis. The cruelty of daily life is transferred to the unhappy victim, but no transformation occurs. This is the Christ who laments the status quo but, instead of challenging it, contents himself with waiting for things to be made right in the next life. This is the Christ of what Romero calls *conformismo*, the Lord of passive resignation.

The other Spanish Christ is the Christ of the mystics. This Christ is the Lord who transfigures all creation.[7] He is a savior, a friend, even a lover. This is the Christ whose followers (like John of the Cross) often found themselves in prison under the suspicion of heterodoxy. He is the risen Christ, the Lord of life, the one who came to transform the world. This is the universal Christ whose passage through the land of Quixote transforms him into the other Spanish Christ. The Presbyterian Mackay highlights the contribution that Protestantism made to the promotion of the other Spanish Christ in both Spain and Latin

America. Mackay's fellow Protestant, the Methodist scholar Baez Camargo, asserts that by preaching a gospel based on grace, not on rituals, Protestants are advancing the day when "the Christ of earth, the dead Christ, the fetish Christ, will give way to the living Christ, the Lord of death and life, the Spanish Christ, American and universal, the true and only Christ."[8]

John Mackay's reading of the two Christs that came to America is clearly polemical.[9] Nevertheless, he is far from alone in questioning the identity of the Jesus who crossed the Atlantic. George Casalis notes that in Latin America Jesus either smells of death or looks like the apotheosis of King Ferdinand I. Yet the real Jesus is neither a defeated king nor a celestial monarch.[10] The different faces of the transfigured Christ in the cathedral of San Salvador represent a common Latin American experience: a plurality of images of Christ, words about Christ, and Christologies. The Peruvian playwright Ricardo Rojas's personal collection of crucifixes includes a mulatto Christ and even an Andean, beardless Christ.[11] Significantly, the Andean Christ was nailed to a cross made of silver plundered from the Andean countryside. Today, the alternative to the Spanish Christ is presented not as another Spanish Christ but as a Christ other than the Spanish Christ. Latina theologian Loida Martell-Otero speaks of the mongrel Jesus whose border-crossing existence is a perennial source of scandal.[12]

The proliferation of faces of Christ in Latin America raises a disquieting, one might say Feuerbachian, question. José Míguez Bonino asks it trenchantly: "Does all this mean, in the last analysis, that Christ is but a projection of determinate social conditions, and the reflection of these conditions in ideology?"[13] If there is talk today of a mulatto Christ or a revolutionary Christ, is it not because there are mulatto Christians and revolutionary Christians? The Feuerbachian question prompts Míguez Bonino to ask a Nicene question: "Have we not come up with a new Arianism? Have we not transported old dichotomies to a new, intrahistorical plane?"[14] The answer that Míguez Bonino proposes is in part hermeneutical. He calls for "a hermeneutics that respects not only the original historicity of the text but also the singularity of the reader's locus."[15] But the hope for escaping the problems of Arianism and ideological projection in Christology does not lie in methodology alone or even principally. The hope is to be found in revelation. Only God can reveal the identity of Christ, and he reveals this identity to those who live in obedience to Christ. This is precisely what happened in the Transfiguration.

The quest for the other Spanish Christ leads to Mount Tabor because there the Spanish Christ is transfigured. Most Latin American Christologies approach contextual questions from the perspective of the birth of Christ. The Incarnation becomes the basis for inculturation. This is not wrong, but the Transfiguration discloses another possibility. For those with eyes to see, Tabor teaches that the glory of God can manifest itself through limited and imperfect representations. To put it another way, the image of a white Christ donated by the Holy Roman Emperor can be transfigured into the face of the Salvadoran Savior. That the possibility of Transfiguration is not seriously considered in Latin American Christologies is not surprising. The Transfiguration has never been a significant feature of Western Protestant or Catholic piety.[16] The event is routinely dismissed as mythological or misunderstood.[17] Nevertheless, it is of great significance for the questions that we have been considering regarding the identity of Christ. The Transfiguration is something that happens in the eye of the beholder and in the person beheld.[18] It is by walking in the light of Christ that we see light (cf. Ps. 36:9). It was because Romero endeavored to obey Christ that he grew in understanding of Christ. The more closely he followed, the more clearly he saw. And the more clearly he saw the shining face of Christ, the more he too shone.

EL DIVINO SALVADOR DEL MUNDO

If for Romero the Feast of the Transfiguration was the icon of God's love for the people of El Salvador and the world, the lectionary lessons from the sixth chapter of the Gospel of John were the biblical frame for this icon. From July 29 to August 26, 1979, Romero's Sunday homilies led his congregants in a patient reading and interpretation of the bread-of-life discourses from the fourth gospel. Five sermons were dedicated to the theme of the Divine Savior as read from a Johannine perspective: "The Divine Savior, Solution to All Our Problems" (July 29, 1979), "The Divine Savior, Bread Which Comes Down from Heaven and Gives Life to the World" (August 5, 1979), "The Divine Savior of the World, Flesh for the Life of the World" (August 12, 1978), "The Divine Savior, Personally Present in Our Eucharist" (August 19, 1979), "The Divine Savior of the World Has Words of Eternal Life" (August 26, 1979). The Divine Savior is not a wooden image to be paraded around the streets of San Salvador every fifth of August. He is a living person who invites people to listen to him.[19] The Divine Savior homilies enrolled the archdiocese in "a true school for the knowledge of Christ" (*Homilías*, 5:240).

The curriculum for this school introduces the congregation to the particularities of the Gospel of John. Romero refers to the Gospel of John as the most ecclesiological, most sacramental gospel (*Homilías*, 5:151–52). These may seem surprising commendations, since the words *church* and *sacrament* do not show up in the fourth evangel at all, but the distinctive eschatology of John, his language of signs, and his understanding of community substantiate Romero's superlatives. For the archbishop, John's gospel presents the church as a sacramental reality that makes the glorified Christ present in history. Romero calls his congregants' attention to some of the differences between the Gospel of John and the synoptics. For example, whereas Matthew, Mark, and Luke include a narrative of the institution of the Eucharist on the eve of the Passion, John does not. The reason for this, according to Romero, is that John knew of the synoptic traditions and did not think it necessary to repeat their work.[20] Instead of presenting one more portrait of the Last Supper, the evangelist used the story of the multiplication of the bread to offer a theological commentary on the Eucharist. "We could say that Saint John gave the presacramental talk and that the other gospels administered the sacrament" (*Homilías*, 5:217). Romero likens John to a catechist. The comparison is provocative. In El Salvador catechists are subject to persecution, so the comparison has political resonances. Furthermore, one of Romero's chief pastoral concerns was the promotion of sacramental literacy among his parishioners. In El Salvador, too many people approached the sacraments with little knowledge of how to read the signs by which these were conveyed.[21] Romero was not questioning the *ex opere operato* power of the sacraments. Nor was he saying that children should not be baptized before they reach the age of understanding. Instead he was emphasizing the importance of catechesis and pushing against a cultural current that did not value the meaning of the sacraments provided that they worked. It is to these that Romero says, "No one is to be baptized who does not know what baptism means; confirmation is not to be given if it is not understood, and also, no one ought to participate in Communion without knowing what Communion is" (*Homilías*, 5:218). John's account of the multiplication of the loaves is ideally suited to meet this pastoral need.

The Bread of Life

John's bread-of-life discourse is rich in signs. These can be understood only if one is well versed in the story of Israel. The location for the miracle is a sign. The mountain on which Jesus sat to teach evokes Mount Sinai and Moses. For those with eyes to see and ears to hear, the church is the Sinai from which the true Moses, the Divine Savior, still leads his Salvadoran people by the law of the Good News. The timing for the miracle is a sign. According to John, "The Passover, the festival of the Jews, was near" (John 6:4). This is an ecclesiological sign that connects the Jewish feast, the Eucharist, and the church. Romero explains, "John, when he mentions the multiplication of the bread in proximity to the Passover, is inviting us to live our ecclesiological sense, to be church and from the church, where Christ lives, to be the solution to our problems" (*Homilías*, 5:162). The twelve baskets are also a sign of the church, particularly of the church hierarchy collaborating with Jesus in teaching the word and administering the sacraments. The signs abound and overlap. They are signs of the times; they diagnose the present situation. They are sacramental signs; they make Christ present. The Divine Savior homilies focus on three mutually interpreting signs: hunger, bread, and flesh.

The hunger of the multitude is the first sign in the bread-of-life discourse. Hunger is not only lack of food. "Hunger is a sign of deeper oppressions" (*Homilías*, 5:174). Paul VI's portrait of the conditions that marginalize people around the world exactly fits the situation in El Salvador: "famine, chronic disease, illiteracy, poverty, injustices in international relations and especially in commercial exchanges, situations of economic and cultural neo-colonialism sometimes as cruel as the old political colonialism."[22] Hunger is a sign of the times in El Salvador. There is hunger for justice for the murdered, the disappeared, the unjustly imprisoned, the unpaid worker, the exiled, and the refugee. Hunger does not only disclose old and present oppressions; it can contribute to new ones. As Jesus found out when in the wilderness, hunger can be an occasion for temptation. Hunger has the power to lock people into dehumanizing conditions of life. Bread, on the other hand, has the power to humanize life by transforming these conditions.

The multiplication of the bread is the countersign to hunger. Romero announces that "in the sign of the multiplication of the loaves we find, according to John, the goods of redemption. All the good that Christ has brought when he came to die for us and to rise again and offer us new life is symbolized in the bread. In it is, then, the true liberation, the true advancement of the human" (*Homilías*, 5:221). Bread is a sign of life. For the campesinos, the recognition of their rights to personal respect, self-improvement, social assistance, and private property is bread. There are two kinds of bread, however: "the bread that perishes" (John 6:27) and "the living bread" (John 6:51). God gives both. God provides for the needs of the body. He feeds Israel manna in the wilderness. "God will also watch over the justice of the claims of the organizations that have the right to organize themselves to defend each other in their rights. God also approves of unions" (*Homilías*, 5:179). The human is not the passive recipient of God's bread. God desires and empowers human participation in liberation, and God looks for collaborators in unlikely places, like the campesino who brought the first fruits of barley and grain to Elisha (2 Kings 4:42). The calculated marginalization of these voices from the national dialogue is slowing down the solution of the problems facing El Salvador. Romero calls on the government to "admit into dialogue not only the people who think like you. Admit the campesinos who are dying of hunger, and who, because they are dying of hunger, organize themselves, not for subversion but for survival" (*Homilías*, 5:168). Christ invites all Salvadorans to join him in solving their problems. Sheer activism and passive quietism are both to be eschewed. Romero finds the right balance in Ignatius of Loyola's wise counsel: "We need to work as if everything depended on us, but we need to wait on Christ as if everything depended on him" (*Homilías*, 5:182).

God cares about the "bread that perishes"; it contributes to ending the dehumanization of life. But this bread cannot bring people to their full humanization; for that another bread is needed, "the living bread" that is Christ. Christ and the church serve the work of human liberation by elevating the efforts for freedom from oppressive structures to the glorious liberty of freedom from sin.[23] The church elevates the "bread that perishes" so that it may be made by the Spirit, the "living bread" for the life of the world. Jesus says that "the bread that I will give for the life of the world is my flesh" (John 6:51).

The Flesh of Christ

Flesh is a sign of human existence. In a homily immediately following the Feast of the Transfiguration, Romero considers this existence in three states: the flesh without Christ, the flesh of Christ, and the flesh in Christ. In scripture, the word *flesh* displays a wide semantic range. The term can be predicated of the human body in distinction from the spirit. "Flesh is a body that is animate by life" (*Homilías*, 5:206). Flesh can also be predicated of the whole person, as when Isaiah says that "the glory of the Lord shall be revealed and all flesh shall see it together."[24] In this latter sense, there are two ways to speak of the flesh. There is the flesh of Adam before the Fall, human flesh without sin, and there is the flesh of Adam after the Fall, sinful human flesh. In this second case, the flesh "is considered by the Bible as the human in his evil inclinations, the carnal human, the selfish human, the hypocrite, the liar, the ambitious" (*Homilías*, 5:206). This is the flesh that Jesus calls "useless" (John 6:63). This is the flesh without Christ.

The flesh without Christ is incapable of seeing the flesh of Christ. To these eyes, Jesus appears to be a common man, a petty criminal who deserves death. And if the eternal Son of God born of the Virgin

Mary is dismissed by the flesh without Christ, what will they not do to his body, the church! The flesh without Christ is a universal reality that Romero holds up as a mirror for self-examination. "Let us analyze our own feeble flesh, when it allows itself to be carried away by bitterness, hatred, rancor, we are honoring the sinful flesh, the flesh without Christ" (*Homilías*, 5:207). This sinful flesh has cut itself off from the fountain of life; it is flesh without transcendence. At the same time, this flesh still hungers for sustenance, and it turns to false bread to sustain its emaciated existence. It develops a craving for the pseudoabsolutes of riches, power, and politics. In brief, the flesh without Christ is sick, and the only cure is the flesh of Christ. "Christ, the second Adam, came to redeem the flesh of sin, he paid for the flesh, for the sins of the flesh, and he cured the evil inclinations of humanity. Thus the redeemed human is the flesh, the human grafted into Christ, who, despite feeling temptations and the inclinations of evil, feels also the saving power of God" (*Homilías*, 5:206).

The flesh of Christ brings life back to the world. Romero delights in the mystery of the Incarnation, *la encarnación*, a word with cultural resonances in Spanish that are not as obvious in English.[25] The "enfleshing" of God ennobles the flesh. No longer can the flesh be seen as something shameful from which humans need to be saved. The remedy for the flesh without Christ is not denigration of the flesh or flight from the flesh. The remedy is the flesh of Christ. This flesh was conceived in the womb of Mary. "God asks her permission to become incarnate, to become a fetus inside her, to be born as a child in Bethlehem, to grow nursed at her breasts" (*Homilías*, 5:214). The Son of God, as truly human, can say, "I have a mother." At the same time, because he is the "flesh-God," the "Word-flesh," he is the "absolute" that the flesh without Christ longed for. All that he did had infinite worth. "Thus, when that flesh-God is crucified and in the agonies of the flesh it renders the merits to God, the redemption is infinite. And when he cries for those who persecute him, because they do not want to understand his own language, his groans are God's groans" (*Homilías*, 5:214).

Romero alludes here to the ancient doctrine of the *communicatio idiomatum*, the communication of attributes. Attributes that could ordinarily be predicated of the human nature of Christ can be predicated of the divine nature because both natures are united in the one person. The hypostatic union is the reason why the flesh of Christ can be revelatory of God. Romero actually uses the Greek term for the personal union of the two natures of Christ in several of his homilies.[26] "Not only will he have a divine nature, the nature of God, but he will also be able to say from his human nature, my hands of God, my cry of God, my tears of God, my blood of God, because in his humanity Jesus has no personhood" (*Homilías* 6:87).

The human nature assumed by the second person of the Trinity was what is technically known as "anhypostatic"; it was a nature "without a person." One implication of the hypostatic union is that the life of Christ in the flesh is a theophany from beginning to end. In his homily of August 12, 1979, Romero reminds his congregation of the story of Elijah in 1 Kings 19:4–8. When Elijah fled from Jezebel's threats, God provided him with a mysterious bread that sustained him along the journey until the prophet arrived at Mount Horeb. There Elijah encountered God not in the classical signs of the old theophanies (earthquakes, fires, whirlwinds) but in a gentle breeze. Romero comments, "It is as if the Lord wanted to teach Elijah: it is not violence, not the force of the elements that will bring the solutions. I will inspire you with the gentleness of my thought, with the breeze of peace" (*Homilías*, 5:215). The mode of this theophany was therapeutic for a prophet who had perhaps become too accustomed to God becoming known through violence, as at Mount Carmel. The therapeutic purpose of theophanies is further fulfilled on Mount Tabor because one of the reasons why God summoned Elijah to Jesus's side at the Transfiguration was the prophet's own history of violence, a history that was transformed by his encounter with God in the breeze. "And so, the God of the breeze is the one that becomes incarnate in our Lord Jesus Christ" (*Homilías*, 5:215). The encounter with the God of the breeze healed Elijah; the encounter with the flesh of Christ transforms the flesh without Christ to the flesh in Christ.

The flesh in Christ is the flesh that has been brought by the Father into communion with his Son. Ultimately, this communion is made possible by the Holy Spirit. The flesh in Christ is "the flesh according to the spirit" (*Homilías*, 5:206). In these homilies, Romero does not trace in detail the pneumatological contours of life in Christ, but neither does John in the sixth chapter of his gospel. In any case, Romero does point to the centrality of Mary, grace, faith, and sacraments to life in Christ, and all of these are traditionally associated with the work of the Holy Spirit. For Romero, there is little doubt that the flesh in Christ is the life that is being sanctified by the Holy Spirit. Echoing Ephesians 4:30, Romero says that "the one who believes in Christ goes as if sealed by the Spirit of God" (*Homilías*, 5:215). These believers are truly "saints in the world"; they are the "holy politicians, holy merchants, holy professionals" that El Salvador needs (*Homilías*, 5:216). Their sanctification is made possible by their Eucharistic sharing. The transformation of the flesh without Christ to the flesh in Christ happens by partaking of the flesh of Christ. Romero explains that "the bread that is eaten becomes the substance of my very life. So should it be with Christ; I should eat him, so that I might become Christ, so that I might be assimilated to Christ" (*Homilías*, 5:216). This is the wonderful mystery that Romero summons his people to ponder. Christ gives his flesh for the life of the world, "but not flesh like that of the human without Christ, flesh of Christ where God became incarnate with all the power, all the love, all the merit of the cross, all the holiness of God, in that insignificant morsel of Communion, the bread that is the flesh of God who comes to fleshen, Christify, and spiritualize all my flesh without Christ" (*Homilías*, 5:218).

The encounter with the flesh-God happens in diverse ways. In the sacraments of baptism, confirmation, reconciliation, anointing, matrimony, and ordination, Christ is present virtually. At the Eucharist he is present personally. Romero cites from the Decree of Trent: "Christ is truly present, really present, substantially present" (*Homilías*, 5:227). He is present as the flesh that was offered at Calvary, flesh united in divine intimacy with the Father. The personal presence of Christ at the Eucharist is revelatory and also transformative; it causes effects. First, his presence gives life. "Whoever eats of this bread will live forever" (John 6:51). That is to say, the Eucharist "makes us immortal, it makes us participants of the very life of God, who does not perish, the life of the risen Christ" (*Homilías*, 5:228). Second, the

Eucharist causes the mutual indwelling of Christ and his disciples. "Those who eat my flesh and drink my blood abide in me and I in them" (John 6:56). The priesthood of the church exists for the purpose of preserving and serving this life-giving flesh and blood. "What a beautiful gesture! The multiplication of the bread is repeated in the churches. In a few moments, we will see the bishop and his collaborators sharing the bread and gathering it, and storing it in the tabernacle with a sense of economy, so that there will always be bread! Bread will not be found wanting as long as there is a Christ and a church that know how to become incarnate in the people of even the most critical times" (*Homilías*, 5:163).

The mission of the church can be termed Eucharistic, provided that this is not limited to distribution of the Eucharistic elements. The reserved host must not become a table ornament, a still life that does not nourish; it must be a sign of messianic abundance for the world and for the church's engagement with it. "If in El Salvador, the 'bread of life' that the church distributes, the word of God, the Christian religion, does not touch the political, social, economic realities of our people, it will be a reserved host, and a reserved host does not feed— only the bread that is eaten, that is assimilated" (*Homilías*, 5:235–36). Properly understood and celebrated, the Eucharist contributes to "redeeming a people, saving human beings, so that when they come to commune they feel that they are truly being elevated" (*Homilías*, 5:231). The Divine Liturgy has the power to transform human life in its totality. The encounter with the flesh-God in the Eucharist leads to prayer: "Lord—we should say at the end—do not allow me to remain one more person without Christ, but having known the beauty of your incarnation, we want to be humans incorporated in Christ" (*Homilías*, 5:218). The answer to this prayer is a Eucharistic form of life.

> Ah, how beautiful life becomes when it is illumined by faith and when one knows that one's body, whether sound or sick, when united to a consecrated host received at Communion, is a life and a body that becomes a host! And all the acts of our life, all the duties that we fulfill, all the sacrifices we make, all the love we spend, all the patience in putting up with the impertinent, all becomes in Christ crucified, the flesh

that saves the world. And I am contributing to this sacrifice, my little host, my little drop of water in the wine chalice that becomes wholly him. You can no longer distinguish the little drop of water and the wine in the chalice. You can only perceive the blood that is poured out for the salvation of the world. Then human life becomes liturgy. (*Homilías*, 5:230)

A Johannine Transfiguration

How does the Johannine framing of the Feast of the Transfiguration help Romero's congregants better understand the Divine Savior of the World? A number of features are worth mentioning. One theme I mention now but treat more extensively later is that of beauty. The gestures of Christ's life are termed beautiful because the flesh of Christ is beautiful. When the flesh without Christ comes into contact with the flesh of Christ, it too becomes beautiful.

First, these homilies present the Divine Savior as the key to read-ing and responding to the signs of the times in El Salvador. God's plan for the transfiguration of El Salvador gains material density by being read with Johannine lenses. As in Caesarea Philippi, the encounter with Jesus provokes questions, but by the Sea of Tiberias in front of the multitude, the questions begin not with the identity of Jesus but with the hunger of the people: "Where are we to buy bread for these people to eat?" John tells us that Jesus already knew what he was going to do but that he asked this question to test them. On Rome-ro's reading, Jesus's test of the disciples is designed with two pur-poses. On the one hand, Jesus's question discloses the limitations of human solutions. Philip answers from an economic perspective: "Six months' wages would not buy enough bread for each of them to get a little" (John 6:7). Andrew offers a technical assessment: "There is a boy here who has five barley loaves and two fish. But what are they among so many people?" (John 6:9). Human analyses and solutions are feeble, limited, and one-sided. Romero warns his congregation of the risk of reductive readings of the gospel: "The false interpretation of today's miracle and of those who interpret the gospel wrongly is called temporal reductionism, and it is just as bad as spiritual reductionism" (*Homilías*, 5:165). Only Christ has the full solution. He cares about his people's hunger. He denounces the unequal distribution of land that makes it impossible for most people to win their bread. He is in the midst of the suffering of the people of El Salvador not only in solidarity but as Divine Savior. Christ offers solutions that touch the present political situations but transcend these. The celebration of the Feast of the Transfiguration calls for breaking free from all one-sided liberations to embrace the universal liberation of Christ. Better yet, Christ takes the earthly liberations and incorporates them into the great, transcendent liberation that only he can bring. He does not want to be king of the earth in a temporal manner. He is the Divine Savior of the World. On the other hand, Jesus's question invites the disciples to join him in diagnosing and addressing the problem. "Because Christ does not want to multiply the loaves alone. He began talking with Philip. He began asking Andrew's opinion. He gathered the five loaves of the poor young man" (*Homilías*, 5:167). Even with their limitations, humans have something positive to contribute to the liberation that only Christ can bring.

Second, the homilies on the Divine Savior underscore the materiality of the Incarnation and by extension the Transfiguration. What is transfigured on Tabor is not the soul of Christ but his flesh. The Gospel of John teaches us more about this flesh. Not only is the flesh of Christ alive, it is life-giving. Romero offers a sacramental account for what the transfiguration of the flesh-without-Christ to the flesh-in-Christ entails. It is by participating in the Eucharist that human flesh becomes transfigured. Romero offers a concrete example of this transfiguration in the life of Peter Damian (*Homilías*, 5:229). When Peter Damian received word that he was being moved from the island of Molokai, where he had been serving among lepers, he asked his superiors to reconsider. His petition fell on deaf ears. So he turned to God and asked for the "grace of leprosy" (*Homilías*, 5:229). The next mass, when he raised the consecrated host, Father Damian noticed on his hand the first signs of leprosy. From then on, whenever he spoke to his congregation, he addressed them in the first-person plural, "We lepers." The transfiguration of the flesh does not necessarily make it radiant and beautiful by the world's standards. After all, even in glory the flesh of Christ bears wounds.

Third, in the Divine Savior homilies, there is a curious silence. Romero does not mention John's omission of an account of the Transfiguration. The archbishop's silence is striking when one considers that he did highlight the lack of a Eucharistic institution narrative from the fourth gospel and that he is making explicit connections between the bread-of-life discourses and the titular feast of San Salvador. Romero could have said that John had no need of a Transfiguration account because he had already given a catechetical explanation of its significance in the prologue to his gospel. Other scholars have advanced arguments along these lines.[27] There is no evidence to suggest that Romero knew of these interpretations. Still, by pairing the transfiguration of Christ with the sign of the multiplication of the bread, Romero schools his congregation in living into the Transfiguration.

LA BAJADA: THE DESCENT OF THE *COLOCHO* CHRIST

The Divine Savior homilies of 1979 served as a school for teaching Salvadoran Christians more about the enfleshed identity of the Transfigured One and the Eucharistic mode of identifying with him. The lessons were not limited to looking at Mount Tabor from the perspective of the fourth gospel. On the eve of the Feast of the Transfiguration that year, Romero invited his congregation to prepare to keep the feast by practicing its rituals in a new way. "I want to transpose this phrase of Christ, 'the bread who comes down,' to give the traditional *Bajada* of this afternoon an evangelical and liturgical orientation. Let us attend not only out of habit, however pious it might seem. Let us give it its deepest sense. The *Bajada* could be explained by Jesus in today's gospel: 'I am the bread who comes down from heaven for the life of the world'" (*Homilías*, 5:173).

The *Bajada* is the most distinctly Salvadoran ritual that takes place during the celebration of the Divine Savior. It is a ceremonial procession of the *Colocho* Christ through the streets of San Salvador, culminating in his being "transfigured" before the eyes of the faithful. The earliest historical records of the celebration of El Salvador's titular feast make no mention of *La Bajada*. Instead these talk about an elaborate "performance" (*función*), dramatization (*simulacro*), or representation of the transfiguration of Christ on Mount Tabor.[28] One account from 1862 speaks of the act of transfiguration as an "unveiling" (*descubrimiento*), a term that became standard in the liturgical lexicon of this celebration. Nineteenth-century accounts of the *Bajada* draw attention to the pomp of the display and the quickness with which Christ was transfigured from the purple robe of the Passion to the white garment of the Transfiguration. The visual spectacle of seeing the image of Christ standing on a pinnacle that rose above the highest buildings in the city, combined with the aural impact of cannon salutes and choirs, made the crowds feel that they too were on Tabor. An 1847 account describes the event in this way: "Thus was the float borne by a hundred men in the midst of a very numerous procession, and upon their arriving at the plaza a cloud covered at the same time the Savior, who still wore a purple tunic, and another cloud opened to unveil him, presenting him before the people in splendor, dressed in fine white linen on the top of the high mountain, ready to be elevated to the very heavens."[29] Spectators became witnesses who could say that they too heard the voice of the Father revealing his beloved Son.[30] The first use of the term *Bajada* appears in an account from 1880 that reads: "Today is the most beautiful act of this popular feast, the *Bajada* of the Savior of the World from Calvary to his transfiguration on Tabor."[31] Jesús Delgado highlights several features of this text. The celebration is termed a *fiesta popular*, that is to say, it is led by the laity (in particular through the Cofradía del Salvador), not the clergy. Also, the mention of the *Salvador del Mundo* refers to the statue carved by Silvestre Antonio García in 1777, which has been paraded in the procession ever since. Delgado highlights the significance of the route for the procession, which began from the church of El Calvario with the statue dressed in purple, the color of the Passion. From the very beginning of its celebration, the *Bajada* represented Christ's descent from the cross into the tomb followed by his glorious resurrection. The *Bajada* links the mystery of the Transfiguration with the paschal mystery and connects the descent of Christ into suffering and death with the ascent into life and glory.

In his Divine Savior homilies Romero associates the *Bajada* with Christ's life-giving descent into the world. The *Bajada* should be celebrated with that same evangelical orientation. Seeing Christ descend before he is transfigured sets the pattern for how Salvadoran Christians relate to their society. They are not to hold themselves back like the reserved sacrament but to go into the places of hunger as the bread that gives life. The connection between liturgy and ethics is an important one for Romero. When Romero became archbishop he invited all diocesan priests and religious leaders to celebrate with him. The priests were also exhorted to invite their faithful to participate in the *Bajada* and the Solemn Mass. The hope motivating these instructions was that the people would continue to grow in their historical awareness and in their conviction that only in Christ is the real way forward shown. Instead of listening to the many voices offering truncated solutions, they should listen to Christ. *Ipsum audite.*[32] The *Bajada* happens in the midst of a crowd not unlike the crowds who followed Jesus. It is a people with its "weaknesses and virtues . . . with its anguish, with a soul bitten by hunger, with lack of work and shelter, lack of physical security, and the violation of their constitutional rights."[33] For all this, these people look to the Divine Savior with irrepressible hope. "The crowds are always thus. It takes longer for them to lose trust in God and their sense of eternity and the transcendence of humanity."[34] In the midst of the shameful violence enveloping the country, the *Bajada* can be a sign of hope that the Divine Savior will transfigure the virtues of the people of God and use them to build a new earth in El Salvador. This transfiguration is not possible without the liturgy.

In an essay on the relation between liberation theology and the liturgy, Ignacio Ellacuría states that "true Christian liberation is discovered and promoted in the liturgy and only in the liturgy."[35] The liturgical assembly is the place where the saving Word becomes alive in community. The liturgical action lifts the movement of liberation from merely immanent ends to the fullness of Christian salvation. "The struggle is fought with guitars and church songs," says Romero (*Homilías*, 4:193). This is the reason why paying attention to the liturgical setting of the archbishop's preaching is crucial. The songs, processions, and prayers are not dressing on his theological vision, they are its lifeblood.

In spite of the significant relation between liturgy and liberation analyzed by Ellacuría and preached by Romero, the paucity of theological studies in this area is striking. The musical expressions of liberation theology are both the most widely known and yet the least studied aspects of Latin American theology.[36] The ancient saying *Lex credendi, lex orandi,* which spoke of a close, mutually informing relation between theology and worship, has not been sufficiently heeded by Latin American theologians. Relatively few people have read the celebrated works of Gustavo Gutiérrez, Ignacio Ellacuría, or Jon Sobrino. Many, many more have heard and sung such protest songs as the "Cristo of Palacagüiña" by Carlos Mejía Godoy or the "Coplas del Payador Perseguido" by Atahualpa Yupanqui.[37]

In the next two sections I want to consider the two movements associated with the *Bajada*, the descent and the *Descubrimiento*. The descent is associated with the passion of Christ, so we will examine how Romero understands Christ's kenosis. The *Descubrimiento* is associated with the Transfiguration, and there we will examine Romero's understanding of Christ's glory. Because Romero's homilies are not academic lectures but liturgical events, I will highlight the contributions of hymns and poems to his Christological reflections.

The God Who Sweats

Romero, like any wise preacher, appeals to popular songs in his sermons as a way of embedding the biblical message more deeply in the souls of his listeners.[38] A particularly fecund example of this practice can be found in Romero's homily from the sixth Sunday of Easter in 1978. The proximity of that Sunday to Labor Day and the feast of Joseph the Worker offered Romero the opportunity to shine the light of the risen Christ on the world of labor. The calendric coincidence is a painful one because on that Labor Day many Salvadoran workers found themselves harassed or even imprisoned for trying to unionize. And yet, Romero insists that all is not lost.

Happy the one who knows that in these dark hours of our history, Christ lives. He lives powerful as God and understanding as human. He is a man of our ways, a man of our history. He is man, as sung in that song that is now in fashion: *the God who appears as a worker, like the one who goes for a walk in the park, like the one who works on the roads and patches tires in the gas station.* God is incarnate in each human and understands each worker, each human who wants to love him and follow him. (*Homilías,* 2:437)

The song to which Romero is alluding when he speaks of "the God who appears as a worker" is the opening song from the *Misa campesina nicaragüense* by Carlos Godoy.[39] Romero references this song on more than one occasion.[40] Its lyrics are vivid and provocative.

Vos sos el Dios de los pobres,
El Dios humano y sencillo,
El Dios que suda en la calle,
El Dios de rostro curtido.
Por eso es que os hablo yo,
Así como habla mi pueblo,
Porque sos el Dios obrero,
El Cristo trabajador.

Vos vas de la mano con mi gente.
Luchás en el campo y la ciudad,
Hacés fila allá en el campamento
Para que te paguen tu jornal.

Vos comés raspado allá en el parque
Con Eusebio, Pancho y Juan José
Y hasta protestás por el sirope
Cuando no le echan mucha miel.

Yo te he visto en la pulpería,
Instalado en un caramanchel.
Te he visto vendiendo lotería

Sin que te avergüence ese papel.
Yo te he visto en las gasolineras
Chequeando las llantas de un camión,
Y hasta patroleando carretaras
Con guantes de cuero y overal.

———

You are the God of the poor ones,
The God human and humble,
The God who sweats on the roadway,
The God who is ruddy faced.
This is why I speak to you,
In the manner in which my people speak,
Because you are God the laborer,
Christ the worker.

You walk hand in hand with my people;
You fight in the field and the city;
You stand in line at the work camp;
So that they will pay your daily wage.

You eat shaved ice in the park
With Eusebio, Pancho, and Juan José
And you even complain about the syrup,
When they do not add enough honey to it.

I have seen you in the store
Set up in a stall,
I have seen you selling lottery tickets
Without being ashamed of that job.[41]
I have seen you in the gas stations
Checking the tires of a truck
And even patrolling the roads
With leather gloves and overalls.

This does not sound like the Christ who stands solemnly in the
cathedral behind the protection of the altar rail. He does not even

much resemble the *Colocho* Christ. This is a Christ who moves to a Nicaraguan waltz. He speaks in the language of the streets because he is more at home there than in the sanctuary. This Christ is the God of the poor, the God who sweats, the God who is a worker. Before studying how Romero treats these themes, a brief historical background is in order.

The windows that John XXIII threw open at the start of Vatican II facilitated the flow of the currents of liturgical renewal and experimentation already circulating in Latin America.[42] People like Pedro Casaldáliga and Ernesto Cardenal were prelates, priests, poets, and also promoters of liturgies that would give voice to the struggles of the poor against oppression. The important examples of these liturgies were the *Misa campesina nicaragüense* (1976) and the *Misa popular salvadoreña* (1980). The way for these militant masses was prepared in 1968 by the *Misa popular nicaragüense*. Its lyrics transpose into song conciliar themes like the conception of the church as the people of God and the centrality of the word of God in scripture.[43] The transposition of these into the lives of the poor in Nicaragua occurred in a relatively irenic manner. Even so, some sectors of the church rejected this mass as too "popular." It was criticized for not being suitably reverent. Its theological expressions were deemed inexact and open to misinterpretation. It was not until the *Misa campesina nicaragüense* of Godoy debuted that the *Misa popular* was embraced by its earlier detractors as the now "traditional" alternative.[44]

Godoy's mass grew within the context of the base ecclesial communities of Solentiname, which were led by Ernesto Cardenal. The language of this mass was not sacred language but street talk. In contrast to the *Misa popular*, this mass presents the poor in an unrelenting class struggle with the rich.[45] This class struggle is supported by Christ because, to quote Casaldáliga, "In Joseph's workshop, God became class."[46] The Christological vision of the Nicaraguan *Misa campesina* is expressed most clearly in two pieces: the opening song and the creed.[47]

Is the Christ of Godoy's mass the same as Romero's Divine Savior? Is the Divine Savior of the World the God who sweats on the street? To answer these questions, we return to his 1978 Labor Day homily. Romero preaches: "Christ is the revelation of the working

God and the working human" (*Homilías*, 2:455). Behind this statement lies the Christological anthropology of *Gaudium et Spes* 22:

> The truth is that only in the mystery of the incarnate Word does the
> mystery of man take on light. For Adam, the first man, was a figure of
> Him Who was to come, namely Christ the Lord. Christ, the final Adam,
> by the revelation of the mystery of the Father and His love, fully reveals
> man to man himself and makes his supreme calling clear. He who is
> "the image of the invisible God" (Col. 1:15), is Himself the perfect man.
> To the sons of Adam He restores the divine likeness which had been
> disfigured from the first sin onward. Since human nature as He assumed
> it was not annulled, by that very fact it has been raised up to a divine
> dignity in our respect too. For by His incarnation the Son of God has
> united Himself in some fashion with every man. He worked with human
> hands, He thought with a human mind, acted by human choice and
> loved with a human heart.

The influence of *Gaudium et Spes* 22 is decisive for Romero's
understanding of Christ and humanity.[48] Humanity has been made
in the image of God, but sin has smeared this image to such a degree
that humans are strangers to themselves. Humanity was meant to bear
God's seal and imprint in creation, but there is no human being who
still bears the image in its original beauty. "That seal will be discovered
only when the imprint returns, the authentic seal, the original of God,
the Word who reflects the divine essence made human. He is the perfect human, the person of human, Christian, and celestial virtues in
which every human being needs to be reflected in order to be worthy
of the dignity of the children of God" (*Homilías*, 2:147). Christ is "the
exact imprint of God's very being" (Heb. 1:3). The questions that
humans have about themselves (Why am I here? Who am I? What am
I going to do with my life?) find their definitive answer in Christ. In
him, human nature is revealed, affirmed, and elevated. The violation
of human rights, the marginalization and destruction of God's image
bearers, constitutes a denial of the Incarnation that must be repudi-
ated. Christ's life of humble obedience reveals the glory of God, and
all people are called to echo the angelic "Glory to God" by leading

lives that glorify God in Christ. "If people want to see their own mystery, the meaning of their pain, of their work, of the anguish, of their hope, get next to Christ. If someone accomplishes what Christ accomplished, doing the will of the Father, being filled with the life that Christ brought to the world, that person is being fulfilled, becoming truly human" (*Homilías*, 4:95).

The Christocentric anthropology of *Gaudium et Spes* 22 is a check against the Docetism pervasive in Salvadoran society. "There are many technocrats, many educated, many professionals, who know their science but are like angels, disincarnate from the reality in which they carry out their profession" (*Homilías*, 2:450). The compartmentalization of life into spiritual zones separated from social zones is an anthropological absurdity. Angelism is a sin. Humans are to glorify God in their enfleshed existence.

Romero applies the Christological anthropology of *Gaudium et Spes* 22 to the question of work. After all, Christ worked "with human hands" (*Gaudium et Spes* 22) as a carpenter (Mark 6:2–3). God created the world as an unfinished opus. He made space in creation for creaturely collaboration. "With their human work, the worker imitates the worker God and is perfecting the creation and transforming the world" (*Homilías*, 2:455). In a world that devalues manual labor, Christ's work as a carpenter became an occasion for misunderstanding and rejection. How can the son of a carpenter be a preacher? Why should one listen to a common worker? Romero notes that "this is the dismissive view of human beings who see in a worker the son of another worker" (*Homilías*, 2:456). For the eyes of faith, the little worker (*obrerito*) of Nazareth dignifies and elevates all work. "There is no insignificant work. All the baptized, however humble they may be—the campesino who earns his livelihood working with a machete is as great as the doctor with the scalpel in the operating room, or the politician, if he knows how to make his work a service to the integral liberation of humanity" (*Homilías*, 2:460).

The fact that Jesus "worked with human hands" invites Salvadorans to self-reflection. "Each human being can look at his hands and say: there were hands that were God's hands, and my workman's hands can also become God's hands if I identify with that Christ . . .

the God who becomes incarnate in a workman" (*Homilías*, 2:456). In this attitude of self-reflection, one is uniquely positioned to hear the call to humanize all work by joining it to Christ's.

> Let us try to find under the label of "work" our own proper vocation. For me, to live the delight of my priestly vocation. For you, to live the delight of your legal, medical, or engineering profession. For you, worker, to feel all the pride of your wood saw, of your masonry spatula. For you, campesino, to also feel the pride of your machete, your plow, your oxen. And for you, market woman, to feel the joy of earning your livelihood under the beating sun. There, in the struggle, each one is a worker. How beautiful it would be to see that the human is the image of God, the God who said like Christ: My Father works. (*Homilías*, 2:455)

Human labor makes Christ present, but note how. It is by the divine movement of ascent through Christ bearing our humanity and of descent through Christ bringing the Spirit that labor can become sacramental (*Homilías*, 2:459). Human life and human work are dignified as they allow themselves to be swept by this divine current. The value of work is also made manifest by the fact that labor is another way of living out the baptismal call. Every Christian can say, "As baptized, my human members have become members of Christ and as members of Christ they have a divine perspective. The sweat of the workman, the worries of the professional, the sincere work of the politician who seeks the common good, all these identify themselves with the thought, the hand, the sweat, the steps of Christ, God made human" (*Homilías*, 2:456).

In Christ the laborer, the God who works is made known. Extending this revelatory relationship, the worker Christ is the revelation of the worker God. Christ is the God who sweats, and he identifies himself with those who earn their daily bread by the sweat of their brow. Is the Christ of the Nicaraguan *Misa campesina*, Christ the worker who lives at the ranch, the factory, and the school, Romero's Christ?

Is Romero's Christ the one who after collecting his daily wage eats ice cones in the park with his fellow laborers Eusebio, Pancho, and Juan José? The answer is yes but with caveats. First, Christ is not just "Christ the worker." He is present not only in the factory but in the convent and the hospital. He lives in just, nonviolent, labor struggles, and also in heaven at the right hand of God. Second, Christ is prolonged in the world by the church, his body in history. True, Christ overflows the church. The vocation of the human is fulfilled most fully in the baptized, but Romero does not limit its scope to the church. Christ's revelation of the human vocation is for all, and the Holy Spirit will find a way to lead people even outside the church to participate in the mystery of Christ.[49] But Christ does not bypass the church, and it is with Christ's presence in the church that Romero the pastor is chiefly concerned. Third, Romero's Christ is more like the Christ of the *Misa popular salvadoreña* and the *Misa mesoamericana*.

The *Misa campesina nicaragüense* has been called a prophetic mass.[50] The *Misa popular salvadoreña* was even more so. Vigil considers that "in the perspective of the popular struggle for liberation, the *Misa popular salvadoreña* is the most expressive of all Latin America."[51] It was composed by Guillermo Cuéllar and the musical group Yolocamba-Ita. The context for its composition was strongly marked by Romero's ministry. It is more ecclesial and less politicized in character than the Nicaragüense.[52] The murder of Romero forced the members of Yolocamba-Ita to flee to Mexico for safety, which ironically but understandably contributed to the quick spread of its music. The *Misa mesoamericana* was written to commemorate the twentieth anniversary of the *Misa popular salvadoreña* and Romero's death. The lyrics were written by Miguel Cavada Diez, one of the editors of the critical edition of Romero's homilies. This mass still sings of a Christ who is very much present among his people, though in a less combative and more diverse way. Christ is not only the worker. He is found not only among the workers but among the seamstresses and the mothers. The Mesoamerican Christ is the "Black Christ, Mayan Christ," "Christ the girl on the street selling chewing gum," "Christ, young and rebellious with a rapper's hat." He is also "Christ the Word, good news; Christ, voice of prophets; Romero of truth."[53] Reading diachronically from the texts of the earliest *Misas populares* of 1950s and '60s to the *Misas campesinas* of the 1970s to the *Misa mesoamericana* of the 2000s, one can see a shift in the Christology. In the *misas populares*, there is an identification of Christ with mainstream popular culture (e.g. "Por la calzada de Emaús" in the *Misa panamericana*). In the *misas campesinas*, Christ is identified with the awakened proletariat (e.g., "Vos sos el Dios de los pobres" in the *Misa campesina nicaragüense*). In the more recent musical productions, Christ is identified with all the people on the periphery, even if they are not fighting for their liberation (e.g., "Cristo mesoamericano" from the *Misa mesoamericana*). In these shifts, it is possible to interpret a corresponding shifting in the implicit application of the Irenaean axiom: *Gloria Dei, vivens pauper.* In the earliest *misas populares*, the glory of God becomes manifest when the culture of the people (who are mostly poor, the pueblo *fiel* of Pope Francis) comes alive. In the time of the *misas campesinas*, the glory of God becomes manifest when the people (particularly the poor campesinos and manual workers) come alive in the struggle for social justice. In the latest musical productions, the glory of God becomes manifest when people who are on the margins (the drug addict, the single mom, the homeless child) come alive. In all cases, it is Christ's gracious self-identification with the least that is the source of a newfound dignity in the midst of undignified, death-dealing conditions. The act by which Christ freely identifies himself with those whom the world regards as of no account is known as *kenosis*, a term whose meaning and range in Romero's Christology need to be explored.

The Kenosis of Christ

The kenosis, the emptying of Christ, is one of the focal points of Romero's theological vision. The word itself comes from a hymnic passage where Paul exhorts his readers to adopt the same manner of life as Christ, "who though he was in the form of God did not regard equality with God as something to be grasped but emptied himself" (Phil. 2:6–7). That the term appears in its Greek form in several of Romero's homilies is characteristic of the archbishop's pastoral approach.[54] He did not dumb down his preaching although his congregation was mostly poor and uneducated. On the contrary, he believed that because so few lacked access to formal schooling the catechetical function of the homily needed to be emphasized. The riches of the church's teaching were to be shared among all, starting with the poor because these are the first beneficiaries of Christ's kenosis.

Christ's whole manner of life is marked by kenosis. In the Incarnation, Christ humbles himself and condescends to be born of his creature, Mary. In Bethlehem, "He cast off his divine rank. As if a sovereign left throne and mantle and everything else behind and clothed himself with the rags of a campesino so as to be among campesinos without bothering them by his royal bearing" (*Homilías*, 3:296). In this Christmas *Bajada,* the infant in swaddling clothes reveals the image of a God reduced to nothing (*anonada*), a God mysteriously void of glory (*Homilías*, 6:105–6). There is a downward arc to Christ's life. Not only does he become human, he becomes poor. He makes his home among the uneducated, the colonized, and the public sinners. Christ blazes the trail for his disciples to follow. Romero avers, "There is a very certain path that Christ chose and that we all must choose. Those of us who want to give a good account at the end of our life must follow it. It is the one that theology calls kenosis, that is to say, undoing oneself, humbling oneself" (*Homilías*, 6:333).

The downward orientation of the Incarnation is purposeful. It is not that God likes abasing his creatures or humiliating his Son. The shape of Christ's life is therapeutic. Outside this way of life, there is no salvation. Romero wants no confusion on this score. "It is necessary to understand that Christ is born to redeem the world and that the redemption of the world cannot proceed except by the opposite direction in which humans have offended God. We have offended him by our pride, our vanity, our selfish wealth, by power, by all that which is called sin and disobedience to God. Thus redemption must be a return through the road of humility, obedience, austerity, and abnegation" (*Homilías*, 4:110).

The downward arc of Christ's life is paradigmatic for the church's movement through history. The glory of the church is "to bear in its bowels the kenosis of Christ, and because of this it must be humble and poor" (*Homilías*, 3:297). Christ's kenosis is more than an example, it is a sacramental reality. When the church walks in the way of Christ, it experiences the presence of Christ. "It feels that that humble and poor Christ, emptied of the greatness of God, goes with this church, which must be marked by that divine kenosis" (*Homilías*, 3:297). The church that imitates Christ in his downward movement of loving service is accompanied by Christ in this very movement.

The archbishop's preaching on the kenosis of Christ is more explicit about what Christ puts on than about what he takes off. What Christ puts on is humanity. In appearance, he is a man like any other. If he walked into the cathedral, neither Romero nor anyone else in attendance would notice him. He would look like any other campesino. Christ puts on (and stretches) humanity. Does Christ lose anything in the Incarnation? Does he take off divinity? The questions revolving around the kenosis of Christ and what the second person of the Trinity "gave up" become most acute in the mystery of the Passion, particularly when we consider his cry from the cross: My God, my God, why have you forsaken me?

The meaning of Jesus's cry of abandonment on the cross along with his experience of agony at Gethsemane has long been discussed. The interpretation of Jürgen Moltmann has been popular in Latin America.[55] Jon Sobrino's treatment of the questions of divine abandonment and suffering on Golgotha in *Christology at the Crossroads* draws heavily on Moltmann's theology of the cross.[56] With Moltmann, Sobrino emphasizes that the manner in which Jesus died on the cross, in total discontinuity with his mission and identity, calls for a revolution in classical conceptualizations of God.[57] In his study of Romero's Christology, Antonio Agnelli hears echoes of the kenotic theology of Moltmann in Romero's preaching.[58] Is Moltmann's Crucified God Romero's *Divino Salvador*? More specifically, how does Romero interpret Jesus's cry of dereliction?

Romero reflects on Christ's words from the cross not as disputed questions but as mysteries that the church proclaims. Of course, the act of proclamation is an act of theological interpretation, and the liturgical year gave him a number of opportunities to interpret this cry. Romero considered Christ's plaintive question when he preached on the seven last words of Christ on Good Friday 1978.

> Dear brothers, when the hour of trial arrives, the hour when even faith seems to grow dark, when hope is eclipsed, when the people seem to be

left without horizons, let us not forget this afternoon of Good Friday. He too felt the anguish, the mystery of being abandoned even by God, he felt *almost* without the love of the Father, hopeless. How strange, brothers, that in the hours of anguish, of tortures, of unjust imprisonments, of situations that have no explanation, we turn to the Father with the confidence of a son to say to him: My God, why have you forsaken me?[59]

Christ's word from the cross draws attention to the parallels between the suffering of Christ on Calvary and the suffering of his people in El Salvador. The darkness of faith in both cases is real, but it is not absolute. Christ *almost* lost hope, *almost* felt unloved—*almost* because in the midst of the agony, he never lost the assurance that "God was only testing the will in its obedience and love" (*Homilías*, 2:358). His cry of dereliction can be confidently taken up by his brothers and sisters in El Salvador because they share the same Father. For Romero, the paradox of Calvary is that it reveals the faithfulness of God. Romero preaches again on Christ's cry of abandonment on Palm Sunday 1979. "My God! My God! Why have you forsaken me? It is *as if* that kenosis, that humbling of the Son of God who became human, had now reached the breaking point, had reached the point that he felt the abandonment of God. How well does Christ identify himself with our peoples! That is how many in hovels, many in slums, many in jail and in suffering, many who hunger for justice and bread cry: My God! My God! Why have you forsaken me! *He has not forsaken us!*"[60]

Again Romero qualifies Christ's *kenosis*. It is *as if* the personal union of the human and divine natures had been torn asunder. *As if* in his humiliation, Christ was no longer divine. *As if* he were only human, or worse, only a sinner rejected by God. Christ's cry results, not from a tension within the Trinity, but from his identification with suffering humanity. In an unmistakable echo of Jesus's words in Matthew 25, the painful hunger of the poor Salvadoran is Jesus's own. In that hour, Jesus does not lose sight of his mission or of God; he carries the sins of the world in obedience to the Father for the salvation of his little sisters and brothers. The Father did not forsake his Son, and he has not forsaken his Salvadoran children. Similar qualifications of Christ's cry on the cross are articulated in Romero's Good Friday homily of 1979.

> And when Christ feels the loneliness, the anguish, the testing of his heroic obedience, *almost like* the abandonment of the Father, a fourth word emerges: My God, my God, why have you forsaken me? *It is not an abandonment,* but Christ does feel all that pain and anguish that the human heart must feel more than once. It is the psychology of suffering; feeling alone, feeling that no one understands me, feeling abandoned. And in that loneliness, Christ has left us that word which will serve as prayer, as religion, as faith in the true God. God is not failing us when we do not feel him! . . . Oh, that before this cry of Christ we would learn that God is always our Father and that he never abandons us and that we are nearer to him than we realize. (*Homilías,* 4:386)

Romero refuses to countenance the divine abandonment of Christ on Calvary. Golgotha is not a window into the inner life of the Trinity but a test of the obedience of the Son and an affirmation of the full humanity of Jesus, which was capable of experiencing the full range of physical, psychological, and spiritual reactions to the trauma of pain. His interpretation of Christ's cry of dereliction approximates that of Aquinas, who also stated that Christ carried the full psychological burden of suffering but without experiencing despair.[61] This interpretation is one that Jon Sobrino deems to have softened Mark's more tragic and authentic account.[62] The cry of dereliction is a confession of faith and a prayer of hope: "It is not an abandonment."[63]

For Romero, the cross is a place of divine intimacy. Christ's cry of dereliction is a sign of his identification with suffering humanity. Antonio Agnelli is wrong. Romero's Christology does not add "a strong pastoral accent" to Moltmann's theology of the cross but challenges it in important ways.[64] Michael Dodds's critique of Moltmann is helpful at this point:

> If we take the Incarnation seriously and so recognize that this human, Jesus of Nazareth, is God, we will not be inclined to postulate some

suffering of the divine nature as belonging more really to God, or being more really God's own, than is the human suffering of Jesus. Instead, we will recognize that there is no suffering closer to God or more really God's own than the suffering of the man, Jesus of Nazareth. In speaking of Jesus, we will not predicate of God some hypothetical sort of "divine suffering," itself alien to our human nature and experience. We will rather predicate of God a human suffering like our own, since "Jesus was made a participant of our affliction."[65]

The problem with speaking of a suffering God in the way that Moltmann does is not simply that a classical (and arguably biblical) divine attribute like impassibility is compromised but that paradoxically the relationship between God and humanity is diminished. A suffering Trinity is both less than God and more removed from humanity. Differently stated, Jesus's cry of dereliction on Golgotha does not result in an even louder cry within the Godhead. The suffering of Jesus on the cross is the deepest, most intimate experience of the suffering of God. It is not only the suffering of Christ that may be identified as the suffering of God; our suffering too is the suffering of God. Confronted with human agony, Jesus does not say, "You were thirsty" but "I was thirsty." The pain that others feel does not evoke a painful reaction in Jesus; he makes their pain his own. Suffering is not constitutive of solidarity. It is not suffering that unites the lover with the beloved but love. Christ's love makes him one with his suffering members.[66] Christ's spiritual agony was an *effect* of his love for humanity. He suffered because he loved, and by his suffering his love became manifest.

God's identification in Christ with the suffering of his people has profound pastoral implications. It is a source of comfort for the afflicted and a call to repentance for those who cause suffering. Michael Dodd presents Romero as an exemplary pastor who oriented his ministry by this gospel light.[67] Indeed, it may be that the life and teaching of Romero contributed to the distancing of Sobrino's appropriation of Moltmann's theology. In *Jesus the Liberator*, Sobrino still emphasizes the themes of God's suffering and divine abandonment that his earlier work *Christology at the Crossroads* appropriated from Moltmann's theology of the cross, but his reception of these themes is more cautious.[68] The language of the German theologian is now described as "exaggerated" and "perhaps extreme."[69] Sobrino also backs away from the more speculative aspects of Moltmann's theology and adopts an approach that is at once more exegetical and more ecclesial than in *Christology at the Crossroads*. The exegetical task finds a centering text in the Gospel of Mark. The ecclesial task finds a pivotal text in the ministry of Romero. The archbishop's way of life under the threat of death models for Sobrino the divine solidarity of Calvary. "What God's suffering on the cross says in the end is that the God who fights against human suffering wanted to show solidarity with human beings who suffer, and that God's fight against suffering is also waged in a human way."[70] This phrase may not sound as "provocative and shocking" as Moltmann's, but it is no less scandalous, because, as Sobrino states, "Solidarity in a world of victims that was not prepared to become a victim would in the end not be solidarity."[71] In brief, Romero helps Sobrino see that the "crucified God" is the "God of solidarity."[72]

Before the mystery of Christ's cry of dereliction the task of the theologian is not simply adoration or silence but the removal of obstacles to adoration and silence. When this happens, the cross becomes the anchor of Christian hope. Christians in El Salvador can sing with the church, *Ave crux, spes unica*, a song that Romero finds beautifully interpreted by the Salvadoran poet Alfredo Espino in his ode to the Feast of the Cross.[73]

Las azules campánulas que visten la pradera;
Todos los frutos rubios, todos los tiernos cantos,
Para adornar con ellos estos brazos tan santos,
Estos brazos tan santos de la cruz de madera. . . .

Y allí, bajo el amor de alguna enredadera,
Cabe un árbol que tienda sus enflorados mantos
Y un amate en que tiemblen—como gotas de Llantos—
Lágrimas del rocío que en la noche cayera. . . .

Allí hubiera una cruz; enfrente los caminos
Donde pasan carretas, entre flautas de trinos,
Bajo la pedrería de esos soles de mayo
Para que así la cruz recibiera homenajes
De pájaros y ríos; de vientos y ramajes,
Y que el sol la besara con el beso de un rayo. . . .

———

The blue little bells that clothe the prairie;
All the blond fruits, all the tender songs,
To adorn with these those arms, so holy,
Those arms, so holy, of the wooden cross. . . .

And there, under the love of some vine,
Fits a tree that spreads its flowery mantle
And a fig tree in which tremble—like drops of Weeping—
Tears of dew that fall in the night. . . .

There would be a cross; in front of the roads
Where the wagons go by, amid flutes of chirps,
Beneath the rhinestones of those May suns
So that the cross may thus receive homage
From birds and rivers, from winds and branches
And that the sun would kiss with the kiss of a ray. . . .

The life of Christ does not end in kenosis unto death. The drama of the Passion climaxes into the resurrection of the dead. The downward arc of Christ's life is followed by an upward movement to the Father. His return does not mean retreat but transformation and beautification of the very places of abandonment. For Romero, the cross, like the *Bajada*, is a thing of beauty, a powerful sonnet.

Confidence in the power of beauty is what I believe lies behind the cultivation of rose bushes in the garden at the University of Central America where the body of Ignacio Ellacuría was found. His brains were scattered over the grass like manure. Violence is an act of desecration, an act of de-creation. The planting of something beautiful at the place where something so ugly happened is born from the prophetic vision. "They cannot conquer forever."[74] The resistance born of this vision is the reason why the gods of money and of power in Cuéllar's *Gloria* are opposed to transfiguration. The power of these idols consists in hiding its horizons and convincing all that the status quo is permanent. The flowers on the *cruz de mayo* in Espino's *Jícaras tristes* say otherwise.

EL DESCUBRIMIENTO—THE GLORIFICATION OF THE *DIVINO SALVADOR*

In the celebration of the *Bajada*, the revelation of the glory of God is termed the *Descubrimiento*, the unveiling. From the perspective of the spectators, the manner in which the *Descubrimiento* unfolds involves first a veiling, where the image of Christ is lowered into some device, and then a reveal when the image is raised again for all to see. Glory is not something that humans discover through investigation or exploration. Glory denotes God's gratuitous self-disclosure or revelation. The *Bajada* is followed by a time of Eucharistic adoration. The liturgical literature explicitly identifies the *Jesús sacramentado* with the *Jesús transfigurado*. This identification is explicit in the hymn of the first Eucharistic Congress in El Salvador and is emphasized in the celebrations during Romero's time as archbishop.[75] On the morning of August 6, the mass of the Transfiguration is celebrated before the image of the transfigured Christ. The order of the mass is what would be expected for a mass on the Feast of the Transfiguration. The Salvadoran accents are evident in the prayers of the people where the mediation of the "Divine Savior, our Patron" is invoked and in the singing of hymns. Before examining how Romero spoke of the glory of the Divine Savior, we would do well to consider how the people sang of this glory.

We begin with the hymn "¡Bendito seas Salvador Divino!"[76] The subtitle of the hymn sums up the titular feast: "A hymn to the Patron of the Republic, which is honored to bear his august name; to him be the praise, love, and gratitude."

¡Bendito seas Salvador Divino!
Los hijos de tu pueblo, como hermanos,
A tus plantas, humildes nos postramos
Adorando tu excelsa majestad.

La tierra que regaste con tu sangre,
Himnos de amor te canta agradecida;
Eres Camino, Luz, eterna Vida,
Eres Rey de los siglos inmortal.

Lleno está de tu gloria el universo.
La falange de apóstoles hermosa
Rodea tu trono y la mansión gloriosa
Resuena con tu cántico eternal.

Allí el insigne coro de profetas
Y el purpurado ejército luciente
De mártires, con gozo indeficiente
Tu nombre nunca cesan de alabar.

La Iglesia Santa por el orbe entero
Pregona tu poder y tu grandeza:
Que eres el Dios de espléndida belleza,
Que eres el Dios de amor y de bondad.

Eres Señor de todo lo creado,
El monarca supremo de la gloria.
De ti espera la Iglesia la victoria.
Sobre el mundo falaz y Lucifer.

Piedad, Señor, piedad para tus hijos
Con tu sangre preciosa redimidos.
Y en la mansión donde están sus elegidos
Te pedimos nos lleves a gozar.

¡Oh Rey de la creación! Tú solo riges
Nuestra vida fugaz; nuestro destino

En tus manos está; muestra el camino
Que nos lleva a la vida eternal.

De rodillas, Señor, te suplicamos
Celebrando tus glorias del Tabor.
Des a tus hijos divinal amor,
unión, fraternidad, eterna paz.

Enarbolado el pabellón sagrado
De la Patria querida. Como hermanos
¡Hijos del Salvador!: alzad las manos
Bendiciendo a Jesús, rey del amor.

Blessed be the Divine Savior!
The children of your people, like brothers
At your feet, humbly we prostrate ourselves
Praising your sublime majesty.

The land that you watered with your blood
Gratefully sings to you hymns of love;
You are the way, the light, eternal life,
You are the immortal king of the ages.

The universe is full of your glory.
The beautiful column of apostles
Surrounds your throne, and the glorious mansion
Resounds with your eternal song.

There the distinguished chorus of prophets
And the shining purpled army
Of martyrs, with joy unflagging
Your name never cease to praise.

The holy church throughout the whole globe
Proclaims your power and greatness:
That you are the God of splendid beauty,
That you are the God of love and goodness.

You are the Lord of all that is created,
The supreme monarch of glory.
From you the church expects the victory
Over the lying world and Lucifer.

Mercy, Lord, mercy on your children
Redeemed by your precious blood.
And to the mansion where your elect are found
We ask you to lead us to enjoy.

Oh, King of creation! You alone rule
Our fleeting life; our destiny
Lies in your hands; show the way
That leads us to eternal life.

Kneeling, Lord, we implore you,
Celebrating your glories of Tabor.
Give to your children divine love,
Unity, fraternity, eternal peace.

Raised is the sacred pavilion
Of the beloved homeland. Like brothers,
Sons of the Savior, lift your hands
Blessing Jesus, king of love.

The hymn reads like a Salvadoran *Te Deum*. The terminology used to describe the chorus of apostles, prophets, and martyrs closely parallels that of the ancient festal song. The hopes expressed in its verses mirror the petitions later added to the *Te Deum*.[77] The contrasts between the two hymns are suggestive. The Salvadoran version is less robustly Trinitarian than the original. Its focus is on the second person of the Trinity, the Divine Savior. Another contrast pertains to the work of salvation. The original *Te Deum* praises the Incarnation, the Passion, the Resurrection, the Ascension, and the longed-for return of Christ. The Salvadoran one highlights the Transfiguration and its consequences for creation, the land of El Salvador, and its people.

This Salvadoran *Te Deum* is perhaps the most popular Transfiguration hymn in El Salvador. It is sung during the *Bajada* as the *Colocho* Christ is paraded around the streets of San Salvador. However, other festal hymns are sung during this celebration. Consider the hymn "The Homes, the Fields, the Nation, Sing to You, oh Saving God."[78]

Los hogares, los campos, la patria
Hoy te canta, oh Dios, Salvador
De entusiasmo y de fe,
Trepidante a tus pies,
De rodillas está la nación.

El himno patriótico y santo
Es el canto valiente, inmortal,
Que resuena en la tierra, gigante,
Y en el cielo se vuelve a escuchar.
Es la voz que los pechos inquietos
De tus hijos candente rasgó;
Es el grito que lanza una raza
Toda fuego, ternura y pasión.

En la guerra tu sangre se funde
Con la sangre inocente y leal;
De la viuda y del huérfano el llanto
Con tu llanto se van a mezclar.
En la paz tu sonrisa de Padre
Nuestros campos inunda de luz
Y el hogar se calienta al embrujo
De tu dulce figura, oh Jesús.

Oh Jesús Salvador, tu forjaste
Nuestra cuna bendita al nacer;
Y hoy que somos un pueblo ya libre
Te aclamamos cual Dios y cual rey.
Al subir nuestro duro Calvario
Tu nos diste la luz del Tabor;

Y ensanchaste después las fronteras
Transformando tu pueblo en nación.

———

The homes, the fields, the homeland
Today sing to you, oh God, Savior,
With enthusiasm and faith,
Trembling at your feet,
The nation is on its knees.

The patriotic and holy hymn
Is the brave, immortal song
That resounds on the earth, powerfully
And in heaven is heard again.
It is the voice that the restless chests
Of your children struck;
It is the cry that spawns a race
All fire, tenderness, and passion.

In war your blood mingles
With the innocent and loyal blood;
The cry of the widow and the orphan
With your cry will be mixed.
In peace your Father's smile
Floods our fields with light
And the home is warmed by the spell
Of your sweet figure, oh Jesus.

Oh, Jesus Savior, you forged
Our blessed cradle at birth
And now that we are a free people
We praise you as God and king.
When climbing our hard Calvary
You gave us the light of Tabor
And widened then the borders
Transforming your people into nation.

This, "the patriotic and holy hymn," alludes to different chapters of Salvadoran history, its origins when "saving Jesus forged our blessed cradle," its independence, even its battles and suffering "where the tears of the orphan and widow are mixed with [Jesus's] tears." The hymn "The Nation Is a Tabor" belongs to this same patriotic genre but with perhaps more emphasis on geography than history as it exalts the skies, fragrances, and colors of this land.[79]

La patria es un Tabor
Y en ella cual fulgores
Irradias tus amores
Divino Salvador.

Esta Patria al surgir soberana
Bajo un límpido cielo de luz,
Te enlazó y proclamó ser cristiana:
Fue una rosa nacida en tu cruz.

De alegría sus horas tu encanto
Con fragancias de cielo impregnó
Y en las horas de luto y de llanto,
Su dolor tu piedad mitigó.

Pues que diste a esta Patria tu mismo
Nombre excelso cuan don singular,
No la dejes rodar al abismo
De la atea barbarie sin par.

Haz que ella oiga tu voz salvadora
De verdad, de justicia y de amor
Y que a ti, triunfador,
Feliz sea tu eterno Tabor.

———

The homeland is a Tabor
And in her like beams

You shine your loves,
Divine Savior.

This land when emerging sovereign
Beneath a clear sky of light
Bound you and declared herself Christian;
She was a rose born on your cross.

Your charm joyfully filled its hours
With fragrances of heaven,
And in the hours of mourning and crying
Your mercy mitigated its pain.

Since you gave this homeland your very
Sublime name as a unique gift,
Do not let it roll down to the abyss
Of barbarous, unequaled atheism.

Make her hear your saving voice
Of truth, justice, and love
And that for you, triumphant one,
She may happily be your eternal Tabor.

One distinctive note in this hymn is that for the poet it was the Divine Savior himself who gave his name to the land; El Salvador is "a rose" born from the cross. This beauty is endangered. Like the rose, it is fragile, and there are those who seek to stamp it out. In these Transfiguration hymns, the enemies are outside threatening to storm the gates. Before these hordes arrived in communist garb, they were identified with the Masons.[80] These two hymns seem to be cut from the same ideological cloth. They resemble more the Salvadoran national hymn than the Salvadoran *Te Deum*. In both cases, the lyrics sing the praises of El Salvador with more gusto than the glories of the Savior.

The final hymn that needs to be included is the one that was mentioned in the first chapter, Guillermo Cuéllar's *Gloria*.

Vibran los cantos explosivos de alegría
Voy a reunirme con mi pueblo en catedral.
Miles de voces nos unimos este día
Para cantar en nuestra fiesta patronal.

¡Gloria al Señor, gloria al Señor!
¡Gloria al Patrón
De nuestra tierra: El Salvador!
No hay redención de otro señor.
Sólo un Patrón: ¡nuestro Divino Salvador!

Por ser el justo y defensor del oprimido,
Porque nos amas y nos quieres de verdad,
Venimos hoy todo tu pueblo decidido
A proclamar nuestro valor y dignidad.

Ahora, Señor, podrás ser tú glorificado
Tal como antes allá en el monte Tabor,
Cuando tú veas a este pueblo transformado
Y haya vida y libertad en El Salvador.

Pero los dioses del poder y del dinero
Se oponen a que haya transfiguración.
Por eso ahora vos, Señor, sos el primero
En levantar tu brazo contra la opresión.

———————

The songs resound, bursting with joy
I am meeting my people in the cathedral
As we join thousands of voices on this day
To sing on our patron feast.

Glory to the Lord! Glory to the Lord!
Glory to the patron
Of our land, El Salvador!
There is no redemption from another lord.
Only one patron. Our Divine Savior!

For being just and defender of the oppressed,
Because you love us and truly cherish us,
We come today as your people committed
To proclaim our worth and dignity.

Now, Lord, you may be glorified
Just as you were once there on Mount Tabor
When you see your whole people transformed
And there is life and peace in El Salvador.

But the gods of power and of money
Are opposed to there being transfiguration.
This is why you, Lord, are the first one
In raising your arm against oppression.

According to Margaret Pfeil, Romero had requested the young musician to write a hymn for the feast of the Divine Savior, but Cuéllar stalled for months, not thinking himself up to the task.[81] Finally, on Friday, March 21, Cuéllar delivered the finished product to Romero, who wasted no time in including it into his Sunday homily as one of the highlights of the life of the church during the past week. Romero's excitement for this hymn is evident in that he included an excerpt from it in his homily of March 23, 1980. It is the only Transfiguration hymn actually referenced in Romero's extant homilies (*Homilías*, 6:445). He expressed particular appreciation for the final stanza of the hymn. Cuéllar intended to debut the hymn for Romero on Monday evening, March 24, but that did not happen.[82] Pfeil correctly notes that "Cuéllar's 'Gloria,' in both content and context, speaks to Romero's desire to contemplate the lived reality of El Salvador from the standpoint of the liturgical and theological meaning of the Transfiguration."[83]

How do these hymns help us understand Romero's theological vision? First of all, they locate his homilies within a liturgical tradition. Romero does not mention any of these hymns in his homilies. However, given the frequent use of these hymns in the *Bajada* and

the Feast of the Divine Savior, their lyrics and tunes must have contributed images and words to the people's theology of the Transfiguration. Many of the tropes of the popularized vision of Tabor
presented in these hymns differed little materially from those offi-
cially promulgated by the archdiocese or Romero. The songs are all
addressed to the second person of the Trinity. All connect Tabor and
Calvary, church and nation, the Savior with the Salvadorans. Where
the theology of the hymns differs from Romero's is in the relative weight that these themes receive. Romero's theological vision
integrates the Christology of the Salvadoran *Te Deum* with the ethics of Salvadoran *gloria* and the historical mind-set of the patriotic
hymns. One more theme emerges in these hymns that needs to be
considered, beauty. The Salvadoran *Te Deum* calls Jesus "the God
of splendid beauty." But the patriotic hymns also sing of the beauty
of El Salvador. The *Descubrimiento*, the unveiling of the statue of the
transfigured Christ, presents the people with a beautiful image of the
Divine Savior that helps people to glimpse the transfiguration of El
Salvador. The "sweet figure" of the *Colocho* Christ dressed in white
points to heights of glory that "the gods of money and of power"
cannot touch.

Ad Majorem Dei Gloriam

The glory of God is a recurring theme in Romero's preaching and
spirituality. His understanding of this theme is strongly stamped by
Jesuit piety. We will study the Ignatian roots of Romero's spirituality
in the next chapter. For now we focus on his adoption of the Ignatian motto of *Ad majorem Dei gloriam*. For Ignatius, greater glory coincides with greater imitation of Christ's humility.[84] The *magis* of glory
is found in the *minus* of daily life. The more transparent one's life
becomes to the divine image, the more God's glory becomes manifest. For Ignatius, the glory of God has a strongly anthropological
dimension.[85] If the goal of the human is to praise and participate in
the glory of God, then the Ignatian *Deus semper maior* makes it clear
that this goal can be attained, not by stretching one's potential, but

by allowing oneself to be stretched. In a homiletical reflection on the Prodigal Son, Romero joins the Ignatian motto to the Augustinian theme of the *cor inquietum*.

> The human has been made for God, said Augustine, and his heart is restless until it rests in God. Happy the innocent person who has never betrayed the law of God! How few they are! But thanks be to God, there are some. God has made me for himself, and the whole reason of my being, the cultivation of my qualities, the development of my faculties, all my life will be happy in its development, if it has the glory of God at its center. Saint Ignatius of Loyola gave the Jesuits the motto: *Ad majorem Dei gloriam.* And this is why the Jesuit works and advances to the dangerous borders of the church. He works. Even if threatened by death he stays and does not go, because he works for the glory of God; if he is surprised by death there, death will not rob him of the glory of God, because he will continue enjoying it forever to the extent that he cultivated it on earth. (*Homilías*, 1:310)

Ignatius's thinking on glory could not help but be informed by chivalric notions of honor and fame.[86] Romero's thinking was informed by his experience of the Salvadoran Jesuits and in particular his relationship with Rutilio Grande. The description of the happy person that Romero offered in the September 11, 1977, homily just cited could be heard as a eulogy for the martyred Jesuit priest. Grande was one of those few innocent ones who stayed at his post and worked for the greater glory of God even under threat of death. But the Ignatian charism is meant to be a model for the laity too. The "sheet metal worker, the carpenter, the street sweeper, the market woman, the student, the professional" live out their priestly vocation in Christ; they are in fact turning their lives into a mass, a worship service to the glory of God (*Homilías*, 2:441).

The Ignatian motto of *Ad majorem Dei gloriam* draws attention to the human response to God's initiative. For Romero reads this motto in conjunction with the Irenaean one: *Gloria Dei, vivens homo.* The glory of God is not simply the praise of the creature to its creator but the participation of the creature in the glory of God. Before it is a creaturely response, the glory of God is God's self-revelation. The glory of God makes manifest the identity of God.

The Epiphanies of God

The term *glory* belongs to the same lexical family as *theophany* and *epiphany*. The term *theophany* is used by Romero in reference to God's great self-manifestations in scripture (Mamre, Sinai, Horeb). These manifestations are accommodated to human capacity. As Romero comments, "We cannot look at God, just as no one can look at the sun face to face. For if we looked at it, we would suffer the effects of the sun. We cannot look at God face to face. We are too small, our pupils are too limited, but we can see his back, his footsteps, his traces" (*Homilías*, 3:159). The term *epiphany* is much more common in Romero's preaching than *theophany*. This should come as no surprise, given that there is a feast that bears this name. In addition to preaching about the epiphany of Christ to the Magi, Romero uses the term to name a profound encounter with God. For the prophets this encounter was crucial for their own sense of vocation and mission. In making himself manifest and present, the Lord invites humans to share his divine intimacy so that "our hope may be buttressed, our efforts strengthened, and our fears abated" (*Homilías*, 6:371). The mysteries of Jesus's life celebrated on the feast of January 6 and the succeeding Sundays of ordinary time (his baptism, the sign at the wedding in Canaan) are all epiphanies.[87] Indeed, all the mysteries of Jesus's life can be understood as manifestations whereby God is known. The Incarnation, the Transfiguration, the Crucifixion, and the Resurrection are all epiphanies of the glory of Christ.[88]

God's unveilings are not limited to the pages of scripture. The epiphanies of Christ continue in the concrete history of the peoples of Central America. Of particular significance for Romero is the Christ of Esquipulas. The figure of a black Christ hanging from a cross in Esquipulas, Guatemala is perhaps the most famous crucifix in Central America. The image was made by Quirio Cataño, a Portuguese immigrant in 1595, out of light wood.[89] Over time, the smoke of votive candles darkened the stain of the wood. The Lord of Esquipulas is an epiphany of how Christ's mystery unfolds in history. The dark hue of the face of Christ was invested with theological significance.[90] In the colonial era, the color represented the sins of the Guatemalans. The divine face has been "uglied and blackened by insults."[91] In the time of independence, creole elites downplayed the blackness of the Lord of Esquipulas because they feared the image could serve as a rallying point for the largely indigenous, dark-skinned population.[92] Protestants were the first to refer to the image as the black Christ because they hoped that the racial weight of the term would drive Guatemalans away from its cult.[93] Ironically, the sobriquet had the opposite effect, as the devotees of the *Señor de Esquipulas* incorporated the term within their piety.[94] In this Black Christ, Romero sees a sign of how God saves within history. "Christ incarnates himself so deeply in our people that we celebrate him in this way like something that is typically ours. That is what Christ wants to be, the Christ of the Epiphany, the God who became a child, and in Christmas we feel that that child belongs to each family, all of us feel him ours" (*Homilías*, 2:204). The Feast of the Black Christ of Esquipulas presented the people with a time to celebrate how the glory of Christ transfigures colonial history into salvation history.

The glory of Christ is the theme of Romero's 1978 homily for the Feast of the Ascension. The title of the sermon, "The Hour of Glorification," proclaims a close connection between the ascension of Christ and his glorification. But Jesus's hour struck earlier. For Romero, "Glorification began in Gethsemane" (*Homilías*, 4:340). In that garden of prayer and betrayal, Christ identified himself fully with the depths of human suffering.[95] Christ did not follow the path of the *homo incorvatum in se* but lifted his tear-drenched face to the one who could deliver him and surrendered himself to the Father's will. In freely doing this, the Son was glorified, and his glorification reveals the glory of God, the human, and the universe. First, Christ is the glorification of God. The lectionary text from which Romero begins his homiletical reflection on the glory of Christ comes from Ephesians 1:17–23, where Paul calls the God of Jesus "the Father of glory." As the Son of the Father, Jesus shared in the divine glory for eternity. When he assumed humanity, this glory was manifested to all.

Romero speaks of the glory of God as beauty beyond comparison. No nobler thought can be treasured in the human heart. By the light of this glory, the glories of the world are reappraised. A Salvadoran who sets his or her sights on climbing the echelons of power would be terribly wanting in ambition. There is no loftier vocation than that of making known the beauty of Christ in whom the fullness of God's glory dwells. Second, Christ is the glorification of humanity. The glorification of the head exerts a kind of magnetic pull on the rest of the body. Where the head goes the body follows. The glory of the head overflows to its members even now; they are vivified by his sacramental presence. There is an eschatological dimension to this presence. The Christ who ascended to heaven without abandoning his members will return again in glory to bring to consummation the glory of humanity. Third, Christ is the glorification of the universe. The *descubrimiento* of the *Colocho* Christ is of import not only for Salvadorans but for all of creation. "Let us not forget that Christ is the ultimate explanation for all that exists" (*Homilías*, 2:476). He is the Lord of history and of the cosmos. Romero's vision does not leave either Christ or the church, precisely because the head and the body cannot be separated. The church is the realm where the glory of God, the human, and the universe begins to be realized. This sounds like an absurd claim. When one considers the long history of the world, let alone the vastness of the universe, can something as insignificant and troubled as the community of the baptized in El Salvador matter so much? The answer for Romero is an assured yes because that community is the church, the fullness of Christ who is the fullness of God.

The glory of Christ is the face of the "God who sweats in the street." The Christocentrism of Romero unites Ignatius and Irenaeus. Christians are called to work *ad majorem Dei gloriam* by imitating Christ. But they can imitate Christ only when he lives in them: *Gloria Dei, vivens homo*. To put it another way, the glory of God is both gift and responsibility. Humans were made to share in the glory of God. This is the end of human existence, and it can be reached only by embracing the cross. To flee from the cross, to empty it of its power, is tantamount to being conformed to this world. A life without a cross is a failed life (*Homilías*, 3:212). When Christians answer the vocation to become more human, the way of the cross and the glory of God are inseparable. A Christian cannot forget that the glory of Christ has a dolorous foundation: the cross. For this reason, the suffering of the church and the suffering of the Christian always have a perspective of glory and hope (*Homilías*, 2:469).

THE BROKEN FACE OF THE SAVIOR

In this chapter we have been considering Romero's Christological vision. We studied his 1979 homilies on the Divine Savior, the chief Christological title in El Salvador, and the liturgical framework for the celebration of the titular feast. The ritual structure of the *Bajada* that culminates in the *Descubrimiento* facilitated the exploration of the themes of kenosis and glory and also served as vehicle for considering the role of hymnody in Romero's vision of Christ. Who was Jesus for Romero? A number of images were familiar to him: the Christ of the four gospels, the Spanish Christ of Charles V, the *Colocho* Christ of Silvestre Antonio García, the Black Christ of Esquipulas, the worker Christ of Godoy, the Divine Savior of Cuéllar, and others. From these images, he formed a vivid mosaic of a beautiful, wounded, *Divino Salvador*. Romero's Jesus was what Ramón Cué called a *Cristo roto*, a broken Christ.

> This is the one. Look at him. *Ecce homo.* Here is the man. Don't you like him? Isn't he really beautiful? Look at the perfect anatomy of his chest, his torso, his stomach. How svelte and proportioned his leg! How elegant and delicate his arm! How manly and tight his musculature! True, he is missing his entire right arm. The left one is poorly attached to the shoulder, and the hand was broken when he was ripped violently from the nail. . . . He is missing the right leg. It was cut off at midthigh. He still has the left one, but it was glued hastily, without care. And, above all, he has no face. It was literally sliced off. Christ without a face; Christ anonymous, a phantom. But he is beautiful, isn't he?[96]

These lines come from Ramón Cué's *Mi Cristo roto*, a 1963 one-man play that recounts the conversation of a priest with an image of Christ that he has purchased at an antique store in Seville. The image has been rescued from the ruins of a church that was destroyed during the Spanish civil war. Consequently, the Christ is broken. He is missing his cross, his right arm, the bottom of his right leg, and his face. In the dialogues, the priest tries to understand the significance of these losses and why Christ did not want to be repaired. Romero references this story in several homilies.[97]

On the Feast of Corpus Christi in 1977, as Romero preached in the cathedral, government troops occupied the church in Aguilares where Rutilio Grande had been the parish priest. Several times Romero unsuccessfully attempted to retrieve the Eucharistic host from the sanctuary, which had been converted into barracks. But neither the chaplain of the national guard nor the archbishop was able to prevent the profanation of the holy of holies.[98] The Christ who had been violated in his ecclesial body and his Eucharistic body was none other than the *Cristo roto*.[99] On his missing face, the faces of all the sinners for whose forgiveness he suffered and died can be discerned: faces of torturers who break bodies to build wealth for their employers, faces of liars who stain reputations to boost their career, faces of politicians who forget the common good, faces of campesinos who are as avaricious as the oligarchs, just less fortunate, faces of priests who preach bravely in defense of human rights but whine when passed over for promotion. The missing face is not an accident: Christ was defaced, yet there is beauty in this because he endures this out of love. His broken body is a token of God's outreach courting humanity. The broken Christ does not want to be pitied, nor does he want to be fixed; he wants to be loved as he is, wounds and all. The way to show love for this shattered glory is by putting away all doubts and fears and embracing the cross as a way of life even if it leads to real suffering.[100]

By human standards, the broken body of Christ is repulsive. There is nothing glorious about a man dying under torture. Romero's *Cristo roto* has neither form nor beauty. What makes Romero's

Jesus beautiful is not how much he suffered but why, namely for love. It was love that gave Romero the eyes to see the death of Father Alfonso Navarro as beautiful (*Homilías*, 1:91). The beauty came not from Navarro's assassination, which was an evil act, but from the dying priest's beautiful gesture of gasping forgiveness with his last breath. The love with which he died conformed him to Christ, and in this way something vile became beautiful. There is a real danger of misunderstanding the Christian claim that the cross is beautiful as a kind of perverted aesthetic that delights in pain. Conversion to love is vital. Luis Pedraja speaks of love as an act that grants value to its object. "God's love for us makes us valuable, both in God's eyes and in others' eyes as well."[101] God loves Christ even at his most unlovable when he hangs naked on the cross. This is what proves God's love for us. Love does not only respond to the value that it recognizes in an object. It also grants value to this object. In other words, things not only are loved because they are lovely; they also become lovely because they are loved.

Dostoevsky's Prince Myshkin claimed that "the world will be saved by beauty."[102] His idea was dismissed as the playful notion of a man in love. When pressed to be specific as to what kind of beauty had this power, the prince remained silent. Romero too was man in love, but his voice could not remain voiceless. The Divine Savior of the World is Christ "the eternal youth, the eternal beauty, the eternal spring" (*Homilías*, 2:369). Romero makes his own Augustine's plaintive plea: "O beauty always new and always old, late have I known you!"[103] He is beautiful in his transfiguration and in his glorification. He is also beautiful in his crucifixion and humiliation. The scourging of his back, the piercing of his brow, the nailing of his limbs, his casting into hell, all this is beautiful because he did it freely out of love for the Father and humanity. "This is the beautiful thing of Christ" and of the church (*Homilías*, 4:339).

The beautiful face of the church was being slapped, slandered, spat upon. Romero cites the example of Father Octavio, whose face was crushed by the treads of a troop transport. The best efforts of the funerary parlor could not restore his face to a recognizable

semblance. Romero comments that "Octavio has already been transformed, because he faced adversity for Christ" (*Homilías*, 4:193). As
Paul found on the road to Damascus, persecution brings together the
face of the broken church and the face of the broken Christ.[104] The
church is truly the body of Christ in history. By the light of Christ's
glory, Romero can see the presence of Christ in the poor and the suffering. It is because Romero identifies with the church that he must
identify with the marginalized.[105] A kenotic Christ can be prolonged
only by a kenotic church, a church that reaches out to embrace the
poor and accepts the world's resulting rebuff as a mark of its fidelity
to Christ.[106] Ultimately, for Romero, the world will be saved by the
beauty of one whose body forever bears the wounds of our transgres-
sions. In this broken Christ, the *gloria Dei* shines forth with the most
splendid beauty, not only because he is a glorified human being (*vivens
homo*), but because he is a glorified poor person (*vivens pauper*).

CHAPTER 5

THE TRANSFIGURED
PEOPLE OF GOD

At the University of Central America (or the UCA, as it is commonly
known) in San Salvador there is a chapel known as the Chapel of the
Martyrs. In it are buried six Jesuit priests who were murdered by death
squads on November 16, 1989. The chapel itself was built in 1985.
Its construction and design were the brainchild of the rector of the
UCA, Ignacio Ellacuría, one of Romero's collaborators and one of
the martyred Jesuits. As with many church buildings in the tropics, the
side walls have many openings so as to let the breeze cool the sanctuary. From the pews, the congregation can see the altar and a series of
panels on the wall behind it showing scenes of the civil war in El Salvador. Romero's own martyrdom is featured along with mass graves,
and yet the scene is a beautiful one; the symmetry of the figures and
the brightness of the colors illustrate the power of the Resurrection to
bring order and beauty to the darkest places. From the altar, the view is
different. The priest looks out on the congregation and behind them,
on the back wall by the entrance, a set of fourteen black-and-white
sketches of tortured, naked corpses. These were commissioned by
Ellacuría, who wanted a set of the Stations of the Cross more in tune
with the realities of El Salvador than the traditional representations.

169

His desire was fulfilled by Roberto Huezo, a Salvadoran artist and student of Ellacuría.[1] Huezo's sister and brother-in-law had been kidnapped years before. While searching for his missing relatives, he saw bodies displayed clinically in morgues and also thrown by the side of the road like garbage. The artist responded to these desecrations by drawing. The more than eight hundred sketches were silent witnesses to the dehumanization of Salvadorans. The white canvas on which the simple charcoal lines were drawn pointed to the void, the nothingness that threatened to swallow the Christian humanist. However, by placing a representative sample of these images within the church, Ellacuría transformed the portraits of suffering into the *via crucis* of the Salvadoran people. Each station marks another step in the journey of the crucified people through history. The images are not meant to encourage fatalism. On the contrary, Ellacuría hopes that by meditating on Huezo's sketches Christians will join Christ in bearing the reality starkly represented by these and take responsibility for it. The *via crucis* of the Salvadoran people intends to form Christians who take the crucified down from the cross. The Christ of the Chapel of the Martyrs is not just the suffering servant of Isaiah, he is Jesus the liberator, Romero's Divine Savior.

In this chapter we will consider Romero's vision of the church. Christology and ecclesiology are distinct but inseparable subjects. Thinking about the transfiguration of Christ leads us to thinking about his transfigured body in history. Thinking about the crucified Lord leads to thinking about his crucified people and vice versa. There is deep wisdom in the display of Huezo's drawings at the Chapel of the Martyrs at the UCA. Romero did not live to see this chapel, but the theology written into its architecture faithfully displays important aspects of his ecclesial vision. Among these aspects, poverty is of special significance. In El Salvador, poverty marks one for death. But poverty is also a mark of the church. The church is the body of Christ, and Christ was poor. The poor have always been with us but often as extras. The relatively recent irruption of the poor as actors in history has prompted the church to consider the poor anew. The exploration of Romero's ecclesial vision begins with an overview of how the church has interpreted the emergence of the poor as a sign of the times that summons the church to action. This section will focus on the development of the preferential option for the poor and the reinterpretation of the classical concept of *loci theologici*. With this background in mind, we will read Romero's ecclesiology by way of his episcopal motto of *Sentir con la iglesia*. The study of the origins of this motto in Ignatius of Loyola and its adaption by Romero for El Salvador will help us understand the concrete catholicity of Romero's vision of the transfigured people of God that is the church. At the center of this vision is the face of the poor. Finally, we will study the pastoral letters that Romero wrote as archbishop. These letters can be read as epistles to the church in Tabor. In these, the archbishop illumines the pilgrimage of the church in El Salvador with the light of the Transfiguration, which is but a ray of the light of the Resurrection, and which offers life to the most vulnerable. These epistles inform a transfigured *Sentir con la iglesia* that can identify with the ugly realities depicted at the UCA with new hope.

THE POOR IN THE THINKING
OF THE CHURCH IN LATIN AMERICA

When the Latin American bishops gathered in Puebla in 1979, they saw the extreme poverty of the continent in a tragic yearbook of faces. These are the faces of the suffering Christ who questions and cries out to the church (*Puebla* 32–39):

> faces of children, stricken by poverty even before they were born, whose possibilities for fulfillment are hindered by irreparable mental and physical deficiencies; the drifting and often exploited children of our cities, the fruit of poverty and the moral breakdown of the family;
>
> faces of young people, aimless for want of a meaningful place in society, frustrated because of lack of opportunities for training and occupation, especially in the peripheries of rural and urban areas;
>
> faces of indigenous people and frequently of Afro-Americans, who living in marginalized and inhuman situations, may be considered the poorest among the poor;

faces of campesinos, who as a social group live in exile in almost our entire continent; at times lacking land, in situations of internal and external dependency, subject to commercial systems that exploit them;

faces of workers, frequently poorly compensated and with difficulties in organizing themselves to fight for their rights;

faces of the underemployed and unemployed, fired because of the hard demands of economic crises and because of development models that subject workers and families to cold economic calculations;

faces of urban, marginalized masses, afflicted by the double impact of lack of material goods in the midst of the flaunting of wealth from other social sectors;

faces of the elderly, each day more numerous, who are frequently marginalized from a society built around progress that has no use for people who do not produce.

The gallery of faces described by Puebla is not a new story. The tragedy of the Latin American situation had already been brutally depicted by Felipe Guamán Poma de Ayala in the late sixteenth century. In his *Nueva Crónica y buen gobierno*, this Andean Christian summed up the plight of the indigenous with a single drawing. The image showed an indigenous person on his knees, surrounded by six savage beasts that represented the dangers that threatened to devour the life of the poor Indian: a snake (the royal administrator), a tiger (marauding Spaniards), a lion (the landowner), a fox (the parish priest), a cat (a notary), and a rat (the native chieftain). The caption of the sketch, written partly in Spanish and partly in Quechua, states: "poor Indians . . . poor Jesus Christ."[2] Poma's pictorial identification of the poor indigenous person with the poor Jesus Christ had been experienced by Bartolomé de las Casas decades before. The Dominican friar wrote of having seen Christ "being scourged, afflicted, struck, and crucified, not once but thousands of times" in the bodies of the indigenous.[3]

The pilgrimage of the crucified peoples in Latin America started a long time ago. The church's reflection on the reasons for this pilgrimage and the implications of it for the proclamation of the gospel received a powerful boost in the late twentieth century. A more critical and self-aware reading of the signs of the times in Latin America helped the church see the centrality of the world of the poor in God's mission. As the church engaged the world of the poor with new eyes, new theological formulas were developed and fresh voices were heard. In this section I want to consider two concepts that capture *in nuce* the place of the poor in the thinking of the church in Latin America: the preferential option for the poor and the poor as *locus theologicus*. I also want to bring the voice of Eduardo Pironio into the conversation. Next to theological luminaries like Gustavo Gutiérrez, Leonardo Boff, and Jon Sobrino, Pironio's light appears dim. But the life and teaching of the Argentine cardinal deeply affected the manner in which Romero thought of God's liberation of the poor and warrants our consideration.

The Preferential Option for the Poor

The term *preferential option for the poor* entered the ecclesial stage at the meeting of Catholic Latin American bishops that took place in Puebla in 1979, but its roots are older. The groundwork for this option was already plowed at the earlier gathering of bishops in Medellín in 1968. One of the main purposes for that meeting was to promote the reception of the teachings of Vatican II in Latin America.[4] At Medellín the bishops found that a significant amount of translation work needed to be done if the indigenous were to faithfully receive the teachings of the council. After all, the chief problem confronting the church in Latin America was not the death of God but the death of the people of God. Themes of poverty and oppression that the conciliar documents treated in passing became the focus of attention. Medellín was a watershed in significant ways. First, methodologically, in the very structure of its report the conference adopted a "see, judge, act" methodology that was inductive and historically grounded.[5] Second, substantively, Medellín promoted a social ethic based on the unity of history. The bifurcation of history into two histories, one sacred and one secular, that ran side by side without touching was repaired. The assertion of the unity of history gave meaning to efforts intended to improve society while safeguarding the transcendental goal of this history in the kingdom of God.

Puebla uses the phrase "preferential option for the poor" seven times in the final document. In lieu of a definition of the phrase, the document offers a cluster of theological themes, social analyses, and pastoral implications. Central to Puebla's deployment of the phrase is the concept of conversion. Those who would opt for the poor must undergo a constant process of repentance and purification. The goal of this conversion is described in the following terms. "The preferential option for the poor has as its object the announcement of Christ the Savior, who will illumine them concerning their dignity, assist them in their efforts at liberation from all want, and lead them into communion with the Father and their brothers and sisters by means of living in evangelical poverty" (*Puebla* 1153).

The preferential option makes a claim about God.[6] It announces that the God of Jesus Christ makes himself known in a special way among the marginalized. Thus the preferential option of God has epistemological, theological, and moral implications for Christians. In effect, the preferential option becomes the criterion for methodology, orthodoxy, and orthopraxis. Opting for the poor requires a radical change in perspective for First World Christians; it means adopting the lived faith of the poor. Opting for the poor entails believing and praying and serving the God of the poor. Roberto Goizueta expresses well what this conversion entails: "The cross, which for the nonpoor is a sign of God's absence, is, for the poor, the assurance of God's presence—not just any god, not just a 'vague' or 'generic' god, but the God of Jesus Christ, the God who accompanies us today."[7] The call to embrace the lived faith of the poor raises significant questions. How does one avoid romanticizing the poor? Granted that God reveals himself preferentially to the poor, is not the response of the poor as ambiguity-ridden as that of any other human being?

The preferential option for the poor has experienced a difficult reception history. Immediately after Puebla, there are signs of divergent interpretations of the term. Rohan Curnow suggests that there are two main lines of interpretation, two versions of the "preferential option."[8] There is a Roman version, whose banner was carried by John Paul II and Joseph Ratzinger and then Benedict XVI, and a Latin American version as exemplified by Gustavo Gutiérrez and

Jon Sobrino. For the former, the option is a principle within moral theology and Catholic social teaching, a topic of discussion within the larger conversation of the universal destination of goods. For the latter, the option is a methodological principle guiding all theology.[9]

The doctrine has been challenged by liberation theologians, who find the term too narrow and exclusive. There are, after all, other kinds of oppression beyond the economic. Moreover, some worry that the principle is insufficiently radical. Its language is vulnerable to cooptation by those who are in positions of power. So even though the preferential option has needled a church that has benefited from the patronage of the rich throughout its entire history, Elsa Tamez expresses concern that the principle "in spite of possibly being subversive, fits perfectly within Christian orthodoxy."[10]

Articulating the basis for the church's partiality toward the poor has proved challenging.[11] At times the basis has been the poor's hermeneutically privileged position. Certain scriptural themes (God's mercy, grace) are believed to be more easily and immediately felt by the poor. True though this is, the epistemic privilege of the poor is partial. There are other social locations from which God may be contemplated that contribute to the Christian understanding of God.[12] At other times, the preferential option is based on the partiality of God, but here too challenges present themselves. Scripture speaks of God showing partiality in the call of Abram, the election of Israel, the covenant at Sinai, and so on. But according to Paul in Romans 2:11, "God shows no partiality."[13] Perhaps the best basis for the preferential option for the poor is the Christological one—Christ became poor.[14]

The Poor as Locus Theologicus

The concept of theological loci began as a Catholic response to the Protestant question of authority. In *De locis theologicis*, Melchor Cano answers the question by offering a theological method. The Spanish Dominican identifies ten places from which the theologian can "draw ideal arguments or prove their conclusions or refute their contraries."[15] These *loci theologici* are sacred scripture, the tradition of Christ and his apostles, the authority of the Catholic Church, the authority of the councils, the authority of the Roman Church, the authority of the holy fathers, the authority of the Scholastics, natural reason, the authority of the philosophers, and the authority of human history. Cano does not consider all ten places as equally authoritative or fruitful for theology. The first two, scripture and the apostolic tradition, are the most proper places of theology. The fathers and the Scholastics offer criteria for interpreting these two, and reason, philosophy, and history play an even more distant role. It is important to observe that although Cano and Philipp Melancthon use similar terminology Cano's usage of *loci* differs from that of Melancthon, for whom the *loci* are theological topics (*loci communes*). For the Catholic, the *loci* pertain to method: What are our sources? For the Protestant, the *loci* pertain to content: What are we talking about?

Latin American theology follows Cano's understanding of *loci* more than Melancthon's. The poor are not a topic that Christians talk about but a place from which one does theology.[16] But what does a *locus theologicus* mean in the Latin American context? The need for clarification is made manifest by the casual and vague manner in which the concept is often used. A quick literature search reveals that a bewildering range of things have been named *loci theologici*: gender, migration, *la familia*, vulnerability, interculturality, Europe, and so on.[17] One way through this morass of *loci* is to introduce the distinction between a *locus theologicus* and a *locus hermeneuticus*. Juan Carlos Scannone clearly distinguishes between the two.

> The *lugar hermenéutico* is not a source or the cause of theological knowledge but a necessary *condition* (*conditio sine qua non*), although not sufficient, by which certain aspects of the sources or the reasons implied in these may be known and recognized. The *lugar* is not the source of the light but may favor or hinder the reception or acceptance of the light. . . . By contrast, when one speaks of *lugares teológicos*, one is speaking, not of a place (hermeneutic or epistemic) that is occupied by the theology or the theologian, but of the *tópoi* (in the Aristotelian sense) or *sources*, be they constitutive (scripture, tradition) or declarative of theological knowledge. They are not the "from where" (neither epistemic

nor hermeneutic-existential, historic, social, or cultural) one reflects, but the "within which" the theology or theologian encounters knowledge and/or theological arguments.[18]

The distinction between *locus theologicus* and *locus hermeneuticus* is helpful in avoiding methodological errors. All theology is done from a certain social location, all *loci theologici* are approached through *loci hermeneutici*, but the social location is not itself the source of theology.[19] At the same time, the distinction enjoys a certain fluidity.[20] The presence of God in some event or experience may be so powerful that its authority cannot be denied. The event is then properly to be interpreted as a *locus theologicus* that contributes its unique sound within the great symphony of faith.

In Latin America, the theologian who most rigorously applies the category of *locus theologicus* to the poor is Ignacio Ellacuría.[21] For Ellacuría, a *locus theologicus* is a multidimensional place where divine revelation happens, true faith is possible, and the conditions are primed for Christian theology. Like Cano, Ellacuría does not consider all times and places to be equally meaningful theological loci. Unlike Cano, Ellacuría names the poor as the best *locus theologicus* on account of the conformity of their life to that of Jesus. They are therefore a privileged place of revelation, the best companions along the way of Christ, and the ideal place for doing theology. Ellacuría refers to the poor as a place of theology, not as a source, but then again he admits that in a sense the place of theology does become a source because only from the poor can God's revelation be truly seen.

From this brief survey, it should be evident that understanding the poor as *locus theologicus* is a complex matter. For Cano, the *locus theologicus* is the material object (*quem*) that is studied. For liberation theology, the *locus theologicus* is the formal object (*quo*) by which something is studied. Under Cano's scheme, one could consider the poor as an auxiliary *locus theologicus* that when illumined by the light of faith becomes a place of revelation. The relation between faith, scripture, signs of the times, and the poor is understood differently by different theologians. Some understand theology as critical reflection on historical praxis in the light of scripture. Others invert this epistemological relation and treat theology as critical reflection on scripture in light of historical praxis. To complicate matters further, there is no consensus as to where the giants of liberation theology stand on this important methodological principle.[22] It is one thing to say that liberation theology starts from the reality of the poor as *locus communis* or as a practical place from which to begin the conversation. It is something very different to make the poor the *locus theologicus* that regulates all theology.[23]

There is a tendency in contemporary theology to absolutize a few theological *loci* (the Bible, the magisterium, praxis), but all loci are in need of integration and broadening.[24] The theological loci and the hermeneutical loci are plural and polyphonic. Neither *sola Scriptura* nor *solo pauper* is enough. The poor as *locus theologicus* can be heard only within the symphony of truth that is the gospel. This is not to say that in a given *locus hermeneuticus* the place of the poor is *the* place from which to do theology. To put it another way, the sign of the times may well be that their part, their contribution to the symphony, is crucial. God may well have called the poor (and particular poor communities) to play the note to which the entire orchestra must listen and tune their instruments.

The Teaching of Eduardo Pironio

The story of the development of liberation theology in Latin America is often told by studying its theologians: Gutiérrez, Boff, Míguez Bonino. This approach is not mistaken. These figures and others like them are central to the story of how Latin America transitioned from being a reflection-church, an echo of European voices, to being a source-church speaking in its own voice. However, if the story stopped there, it would be incomplete. Professional theologians attended Medellín and Puebla, but these meetings were not academic conferences; they were first and foremost gatherings of bishops. Not only did bishops, especially the bishop of Rome, have a large role in setting the agenda for the conversation; they also had the power to shape the reception of these meetings. One of the bishops who contributed positively to the theological conversations in Latin America was Eduardo Pironio.

Throughout his more than five decades of ordained ministry, Eduardo Pironio served as bishop in Argentina, secretary general and also president of CELAM, and cardinal prefect of the Congregation for Institutes of Congregated Life and Societies of Apostolic Life.[25] Pironio was not a prolific writer, but as bishop he was frequently called to lead spiritual retreats for other bishops. The published meditations from these retreats are among his chief and best-loved literary productions. The voice of Pironio did not achieve the continental reach of those of other bishops like Hélder Câmara or even Alfonso López Trujillo, but his ministry touched Romero intimately.

In Romero's eyes, Pironio was "a holy bishop" (*Homilías*, 1:100). The Argentine prelate modeled the essential qualities and responsibilities of an episcopal leader.[26] So highly did Romero regard the spiritual leadership of Pironio that abridgments of his meditations were regularly published as columns in *Orientación*.[27] The title of Romero's salutatory letter to his archdiocese, *The Paschal Church*, echoes an essay by Pironio titled "Latin America: Paschal Church."[28] The similarities between these two writings are not limited to their titles. In his letter, Romero appeals to Pironio when characterizing the crucial time through which El Salvador and Latin America are passing as an hour of "cross and hope, possibilities and risks, responsibility and commitment."[29] Romero also finds Pironio helpful in selecting the right language of conversion required in the present hour. For too long, the church in Latin America had lived in a shallow relationship with Christ, separated faith and life, and was insensitive to the problems of Latin American existence. The hour of the Latin American Church called for "savoring Christ in his mystery," making the faith "concrete in love and justice," and contributing "to the positive construction of history."[30] The relation between the Salvadoran archbishop and the Argentine cardinal is not exhausted by these textual references.

Romero calls Pironio "a great friend" (*Homilías*, 3:80). During his visits to Rome, Romero usually set time aside for visiting Pironio.[31] In their time together, the archbishop and the cardinal would open their hearts to each other and share their concerns for the church in Latin America. When Romero felt persecuted and slandered by his opponents in and out of the church, Pironio offered words of encouragement. The cardinal too had been called a communist and had even received a book titled *Pironio, Pyromaniac* (*Homilías*, 3:80). Romero also considered Pironio "a great promoter of authentic liberation in Latin America" (*Homilías*, 1:298).

To understand how Romero thinks of liberation theology it is important to read Pironio. In fact, Romero himself preached from the pulpit that Pironio was one of the solid theologians through whom he studied liberation theology (*Homilías*, 1:215). Pironio's most extensive treatment of the subject is an essay titled "Theological Reflection Regarding Liberation."[32] We know that Romero read this essay because he cites from it in one of his homilies.[33] A number of themes from that essay work their way into Romero's theology. First, Pironio interprets the longing for liberation as one of the signs of the times. The Spirit is speaking to the church through the deafening clamor for liberation of so many poor and marginalized voices in Latin America. This longing is experienced as a desire for freedom from all kinds of bondage and as a vocation to become new creatures. Latin Americans long for a liberation that is temporal and eternal, spiritual and material, personal and social. Second, both Pironio and Romero understand that liberation is a rich theological theme. It needs to be considered from different but inclusive perspectives: salvation history, new humanity, and hope. The plurality of perspectives gestures to the fecundity of the mystery of Christ and his saving work. Third, Pironio warns that for liberation theology to flourish certain caveats must be observed. Focusing all attention on the theme of liberation eclipses other aspects of the mystery of Christ. Indeed, the attempt to reduce theology to one master theme cannot help but obscure other aspects of theology whose object is the uncontainable Triune God. Against all one-sided, superficial interpretations, the theme of liberation must be understood from the perspective of the history of salvation as manifested through Israel and finding its fulfillment in Christ.[34] In addition to these caveats regarding the theme, Pironio offers a caveat for the agents of liberation. Human beings have a real role to play. However, this role must not be reduced to mere activism or to structural changes. The reformer of society must first be reformed by the Spirit.[35]

By entering the world of the poor, the Latin American church deepened its faith in Christ and developed important insights regarding liberation and the proclamation of the gospel. As Pironio said, "The Latin American church is living its hour."[36] At the same time, the Latin American church had to be on guard against becoming "Latin Americanized."[37] That is to say, it had to keep from exaggerating its gifts and accomplishments or becoming self-absorbed. The hour of the Latin American church called for a concrete catholicity, an incarnation in the realities of the continent that remained connected to the universal teaching authority of the church represented by Rome. For Romero, the right posture for living into this hour was found in the Ignatian phrase *Sentir con la iglesia*.

Sentir con la Iglesia

During a spiritual retreat in preparation for his episcopal consecration, Romero writes in his diary: "My consecration is synthesized in this word: *Sentir con la iglesia*."[38] It may seem curious that Romero chose an Ignatian saying as the motto for his episcopacy. After all, Romero was not a Jesuit, but he did have the highest esteem for Saint Ignatius of Loyola. The testimony of Jesuits such as his friend Rutilio Grande and others moved him deeply. He considered the Society of Jesus as the vanguard of the church (*Homilías*, 1:64). Their commitment to live and work *ad majorem Dei gloriam* manifested itself in their movement from the center "toward the dangerous frontiers of the church" (*Homilías*, 1:310).[39] For this reason, "It is natural that they are always placed in the line of fire when there are attacks on the church" (*Homilías*, 1:64). If persecution is one of the marks of the church, the Jesuit order has the privilege of carrying this mark in a specially conspicuous way (*Homilías*, 1:117–18). Romero was inspired by the Jesuit way of life. It is significant that although Romero was a lover of the Spanish mystics in general, he decided to write his dissertation at the Gregorian on the Jesuit Luis de la Puente (1564–1624). The mystical vision of this heir of Ignatius drew on the theological currents flowing through Spain at the time: Augustinian, Pseudo-Dionysian, Thomistic. Even the Benedictine strand of spirituality found its place here, as the Nursian's vow of stability (*stabilitas loci*) anchored this version of Ignatian spirituality. Rady Roldán Figueroa explains that "for de la Puente, stability no longer depended exclusively on physical location but consisted of internalized routines and habits of mind that could preserve the integrity of the self even in the midst of considerable mobility or situations requiring extreme suppleness."[40] Since Romero's work on de la Puente never really got under way before he was recalled to El Salvador, it is difficult to assess the contribution of the Spanish Jesuit to the Salvadoran priest's thinking and doing. But Romero's lifelong attraction to the work of the mystics and to the quest of union with God would have found ample sustenance in de la Puente's writings.[41]

The Spiritual Exercises of Ignatius

In addition to his high regard for Saint Ignatius and his followers, Romero was an avid promoter and practitioner of the Spiritual Exercises. Romero's encounter with Ignatian spirituality dates to his first years of seminary in San Salvador and in the Gregorian in 1937 and continued to the final days of his life.[42] In an interview with Father Enrique Nuñez Hurtado during the gathering of Latin American bishops in Puebla, Romero articulated his thoughts regarding the significance of the Spiritual Exercises not only for him but for the continent.[43]

For Romero, the Spiritual Exercises in Latin America were instruments of evangelization. Latin America needed agents of social transformation and renewal. The Spiritual Exercises were a wonderful school for instilling the disciplines of discerning the will of God for the here and now. At Puebla, John Paul II pointed out the doctrinal constellation that was to guide the people of God's journey through the history of Latin America: the truth about Christ, the truth about the church, and the truth about the human. When the Spiritual Exercises take their bearings from these three lights, then they are eminently suited to the formation of these new evangelists.

First, Romero says that "the Spiritual Exercises should learn to read a Christology from our Latin America that helps us feel [*sentir*] in the humanity of the eternal Christ the hurts, the anguishes, the hope of our Latin American people."[44] As "true God and true human," the Christ of the Exercises identifies himself thoroughly with the Latin American realities of poverty, oppression, and marginalization and invites participants to do the same.[45]

Second, the identification of Christ with the Latin American people injects new meaning into the famous Ignatian motto. The feeling of ecclesial solidarity is not limited to the magisterium but is extended to the entire people of God, a people that is acquainted with suffering and turns to the church in hope. The church whose participants are enjoined to *sentir* is not just any church. It is the church that the Spirit is raising on the continent, a church characterized by fidelity to the magisterium and service to the people.

Third, as far as the Ignatian vision of the human is concerned, Romero longs for the development of a theocentric anthropology. In Latin America the Ignatian *Ad majorem Dei gloriam* must be interpreted alongside an Irenaean conviction that "the human is the glory of God to the extent to which he is fulfilled, liberated, and promoted."[46] The theocentric anthropology teaching that "humans are the glory of God on earth" encourages the church in its humble yet firm defense of the dignity of those whose worth is so frequently discounted.

Romero believed that if the Spiritual Exercises were going to succeed in forming the agents of transformation that the continent needed, then the priests leading the exercises would have to be immersed in the spirit of Ignatius and in the life of their local communities. Knowing the social, political, and economic framework for the call was crucial. "A life that does not commit itself to God's project in history would denote a poorly understood vocation."[47] The laity too had to embrace their vocation. In the present hour of Latin America, God called the laity to be messengers of that "integral liberation that understands how to give earthly liberationist movements their true horizon, their true strength, their originality, their highest reach."[48] This did not mean that all lay people were called to embrace a political vocation. There are many calls, and the Spiritual Exercises might be one of the most important ways in which to learn to discern what God wants from us. But *Sentir con la iglesia* could not avoid having a political dimension.

An Ignatian Rule

The phrase *Sentir con la iglesia* appears in the section of rules that concludes the Spiritual Exercises of Saint Ignatius. The text reads: "Para
el sentido verdadero que en la Iglesia militante debemos tener" (For
the true *sentido* that we should have in the militant church).[49] I leave
the word *sentir* untranslated because it is difficult to convey its semantic range in English. *Sentir* can be translated as "to think." Indeed,
one of the most common English translations of the Ignatian saying is "To think with the church." But *sentir* can also be translated as
"to feel," "to perceive," or "to sense." Two points are worth noting.
First, the series of rules headed by the Ignatian saying are found at the
end of the Exercises rather than at the beginning. *Sentir con la iglesia*
is not a point of departure for Ignatian spirituality but its point of
arrival.[50] Second, the *sentir* that Saint Ignatius desires to inculcate has
as its object the church militant. Doubtless, it would be easier to *sentir
con la iglesia* if the *iglesia* were removed from the historical legacy of the
Crusades and the sale of indulgences that complicate her testimony
and thus our *sentir*. But Ignatius's *Sentir con la iglesia* is a concrete commitment without emergency exits toward a golden age lost in the past
or hidden above in the heavens. The basis for the ecclesial commitment that Ignatius teaches is found not in the history of the church
but in the mystery of its union with Christ. Therefore, *sentir con la iglesia*
is the fruit of *sentir con Cristo.*[51]

Ignatius structures the rules for *sentir con la iglesia* into three
groups.[52] The first group concerns worship and Christian devotion.
It may seem curious that in the midst of fighting so strenuously to
internalize Christian piety, Ignatius dedicates the majority of the rules
for *sentir con la iglesia* to the external practices of piety.[53] Against the
luminosity of the *alumbrados* and the cynicism of the humanists, Ignatius proposes the practices of popular piety as the backbone for the
spirituality of those who seek to *sentir con la iglesia*. The second set of
rules concerns the diverse authorities to whom those who seek to
sentir con la iglesia need to adhere. *Sentir con la iglesia* is *sentir* with the *magisterium* as taught by the theologians and lived by the saints.[54] Ignatius
proposes an innovative and radical union between the inclination to

obedience and the desire for reform. In the church there is always need for reform, but true reform must proceed with prudence if it is to be efficacious and not result in a remedy worse than the infirmity.[55] The third set of rules concerns the dogmas that must be believed and preached concerning God and humanity, faith and works, grace and freedom, and love and fear. Ignatius believed that the loss of due proportion in these pairings provoked the ecclesial crisis of the Reformation. The proper balance will be found only by adopting a posture of both filial love and servile fear.[56]

In summary, for Saint Ignatius, if the Spiritual Exercises have as their object vocational discernment, then the decision of how Christ wants one to serve him, the *Sentir con la iglesia*, makes this calling concrete. Against spiritual elitism, the *Sentir con la iglesia* requires Christians of all walks of life to unite in prayer and adoration, especially in those practices that are more at home in the village than in the monastery. This *sentir* with the people becomes true when united to a *sentir* with the tradition. Finally, *Sentir con la iglesia* is not a passive attitude but one that requires action; it calls for a commitment to proclaim the faith with vigor, prudence, and fearfulness. The density of the Ignatian *Sentir con la iglesia* was the object of adoption, adaptation, and accretion by Óscar Romero.

A Salvadoran Ressourcement

Romero's appeal to the Ignatian motto predates his episcopal consecration. In an editorial in *Chaparrastique* from 1965, Romero affirmed the importance of *Sentir con la iglesia* for implementing the *aggiornamento* encouraged by the Second Vatican Council.[57] According to Santiago Mata, the 1965 editorial may be Romero's first invocation of what would become his motto.[58] The timing of his usage may be due to the release of the encyclical *Ecclesiam Suam* on the Feast of the Transfiguration in 1964. In that letter, Paul VI writes that awareness of the mystery that is the church produces in Christian souls a *sentir de la iglesia (sensus ecclesia)*.[59] Even if this encyclical is not the textual inspiration for Romero's adoption of the phrase, it is without a doubt the text that furnishes the structure for how Romero later on appropriates the Ignatian saying. Following Paul VI's encyclical *Ecclesiam Suam*, Romero speaks of two opposing forces resisting the longed-for goal: a fixation on the immobility of traditional forms and dreams of false reforms. On the one hand, unconditional adherence to the traditional forms impedes the progress of the church and reduces its catholicity. The catholicity of the church is multidimensional; it has a geographic aspect and a historical one. The dynamism of the church's catholicity is what allows it to be attuned to all kinds of civilizations and historical periods. On the other hand, when an exaggerated spirit for novelties captures the imagination of people in the church, the understanding sought by the faith easily degenerates into an imprudent exploration of the unknown that betrays the rich patrimony of experiences from the past. The opposing forces of theological rigidity and a false spirit of reform encourage dissension in church life. In a letter to *Orientación* in 1972, Romero speaks of the danger of separating renewal from adaptation. "Renewal is a return to basic values, an inward look, an examination of conscience. Adaptation is an outward look to the present times, the needs and hopes of people today."[60] The former roots Christians in tradition; the latter opens the church to the new. When renewal and adaptation are set against each other, they become dangerous words. Conservatives mistake Tradition (capital T) for traditions that are but the particular and passing realizations of Tradition. Progressives confuse change with the movement of the Spirit. The true path lies in the mean between these two errors, and the mean itself is found by living into the Ignatian aphorism *Sentir con la iglesia*, which Romero interprets here as "unconditional adherence to the hierarchy."[61]

After his selection as auxiliary bishop (but before his consecration), Romero participated in a spiritual retreat where he voiced his concerns and hopes about his new assignment. During this time of renewal and reflection, Romero reread the church's magisterial documents. In particular, he mentions reading the first chapter of *Gaudium et Spes*, which treats the subject of human dignity, and chapter 5 from *Lumen Gentium*, which talks about the call to holiness, a call that culminates in martyrdom. Romero could hear the council father reminding him of the story of the church: "All must be ready to confess Christ before men and follow him by the way of the cross in the midst of the persecutions that are never absent from the church" (*Lumen Gentium* 42). These readings confirmed the orientation of Romero's consecration. "I would like to be distinguished by this," vows Romero, "by *being the bishop of the heart of Jesus*."[62]

Devotion to the Sacred Heart ran deep in Romero's piety. By some counts, as a young seminary student, Romero kept over two hundred index cards on the subject, making it the third most popular topic in his files after ascetic theology and Christology.[63] On February 25, 1980, in what turned out to be his final spiritual retreat, Romero concluded his notes to the exercises with a prayer of consecration to God where he rededicated himself to the Sacred Heart of Jesus. "Thus I consent my consecration to the Sacred Heart of Jesus, which was always my source of inspiration and Christian joy of my life."[64] At the hour of his consecration as bishop, the dedication to the heart of Jesus expressed a desire to receive a new infusion of the Holy Spirit that would renew his baptism and ordination. At the hour of his death this dedication denoted an act of entrusting himself to the will of God. Romero's consecration to the sacred heart was sealed by his commitment to *sentir con la iglesia*. "My consecration is synthesized in this word: *Sentir con la iglesia*. This means I will make the three ways of the church according to the encyclical *Ecclesiam Suam* my own and after examining my personal reality according to the criteria of the glory of God and the eternal health of my soul."[65]

In appropriating the Ignatian motto, Romero claims for his episcopate the three chief tasks of Paul VI's pontificate as outlined in the aforementioned encyclical *Ecclesiam Suam*. First, *sentir con la iglesia* denotes a posture of self-awareness. The self that Romero is seeking to understand and be true to is ecclesial. His episcopal motto leads him to commit himself to "know[ing] the church more each day and my place and duty to her."[66] In order to carry out this commitment, Romero pledges himself to being up to date and faithful to ecclesial pronouncements. His persistent appeal to ecclesial documents in his teaching and preaching is an expression then of his *sentir con la iglesia*. Second, *Sentir con la iglesia* entailed for him a strong commitment to renewal. Romero writes: "The church demands holiness and is always in need of conversion. I will be before I act. I have examined the many things that ask for penitence, caution, and reform within me."[67] The things that need to be reformed in Romero are his sensuality, his bad examples, his sacrileges, his lack of order, and his pride. Some of the things that Romero proposes to do in order to renew his inward being involve simple, ordinary practices like short naps and early bedtimes ("no later than ten"). Other practices pertain to priestly activities like celebrating mass with more fervor, praying Matins at midnight, preparing better for confession, and the like. Still other practices belong to the ascetic life. Romero fasted regularly and wore a cilice for one hour each day. In all, Romero understood that only to the extent to which he experienced the renewal of his passions and actions could he be identified with a church that was also in a constant process of renewal. Third, *sentir con la iglesia* requires dialogue. "The church becomes self-aware [*toma conciencia*] and is renewed not for itself but rather to be attractive and bring redemption to the world. Being in order to act. I too need to be apt for dialogue with men." Bishop Romero understands that he is called to engage everyone. Even those outside the church are to be approached. "They too are sheep of Jesus . . . *in spe*. . . . The bishop also has responsibility for them." Romero singles out the importance of "dialogue with the poor." All, especially the parish priests, are exhorted to "love them as images of Christ. Encouraging works of charity and advancement in their favor. Visiting the sick, hospitals, slums. Encourage secular priests towards them." Romero recognizes that his natural timidity can be an obstacle to this *sentir con la iglesia*. He warns himself: "Beware of feelings of insecurity." Confronted with the scope of the task facing him, Romero tells himself: "I will contribute my opinion. I have the courage to intervene. . . . I will consult."

The *sentir con la iglesia* that characterized the ministry of Archbishop Romero adapted the Ignatian rules. It was not a simple translation but a complex act of rereading, a *ressourcement* from the margins. "Everything is received according to the mode of the receiver," says Thomas Aquinas.[68] Romero received Ignatius (and Irenaeus) as a Salvadoran priest. He contextualized what the true *sentir* that Ignatius spoke of consisted in. The contextualization of the Spiritual Exercises in light of a fresh reading of the signs of the times is nothing new or unique to Romero.[69] Ignacio Ellacuría advanced a robust interpretation of the Spiritual Exercises based in Latin American reality. Ellacuría discerned the signs of the times not as underdevelopment (the reading of the North) but rather as dependence and oppression whose solution was liberation.[70] Romero, like Ellacuría, discerned oppression as one of the signs of the times, and his true *sentir con la iglesia* was characterized by an assiduous reading of these signs. Discerning the signs of the times is one of the hallmarks of the contextualization of the Spiritual Exercises in Latin America and in other parts of the world.[71] According to Sobrino, Romero's *sentir* "goes further than adherence to truths. It truly means *sentir*, enjoy, anticipate, and, above all in those days, to suffer."[72] *Sentir con la iglesia* denotes the posture that Christian people must adopt if they are to find their way among the waves that threaten to sink the ark of the church. The collisions of tradition and innovation, action and contemplation, individual and society strike fear in the hearts of many Christians. *Sentir con la iglesia* involves an act of judgment. It may be necessary to turn the rudder of the ecclesial ship in order to maintain the original bearing. In addition to contextualizing *sentir*, Romero contextualized the church that was the object of this rule. The church had to be "a church interpreted not only as magisterium but as people; a people that puts its hope in the church, a people that is the church and Christ, who has become flesh in the Latin American church of the poor, the oppressed, and those who suffer."[73]

THE TRANSFIGURATION LETTERS

Sentir con la iglesia binds the Christian to today's church. Romero's solidarity was expressed in a historical and spiritual reading of the signs of the times and in a commitment to identify himself with the church in El Salvador even unto death. His *sentir* with the church was a *sentir* with the campesinos, but also with the soldiers who lived in opposition to the love of God. This *sentir* with the church was a *sentir* with Vatican II and with Medellín, with Aquinas and with Sobrino.

The *sentir* was hard but not burdensome because with the people of God in El Salvador it was not difficult to be a good pastor (*Homilías*, 5:543). The pastoral letters that Romero released on every Feast of the Transfiguration during his years as archbishop were one expression of his *sentir con la iglesia*. Each reads like a "love letter" to the Divine Savior and his transfigured body on the feast of Tabor. I place the term *love letter* in quotation marks because although the words flow from a heart moved by love, the reality that these words name is not altogether lovely. We will consider each letter in chronological order, paying particular attention to the ecclesial notes that can be heard in them.

"The Church, the Body of Christ in History" (1977)

The title for Romero's first Transfiguration letter sounds one of his strongest ecclesiological notes: "The Church: the Body of Christ in History." The archbishop finds in the feast of the Divine Savior an invitation to all Salvadorans to identify with their namesake. The goal of this identification is "sentirse cuerpo histórico" (to think and feel oneself a historical body) (*Voz*, 76). The body of Christ has a history and Romero's second pastoral letter to the archdiocese of San Salvador addresses the question of continuity and change in this history.

After years of apparent immovability, the landscape of church life in Latin America was shifting rapidly. Some greeted these changes with joy but others with confusion and anger. Many conscientious Catholics expressed doubts about the new direction that the church had taken. In any case, the reality of change was undeniable. The church's liturgy, its understanding of the role of the laity, and many other aspects of church life were barely recognizable from those of previous decades. The change that was most jarring was the new posture that the church adopted vis-à-vis society. Indeed, this was the change that accounted for all the others. The church had gained a new awareness of the implications of its presence and service in the world. Romero wrote this pastoral letter in order to explain the implications of this newfound awareness for all the people of El Salvador: Catholics, Protestants, and others.

One might lay the credit (or blame) for the changes in the church at the feet of Vatican II or Medellín, but Romero sees it differently. It is because the church is the body of Christ in history that these changes are necessary. "Christ has wanted to become the life of the church in all the periods of history" (*Voz*, 75). As Christ marches through history, a history replete with twists and turns, the church must follow and adjust accordingly, now leaning one way, now leaning another way. Historical Docetism that deems changes illusory and ecclesial deism that deems changes unnecessary are both ruled out. "The church is the flesh in which Christ makes concrete his own life and his personal mission through the centuries" (*Voz*, 76). Christ, the Lord of history, is also a subject of history. The incarnation of the Word occurs in a discrete historical moment within a concrete society. The particularities of this context belong to the material reality assumed by the Son of God and are carried over into his mission.

The mission of Christ begins with the announcement of the kingdom, especially to the poor. His preferential love for the outcasts is evident in all four gospels. Many of Jesus's healings and teachings exalt those whom the world calls last and least. The manner in which Jesus relates to "the people who were marginalized by the society of his time is the sign that he gives to guarantee the content of what he preaches, that the kingdom of God draws near" (*Voz*, 77). This kingdom was for all. The manner in which Jesus drew near to Zacchaeus, the Roman centurion, and other people in power is evidence of the universality of this kingdom. No one was excluded unless they excluded themselves. Jesus loved all his fellow human beings, "and because he truly loved them all, he demanded their conversion. In other words, he demanded that change of heart which humanizes all people and which was obscured and drowned by riches, by power, by pride, and by trust in the traditions of the law" (*Voz*, 78).

The church as the body of Christ in history continues Christ's presence and mission. Romero claims that in its renewed engagement with the world the church has rediscovered the centrality of the poor to the message of the gospel and in so doing has gained a new awareness of the insidious power of sin. Traditionally, the church has been strong in its condemnation of sin as an individual act, as a turning away from God. The church has also been sensitive to how the denial of God by the individual has immediate social ramifications. So, for instance, the sin of the adulterer breaks covenant with God and damages the network of family relations betrayed by this act. Now, Romero writes, the church "has remembered again that which from the beginning was basic, social sin, that is to say, the crystallization of individual selfishness into permanent social structures that maintain this sin and make its power felt over the masses" (*Voz,* 74). As long as the church stuck to preaching against personal sins, it remained beyond reproach; this was its divinely assigned and socially expected role. What was seen as new by all and unsettling for some was its denunciation of structural sins and its admission that the church too must convert. The old motto *Ecclesia semper reformanda* gained a new level of concreteness and urgency as the church listened to the questions and complaints of the poor, the weak, the hungry, and the oppressed. Throne versus altar disputes were not new; what was new were the rancho versus altar encounters. As it serves in the world, the church develops also a new sensitivity to the unity of history. Salvation history and world history are not two separate things unfolding on their own parallel chronologies. Scripture itself teaches that God acts in human history, and for this reason the church is concerned with human affairs.[74]

Romero hopes the Feast of the Transfiguration will help his congregation deepen their identification with the *Divino Salvador* and thus their *sentirse cuerpo histórico*. In his homilies, Romero gives this claim its due Christological weight. *Sentirse* one with the body of Christ means sharing in his two natures, human and divine. The church "prolongs the humanity, the flesh of Christ in history" (*Homilías*, 2:150). It should come as no surprise, then, that throughout history the church is vulnerable to the weaknesses of life in the flesh. The church grows weary; it stumbles; it hates. The church does not need to hide its many deficiencies. As Romero explains, "When the bitter criticism of our enemies wants to air our dirty laundry, it falls short, and it is nothing in comparison to all the sinfulness we have in the church" (*Homilías*, 2:150). In its journey through history, the church has been beset by the temptations of power, wealth, and prestige. Romero is bold to exclaim: "How many times has the poor church fallen into these temptations!" (*Homilías*, 2:271). *Sentirse* Christ's body in history is one way of living out one's baptism. It is by baptism that Salvadorans become the flesh of Christ, and it is by baptism that a life of constantly turning to God becomes possible and necessary. "We are rotten flesh, we are fragile flesh, we are the flesh of Christ in history. No one can say that he or she can throw the first stone when all of us are sinners. This is why we said that if the church has the courage to denounce the sins of the world, it is not because she thinks of herself as unpolluted but because the one who denounces must also be willing to be denounced and has the obligation of being corrected and converted to God" (*Homilías*, 4:71).

The body of Christ in history bears wounds and imperfections. At the same time, this historical body participates in the divinity of Christ. The church is holy; it is without sin; it is indefectible. "The church is the emissary of Christ and the Holy Spirit to the men and women of each and every time" (*Homilías*, 1:418). As a divine institution, the church has never failed in its mission; it has never lied, or hated, or sinned because, as the prolongation of Christ in history, the church is protected by God. It is always ready to be used as God's instrument for preparing the kingdom. *Sentirse cuerpo histórico* confirms the church's status as being on the way. The church's status as a pilgrim church has implications for how Christians in El Salvador live. "No one needs to settle down. All of us have to walk with the pilgrim's staff, for though we have to gladden the land in which we live, we also know that we are only passing through. Today we occupy it. Yesterday it was our grandparents, who no longer live; tomorrow it will be the future generations, and we will no longer be. Humanity is in constant pilgrimage. And Christ wants to walk with that history, with the history of all times" (*Homilías*, 1:272).

Passivity is ruled out. The church is commissioned to be "Christ in this time and in this country. It must speak as Christ would speak here, today" (*Homilías*, 1:286). It cannot talk the way that it used to in the Middle Ages or in the patristic era. It must find new words to preach Christ, even as Christ remains unchanged. The realism of Romero's language is striking. The incarnation of Christ ripples throughout history. Mary's great vocation was to incarnate Christ in history, and her work also ripples into the present. "Mary becomes Salvadoran and incarnates Christ in the history of El Salvador, and Mary takes on your last name and my last name to incarnate the story of your family, my family, in the eternal life of the gospel" (*Homilías*, 4:96). *Sentirse* the historic body of Christ identifies one with Christ's unfolding history. Weeks after his first Transfiguration letter, Romero reminds them again of its message. "All of us who live now, we are the church, we incarnate with our flesh the Christ who lives here now, in El Salvador, in 1977, in this church of today. Just as the church of other centuries was incarnated by our ancestors, and the church that will come after we have died will be incarnated by other generations. Christ continues incarnating himself in this church" (*Homilías*, 1:358).

Romero believed that the life of the church in El Salvador confirmed the message of this Transfiguration letter. Against all odds, the church had steered clear from preaching hatred or partisan politics. It had been provoked mercilessly, and the murders of priests and laypeople had sorely tested its resolve, but the church had remained true to its prophetic mission of denouncing sins and announcing the kingdom of God. The evangelical trajectory initiated in 1977 continued throughout Romero's term as archbishop. About a month before he was killed, Romero recalled an encounter he had had with a former politician from Venezuela, Doctor Jiménez. Doctor Jiménez was under the impression that the masses celebrated at the cathedral were political meetings dressed up in liturgical garb, but when he actually attended the Sunday mass on February 10, 1980, what he saw was a devout congregation in worship. He was impressed by the strongly spiritual yet politically relevant message and by the huge number of communicants at the Eucharist (*Homilías*, 6:273).[75] Romero recalled the encounter because he wanted his people to understand that the chief end of the Sunday mass was the adoration of God. The Church preached the love of Christ, a love that became concrete in different ways to different people according to their particular situation. The church in El Salvador prolonged Christ: "To the people who have become dehumanized through love of wealth, he showed clearly, through love, the path to recovering their lost human dignity; with the poor, dehumanized by their marginalization, he sat down, also through love, at their table, to give them hope again" (*Voz*, 82).

Sentirse the historic body of Christ in El Salvador calls for expecting (but never accepting) persecution. On Pentecost Sunday of 1977, the traditional birthday of the church, Romero called strongly for an expanded list of marks of the church. The Nicene-Constantinopolitan Creed professes the church to be one, holy, catholic, and apostolic. These classic marks of the church have been used polemically in distinguishing the true church from its counterfeits and catechetically in explaining the nature of the church. In the Latin American context two more marks are conspicuous and in need of elucidation: persecution and poverty.

> Persecution is something necessary in the church. Do you know why? Because the truth is always persecuted. Jesus Christ said, "If they persecuted me, they will persecute you." And thus, when someone asked Pope Leo XIII, that prodigious intellect from the early part of this century, which are the notes that distinguish the true Catholic Church, the pope said, "There are the four already known: one, holy, catholic, apostolic. Let us add another," said the pope, "persecuted." The church that fulfills its duty will not be able to live without persecution. The church preaches the truth just as God ordered the prophets to announce the truth against the lies, injustices, and abuses of their time. And how much did this cost to the prophets! They even wanted to run away from God because they knew that going out to speak the truth was a death sentence. (*Homilías*, 1:117)

Sentirse cuerpo histórico in El Salvador in 1977 required embracing the poor and expecting persecution. In one of his final homilies, Romero states, "Only the church that converts and commits itself with the poor, suffering people can be the true church" (*Homilías*, 6:276). Since Christ's movement was from majesty to poverty, since he died a slave's death, the church too must walk as he walked and with whom he walked. This commitment is costly. Christians who commit themselves to serving with the poor suffer the fate of the poor, which in El Salvador meant disappearance, torture, and death.

Poverty and persecution mark the church in El Salvador as being truly the one, holy, catholic, and apostolic church, Christ's body in history.

"The Church and the Popular Political Organizations" (1978)

The celebration of the titular feast of the nation in 1978 was marked by growing violence and also by the death of Paul VI. The passing of one of Romero's favorite popes on the very Feast of the Transfiguration gave fresh meaning to the theophany on Mount Tabor. The archbishop claimed the words that the pontiff had prepared to deliver at the Angelus on August 6 as an inheritance for the people of El Salvador. The pontiff's final address was inspired by the vision of the transfigured Christ.

> The transfiguration of the Lord remembered in the liturgy of today's solemnity throws a ray of dazzling light on our daily life and makes us turn our minds to the immortal destiny that this event prefigures. On the summit of Tabor, Christ reveals for an instant the splendor of his divinity, and he manifests to the chosen witnesses who he really is, the Son of God, "the irradiation of the Father's glory and the imprint of his substance" (cf. Heb. 1:3). But he also makes us see the transcendent destiny of our human nature that he has assumed in order to save. Because it has been redeemed by his sacrifice of irrevocable love, this nature too has been destined to participate in the fullness of life, in "the inheritance of the saints in the light" (Col. 1:12). That body which is transfigured before the astonished eyes of the disciples is the body of Christ our brother, but it is also our body that is called to glory. The light that overwhelms it is and will also be our part of the inheritance and splendor. We are called to share so much glory because we are "partakers of the divine nature" (2 Pet. 1:4). An incomparable destiny awaits us if we have honored our Christian vocation, if we have lived according to the logical consequences of word and deed that our baptismal vows impose on us.[76]

It is easy to see how the pope's message resonated with Romero's own vision of the Transfiguration, not least in that Paul VI saw social implications to this festivity. In Italy, the August celebration occurs during the season of vacations, and Paul VI hoped that vacationers would take time to reflect on the light of Christ so as to transfigure the time of rest and enjoyment into one of spiritual maturation. At the same time, Paul VI understood that vacations were a luxury that too few could afford, and he closed his Angelus prayer and his life lifting up the cares of the unemployed, the hungry, and all those who found themselves at the margins of social and economic life. Romero captured the beautiful solemnity of the pontiff's message with heartfelt words. "Following the ecstasy of the transcendence that illumined the last day of his mortal life, the gaze of the pontiff turned to earth in anguished concern for the poor and in a cry of social justice for the world" (*Voz*, 94).

Romero's second Transfiguration letter could be read as a eulogy to the Petrine ministry of Paul VI. It was written a few weeks after Romero's *ad limina* visit, where he received personal words of exhortation from the pope. Moreover, the writings of Paul VI, particularly *Evangelii Nuntiandi* and *Octogesima Adveniens*, are featured prominently throughout the letter and serve as guideposts for Romero's ecclesiological thought. Romero's reverence for the bishop of Rome is sincere and also strategic. By showing how closely his thought cleaves to the authoritative teaching of Paul VI, Romero pushes back against his detractors' charges of Marxism. At the same time, Romero locates his letter within a long tradition of Christian social action in Latin American history. The church in Latin America has always counted on "apostles like Fray Antonio de Montesinos, Fray Bartolome de las Casas, Bishop Juan del Valle, and Bishop Valdivieso, who was murdered in Nicaragua for his opposition to the landowner and governor Contreras" (*Voz*, 94). In other words, Romero turned to Paul VI not only because this pope was the faithful interpreter of Vatican II but because his teaching grew from a tradition that had dug itself deeply in the soil of Latin American history. By extension, the teachings of Medellín and Romero's own episcopal practice were not newcomers on the scene but the fruit of a long line of pastors who sought to illumine the injustices of the Latin American situation with the light of the gospel. The convergence of dates—the death of the pontiff, the Feast of the Transfiguration, and the titular feast of El Salvador—offered Romero fertile ground for theological reflection. For both the bishop of Rome and the archbishop of San Salvador, the transfiguration of Christ illumined the glory to which humanity had been called and the shameful conditions in which most of humanity lived.

In this Transfiguration epistle, there are two topics that Romero seeks to elucidate with the light of Tabor, the question of popular organizations in relation to the church and the problem of violence. The authorship of this letter is shared with Romero's successor at Santiago de María and later San Salvador, Bishop Arturo Rivera y Damas.[77] Their joint letter builds on the ecclesiology of the two pastoral letters of 1977. Differently stated, *sentirse cuerpo histórico*, identifying themselves as the historic body of Christ in 1978, the Salvadoran Christians need to read the signs of the times, denounce what is wrong, and defend what is right. We have studied the problem of violence previously, so the focus here will be on the popular political organizations.

The body of Christ in history is the church militant. Against government attempts to have exclusive control over the well-being of the nation, the archbishop defends the right of people to organize themselves for common social ends. Faithful to Catholic social teaching, Romero bases this right on the principle of sociability that is intrinsic to human nature. Humans are naturally constituted to cooperate in order to attain and secure the goods that are integral to human flourishing. This cooperation is particularly urgent when the goods appear to be difficult to attain or secure by oneself. Hence, the right of people located at the margins of society to organize themselves and to be heard as contributing members to the national discourse carries great social weight. This makes the defense of the right of the poor to organize a priority for the church. "All that is human that is represented in the causes and struggles of the people, above all in the causes and struggles of the poor, is of concern to the church" (*Voz*, 105).

The present Transfiguration epistle outlines three principles that orient the church's militancy. First, the church exists for God; it has a religious goal, namely "the evangelization which by the Word of God creates a community-church united in itself and with God through sacramental signs, the chief of these being the Eucharist" (*Voz*, 103).

Second, the church best serves the world by proclaiming the gospel. This is the contribution that is unique to its mission. Third, the gospel that the church proclaims is a gospel of liberation. The liberation that Romero promotes is an integral liberation that encompasses the whole human and is oriented toward the kingdom of God. Conversion of mind and heart are necessary for this liberation, but violence is ruled out. The application of the three principles of the church's nature, mission, and theology to the church's engagement with the popular political organizations presupposes that careful distinctions be drawn between the people of El Salvador, the people of God, and the political community. The distinction between the people and the people of God is a recurring theme in Romero's homilies.

> When we call our church "the people of God here in El Salvador," it must not be confused with a democratic understanding, as if all Salvadorans formed the people of God. Only the baptized are the people of God, "only those who have not forgotten my promises, only those who remember how I led them on eagle's wings, only those who have faith," which is what marks the true descendants of the people of God (cf. Exod. 19:4). Not all Salvadorans belong to the people of God, just as in the time of Moses not all the peoples of the world belonged to the covenant that God had made with one people. (*Homilías*, 4:288)[78]

All Salvadoran Christians belong to the people of El Salvador and to the people of God. Moved from concern for the common good and discernment of God's will, a Christian may enter the political community represented by groups like the popular organizations. In these organizations, Christian faith and politics are united, but they must not be confused. The unity of the two comes from the shared aspirations of both the political and the baptismal communities—the promotion of the human being. Their distinction comes from the transcendent end for which the gospel is proclaimed—eternal life with God. The confusion of faith and politics can lead to significant errors. Some may reduce the faith to the political ideology of a particular popular organization. Others may believe that only by joining with a certain political organization can one truly witness to the justice of Christ. Christians may become involved in party politics, but they must do so as Christians without making membership in the organization the litmus test of true Christianity. In a homily preached in October 1979, Romero revisits and deepens this theme of his pastoral letter. "It was the desire of my third pastoral letter to distinguish between the Christian community where faith is cultivated, where Christian virtue is grown, and the political organization where a Christian from this community may act and bring—as the council says—a germ of Christianity" (*Homilías*, 5:471).

In the same homily, Romero defines the three different kinds of communities not to separate them but to understand their proper relations. The relationship that Romero envisions between the organizations and the church can be characterized by mutuality. When relating to popular organizations, the church's chief criterion is the truth and justice of their cause, not their religious affiliation. This is why Romero is more critical of Christian organizations who labor to defend the entitlements of the wealthy than of leftist popular organizations who work on behalf of the poor. The church expects that these organizations will work for the common good of the society, especially of the poor, while keeping themselves open to dialogue and collaboration with the church. In return, the organizations can expect and demand that the church fulfill its duty to be a defender of the rights of freedom of association and expression, strike and protest, for all popular organizations, be they Christian or not. What the organizations cannot ask from the church, even if these are Christian organizations, is the cooptation of its ecclesial symbols as propaganda instruments. The church has strong theological reasons for supporting popular organizations. "Beyond the boundaries of the church there is much strength from the redemption of Christ, and the liberationist efforts of individuals and groups, even if they do not profess themselves Christian, are driven by the Spirit of Jesus. The church tries to understand them thus in order to purify, encourage, and incorporate them—as with all Christian efforts—into the global project of Christian redemption" (*Voz*, 113).

Romero finds remnants of the people of God outside the visible community of the Catholic Church and even outside Christianity.

"Christ overflows the Catholic Church and is present in a saving way in the Protestant, in the Muslim, in the Jew of goodwill" (*Homilías*, 1:129). Romero offers a comparison to account for this presence. It is as when one fills a cup of water from a fountain. The glass may be full but there is a lot more water outside the glass. The comparison does not minimize the importance of the church. It goads her to service. "Even though the church does not contain all of Christ, it is a sign that Christ is in the world. Let us return to the comparison. The glass of water drawn from the fountain does not contain all the fountain, but it is a sign that the water comes from that fountain, that there is a fountain from which the glass of water could be drawn" (*Homilías*, 3:166).

The overflowing presence of Christ encourages the church to engage people of goodwill wherever they may be found. The church can expect to find the power of Christ already at work among Protestants and secularists, energizing their work for justice. In these encounters, the church seeks to water the seeds that God has already sown and also to point these groups to the fountain who is Christ and to his clearest, fullest glass, which is the Catholic Church. The efficacy of Christ's overflowing power is not limited to the attainment of historical goals but extends to salvation. Contra Cyprian of Carthage, Romero does not believe that outside the church there is no salvation (*Homilías*, 1:478–79). *Lumen Gentium* 14 taught Romero to draw a distinction between the body and the heart of the church. Those who lead morally just lives and seek to follow God according to the best of their understanding are in the heart of the church even if they are not in the body by confession of faith and baptism. Conversely, those who have professed themselves to be Christian and participate in the church's sacramental life but worship the idols of this world are in the body of the church but not in the heart. "It is much better to belong to the heart, but even better still to belong to the heart and the body of the church" (*Homilías*, 5:224).

Sentirse cuerpo histórico calls for identifying oneself with the body of the church through the sacraments and with the heart through love, a love that also receives sustenance from the sacraments. The church militant marches side by side with popular political organizations and

Protestant groups in defending the rights of the Salvadoran people from those who would trample them for self-benefit. In this fight, the church has something to offer, the water of Christ that is the Holy Spirit, and it offers it in humility because there is more of Christ and the Spirit outside the church than inside—*etiam extra ecclesiam.* Romero fervently hopes that the light of the transfigured Christ will channel the militancy of the people of God in El Salvador in a healthy direction, but he knows that the attainability of this hope depends on their willingness to listen to the voice of Christ that still speaks from Tabor.

"The Mission of the Church in the Midst of the National Crisis" (1979)

Romero's last Transfiguration letter begins with an echo of the greeting that opened his 1976 Transfiguration sermon at the Cathedral— the name of El Salvador. Pius XII's words to the Eucharistic Congress in El Salvador of 1942 ring prophetically true in Romero's ears. "It was not just . . . the burning piety of Pedro Alvarado that in the dawn of the American conquest baptized you so highly, but it was above all Divine Providence!"[79] God the Father condescends to allow this country to bear the name of his only begotten Son.

Like the previous Transfiguration letters, this one was written from within the accelerating spiral of violence into which the country had fallen, but three things stood out as new with respect to previous letters. First, this letter included feedback from a survey of the priests and base ecclesial communities of the archdiocese. Romero attributed the inspiration of this survey to the calls for communal discernment voiced by Vatican II and Paul VI. By cultivating the prophetic ministry of the people of God as a whole, the bishop could better hear what the Spirit was saying to the church. Thus the survey was one more concrete application of Romero's *sentir con la iglesia.* Second, the third Latin American Episcopal Conference had taken place in Puebla, Mexico, earlier that year. Romero attended this meeting and found there vindication for the pastoral direction that he was giving to his archdiocese as well as illumination for how best to confront its present challenges. Indeed, the chief purpose for this pastoral letter was to apply the teaching of Puebla to San Salvador. Third, John Paul II was now the bishop of Rome. Romero had enjoyed a warm and close relationship with Paul VI. John Paul I was not bishop of Rome long enough to affect Romero's ministry, though the archbishop preached poignant sermons about his tragically brief pontificate.[80] Romero's relation with John Paul II was more complicated than that with Paul VI, at least at first, but the pope's leadership at Puebla and his first encyclical *Redemptor Hominis* contributed significantly to the theology of this final pastoral letter from Romero.

At Puebla, Romero received confirmation regarding the church's service to El Salvador. "This is the main contribution that our church should offer to the life of the country—being herself" (*Voz*, 140). It is as the church embraces her own identity that she contributes something new and unique to the world. The call for the church "to be the church" must not be misunderstood as retrenchment in the face of a hostile world or as an obsessive concern for maintaining a pure ecclesial identity. It is instead a call to conversion. Conversion is necessary if the church is to avoid the reductionist visions of evangelization prevalent in the Salvadoran context. The proclamation of strictly transcendent hopes or of historically realized kingdoms makes for simple messages but poor gospel. The church best serves the world by working from a solid doctrinal orientation. The truths that tradition has bequeathed to the church are like the vertebral column that keeps the body of Christ upright in its pilgrimage through history. From the firmness of its teaching on Christ, the church, and humanity, the church denounces sin in the world and unmasks the national idols. The church, then, is the herald of a holistic message of liberation, but it is more than that: it is also a companion who walks with the oppressed on their exodus. However, the credibility of the church's proclamation and solidarity is undermined by the mystery of sin at work within her too. The disunity of the clergy, the polarization between progressives and traditionalists, turns the church's attention inward and limits the effectiveness of its mission. The remedy that Puebla proposes and Romero embraces is the preferential option for the poor. Only as the church rediscovers the Lord's call to convert to the poor will it find its true ground of unity (*Voz*, 137).

Since the precise formulation of the *preferential option for the poor* first became widely known only at Puebla, it is not surprising to see it used by Romero upon his return to El Salvador. In the Sunday homily that he delivered immediately after the end of the CELAM gathering, Romero brings the message of Puebla to bear on the realities of the archdiocese. Against church critiques who see the pastoral approach of Romero as partisan, Romero says, "The preferential option for the poor does not mean the exclusion of the rich but rather a call also to the rich to feel the problem of the poor as their own" (*Homilías*, 4:216). Romero does not introduce the preferential option as a new social doctrine. He does not even call attention to the novelty of the formulation. Instead, Romero speaks of the preferential option as something that the archdiocese has been practicing all along and of Puebla as its interpreter and guarantor.

The preferential option for the poor features prominently in many of Romero's homilies.[81] Romero's commitment to the option was so noticeable that his fellow Latin American bishops sent him a congratulatory note to that effect (*Homilías*, 5:303). One of his richest expositions of the topic is found in a sermon that he preached on July 1, 1979, "Christ, Life and wealth of the Human." This homily predated his fourth pastoral letter by just about a month. Thus a consideration of the themes of the homily can throw light on how Romero appropriated the teachings of Puebla featured in his letter. The reflection occurs in the context of the lectionary reading from 2 Corinthians 8:7–9, 13–15, which exhorts Christians to be generous like Christ, who "for your sakes became poor, so that by his poverty you might become rich."[82] Romero reads in this passage the seeds of the social doctrine of the church. The Lord's instruction to Israel in the desert concerning the gathering of manna to which Paul appeals at the end of the passage cited and his commendation to the Corinthians to be generous in their offering to the church in Jerusalem set the stage for *Rerum Novarum, Populorum Progressio*, Vatican II, Medellín, and Puebla.

The message of the bishops at Puebla illumines the realities of the Latin American continent and offers the preferential option for the poor as the pastoral response to these realities. The scandalous gap between rich and poor was rending the social fabric of the continent. The poverty of the majority has many causes, and the bishops at Puebla and Romero do not shy away from saying that "some are poor because of their own actions, because of their vices" (*Homilías*, 5:68). However, the flaws of the poor are not the main source of the problem. "There are horrible, brutal structures that impede the best-intentioned progress" (*Homilías*, 5:68). The economic and political systems governing El Salvador are animated not by humanism but by a materialism that promotes the good of the few.

In such a fundamentally unjust social climate, the preferential option becomes for Romero a criterion of Christian discipleship. The fidelity of the church can be measured by its commitment to the poor. This mark is a sign of contradiction and elicits opposition. The murdered priests of the archdiocese are "the glory of the preferential option for the poor" (*Homilías*, 5:69). Against those who reject the preferential option as partisan or sectarian, Romero underscores the universality of the message. "God wants to save the wealthy as well, but precisely because he wants to save them, he tells them that they cannot be saved until they are converted to the Christ who lives in particular among the poor" (*Homilías*, 5:70). The preferential option denotes a spiritual attitude. It is not a counsel of perfection but a call to holiness that all must answer, from the campesino to the bishop. The poor must understand that "not having is not enough; if you do not put an evangelical spirit to that poverty, it is not the poverty that Christ wants" (*Homilías*, 5:70). The rich must understand that a vague spiritual poverty is not enough either. "As long as they do not embody those desires of evangelical poverty in actions that are as concerned for the poor as for their own welfare, as if it were for Christ, they will continue being called the rich whom God disdains because they put their trust in their money and separate themselves from others whom they look upon as second-class humans" (*Homilías*, 5:70). Rich and poor are called to embody a spirit of evangelical poverty. Romero interprets Paul's address to the Corinthians as a summons to a new way of living justly amid social asymmetries. The rich are called to give without paternalism and the poor to receive without dependency. The spirit of evangelical poverty makes it possible "for the rich to feel very much a brother to the poor and the poor to not feel inferior to the rich" (*Homilías*, 5:71). The preferential option is a call that Romero longs his congregation to answer wholeheartedly.

> How great would be the day, then, in which we understand this beautiful evangelical doctrine of poverty! Persons who, like Christ, trust only in the Father; persons who, like the Virgin, know how to be the poor of Yahweh, with the holy liberty of denouncing sin wherever it may be found. The poverty of the church! It will be more authentic and effective when it truly does not depend or seek the support of the powerful, the shelter of the powers, when evangelization does not consist in getting power but in being evangelical and holy, when it leans on the poor, who with their poverty enrich—Christ. (*Homilías*, 5:71)

This encomium brings to the fore a number of leitmotifs in Romero's understanding of the preferential option. First and foremost, it is a Christological option. The preferential option is born in Bethlehem with the poor shepherds gathered around the manger (*Homilías*, 6:231). The preferential option as taught by Puebla was also applied to the youth.[83] Romero does not foreground this dimension, but glimpses of it are visible in his linkage of the poor child with the poor Christ. The "child is the most eloquent figure of poverty," and this is why a preferential option for the poor is also an option for children (*Homilías*, 5:352). Opting for the poor implies making their cause one's own in a concrete, practical way because the poor and the weak "represent Jesus" (*Homilías*, 5:387). Romero reminds his readers that at Puebla the bishops said that the poor and the young were the signs of God's presence in Latin America. The church was called to make a preferential option for the poor and for the young whom God was calling to be the founders of a more just society. If the poor and the young were signs of God's presence, then they were signs of hope, and if so El Salvador was truly blessed. Romero states: "Let us not despair, because if this is the hope of Latin America, then there is a lot of hope in El Salvador because there are many poor and many young" (*Homilías*, 6:276). If the preferential option was born in Bethlehem, it achieved fruition in Calvary. It was in the Passion and Resurrection that the drama of redemption summed up by Paul in the formula "He became poor" climaxed. The preferential option is an option for the crucified and for the crucified people.

The term *crucified people* may well have its origins in the ministry of Bartolomé de las Casas. In the suffering of the indigenous, the bishop of Chiapas claimed to have seen "Jesus Christ our Lord in the Indies, being beaten, whipped, afflicted, and crucified not once but thousands of times."[84] Las Casas is among the first to extend Jesus's identification with the "least of these my brothers and sisters" to a whole hemisphere of unbaptized peoples. In Romero's preaching, this tradition is mediated through the history of contemporary biblical interpretation, which speaks of the suffering servant of the Lord as mysteriously united and identified with the people of God. Romero invites his congregation to see the people of El Salvador on the cross. It is their body, their members that are being pierced, their face that is being spat upon and humiliated.[85] "*Sentimos* in the Christ of Holy Week carrying his cross that it is the people who are carrying their cross. *Sentimos* in the Christ of wide-open and crucified arms the crucified people, a crucified and humiliated people, who from Christ find their hope" (*Homilías*, 2:333). The identification of the crucified Christ with the crucified people might be interpreted as fatalistic, as supporting the status quo. Romero believes that a true identification with the crucified has exactly the opposite effect. *Crucified people* is a hopeful term. He explains, "The call of Holy Week, of Palm Sunday, is not to preach to you conformity. Instead it is a summons to give to your tribulation a sense of divine poverty; give to your suffering a sense of redemption; accept the cross, embrace it like Christ, not passively but indeed with the love that builds a civilization of freedom and love" (*Homilías*, 2:333). These are hard words, hard as the cross. When seeing the crucified people, it is tempting to want to avert one's eyes from this wounded body and like the priest and the Levite walk by on the other side. Romero invites his congregation to freely embrace the wounded man and offer themselves as members of Christ's suffering body. With Christ they speak from the cross, and with Christ they long to be taken down from the cross; they long for liberation, but not just any kind of liberation; the crucified people long for resurrection.

The preferential option was supremely embodied by Christ and is an option for Christ.

The option is also Mariological because this was the path followed by the "the poor of Yahweh." This is one of the terms that Romero and CELAM repeatedly use to name the spiritually poor.[86] These are those poor persons who from their material poverty have embraced spiritual poverty. There are clear Old Testament antecedents for these poor ones. Poverty was a marker of God's people from the beginning. There was the poverty of childlessness that befell Abram and Sarai, a childlessness that contradicted the Lord's promises. There was the poverty of landlessness that afflicted the descendants of Israel from their bondage in Egypt to their exile in Babylon. The poor one of the Lord is the one who responds to these markers of poverty with faithful trust, and the paradigm for this response is Mary. Her song of praise, the Magnificat, forcefully expresses the hope of the poor of Yahweh.[87] Mary lived the political dimension of faith of which Romero spoke at Louvain. So did Paul. His encounter with the risen Christ upended his way of life. The proclamation of the Resurrection of the Dead is the wellspring of the "great spirituality of the poor." The risen Christ is the God of the poor.[88] The belief in the resurrection of the dead animates the Christian struggle for justice because liberation from death is the great liberation. The struggles for better wages and new structures are needed skirmishes next to Christ's victory, and these derive their meaning only when seen from that vantage point. The spiritual poverty that the option entails finds sustenance in Marian piety, which Romero describes as a "liberating devotion, a devotion that makes us learn from Mary the freedom with which she spoke, a devotion to the Virgin that . . . knows how to be bold for Christ, even when because of the injustice of the world he is nailed to the cross and everyone else flees," a devotion to the one who in the words of Pironio, whom Romero cites, "visits America barefooted, with a poor child who makes us rich, with a homeless child who makes us free."[89]

Finally, the preferential option is an evangelical doctrine. It is the best response to communism and the medicine for lack of unity in the church.[90] The preferential option is the path to happiness for the people of El Salvador (*Homilías*, 5:424). It is a path that also leads to peace, as was shown by Mother Teresa of Calcutta.[91] The option commits the church to be the defender of human rights and is a basis for building the civilization of love; it is not demagogy.[92] The preferential option is the fitting response to the good news of the integral liberation accomplished in the paschal mystery.

As he finishes this homily, Romero informs his congregation that after mass on that very Sunday afternoon there will be a gathering at the Hospital de la Divina Providencia. Everyone is invited to come and see the patients at this cancer hospice center. A collection will be taken then to support the children left orphaned when their parents die at the *Hospitalito*. The main reason for going is not to write a check but "to support this work, which, as Paul says, invites us to see Christ and thus to work with greater zeal" (*Homilías*, 5:74).

Toward the conclusion of his third and final Transfiguration letter, Monseñor Romero reflects on the pastoral response of his archdiocese to the national crisis. As archbishop he walked with the people of a God in a *pastoral de conjunto* (*Voz*, 165, 167–68). In other words, he was attentive to their *sensus fidelium*, especially as it was found in the base ecclesial communities, without neglecting the voice of the *magisterium*. Romero did not only walk with the people of God; he also demonstrated a willingness to walk with persons or groups who from their faith (or even without faith) made a concrete political option that promoted the life of the Salvadoran. Romero refers to this as a *pastoral de acompañamiento* (*Voz*, 168–70). Naturally, the church cannot allow itself to be tied to a particular political platform, but it can and must walk alongside Christians who have. Romero also walks with the people of El Salvador in what he calls, for lack of a better term, a *pastoral masiva*, a pastoral for the masses, the multitudes. The goal of this service is "helping the masses to become a people and helping the people to become the people of God" (*Voz*, 166). In all cases, the pastoral response of the archdiocese needs to be characterized by a willingness to test the spirits and by a firm commitment to the preferential option for the poor. Indeed, the commitment to learning about and living out the preferential option for the poor is the thread that ties together Romero's final Transfiguration letter.

ROMERO'S TRANSFIGURED *SENTIR*

The light of the Divine Savior transfigures Ignatius's *Sentir con la iglesia* into Romero's *Sentirse cuerpo histórico*. *Sentir* implies a mode of reflection and at the same time a mode of identification with the object of reflection. For Romero the true *sentir con la iglesia* is an act of social analysis and spiritual discernment. It is action and contemplation with the church and in the church. Ricardo Urioste offers a translation of the episcopal motto that sums up its essence. *Sentir con la iglesia* means "being one with the church."[93] The church to which Romero is inextricably bound is Roman, ecumenical, poor, and Salvadoran.

First, *sentir* with the church in El Salvador means being one with the church in Rome. The emphasis on ecclesial obedience present in Ignatius's original rule for a true *sentir* within the church militant is by no means downplayed in its Salvadoran translation. If anything, it is placed in all caps. The homilies of Romero are saturated with citations from the magisterial documents of the church. Romero's final homily includes an extensive reference to a paragraph from *Gaudium et Spes* (*Homilías*, 6:456). *Sentir* with the church means *sentir* with the *magisterium* of the church. Even more, the true *sentir* with the church is a *sentir* with the pope. In his homilies, Romero never passed up an opportunity to demonstrate his fealty and even affection for Peter's successor. He wished Paul VI a happy birthday and preached a tender and sorrowful sermon upon the death of Pope John Paul I.[94] Even in the case of John Paul II, whose interactions with Romero were more difficult, Romero refused to criticize the pontiff. Instead of whining about being misunderstood, Romero listened with appreciation to what the pontiff had to say without neglecting his responsibility to speak the truth to the pope about the situation in El Salvador.[95] The depth of Romero's identification with the bishop of Rome is undeniable. Faced with death threats on one side and questions about his orthodoxy on the other, Romero declared: "I shall die, God willing [*primero Dios*], faithful to the successor of Peter" (*Homilías*, 3:60).[96]

Second, *sentir* with the church in El Salvador means being one with the struggles of the church. Romero is a faithful disciple of Ignatius on this version of his translation. *Sentir* is not a passive feeling but an intellectual and volitional act that empowers resistance against the powers of the world that threaten the church. On seeing the weakness of the church militant, its cowardice before the fights of the present time, many Christians feel horror and attempt to flee from the contradictions by seeking refuge in the golden age of the past, in the utopias of the future, or in a spiritualism of the present. *Sentir con la iglesia* implies an irrevocable commitment to the church that exists now. Adopting the motto *Sentir con la iglesia* requires an act of discernment and commitment. In the time of Saint Ignatius, *Sentir con la iglesia* led the Society of Jesus to fight against the challenges of Renaissance humanism and the Protestant Reformation. In the time of Romero, the archbishop and his people judged that the church in El Salvador had to fight the pedagogy of death with the violence of love. Romero's militancy does not bear hatred toward anyone. As Romero said on various occasions, "I do not want to be 'anti,' or 'against' anyone. I simply want to be the builder of a great affirmation: the affirmation of God that he loves us and wants to save us" (*Homilías*, 4:234). *Sentir con la iglesia* rules out any type of partisanship within the church. There are not two churches, one of the poor and one of the rich.[97] In response to the accusation that he worried only about the victims from one side of the conflict, Romero confessed: "Death pains me the same in whatever man it might be! During this week three police officers have died, and I might say more is the pity, because they died precisely by serving the god Moloch" (*Homilías*, 5:64, 269). Thus *sentir con la iglesia* moves the archbishop to weep for the enemies of the church.

Third, *sentir* with the church in El Salvador means being one with the ecumenical church. In this case, Romero's adaptation of the Ignatian saying certainly cuts against the grain of the original. The *sentir con la iglesia* of the spiritual exercises was intended to be worn as a shield in the battle against the Protestant reformers. In the context of El Salvador *sentir* became a bridge to those outside the Catholic Church. The generosity of Monseñor Romero's ecumenical spirit is one of the characteristics that commends him as a father of the Latin American church. A study could be dedicated to this topic alone, but here I limit myself to a few brief comments.

Romero did not always identify with the Protestant churches. The manner in which he speaks about the week of prayer for Christian Unity in 1951 is revealing and typical of his early attitude toward those outside the Catholic Church.[98] He describes the Orthodoxy and Protestantism as apostasies that have rent the fabric of the church and spread all manners of evils in the world. In particular, he blames Protestants for weakening the church's witness in El Salvador. At the time, his hope for Christian unity was that the prodigals would return to the arms of Mother Catholic Church.

Romero's *sentir* with the Protestant changed after Vatican II. A 1965 column he wrote for the *Chaparrastique* newspaper ties unity to conversion.[99] But the conversion of which he speaks is no longer that of Protestants becoming Catholic but of both Catholics and Protestants turning to Christ and growing in holiness. This turn to Christ would entail a "return to humility, obedience, and charity" in relating to other Christians.[100] The following year Romero accentuated the importance of sincerity and prudence in ecumenical dialogue, as stated in the conciliar document *Unitatis Redintegratio*.[101]

As archbishop, Romero's identification with the ecumenical movement grew. The desire for unity was now not something that Romero felt simply out of loyalty to the teachings of the council or pity for the deluded heirs of Luther but from the expressions of support that he had received from Protestants during the turbulent times faced by the archdiocese. The week of prayer for Christian unity in 1978 was one that Romero recalled with particular fervor. "They were eight unforgettable nights. The temple in which we gathered each night, whether Catholic or Protestant, acquired the human warmth of a true home where all felt that they were in their own house. There, while remaining faithful to the various personal convictions that still prevent a full communion, we felt that there was a common denominator that glued us together: being Christians."[102]

Sentir these experiences of imperfect but fervent communion with each other resulted in the formation of a standing ecumenical committee. This new committee would serve as the instrument for coordinating Catholics' and Protestants' efforts "to incarnate their Christian faith in works that give witness to the social dimension of the gospel."[103] Romero's *sentir* with the Protestants did not cause him to abandon his teaching office as bishop of the Catholic Church. Romero's views of Luther remained overwhelmingly negative.[104] He criticized the individualist piety of many Protestants, and he never gave up on encouraging Protestants to receive the gift of Marian piety.

> Let us feel a lot of devotion for the Virgin, brethren. And since my friendship with the Protestant brothers leads me to address words to them from our greatness and Catholic truth, I tell you, dear Protestant brothers, that we feel that nostalgia in you. You lack more love for Mary, and there are some among you who in your zeal even remove her from the worship of Christ. But Mary takes nothing away from Christ! On the contrary, Mary makes Christ more sympathetic, more beautiful, more attractive. It is just like when then the smith sets a very precious jewel on a gold frame. The gold frame makes the stone even more beautiful. Christ is the precious pearl; there is no comparison. He is the savior between God and humanity. Mary has not saved us. Christ has. But God wanted there to be next to Christ, the precious pearl, a gold frame. Mary is like the gold frame that God used to present Christ our Lord to us. (*Homilías*, 2:182)

Romero's *sentir* with the Protestants led him to form close friendships with Brother Roger of Taizé.[105] Romero notes that Taizé's ecclesial vision represented something new, a space that was Christian without being strictly Catholic or Protestant.[106] Even as Brother Roger's works inspired him, Romero's *sentir* was never able to imagine a vision of unity different from ecumenism of return. Still, Romero's sense of ecclesial unity overflowed the bounds of Catholicism. He reached out in concrete ways to his "dear Protestant brothers."[107] During one of his Sunday homilies he even shared the microphone with the Presbyterian pastor Jorge Lara Braud.[108] The *sentir* was mutual. Romero received letters of support from Protestant organizations like the Concilio Latinoamericano de Iglesias (CLAI) (*Homilías*, 3:427). Salvadoran Protestants like the Lutheran Medardo Gómez Ernesto grew to consider Romero their saint.[109]

Fourth, *sentir* with the church in El Salvador means being one with the church of the poor. The prioritization of the poor in Romero's adaptation of Ignatius's saying does not betray the spirit of the exercises. On the contrary, in discerning that the poor are among the chief signs of the times in Latin America and directing his energies and those of the church he serves toward the Church of the poor, Romero is being very Ignatian. *Sentir* with the church of the poor entails speaking on their behalf, being a voice for those without voices (*Homilías*, 2:172). But it is not possible to speak for someone if you do not first listen to that person, and for this reason, a practice of *sentir con la iglesia* requires listening to the people who constitute the church. It is necessary "to listen to what the Spirit is saying by means of his people, and, then, having received this from the people, to analyze the message and, together with the people, make it be for the building up of the church" (*Homilías*, 5:372). Romero believed in the *sensus fidelium* at work in his congregation, and he consulted this *sensus* as a guide for his episcopal service.[110] Listening to the people does not mean discarding the hierarchy (*Homilías*, 5:372). To be sure, Romero knew that speaking of the church of the poor was in fashion in some circles who used the term as an ideological wedge for dividing the church. Romero refused to play that game. There were not two churches, one of the poor and one of the rich; there was only one church.

On account of the manifold ways in which the church of the poor is announced, Romero teaches his people to recognize it through a dynamic catechesis that first walks them through the *via negativa* before leading them on *via positiva*. First, he teaches them what the church of the poor is not. The church of the poor is not simply a gathering of poor people. We already saw that Romero refuses to separate membership in the people of God from participation in the sacraments; he also refuses to separate this membership from holy living. Romero is not one to wink at sin among the members of his church, even among the poor (*Homilías*, 1:313). The church of the poor is not the assembly of "those who lack fortune but are ambitious, nor of those who lack material goods but kidnap to make money, nor of those criminals who vent their resentments in hatred against their harassers, nor of the terrorist" (*Homilías*, 3:88). The poverty of the Prodigal Son who misspent his inheritance is not blessed. These may seem extreme cases, but behind these descriptions were names of people personally known to Romero. Of course, the church is open even to sinners such as these, provided that they repent. The church of the poor is not the Communist Party at prayer. Time and time again, Romero pushes back against those who see this language as demagogical as the result of a Marxist dialectic (*Homilías*, 4:28). The church of the poor is not a church of the proletariat engaged in class warfare against the rich.

If this is what the church of the poor is not, then what is it? The church of the poor is the church professed in the Nicene Creed; it is an evangelical reality that is good, if challenging, news for all. The true poverty embodied by the church is that of Paul who cries, "The world has been crucified to me, and I to the world" (Gal. 6:14). It is the poverty of the person who looks on the naked Christ hanging on the cross and says: "Lord, I will follow you wherever you go, by the paths of poverty, not because of demagogy, but because I love you, because I want to be holy from my own holiness" (*Homilías*, 1:176). The church of the poor is the church of the Beatitudes. It is the church of those who have learned that "their poverty, their ranch, their field is not a context that should make them feel different from other people, because the Lord has made all of us in the image of God. And we must respect and promote that dignity" (*Homilías*, 2:423). The church of the poor is the church of "the poor who hunger for God, of those who feel that without God all things are empty and impure" (*Homilías*, 4:29). This is the church of the true peacemakers. They understand that although there is no peace without justice (*Opus justitiae, pax*), justice alone is not enough. Love is necessary. Love of Christ is the source of true poverty, justice, and peace. Hence, the church of the poor is the church of love. This poor church is the true preacher of Christ that invites all people "to find in the poverty, in the misery, in the hope of the one who prays in the slum, in pain, in not being heard, a God who hears, and only by drawing close to that voice can God also be felt" (*Homilías*, 3:362).

In Romero's theological vision, it is not possible to separate the flesh of the people from the bones of the hierarchy when both receive their life from the head that is Christ. Even if it is true that many times these bones have become as dry as those that filled the valley that Ezekiel saw in his prophetic vision, it is also true that the Holy Spirit can make these bones live (cf. Ezek. 37:1–14). Romero himself is evidence of the Spirit's power to vivify dry bones and cover them with sinews and skin; he is a hierarchical figure whom God moistened and molded to *sentir* with his people. In his ecclesial vision, theological poles are paired harmoniously: Medellín and Vatican II, solidarity with the poor and joyful obedience to the pope. He cannot be easily categorized along the usual lines of conservative or liberal, traditional or progressive. Margaret Guider helpfully speaks of Romero as an ecclesial mystic for whom identifying himself with the crucified people of El Salvador and loving the pope were expressions inseparable from *sentir con la iglesia* because both parties were essential members of the body of Christ.[111] As Romero says, "I am neither on the right nor on the left, I am trying to be faithful to the word that the Lord has sent me to preach" (*Homilías,* 4:503). Romero is difficult to place on the theological world map, not because he floats abstractly above it, but because his commitment to his historical and geographical context does not exhaust his localization. His *sentir* is certainly political, but it is never partisan or parochial. His sense of location is dictated, not by the magnetic forces that unrelentingly polarize all things between right and left, but by the Holy Spirit who descends from above and unites all things in the bond of love (cf. Col. 3:14). Analogously, Romero's church is difficult to place, not because it floats in space far from the realities of the world or because it is incoherent, but rather because what is concrete in its mission is a prolongation of the Word's *incarnatus est.*

A MOSAIC OF CHRIST

The journey of the church through El Salvador's history is indeed a *via crucis.* Roberto Huezo's drawings in the chapel at the UCA are true depictions of the reality of El Salvador in the time of Romero. They are visual representations of the troubling yearbook opened up at Puebla. These are the faces of the crucified people whose suffering is an offense crying out to heaven. *Sentir con la iglesia* commits Romero to make their cry his own and denounce their dehumanization. The image of God shining from these faces has been eclipsed by the idols that have been made in and also imported to El Salvador, idols like national security and private property. The absolutization of these values cemented the ideological underpinnings for the violent repression of dissidence.

The faces of the poor in Latin America are signs of the mystery of sin whose ultimate consequence is shown in Huezo's drawings. But in Romero's vision of the church, the faces of the poor are more than death masks: they form a mosaic of Christ. *Sentir con la iglesia* unites Romero to the paschal church. The chapel at the UCA is the Chapel of the Martyrs. Huezo's drawings are not the only images on the walls of the church. On one side wall hangs Miguel Antonio Bonilla's *Requiem to the Martyrs*, which shows the victims of the massacre of November 16, 1989, no longer as cadavers but as risen. On another side wall, there are the plaques by the tombs of the martyrs who scripture tells us stand "before the throne and before the Lamb, robed in white, with palm branches in their hands" (Rev. 7:8). The portrait of these witnesses and their graves are a constant reminder that the final word of the church is not death but life. The *via crucis* of the Salvadoran people ends, not in Golgotha, but in the kingdom where the light of Tabor shines without interruption, bringing life and beauty to all who see its dazzling rays.

CHAPTER 6

THE VISION
OF GOD

POSTCARDS FROM TABOR

In the spring of 1956, Óscar Romero traveled to the Holy Land. He left Venice on March 15 and arrived five days later in Jaffa within sight of Mount Carmel. By the slopes of this mountain, in the grotto where Elijah lived and under the maternal eye of the Virgin of Carmel, Padre Romero celebrated his first mass in the Holy Land. His travelogue records with special joy the places where he had the opportunity to celebrate mass while walking in the land of the Bible: Carmel, the Basilica of the Annunciation, Gethsemane, and so on. Among the many places that he visited in this trip was the mountain that tradition identifies as the site of the Transfiguration.

In a letter to the *Chaparrastique*, he speaks of Tabor as more than a mountain: "It resembles an altar raised to the glory of God."[1] When he reached the top after climbing its long slope, Romero commented, "God is felt in this divine landscape of mountain and plain. When the Creator built it, he thought that one day on that mountain he would allow a stream of his glory to cover in splendor of cloud and sun the beloved Son in whom he is well pleased."[2] The consonance of

the land with its divinely appointed purpose was a source of unending wonder for Romero. His amazement at the beauty of the setting
for the story of salvation was one that he learned in El Salvador, the
American Tabor. After all, this watchtower of scripture was the sight
of the theophany of the Transfiguration.

> The Basilica of the Transfiguration is a true poem in stone to the
> glory of the Transfigured One. When the sun strikes the polychromic
> stained glass of the apse, it seems as if the "luminous cloud" has again
> descended on Tabor. . . . The lovely mosaics that represent the other
> four transfigurations of Jesus (his birth, his Eucharist, his passion, and
> his resurrection) are illumined. And when the priest cloaked in the glory
> of that basilica receives the privilege of celebrating the mass of the sixth
> of August it seems as if he feels something akin to the ecstasy of Saint
> Peter: Lord, it is good to be here. How I remembered that morning
> the Divine Patron of my country and committed unto him this beloved
> Salvadoran soil, the Tabor of America.[3]

Departing Tabor was not easy. "Saint Peter must have felt all
through his life the nostalgia for this mountain where he learned to
know and love Jesus better, because in the presence of the Transfigured One the promises of the prophets gained new lights and
hopes."[4] Even so, it was necessary to descend the mountain because
"the definitive glory of Tabor must be earned by the pain of the transfiguration of Calvary."[5] Holy Week drew close, and Romero planned
to celebrate it in Jerusalem. His last entry of his Holy Land pilgrimage
tells of a side trip he took to the place where Jesus wept over Jerusalem. "But this time, after the days of redemption, I desired to see it as
Saint John did in the Apocalypse, a beautiful image of heaven and the
church. . . . When seeing Jerusalem thus, after Holy Week, the symbol
of a paradise regained, I am filled with feelings of singing to it with the
nostalgia of the old Israelites."[6] For Romero, the best part of a journey
was the return home, but as Salvadoran as he was, Romero never forgot that he was a pilgrim. The consonances between the topography
of El Salvador and that of Palestine filled him with longing for his true
home. The view from Tabor was a postcard of the kingdom of God.

In this chapter, we will explore Romero's vision of the end, his eschatology. In particular, I will draw our attention to Romero's account of the beatific vision, martyrdom, and hope. Two texts from the end of Romero's life will anchor these explorations: the Louvain address and his final homily. Tying this chapter together and in a sense this whole book is Romero's adaptation of the Irenaean saying *Gloria Dei, vivens homo*. Romero's theological vision can be termed Irenaean not because the archbishop of San Salvador was textually indebted to the bishop of Lyons but because, in effect, their resolute battle against the heresies that debased the goodness of life in the flesh was fought from the same high ground—Tabor. On that mountain, the Irenaean vision of the scandal of the Incarnation becomes sharpened in Romero's vision of the scandal of the Transfiguration. Let us see how.

AN IRENAEAN APHORISM

On January 28, 1980, Monseñor Romero departed El Salvador aboard a Pan American Airlines flight. He was bound for Belgium, where he would receive a doctorate *honoris causae* from the University of Louvain.[7] Romero traveled reluctantly. He had been agonizing for weeks as to whether he should attend. The intensity of the crisis in El Salvador seemed to render foreign academic honors superfluous. The place of the shepherd is with the sheep, especially when these are being rounded up and slaughtered. Nevertheless, in the end Romero decided to go. He was transparent with his congregation regarding his rationale. "For myself, I would have preferred to remain here, where I felt the anguish of these difficult situations. But others persuaded me that I had to go and carry there the cause that we support and defend. I also felt that it was not an honor given to me alone, but that all this overflowed and served this entire community, and that I presented myself to receive the hood of the doctorate *honoris causae* in your name" (*Homilías*, 6:249).

The ceremony at Louvain would give him the opportunity to speak to an international audience about the tribulations that El Salvador was undergoing and the fidelity of the church in this context.

Also, Romero planned to make a side trip to Rome. Rome always meant for him "the cradle, the home, the fountain, the heart, the brain of our church."[8] There he had the opportunity to spend time in prayer before the tomb of the beloved Paul VI and also to have conversations with the likes of Eduardo Pironio and John Paul II.[9] After concluding his business in Rome, he headed off to Louvain for the hooding ceremony. The topic for his acceptance address was "the political dimension of the faith from the perspective of the poor." Romero began his speech with a greeting in halting Flemish before switching to his native Spanish. For forty minutes he spoke of how the church's engagement with the politics of El Salvador from the perspective of a preferential option for the poor had deepened the church's understanding of the central mysteries of the faith. Romero ended his address with a reference to the church fathers. "The early Christians used to say, *Gloria Dei, vivens homo*. We can make this concrete by saying, *Gloria Dei, vivens pauper*" (*Voz*, 193).

What does Romero mean by this aphorism? How significant is it for understanding his theological vision? As I said, the fact that the phrase appears only at the end of his speech at Louvain may lead us to think that it was a rhetorical flourish or a nod at erudition. However, the role played by the Irenaean aphorism in Romero's ministry militates against this interpretation. Before turning to Romero's exercise of *ressourcement* from the margins and his rewriting of Irenaeus, we need to consider what the bishop of Lyons said.

Gloria Dei, Vivens Homo

The famous phrase appears in book 4 of *Against the Heresies*, where Irenaeus endeavors to demonstrate the unity of the Old and New Testaments. The argument continues that of the previous chapter of his book, where Irenaeus defended the unity of the Father and the incarnate Son. Both forms of unity were denied by Irenaeus's foes. In Gnostic thought, God is not the creator but the demiurge. The demiurge is a lesser god; it creates so as to receive from creatures the glory that it lacks by nature.[10] For Irenaeus, the situation is very different. The communion of Father and Son in the Spirit is one of mutual glorification from eternity. God lacks nothing that he can then receive from creatures. He creates, not because he needs something from creatures, but because he wants to give freely.

> And for this reason did the Word become the dispenser of the pater-nal grace for the benefit of men, for whom He made such great dis-pensations, revealing God indeed to men, but presenting man to God, and preserving at the same time the invisibility of the Father, lest man should at any time become a despiser of God, and that he should always possess something towards which he might advance; but, on the other hand, revealing God to men through many dispensations, lest man, fall-ing away from God altogether, should cease to exist. *For the glory of God is a living man; and the life of man consists in beholding God.* For if the manifesta-tion of God which is made by means of the creation, affords life to all living in the earth, much more does that revelation of the Father which comes through the Word, give life to those who see God.[11]

The Latin text for the sentence in italics reads: *Gloria enim Dei vivens homo, vita autem hominis visio Dei.*[12] The first part of the sentence became the basis for the famous saying that became a pillar of genera-tions of post–Vatican II Christian humanism. We will consider this part first, before turning to the lesser-known but crucial clause that ends the statement.

The *gloria Dei* of which Irenaeus speaks is not the glory that humanity renders to God but rather the glory that God reveals to his creatures.[13] Throughout the history of salvation, this glory is mani-fested to creatures through different economies: the economy of the Holy Spirit in the Old Testament; the economy of the Son in the New Testament; the economy of the Father in glory. In spite of the appro-priation of different times of salvation history to one person of the Trinity or another, the Son is present and active at all times in mak-ing the Father known. The *gloria Dei* is not the glory that God wants from the living human (not *gloriam enim Dei quaerit vivens homo*). The glory that God wants *is* the living human (*gloria enim quam Deus quaerit est vivens homo*).[14] Who is this *vivens homo*? This is the question to which we now turn.

Irenaeus distinguishes between two vital principles: one creaturely, the other divine.[15] The first principle is the breath of life (πνοή)
that God breathed into the nostrils of the first human (cf. Gen. 2:7).
Irenaeus describes the creation of the human being as a process of
"plasmation," a technical term used to describe the art by which a
potter shapes clay. Everything else in creation was created solely by
divine fiat: God spoke and it was so. By contrast, the human being was
molded by God's hands. This molding occurred in two movements,
two acts. First, God took the finest dust (χοῦς) of the earth. However,
as Rafael Amo Usano explains, "This dust was not sufficient of itself
to allow for plasmation. Just as the work of the potter needs water
to prepare the earth, so the dust needs an element to allow its molding."[16] The element that prepares the dust for plasmation is power
(δύναμις). The mixture of dust and the power of God constitutes
"the flesh," by which Irenaeus means the entire human body with
its diverse members and organs. The molding of the human continues with a second divine act, the infusion of the breath of life (πνοὴ
ζωῆς). This breath prepares the flesh to receive a second vital principle, the Spirit (πνεῦμα).[17]

Human life is differentiated according to its vital principle. One
kind of life is temporal, the other eternal. One kind of life "animates,"
the other "vivifies." The first kind of life has a pedagogical role with
respect to the other. The first habituates the flesh for the second. The
creation of the human is not complete until the human grows from
image into likeness, that is to say, until the human is conformed to
the stature of Christ, the archetype of the *vivens homo*. Christ is living and perfect from his conception. In other humans perfection will
happen gradually as they follow Christ and open themselves to the
life that comes from the Father. Contrary to Gnostic claims, humans
are not naturally divine. They become divine by grace as their spirit is
united to flesh. The Spirit does not do away with human nature but
strengthens it so that it may participate in the glory of the Father.[18]
The spiritualization of flesh is not instantaneous. The cycles of inhal-
ing and exhaling the breath of life prepare the flesh for the inspiration
of the Spirit. It takes time to transform the human, not on account of
any weakness in the Creator, but because of the temporal nature of

corporal creatures. Herein lie the anthropological roots of Irenaeus's vision of history. The purpose of history is to acclimatize humans to the indwelling of the Holy Spirit who is the principle of eternal life.[19]

To recap the argument thus far, when Irenaeus says, *Gloria enim Dei vivens homo*, he is saying that the human being in whom the Holy Spirit dwells is the best image and likeness of God's glory in the flesh. Now the second part of the phrase needs to be considered: *Vita autem hominis visio Dei*. Humans become alive in the Spirit as they see God.

Irenaeus's vision of human life abounds in dramatic tensions. Without seeing God humans cannot really live, yet by itself the flesh is incapable of seeing God. Indeed, scripture speaks of the vision of God not as life-giving but as lethal: "No one shall see God and live" (Exod. 33:20). For Irenaeus, God's word to Moses was the truth, but it was not the whole truth because it glossed over the pedagogic purpose of history. God reveals himself in different ways in manners befitting the different stages of human receptivity to the light of his glory. In the theophanies of the Old Testament, the prophets saw God's glory in likenesses and figures. Moses saw God's "back" (cf. Exod. 33:23). Elijah heard God's still small voice (cf. 1 Kings 19:12). The centuries of covenant relationship with the Lord who made heaven and earth prepared the people of God for something more. On Mount Tabor, Moses and Elijah and the chosen disciples saw the glory of God face to face. The vision of the transfigured Jesus revealed the glory of God and of humanity.[20] For the bishop of Lyons, human dignity stems from the human capacity and vocation to see God and live. The vision that the Gnostics thought was available to an elite and small portion of humanity is made available to all human beings, starting with those whom the world regards as refuse. A living translation of Irenaeus's book would surely catalog classism and racism among the heresies.

Gloria enim Dei, vivens homo. Vita autem hominis, visio Dei. Humans live as they see the light of life that is the glory of God. Since this glory is made known through different economies (the Spirit in creation, the Son in adoption, the Father in glory), the life of the human will vary accordingly. The clearer the vision of God, the more alive the human becomes, and the more the glory of God is made manifest. The orientation of Irenaeus's maxim is eschatological. Amo Usamos captures the Irenaean vision: "The goal of life is Life."[21] However, its heavenward orientation does not disconnect Irenaeus's vision from earthly realities. God is known not only in the light of glory but in human history. He has revealed himself through many created signs and has spoken in many different voices; these are meant, not as consolation prizes for a paradise lost, but as promissory postcards. As Irenaeus states, "If the manifestation of God which is made by means of the creation, affords life to all living in the earth, much more does that revelation of the Father which comes through the Word, give life to those who see God."[22] In the Irenaean vision, events are interpreted from their final cause; they are seen eschatologically. Learning to see eschatologically means learning to read the entirety of the economy of God through Paul's Adam-Christ typology. The end comes first. Historical happenings are interpreted from their recapitulation in Christ. You start at omega and work your way back to alpha. Seeing from the end makes it possible to live from the end, which can be confusing and even disturbing for those used to time marching on.[23] But without the "second sight" made possible by the second birth of baptism, the book of life becomes a closed book of efficient causes rather than the open score of God's symphony of salvation.

Reading Irenaeus from El Salvador

How well did Óscar Romero understand the theological density of the Irenaean vision? It is impossible to know. Irenaeus was certainly high on his reading list. According to Jesús Delgado, "Romero became very interested in the reading of this church father on account of his distinguished service to the church in the defense of the Catholic faith."[24] Even so, Romero was not a scholar of Irenaeus or of any of the church fathers. It is unlikely that he would have engaged secondary literature on the bishop of Lyons to any significant extent. Romero's reading of Irenaeus was probably based on reading selections from *Against the Heresies* with the guidance of the humanistic appropriation of the Irenaean aphorism that was characteristic of the time following Vatican II.[25] Still, it would be a mistake to downplay Romero's knowledge of Irenaeus because what the Salvadoran cleric lacked in terms of technical expertise he more than made up for in pastoral and spiritual experience. The bond tying Romero to Irenaeus was not simply textual; it was theologal. The same Spirit that spoke through Irenaeus to defend the goodness of the flesh spoke through Romero to defend the goodness of the poor. With these caveats in mind, we can now consider how Romero retrieved and rewrote Irenaeus for his context.

Romero came across Irenaeus's saying as early as 1975, during a spiritual retreat in Guatemala. At the Posada de Belén, Romero heard a series of reflections led by Cardinal Pironio. The purpose of these was to foster an encounter with Jesus from within the Central American reality.[26] The first meditation was based on John 12:20–27. This text, which would turn out to be Romero's martyrial biblical text, was the springboard for plunging into the theme of the hour of Jesus. Pironio describes it as an hour of passion and glory. Christ trembled before the coming hour, yet he committed himself fully to the hour; he drank the cup of suffering to its dregs, assured that he would be vindicated and raised by God. The dynamism of the hour of Christ as sorrow and joy, death and life, is carried over to the life of the church. In Central America this hour has positive and negative elements. On the positive side, the hour contributes to an ever-deepening understanding of the mystery of the church. At its heart, the church is constituted by the life of Christ and the activity of the Holy Spirit; their supernatural dynamism impels the church to grow in its purity, poverty, communion, conscience, and freedom. From the heart of God, the church flows in mission to the world. There the church is "the soul of society, the leaven of history."[27] The present hour of the church is also one of renewal: renewal of the liturgy, renewal of the communion among bishops and the people of God, and renewal of holiness. The hour of the church in Central America is also the hour of the youth. The young people of Central America, despite their confusions and misunderstandings, want to see Jesus, and they look for him in the church and in Christian spirituality. In sum, there is much that is positive about the present hour of the church, but on the negative side, it is an hour of persecution. This persecution is felt most keenly by those who want to live in fidelity to the gospel among the poor. These evangelical souls need the support of the bishops, who must in turn support each other. The hour of persecution is compounded by the loss of a number of foundational postures within the church. Many have lost a sense of the presence of God in the church. The result has been the darkening of the faith, a faith that tends to abstraction, a faith that lacks commitment. Paradoxically, at the same time that there has been a loss of the sense of God's nearness, there has also been a loss in the sense of God's absoluteness. Romero wrote in his journal: "We have discovered the human, history. But in the end it is God that matters. The human being is of concern on account of being the glory of God. *The glory of God is the living human.*"[28]

Listening to Pironio, Romero came to understand that the Salvadoran context had rendered the Irenaean maxim unintelligible. A dulling of the senses had pushed God to the margins of the Central American worldview; his immanence and transcendence were hidden by idols. The marginalization of God had logically led to the immanentization of the human being. The mystical dimension of theology had been forgotten. A diminished capacity for silence and prayer hardened the ground from which true prophecy could flourish. Symptomatic of the decoupling of human life from the glory of God was the loss of retreat places, or more accurately a loss of purpose for these places. The mountain, the lonely place, was not meant to be a place of withdrawal from the world in order to feel good, but a place where one learned to live within history. Pironio challenged Romero to find the opportunity in the difficult times. In this hour, the peoples of the world still wanted to see Jesus. The offering of the paschal Christ was the church's most important contribution. For many, the sacramental reality of the church was an obstacle that got in the way of seeing the Savior: "The sign of the bread hides the immensity of Jesus."[29] But this same reality "expresses and communicates the Savior."[30] In order to help people to see Jesus, the church must pursue the renewal of its conduct and structures, but the starting and ending points for this renewal are Christ. In other words, the success or failure of a renewal will be measured by the church's transparency to Christ. One might say that the task of the church is the performance of the Irenaean saying, embodying the union of the glory of God and the life of the human.

A few years after this retreat in Guatemala, the Irenaean maxim played a pivotal role in how Romero responded to the murder of his friend Father Rutilio Grande. His decision to celebrate the *Misa única*, a single mass for the entire archdiocese, was not one at which he arrived easily. Sobrino recalls the archbishop's vacillations: "If the Eucharist gives glory to God, will not God have more glory in the usual number of Sunday masses than in just one?"[31] The intervention of Father Jeréz won over the archbishop. "I think Monseñor is absolutely right to be concerned for the glory of God. But unless I am mistaken, the Fathers of the Church said, '*Gloria Dei, vivens homo*'—the glory of God is the living person."[32] The Jesuit provincial's words struck a chord in the archbishop's heart and gave him the theological rationale to move forward with the single mass. Jon Sobrino, who overheard this exchange, wondered whether Romero knew the second part of the Irenaean maxim, *Vita autem hominis, visio Dei.*[33] Since Irenaeus was one of Romero's most read authors, he probably did know the full saying.[34] Whatever the case may be regarding the extent of Romero's familiarity with Irenaeus, the theological view of the bishop of Lyon was congenial to that of the archbishop of San Salvador. The anthropology expressed pithily by his aphorism pulsated like a bass note in the theology of Romero. Almost two years after the *Misa única* for Grande, while Romero was attending the gathering of Latin American bishops in Puebla, the *vivens homo* of Irenaeus gave him the language with which to describe the Salvadoran crucible. He unfolded the scene tersely to the Brazilian theologian Leonardo Boff: "In my country, people are being horribly murdered. We must defend the minimum gift of God, which is also the maximum: life."[35] In sum, it was the practice of ministry in a structurally unjust society that led Romero to conclude his discourse at Louvain by revising Irenaeus's dictum of *Gloria Dei, vivens homo* to *Gloria Dei, vivens pauper.*

The Louvain Address

The address at Louvain on February 2, 1980, was arguably Romero's most important and carefully crafted lecture. Romero credited Father Delgado and Aníbal Romero with helping him articulate his reflections.[36] Sobrino too contributed to early drafts of the address.[37] This lecture is distinctive for the explicit references to theologians both ancient and contemporary. It contains not only a direct quote from Ellacuría's work but also indirect references.[38] At Louvain the archbishop expounded on the relation between faith and politics, the church and the world, as experienced in El Salvador. To be sure, the story of the church engaging the world and exerting sociopolitical pressure was not news. Romero states: "Jesus lived, worked, struggled and died in the midst of the city, the *polis*" (*Voz*, 184). In other words, there has always been a political dimension to the faith. What is news is the church's critical reflection regarding the kind of political influence that is most harmonious with the Christian faith. Romero defines the political dimension of the faith negatively and positively. The church is not a political institution jockeying for power with other political parties. The church has a political dimension. It makes an option for the poor by making them the privileged audience of the gospel and defending their rights, chief of which is the right to life with dignity. To display the fruitfulness of this critical engagement, Romero approaches the topic from two angles. First, he examines how the church in El Salvador has engaged the world, which, in the Salvadoran context, is the world of the poor. Second, Romero examines what the church has learned from this engagement.

The human misery of poverty is the "primordial fact" that defines the Latin American world and El Salvador. For centuries, this reality remained largely hidden from the eyes of the church, but now the church makes its own the words of God to Moses: "I have observed the misery of my people. . . . I have heard their cry on account of their taskmasters" (Exod. 3:8). The church in Latin America has heard the cry of those whose poverty implores heaven for justice.[39] For many people, the poor appear to be a faceless mass, but to the eye of faith poverty is "a contemporary sacrament of the suffering servant of Yahweh" (*Voz*, 186). The faces of the poor reveal the reality of the continent as a gargantuan road to Jericho where the bodies of those who have been beaten and left for dead can be found around every curve. Confronted with this reality, the church in El Salvador has not passed by on the other side like the priest or the Levite. Like the Good

Samaritan, it has allowed itself to be moved by the realities of the victims and to become incarnate in their midst. Romero understands that speaking thus could be heard as boastful, but it is for this very purpose that he has traveled to Louvain, to inform them about the heroic if halting witness of the church in El Salvador. For the first time in a long time, the poor have been finding "a fountain of hope and a support for their noble struggle for liberation" in the church (*Voz*, 186).

In El Salvador, the church has rediscovered that its chief service to the world is the proclamation of the good news of salvation starting from the poor. To the poor who have heard only bad news, the church preaches the good news that the kingdom of God is theirs. To the rich, the church preaches the good news that they are invited to share in the goods of the kingdom that have been handed to the poor. Romero leaves no room for ambiguity with respect to the demands of conversion. For the rich, conversion means turning to the poor. For the poor, conversion means taking responsibility for their own liberation under the guidance of the word of God. Romero traces the roots of the preferential option for the poor to the Second Vatican Council, which called for the church to follow Jesus in evangelizing the poor and raising the oppressed.[40] The experience of the church in El Salvador has put flesh on the conciliar declarations and has clarified the implications of ministering among the poor for the life of the church. By serving among the poor, the church has gained new eyes. It now sees the depth of humanity radiating from the faces of the landless campesino, the unemployed laborer, the political prisoner, and the disappeared. Their faces unmask the paternalism implicit in many of the church's ministries. The poor are not simply the destination of the church's mission or the recipients of its charity. They are partners in mission. From the side of the poor, the church preaches the good news of God's love to the poor even as it commits itself to their defense. It is on account of this defense that the church is being persecuted in El Salvador, and in this way the poor are the interpretive key to the complex political situation of this small Central American republic. "The true persecution has been directed toward the poor, who are today the body of Christ in history. They are the crucified people, like Jesus, the persecuted people, like the servant of Yahweh. They are the ones who complete in their body what is lacking in the passion of Christ" (*Voz*, 188).

The church is being persecuted not simply out of *odium fidei* (hatred of the faith) but out of *odium pauperis* (hatred of the poor). Not all churches are being occupied by the military, nor are all priests subject to persecution. Only the priest and parishes that have drawn so close to the poor as to become incarnate in their world suffer the fate of the poor, which in El Salvador means death.

Removing the faith from the security of its ecclesial greenhouse is dangerous but necessary. Only if that faith is planted in the rich, bloodied soil of the people of God in Central America can it become fruitful. The first fruits of this new field are a new understanding of sin, the Incarnation, and discipleship. For an adequate measure of the first of these fruits, Romero enlists the help of the Jesuit Ignacio Ellacuría, whom Romero does not name in his address but simply refers to as "one of our theologians" (*Voz*, 189).[41] According to Ellacuría, "The worst secularism is the negation of grace by sin, the objectification of this world as the active presence of the powers of evil, as the visible presence of the negation of God" (*Voz*, 189). Differently stated, sin renders the world antisacramental. The structures of sin that are propping up the crumbling Salvadoran economy have defaced the road signs that God placed in El Salvador. The campesinos, instead of being pointers to the glory of God, are signs of the wages of sin. Hence, the church's preaching against sin requires speaking against the social structures that protect riches, property, and national security as the private good of the few. Entering into the world of the poor, the church's awareness of the power of sin has grown, but where sin has abounded, grace has abounded more. From the world of the poor, the church's faith in the mystery of the Incarnation has been also illumined. Romero avers: "Jesus took truly human flesh and expressed solidarity with his brothers in suffering, in cries and moans, and in surrender" (*Voz*, 190). The false universalisms that the church has from time to time ingenuously pronounced serve only the powerful. The church must reject these both theoretically and practically by becoming incarnate among the poor. When it becomes incarnate among the poor, the church finds that the words of the prophets speak powerfully to their contemporary situation. The new heavens and new earth that Isaiah saw can be ushered in only by God. The transcendent dimension of Christian hope must never be forgotten. At the same time, the proclamation of this eschatological hope must be accompanied by the affirmation of historical hopes. Romero references Isaiah 65:21, "They shall build houses and inhabit them; they shall plant vineyards and eat their fruit." Dignified employment and housing can be signs of the new creation. These signs do not rob eschatological hope from its orientation but rather confirm it by pointing to the inbreaking of the kingdom.

From the world of the poor, the church has understood more clearly that professing faith in the God of life has implications for the life of discipleship. Like Irenaeus, Romero speaks of life as an analogous term that allows for different degrees of fullness. The primary levels of life consist in having bread, roof, and work. These are the very material needs whose satisfaction Isaiah interpreted as signs of the new creation. A fuller degree of life is enjoyed when one surrenders oneself to God in service to his kingdom. Fullness of life is only attained in the kingdom of the Father. The church is concerned with life in all its stages because wherever there is life, God manifests himself. The universality of God's presence is affirmed by pointing out his preferential manifestation among the poor. "Where the poor begin to live, where the poor begin to liberate themselves, where humans are able to sit around a common table to share, there is the God of life" (*Voz*, 191). The church's proclamation of abundant life in Jesus would be absurd without an equally strong affirmation of the dignity and worth of the primary levels of life. The defense of the life of the poor does not exhaust the message of the gospel, but take it away and the Christian faith collapses like a house of cards. Because the human being is made for eternal life with God, the Christian must be for the life of the poor and against their untimely death. The orientation of the church toward the poor is not limited to a Hippocratic *Primum non nocere*. Romero insists that the call to discipleship commits Christians to supplying for the needs of the poor from the goods that they possess to the extent of being willing to lay down their own lives for the sake of the lives of the poor. It is in the context of these reflections on the God of life and the life of the church that Irenaeus's aphorism serves as the capstone for Romero's address on the political dimension of the faith. "The early Christians used to say, *Gloria Dei, vivens homo.* We can make this concrete by saying, *Gloria Dei, vivens pauper.* We believe that from the transcendence of the gospel we can judge what the life of the poor truly consists in, and we believe also that by placing ourselves on the side of the poor and trying to give them life we shall know what does the eternal truth of the gospel consist in" (*Voz*, 193).

Romero's revision of the Irenaean quote is not a correction; it is a *concretar*, a contextualizing, making it real within a particular history. The fight against heresies is no longer being waged against second-century Gnostics but against twentieth-century idolaters of capital. Against these foes, the simple repetition of Irenaeus would miss the mark, the power of his theological vision would be an abstraction. If Romero is going to be Irenaean, then he must rewrite Irenaeus. In concretizing Irenaeus for El Salvador, Romero shifts the optic of the bishop of Lyon's anthropology. The life of the poor serves as the *locus hermeneuticus* for approaching the church father's theological vision. The key terms in the aphorism, glory and life, are resituated. The eschatological orientation remains, but the emphasis falls on a realized eschatology that affirms the dignity and value of the basic levels of human life. This is why Romero says that although abundant life can be attained only in the kingdom of God, neglecting the less than final but necessary and real goods that make life possible in history would be ironic and blasphemous. In God's divine economy the bread that perishes matters and is good; it too is the object of hope and prayer. At the same time, the future eschatological horizon is never out of sight. The life of the poor finds its meaning and sustenance in the life of God. The ultimate purpose of the incarnation of Christ among the poor is the deification of the poor. For the bishop of Lyon and the archbishop of San Salvador, the end of *kenosis* is *theosis*.

GLORIA DEI AND THE PROMISE OF DIVINIZATION

Like the Transfiguration, the topic of *theosis* or divinization is commonly associated with Eastern Orthodox theologies. But in fact the theme runs deep in Western Christianity even if with its own linguistic and conceptual particularities.[42] To be sure, the term *theosis* does not appear in Romero's sermons. Its absence cannot be attributed simply to its Greek provenance. As we have seen, Romero is not afraid to introduce his congregation to Greek terms like *kenosis* that he thinks will facilitate their understanding of the biblical text. Instead of the Greek *theosis*, Romero uses its Latinized counterpart, *divinizar*. The term denotes the transformation that God seeks of all things human from conscience to culture.[43] Romero does not use *divinizar* very often, nor does he explain or define it. Still, his association of the term with participation in the Eucharist displays a robustly patristic logic at work in his thinking.

At the end of a novena for the murder of Father Rafael Palacios, Romero invites his congregants to draw near to the Eucharist, "where the body and blood of our Lord gather the meaning of so much spilt blood, divinize it, ennoble it, purify it of any stains that it might have" (*Homilías*, 5:58). In interpreting Jesus's command to eat his flesh (John 6:41–43), Romero explains that "the flesh divinized in the sacrifice of the cross and united with God in the mystery of the Incarnation, that flesh is divine, and that is the flesh that the Lord offers us" (*Homilías*, 5:231). The divinization effected at the Eucharist is not limited to the bread and wine. Contact with the divinized flesh and blood of Christ divinizes the people of God and empowers them to go into the world to fight for the divinization of all Salvadorans.[44] Escobar Alas affirms Romero's teaching on the divinizing power of the Eucharist: "Whoever eats the body of Christ and drinks his blood must undergo, little by little, a process of conversion or transfiguration, those of us whose Patron is the Divine Savior of the World would say, until we are like Jesus."[45]

The depth of the patristic logic at work in Romero's theology cannot be measured by a simple word count. In a homily that he preached on July 17, 1977, Romero speaks of divinization as the better part chosen by Mary that draws humans into the mystery of Christ. "Blessed is the one who finally understands that God became human in order to save humans and that each human life that is incorporated into this stream of redemption and turns to Christ is divinized. For God became human in Christ so that humans who believed in him would become God" (*Homilías*, 1:200).

For Romero, divinization is the one thing needful and is possible on account of the divine exchange expressed pithily in the patristic formula: "God became human, that the human might become God." This theological motif is heard in a number of his homilies.[46] On the Feast of the Holy Family on December 30, 1979, Romero speaks of the Incarnation as a mystery of immanence and transcendence.

> God comes down to history. He assumes all the problems of humanity. He becomes incarnate in all peoples, in all families, not to remain there but in order to transcend. It is also then a mystery of transcendence. If God became human, it is so that we humans may become God, so that we may be lifted up, and so that all human, political, social, historic problems may be carried away by that current of transcendence toward the Word that became flesh so as to give divine life to humanity and make humanity sharers in the happiness of God for eternity. (*Homilías*, 6:112)

The divinization of human nature begins with the incarnation of the Word and ripples from the flesh of Christ to touch all human things. Romero's language is strongly evocative. He likens the Incarnation to a divine flood that lifts and carries human nature toward the ocean of Triune life. The human who wades into the stream of God's redemption is swept by its powerful current. For Romero, the church as the body of the Christ in history is a kind of Holy Midas transfiguring everything it touches. Immanence becomes buoyed by transcendence. The family becomes an epiphany of the Trinity. The person becomes an icon of Christ who thinks with the mind of Christ, feels with the heart of Christ, and works with the hands of Christ. Reading humanity from the end, Romero teaches that in the divinization of Christ, Christians hear their supreme calling: "Dear sisters and brothers, as long as we do not have this idea of a Christ who is true God and true human, we have not understood our church or the saving mystery of the Lord. For this reason God became human, so that through the figure of that God-human, we would enter deeper into the divine mystery" (*Homilías*, 2:437).

It is through Christ that humans enter into the life of the Trinity. Divinization is always Christocentric. It is telling that some of the traditional scriptures associated with *theosis* like 2 Peter 1:4 and Psalm 86:2 are not commonly found in Romero's cathedral sermons.[47] The chief textual anchor for Romero's theology of divinization is 2 Corinthians 8:9—"For you know the generous act of our Lord Jesus Christ, that though he was rich, yet for your sakes he became poor, so that by his poverty you might become rich." Jesus's act of casting aside wealth to enrich others offers an example for all his followers, a criterion of true conversion and discipleship.[48] In the pilgrim's progress through the history of salvation, the way of *theosis* looks like *kenosis*. The logic of salvation for Romero is marked by what Jon Sobrino calls trans-descendence.[49] The God to whom humans are being conformed by grace is the God of the poor, and this God calls humans to find their transcendence by way of descent and solidarity with the lowly ones. "The God of the Christians cannot be another than the God of Jesus Christ; the God of the one who identified himself with the poor and gave his life for others; the God who sent his Son, Jesus Christ, to take a preference, unambiguously, for the poor. Without disdaining the rest, he called all to the field of the poor so that they could become like him."[50]

The Problem of Conformismo

The identification of the way to life with the way of the cross prompts a question: How does the conjunction of glory and suffering not devolve into the glorification of suffering? Romero terms this the problem of *conformismo*. The archbishop ceaselessly chastises a dangerous and illicit complacency with things being as they are. This *conformismo* can manifest itself in different ways. At the individual level, Romero speaks of the sin of those who having nothing "are *conformistas*, lazy; they do not fight for their progress" (*Homilías*, 1:381). Yet if many poor people settle for things as they are, it is because they see no alternative: "There is a series of conditionings, of structures, that do not allow him to progress" (*Homilías*, 1:381). What *Medellín* refers to as institutionalized sin is very often institutionalized *conformismo*. Structures are erected that keep marginalized people in their place. These structures inculcate a pedagogy of self-exclusion that teaches the poor that their chief contribution to the common good is to be neither seen nor heard. "*Conformismo* is a pessimist, a determinist who believes that everything comes from above and that he has no role" (*Homilías*, 6:55). *Conformismo* is supported by a distorted theology of history. The separation of God's history of salvation from human history relegates the latter to being a waiting room or test center for the former. The only thing that matters is preparing for heaven. Whether one lives in a mansion or a shanty is irrelevant provided one prays and obeys. Among the poor, *conformismo* encourages a fatalistic outlook that sees suffering as part and parcel of life, or an escapist one that waits for things to be better in heaven. Among the powerful, *conformismo* is the ally of a conservative impulse that mistakes the income gap as a divinely ordained status quo. The more cynical among them might actually seek to take advantage of the *conformismo* of the poor and promote it in order to strengthen their hold on power and wealth. After all, they profit from having "anesthetized masses, people incapable of raising critiques, people unable of reconstituting themselves, of making their own history" (*Homilías*, 1:234). Since *conformismo* is supported by a flawed understanding of history, it is no surprise that it works as antiecclesiology. It reduces Salvadorans to an amorphous mass inimical to the formation of the pilgrim people of God. It also works as a reductive anthropology where being human is reduced to subsistence levels of existence. *Conformismo* deafens persons to their divine calling.

The church has a duty to preach against the *conformismo* of the rich and of the poor. It denounces the *conformismo* of the rich as opportunistic. It counters the *conformismo* of the poor by encouraging their personal responsibility and by promoting their dignity through reflection groups and local associations for campesinos and workers.[51] In both cases, the church preaches conversion from the sin of *conform-ismo* to an Irenaean vision of God. The aphorism *Gloria Dei, vivens pauper* puts the lie to the minimalist anthropologies and antiecclesiologies entrenched in El Salvador. All humans, starting from the poor, were made for communion with the Triune God. They cannot settle for mediocrities when they were made for divinity; they cannot be *conformistas* when they were made for transfiguration. The church is tasked with announcing to the poor person the good news of their transcendence as a present reality. Countering *conformismo* among the poor entails the following:

> engaging the child, engaging the poor, engaging the person in rags, the sick, the person in the shack, the hovel, it means going to share with them. And from within the very bowels of his misery, his situation, transcend him, raise him, promote him, and tell him: "You are not garbage, you are not a marginalized person." In fact, it means telling them the opposite: "You are worth much. You are worth as much as the master who lives in the great mansions that you see but will not possess. You are equal; you are a human like all others, image of God, you too are called to heaven." (*Homilías*, 5:353)

The most powerful antidote in Romero's medicine bag for countering the poisonous effects of *conformismo* in El Salvador is the example of Mary. She was acquainted with suffering. She was born to a people under imperial occupation; she knew poverty; she experienced the plight of the refugee; she underwent a parent's worst fear, not just outliving her child but seeing him killed before her. She bore all this courageously without *conformismo* (*Homilías*, 5:348). Romero terms her song of praise, the Magnificat, a "cry of holy rebelliousness," a protest and plea to the God who has the power to pull the mighty down from their thrones (*Homilías*, 6:107). Were she to sing that song in El Salvador, she too would be labeled subversive. For Romero, Marian devotion should come with a warning label; it is not for the weak hearted. Her *fiat* was not a passive surrender to an inexorable divine will. Her "yes" was the faithful, open-ended assent of a young girl, and it was also "the cry of agony of all the peoples in need of redemption" (*Homilías*, 6:86). Mary was in effect saying: "Here I am the slave; come save this people. Come! El Salvador needs you. History needs you. The peoples need you" (*Homilías*, 6:87). Here we have another example of Romero's Irenaean perspective. He listens to Mary's song from the end, the recapitulation of all things in Christ. Romero insists that her submissive attitude is not alienation. Alienation is the attitude of the one who like Satan refuses to serve God. When someone severs the bonds to the Creator, life begins to unravel (*Homilías*, 4:94). Ultimately, freely conforming to the will of the Father is the answer to the *conformismos* of earth. Conformity to the will of the Father does not deaden the spiritual and physical senses. On the contrary, the person whose flesh is raw because of the lacerations that the wild beasts of wealth, power, and national security have inflicted finds that turning to God does not dull the pain but gives it a purpose. The dissonance between the current situation of shameful injustice and the divine vocation to glory fuels protest and guides action. When freely offered up to God, one's poverty, marginalization, and underdevelopment become forces of true liberation (*Homilías*, 5:348).

Gloria Dei, vivens pauper. The Irenaean aphorism capped what turned out to be a very well-received lecture. Romero had the opportunity to reprise his address at an ecumenical gathering in Paris on February 4. There he described his message as a bifocal reflection on "what the Christian faith can offer to the world in service and how the Christian faith is enriched as it receives from the world the reflections of what she cultivated in the world."[52] Monseñor Romero departed Europe on February 6, 1980, satisfied that he had fulfilled the purpose of the trip. His only regret was that news of the event received little coverage in El Salvador. Perhaps this news blackout was the reason why Romero offered an encore of the address during his Sunday homily of February 10. In that sermon he offered a paraphrase of the Irenaean saying: "In the glory of God human beings find their human dimension" (*Homilías*, 6:254). Ignorance of God results in ignorance of humanity, the manufacture of idols, and the death of the poor.

The Salvadoran version of the Irenaean saying occurs only once in Romero's homiletical corpus, and yet it is like a lightning flash that illumines an entire room, revealing previously unseen art and furnishings. We have already examined the theme of *theosis*. In the next section, we will consider how Romero's *ressourcement* from the margins informs his theological aesthetics and his theology of martyrdom.

VISIO DEI AND THE BEAUTY OF EL SALVADOR

If seeing God is integral to life, then salvation has an aesthetic dimension. According to Alejandro García-Rivera, "Irenaeus tells us that we were made to see God, our very life depends on seeing God, and thus in a sense our very lives depend on seeing truth, goodness, and beauty."[53] A long, venerable tradition connects *theosis* with beauty.[54] One can find representatives of this tradition among Eastern fathers like the Cappadocians and Denys the Aeropagite and among Western doctors of the church like Augustine and Aquinas. Because there is a connection between divinization and beauty, there is also a connection between liberation and beauty.[55] The Latin American fathers of liberation theology understood this. Gustavo Gutiérrez played classical music while his congregants gathered for mass because he believed that the "poor have a right to Beethoven."[56] Rubem Alves came to see this connection too and traded in liberation theology for poetry. "If we want to change the world, we need first of all to be able to make people dream about beauty."[57] The mothers and fathers of Latino/a theology also underline this connection. Michelle Gonzalez asserts that "the loss of aesthetics has resulted in rendering the Christian message unattractive and undeliverable."[58] Roberto Goizueta agrees: "If the wounded, risen Christ is to be the source of a new, reconciled *communio*, his figure (form) must have the power to draw us to Christ and his cause."[59] Only the aesthetic character of truth has the power to break the barriers "between the crucified and risen Lord and the millions of crucified victims for whom Christ would otherwise be simply another abstract theological concept incapable of generating hope."[60] For the truth to set us free, it must first capture the mind, which is possible only when goodness inflames the heart. Another term for the attractive power of truth and goodness is *beauty*. Óscar Romero understood the liberative power of beauty.

The Beauty of the Salvadoran Tabor

Monseñor Romero spoke of the beauty of El Salvador on many occasions. This is not surprising. El Salvador has been gifted with a lush landscape of soaring volcanoes and gentle lakes. Romero states that "the beauty of creatures has been given by God" (*Homilías*, 1:247). The chief characteristic of the beautiful is to be found not in the classic attributes of proportionality and clarity but in its transparency to the giver. El Salvador is beautiful because its Divine Savior is beautiful. The loveliness of the land evokes a grateful response toward God and patriotism toward the country. As we have seen, Romero was proud to be a Salvadoran, but he steered clear of the nationalism that brooks no questions and the cynicism that allows no affirmations. His comments about the Salvadoran national anthem exemplify the path he charted for himself and the church: "The national hymn is no dogma and yet it has much that is beautiful and true. We need to translate that truth and beauty to the reality of the country, so as to not sing what in reality is not true" (*Homilías*, 3:266). The church has a stake in the promotion of a Christian patriotism that facilitates the translation of the hymn to the national reality, and an exemplary translator, the model patriot, is Mary. "Mary was chosen for her holiness and her patriotism" (*Homilías*, 2:179). A bold claim! But the basis is Christological. If Jesus is to be the son of David, then in a manner of speaking, his mother must be the bearer of that whole heritage. The landscape of the Holy Land, the stories of the patriarchs, kings, the prophets, and the daughters of Zion, all beat in her heart. "Mary is the expression of an entire people" (*Homilías*, 2:179). Mary's *fiat*, her "letting be," should characterize the grateful response of the people to the beauty of El Salvador. The cultivation of this vision is an urgent task for the church because the beauty of El Salvador is endangered. "What beautiful coffee fields! What beautiful sugarcane fields! What beautiful cotton fields! What lands has God given us! What beautiful nature! But when we see it groan under oppression, under iniquity, under injustice, under violations, then the church hurts and hopes for a liberation that comes not just from material well-being but from the power of a God who will liberate nature from sinful hands so that nature together with the redeemed humanity will sing for joy of God the liberator" (*Homilías*, 2:93).

Salvadorans have forgotten how to see beauty. From an Irenaean perspective this is a serious problem, because being truly alive is dependent on seeing beauty. It is common among intellectual historians to attribute the eclipse of beauty in the Western imaginary to a matrix of factors including the rise of nominalism, the influence of the Renaissance, and the debates over justification by faith.[61] This is no doubt correct, but in El Salvador the most important cause of blindness to the beauty of God, creation, and the human was the proliferation of idols peddled by the pedagogy of death. Human worth became devalued to whatever manifested a fallen *gloria mundi*. Instead of a life-giving *visio Dei*, a death-dealing *visio idoli* filled the imagination of the Salvadorans.

Romero looks at El Salvador eschatologically. It is the "land of hope" because Isaiah's prophecy of the "new heavens and new earth" (Isa. 65:17) will be fulfilled in it (*Homilías*, 2:42). The eschatological perspective on life in the land as marked by justice (where they build houses and live in them, plant vineyards, and eat of their fruit) informs how Romero thinks of the land in the present. Matthew Whelan argues that, for the archbishop, agrarian reform is not simply a social program for just land redistribution but a reordering of the goods of the earth in accordance with their final end—communion with God in the kingdom. "When Romero speaks of creation, it often seamlessly opens into new creation. In other words, it opens into the theological landscape of God's work of salvation in Israel and in Christ, and humankind's calling to share in the common life of God through Christ and in the Holy Spirit—the communion that creates and sustains all created reality."[62] The beauty of El Salvador was made, not to be hoarded by the few, but to be shared by all. When the oligarchy claim exclusive ownership over the land and ignore the social purpose of private property, they are setting themselves against the grain of the universe. In so doing, they wound their capacity for communion with God, which is in fact the goal of the cosmos.[63] Instead of opening themselves to God in praise (*homo adorans*), they turn in on themselves (*homo incorvatus in se*). The unbridled acquisitiveness that is at the root of the idolatry of wealth misshapes the person, society, and even the land. By contrast, the eschatological light of glory transfigures the people of El Salvador into the people of God and the land of El Salvador into the Salvadoran Tabor.

Romero's Taboric vision of the beauty of the land shares commonalities with theologians of the Eastern Church like Sergei Bulgakov. Introducing this Russian Orthodox theologian at this point in our work may seem like a pointless detour, but I do so for two reasons. First, the manner in which Bulgakov expresses his theology of the Transfiguration sharpens Romero's eschatological view of the beauty of the land and the Christian's responsibility for orienting it toward its end. Second, I wish to suggest that the theological vision from the Salvadoran Tabor is rich in potential not only for North-South ecclesial relations but for East-West ecumenical rapprochement.[64]

Willis Jenkins finds in Sergei Bulgakov the roots of a spirituality that can undergird the church's witness to the integrity of creation in a time of ecological crisis.[65] Of course, the situation that Bulgakov faced in Russia was very different from the one that confronted Romero. And yet both understood that at the foot of Tabor lie the kingdoms of the prince of this world, the unenlightened land. Both the Marxist and the capitalist were seeking to build a better earthly city by flattening it and stripping it of transcendence. But real progress in the world requires adopting a new vantage point; it requires "thinking like a transfigured mountain."[66] According to Jenkins, this means that before making plans for transforming the world, people need to "first, look up to the hills and see how the mountains reveal God's glory."[67]

For both the Orthodox theologian and the Salvadoran prelate, Tabor occupies a prominent place in the spiritual cartography of Christianity.[68] Mount Tabor, like the Jordan River, marks boundaries in the terrain of Jesus's life. At the Jordan, Jesus freely crosses the threshold from his hidden life to his public ministry. At Tabor, Jesus crosses another threshold, from a life of teaching and healing to the Passion. To put it in terms more at home in Romero's view, Jordan made manifest Jesus's desire to preach good news to the poor. Tabor manifested his desire to suffer with and for the poor. More than that, in that Christ freely sets his face toward Jerusalem and the cross, his final glory is anticipated at Tabor. Bulgakov avers that "events cast their light from the future into the past and the present, already pregnant with the future."[69] The light of glory shines in the Upper Room and casts the scene of the Last Supper in the *chiaro* of Christ's resurrection and return and in the *oscuro* of his passion and death. The present age is already transpierced by the glory of the age to come. The small company of prophets and apostles experience a taste of the communion of saints. On Mount Tabor the disciples learn to live backwards; the light of Christ helps them read Creation from consummation, the land of El Salvador from the kingdom of God. Bulgakov considers the Transfiguration to be a decisive event in the life of Christ, a foretaste of the kingdom for the five witnesses gathered with him, and the revelation of beauty. As we saw in Romero's sermons on the Transfiguration, by the light of Tabor, El Salvador's beauty is revealed even in the midst of the ugliness of a history of violence. Bulgakov too preaches about this crucified beauty: "Beauty does not yet reign in this world, though it has been enthroned in it through the divine Incarnation and Pentecost. It follows Christ on the way to the cross; in the world beauty is crucified. It is sacrificial beauty, and the words about 'going forth to suffer' are said in reference to it. Yet it is beauty. And it is the feast of this sacrificial beauty that we celebrate on the day of our Lord's Transfiguration."[70]

The beauty celebrated on the Feast of the Transfiguration is an anticipation of the beauty and light of the new creation. The beauty that will save the world is the eschatological beauty of Christ that the Holy Spirit reveals. The Holy Spirit gives God's elect the eyes to see the glory of God already shining in the present. The future renewal of all things has already begun; to those who listen to Christ, creation already appears transfigured. This is the reason why even in a time of national crisis Romero and Bulgakov could say with Peter, "It is good to be here." The Spirit had given them eyes to see with God that everything that had been made was "very good" (cf. Gen. 1:31).

The beauty of the Salvadoran Tabor illumines the manner in which the church lives in the land as it journeys through the dark night of history. On Bulgakov's terms, the church in El Salvador practices transfiguration by humanizing the country after the image of Christ revealed on Tabor. In the words of Paul, "The creation waits with eager longing for the revealing of the children of God" (Rom. 8:22). The longing of creation for liberation is one of the signs of the times in Russia and El Salvador.[71] The liberation of the Salvadoran also liberates El Salvador from its subjection to futility. The transfiguration of the cosmos is not a Promethean project that seeks to tame or manage creation. Christians practice transfiguration by creatively working in the world so that God's "wild glory" shines through everything.[72] Intrinsic to this creative act is an ascetic practice, a kenotic gesture. Approaching the world as if it were a depository of resources for human projects, even if these projects seek to promote human welfare, ends up being dehumanizing and destructive. Human creativity that does not confess sin and give thanks for finitude will inevitably enthrone itself as the divine savior of the world.

As I mentioned, this sidebar conversation between Bulgakov and Romero is meant only to illustrate the fruitfulness of a richer encounter between Eastern theologians and Salvadorans on the summit of Mount Tabor. The engagement also helped us to understand better that projects of liberation will succeed only when Salvadorans learn to see like a transfigured people.

Seeing Like a Transfigured People

The church has the responsibility to form a people who learn to liberate beauty from its captivity to idols. For Romero, contemplatives are the great liberationists in this struggle.[73] Their practice of taking time away from work to contemplate has taught them how to see signs of God's presence and love everywhere. The hours of prayerful attention before the face of God have helped them recognize his silhouette in his passage through history even when all that is visible is his back. The contemplatives help build up the church by communicating what the Spirit is saying in the present hour. "The equilibrium of that voice of the Spirit that cries from the human misery of our peoples and the voice of the Spirit that cries from contemplation and prayer are what makes the church the authentic liberator of Latin America, a liberator without demagogy, without class warfare, a liberator based on the strength of the wisdom of God, a liberator from the Holy Spirit" (*Homilías*, 1:298).

The vision of God that the Holy Spirit makes possible comes into focus on the face of Christ. We already touched on this topic at the end of chapter 4 when we considered Romero's adoption of Ramón Cué's *Cristo roto*. The missing face on that figure made room for the faces of his crucifying foes and crucified friends. If anyone sees Jesus, they see the Father. But also if anyone sees Jesus, they see the face of "a suffering man, the face of a crucified, the face of a poor person, the face of a saint" (*Homilías*, 1:180). The Holy Spirit opens the eyes of Christians so that in the face of each poor person they can see the face of Christ. The Spirit accomplishes this transformation in several ways.

The Holy Spirit can liberate the beauty of Salvadorans by uniting their suffering to Christ's self-offering. Romero recalls how Good Pope John spoke of his sickbed as an altar on which he was the host. "In the final moment how beautiful is the body, even if it is an obese and ugly one like that of John XXIII, but converted into a pleasing host by the beautiful spirit that that body enclosed" (*Homilías*, 3:218). Yes, Romero called the dying pope fat and ugly but beautiful, because the sacrifice that is pleasing to God is that of the contrite spirit. Everyone has something to offer. "Each body is a host when one lives to offer God one's energies, voice, walk, hands, intelligence."[74] Even in the direst hour of need, everyone has something beautiful to offer. "The poor one who comes to him to say, 'Lord, I have no work. I spent the whole week looking and I bring nothing but anguish. I have no work.' That too is a service, an offering, a sacrifice. Or the mother who comes to tell of the illness of her son or that they disappeared him. Or the tortured one who comes to offer to the Lord, "Today I endured prison. I bring you my lacerated back" (*Homilías*, 3:85–86). The point is not that being imprisoned or tortured is a good and beautiful thing; that would be either masochism or *conformismo*. The point is that when the body has been consecrated to God, then the hospital bed, the jail cell, even the bloody street becomes an altar from which the irrepressible beauty of the human being as a creature made in the image of God blazes forth.

The Holy Spirit can correct the Salvadoran's visual impairment through the gift of tears. On a number of occasions, Romero appealed to the closing address of Vatican II in which Paul VI exhorted the gathered bishops that "in everyone we can and must recognize the countenance of Christ, the Son of Man, especially when tears and sorrows make it plain to see."[75] In a mysterious way, tears render the face of humanity more transparent to the face of Christ. Tears clear the eyes of the beholder and wash the face of the sufferer; they make the poor translucent to Christ. Thanks to this gift, the beauty of Christ can be sought and seen in the places that the world looks down upon: "Face of Christ between the burlap bags and baskets of the harvester, face of Christ amid tortures and mistreatments in the prisons, face of Christ dying of hunger in the children who lack food to eat, face of Christ in the needy who cry out to the church with one voice" (*Homilías*, 3:432). Tears have rendered these faces transparent to the suffering servant of Isaiah. "It is there where we know most intimately the mystery of Christ who becomes human and becomes poor for us" (*Homilías*, 6:278). The liturgical calendar can habituate Christians to seeing the mystery of Christ in the mystery of human suffering. For instance, "Advent should alert us to discovering the face of Christ in each brother we greet, in each friend with whom we shake hands, in each beggar who asks me for bread, in each worker who wants to use his right to organize in a union, in each campesino looking for work in the coffee fields" (*Homilías*, 4:34). It is the presence of the Holy Spirit in the church that allows Romero to discern and announce the union of the crucified Christ with his crucified people. On Good Friday, it is not just Christ who walks to Calvary. The people of God walk with him, and not just as spectators or even as characters in the drama, but as the body that is carrying the cross (*Homilías*, 2:334). If the gift of tears helps one see the face of Christ, then it should come as no surprise that Romero frequently invites members of his congregation to visit the *Hospitalito*, because this cancer hospice center was an admirable school of tears. It was a place where Christians learned to be "honest with reality."[76] In a diary entry from May 14, 1979, Romero tells of one of those invitations.

The invitation that I made to the nurses during the Sunday homily to celebrate a Eucharist at the chapel of the Hospital of the Divine Providence was heeded with great enthusiasm, and the chapel was full of nurses. Monsignor José López Sandoval, ecclesiastical adviser to the nursing national movement, celebrated with me. I addressed to them a message where I invited them to see in each sick person the twofold face of Christ—the suffering, painful, dying face and the glorious face given to him by that very passion. He learned obedience through suffering, but because of this he was constituted the principle and cause of hope for all who believe in him.[77]

Vita autem hominis, visio Dei. The life of the human, says Irenaeus, is the vision of God. A Salvadoran retrieval of this second clause of the Irenaean aphorism would render it as *Vita autem hominis, visio Dei pauperum*, "The life of the human is the vision of the God of the poor, Jesus Christ." The Holy Spirit, through the hallowing of a Christian's self-offering and through the gift of tears, makes it possible to see the twofold face of Christ as suffering servant and Lord of history in the faces of the poor. The mystical union between Christ and his people is the basis for his epiphany among the poor.[78] The members of his body may be unaware of this union, yet the very fact of this communion is life-giving (*Homilías*, 2:211–12). When united to the head, the humiliated body becomes the glorified face (*Homilías*, 3:147). The vision of the wounded beauty of Christ makes it possible to read the tragic history of El Salvador as what tradition calls a *felix culpa*, a happy fault. In these words from the ancient hymn known as the *Exsultet*, Christians announce their most profound answer to the problem of evil. García-Rivera explains it thus: "Sin is a *felix culpa* when, in overcoming it, the world is made better than if the sin had not been committed."[79] It is crucial to note that the *Exsultet* of the *felix culpa* is not sung on Good Friday. It is an Easter hymn! It is not something that Christians sing before the Stations of the Cross but at dawn when the risen Christ shows his wounds. When this happens, the *felix culpa* is also a *pulchra culpa*, a beautiful fault that merited such a beautiful redeemer, a *Divino Salvador*.

Will beauty save the world? It seems impossible to answer "yes" when the images like the stations of the crucified people that hang at the UCA are broadcast around the world in high definition and surround sound day in and day out: drowning Syrian refugees, kidnapped Mexican students, black bodies bleeding on city streets, and on and on. The difficulty in answering "yes" is compounded by contemporary skepticism of the existence of universals like beauty, goodness, and truth. The skepticism is understandable. There is a history of weaponizing the universals as homogenizing stereotypes.[80] But without universals, what is the basis for the prophetic challenge of evil and injustice? What is truth? What is justice? Faced with this cynical posture, a Christian apologetics centered on the declaration of human rights is necessary but insufficient. The aesthetic turn, the liberating power of beauty, can help if it is rightly understood. The beauty that will save the world is not the beauty of art, though this has its place. The beauty that will save is the beauty of holiness, and this beauty shines most brilliantly from those who are most fully alive. For Romero, the *vivens homo* par excellence is the martyr.

VIVENS HOMO AND THE GIFT OF MARTYRDOM

The focus of this study on Romero's homilies and speeches may give the wrong impression about him. He was not an academic. He did not spend his days in the library preparing weighty theological addresses. God calls people to edify the church by devoting their lives to study, but this was not Romero's call. He was first and foremost a pastor, and his delight was to spend time with his sheep. Monseñor Romero often traveled to the parishes of his archdiocese in order to encourage them in their discipleship and to learn from them how the archbishop might better serve them. On Monday, February 11, 1980, Romero visited the parish in the town of Colón and preached a sermon on the Virgin of Lourdes, whose feast day fell on that date. In contrast with his experience during a prior visit to this canton, he was warmly received.[81] The parish priest, Nicolás Menjivar, interpreted for his congregation the significance of the honor that had been bestowed to Romero in Louvain the week prior. After the mass, Romero had an opportunity to talk one on one with the parishioners. He gathered from them "testimonies of their *sentir* of the church."[82] These testimonies were a vital source of information for Romero's theological advocacy as well as yet another concrete expression of his *sentir* with the church. On March 8, 1980, Romero visited the canton of El Salitre to celebrate the blessing of the parish church. So eagerly was his visit anticipated that a group of the faithful waited for him at a crossroads an hour away from the church and accompanied him on foot along the dusty road. During the mass, Romero preached a homily on the nature of the church as the nucleus of the Christian family, the place of encounter with the Lord, and the giver of a sense of transcendence to life. After the blessing of the church and a time of fellowship with the members of the congregation, Romero tended to the sheep who were homebound. He states in his diary, "I visited the elderly father of Felipe de Jesús Chacón, who was violently killed, a catechist whom the people there consider a martyr of our faith. These are very friendly people. They welcome you with much affection and love to give and share what little they have."[83] Romero had visited this canton the previous year for the celebration of a mass on the second anniversary of the death of this catechist.[84] So many people attended that the mass had to be moved outdoors. The archbishop does not describe the circumstances of his death other than saying that the skin of his face was removed.[85] From the testimony of the people who knew him, Romero drew a sketch of Felipe de Jesús Chacón: "An admirable man who left a wondrous testimony that is remembered, above all, by the Christian *cursillos*. It was from his involvement in the Christian *cursillos* that he dedicated himself to work for the kingdom of God in a very edifying manner."[86]

From as early as the murder of Father Grande, Romero understood that he was pastor of a martyrial church. In fact, Romero can be considered the first martyrologist of the church in El Salvador.[87] José Ignacio González Faus refers to martyrdom as double gift: "Martyrdom is the gift of God for the martyr, and the martyr is the gift for the people of God."[88] Romero's funerary homilies were among other things the church's act of thanksgiving to God for the indescribable gift of the martyr. During his time as archbishop, celebrations of the Salvadoran martyrs were ecclesial events of the utmost importance. As the first anniversary of the deaths of Rutilio Grande, Manuel Solórzano, and Nelson Rutilio Lemus drew near, Romero invited the entire archdiocese to join him in El Paisnal for mass. "We have, brothers and sisters, an obligation to gather the memory of our dear coworkers, and if they have died under the martyrial sign, to gather also their example of integrity, of courage, so that the voice that they tried to silence with violence does not die but continues being the cry of Jesus Christ: Do not fear those who can kill only the body but leave the word of the eternal gospel resounding" (*Homilías*, 2:293).

What good are these memories? Are martyrologies the Christian equivalent of "Precious Moments"? Are they saccharine pieces of theological kitsch? No. The stories of the martyrs serve as signs of God's presence in the history of the churches and communities from whence they came. The church is both a church of martyrs (*ecclesia martyrum*) and a martyr church (*ecclesia martyr*). The martyrs make manifest the reality of the church's conformity to Christ the martyr. Rino Fisichella speaks of the martyrs as a kind of eye chart against which the church can measure its visual acuity. "Through their testimony, the church verifies that only on this path can the announcement of the gospel be rendered fully credible. This also explains the fact that the church has from its earliest years understood martyrdom as a privileged place for verifying the truth and efficaciousness of its proclamation."[89] Roberto Casas Andrés agrees: "Monseñor Romero, Rutilio Grande, Alfonso Navarro, and so many other Salvadoran martyrs can prepare our vision to discern the saving passage of God through our latitudes in the lives of so many witnesses who are still almost anonymous."[90] Like John the Baptist, they point away from themselves to the God who walks through history. For the stories of the martyrs to achieve this goal they have to become traditioned: that is to say, ritual and narrative practices need to develop that allow others to participate in the life and values of the martyr. The local practices by which the canton of El Salitre honored Felipe de Jesús are one stage of that tradition. Romero's homiletical martyrologies mark another stage. The retrospective reflection on these practices paves the path for still another stage in the traditioning of the martyrs—a theology of martyrdom.

Romero as Theologian of Martyrdom

The archbishop was more than a martyrologist. His homilies disclose a theologian of martyrdom at work. Jon Sobrino aptly describes El Salvador as a place where the *Sitz im Leben* (the context or place of life) is also the *Sitz im Tode* (a context or place of death).[91] In this context, reflection on martyrdom becomes intrinsic to the theological task.[92] The pedagogy of death at work in his country urged Archbishop Romero to understand the sacraments as matters of life and death. Confirmation was not simply a booster shot for baptism but "the sacrament of the martyrs" (*Homilías*, 2:61). "A martyr means a witness. A witness of a life that the world does not know. A witness of a life that the world does not know and for this reason persecutes and slanders. The one confirmed must be a brave young man or woman so as to give his face for Jesus, like the martyrs. We would not have the glorious pages of martyrdom in the church of Christ were it not for this gift of the Holy Spirit that you are about to receive" (*Homilías*, 2:486).

Confirmation is like an oasis where the confirmand finds refreshment for the *via dolorosa* that lies ahead.[93] The gift of the Spirit that comes through the bishop's laying on of hands strengthens the baptized so that they may produce fruit even in adverse conditions. It was the Holy Spirit that gave the disciples the courage to speak of Christ in the face of entrenched opposition from their fellow Jews. The celebration of this sacrament pointed the congregation to the same oasis that sustained the apostles. "Dear brothers and sisters, parents, starting with me, the bishop, may this morning be for us, then, like our renewal of the Holy Spirit, may confirmation become for us a sacrament of martyrdom. Let us also be ready to give our life for Christ and not betray the Lord with the cowardice of today's false Christians" (*Homilías*, 2:66).

For the sacrament of confirmation to be effective in this manner, Christians need to cultivate an attitude of receptivity. Old habits need to be unlearned and new ones acquired. In El Salvador it was customary to confirm children as infants, prompting Romero to ask: "Why were we confirmed?" (*Homilías*, 2:61). Without lay catechists like the martyred Felipe de Jesús, the people of God will be unformed and all the more easily conformed with the unjust situation in El Salvador. The Spirit given at confirmation makes the baptized more: more fruitful, more incorporated into Christ, more committed to the kingdom, more dedicated to the proclamation of the good news.

Romero's theology of martyrdom calls for the reinvigoration of church practices and also for expanding the categories by which the martyrs are recognized. As Romero told his confirmands, the word *martyr* means "witness." It is from the Greek term *martyrios* that the word is derived, as when the risen Christ tells his disciples: "You will be my *martyres*" (Acts 1:8). During the Christian era, the term *martyr* underwent a semantic evolution from the juridical realm to religious arena. Although the phenomenon of "martyrdom" in the sense of being killed for refusing to abandon the faith was well known, the "Martyrdom of Polycarp" (155 AD) was among the earliest uses of the word *martyr* in its current understanding.[94] It was in this time that the category of *odium fidei* became interlaced with the concept of martyrdom. For although a Christian might kill another Christian for a variety of reasons, it was taken for granted that only pagans, Jews, and heretics could kill Christians out of hatred of the faith.

In El Salvador, the persecutors of the church were other Christians, which complicated the application of the traditional categories. By their self-understanding, the "brother criminals," as Romero calls them, were not acting out of hatred of the faith (*Homilías*, 1:35). The oligarchy and its boosters saw themselves as true defenders of the faith. Yet they were fundamentally incoherent persons whose lives were countersigns of the kingdom. Romero's martyrology was populated with the names of people who were not killed out of *odium fidei* in the ordinary sense of the term, an animus against the creeds or the sacraments. "Why were they killed? They were killed because they were in the way" (*Homilías*, 5:354). They were killed out of *odium justitiae*. Jon Sobrino refers to the Salvadoran martyrs as Jesuanic martyrs. "The Jesuanic martyrs are not only, or even mainly, those who die *for* Christ or *because of Christ*, but those who die *like* Jesus and *for*

Jesus' cause."[95] Romero would agree with this provided the first part of the clause is not set over against the second one. Those who die for the cause of the kingdom of God die for Jesus Christ because he was the kingdom in person. The extension of the category of *odium fidei* is one that scripture itself encourages. Jesus himself teaches that "those who are persecuted for righteousness' sake" are blessed (Matt. 5:10). This teaching was handed down by the Christian tradition, and theologians as renowned as Thomas Aquinas asserted that hatred of the Christian faith was not the only direct source of martyrdom.[96] Thus Romero stands on very firm ground when he calls the murdered priests and catechists martyrs "in the popular sense" (*Homilías*, 5:354). Even as he stands on this firm basis, Romero does not presume to exceed his authority to adjudicate the merits of these particular cases and submits his martyrology and his theology of martyrdom to the judgment of the church.

Romero's theology of martyrdom emphasizes the love animating the martyrs and the community that honors them. Martyrs are remembered for their courageous resistance to evil and compromise.[97] They are praised in proportion to the justice of the cause to which they witnessed. But the distinguishing mark of the Christian martyrs is love. Without love, the sacrifice of their life and limbs would mean nothing (cf. 1 Cor. 13:2). It is love that animates their faith (cf. Gal. 5:6), and the greatness of their love is made visible in their willingness to risk losing life not for noble ideas but for friends (cf. John 15:13). According to Hans Urs von Balthasar, "The Christian does not die for an idea, however sublime, like human dignity, liberty, solidarity with the oppressed (even though this is all in play and included). The Christian dies for someone and for someone who previously died for him."[98] Romero would agree, but he would amend the Swiss theologian. The Christian martyr may not die for the idea of "solidarity with the oppressed" but may well be killed for teaching this idea and may die in loving solidarity with the oppressed and the God of the oppressed.

If love is the hallmark of the Christian martyr, then martyrdom cannot be reduced to an individual's heroic act of love; it has an ecclesial dimension. Escobar Alas states that martyrdom "helps cement the unity of the church around Christ and issues through its testimony an invitation into the body of Christ."[99] Martyrdom turns death squads' motto *Haz patria, mata un cura* (Build the fatherland, kill a priest) on its head. As witnesses of the sacrificial love of Christ, the martyr's act of love builds the church as an outpost of the land of the Father, the kingdom of God. Romero's word to the eavesdropping assassins of Rutilio Grande on All Saints Day 1977 enacts this theology. "We do not hate you . . . because the Christian does not hate. I imagine Father Grande and the martyrs of our persecution in heaven asking intently to the Lord for their executioners so that they may be converted and one day enjoy the happiness that comes from having been faithful to the Lord" (*Homilías*, 1:431).

Romero's message of love does not gloss over the crimes of the guilty and the injustice of the situation. He condemns the executioners as cowardly and deluded. Nor does Romero wink at the sins of the martyred. He admits that the Salvadoran martyrs are not without sin. The murdered priests had their flaws too.[100] Yet their endurance of hardship, their identification with the poor, and their baptism by blood were effective in washing their stains away (*Homilías*, 5:355). For Romero, though purity of life was vital, the holiness of the Salvadoran martyrs shone more clearly through the abundance of their love.[101]

Rereading the Vivens Homo

In Irenaeus's theology, the best paradigm of the *vivens homo* is the martyr. These witnesses are the ones who have allowed themselves to be vivified by the Spirit and led to whatever end would make them most transparent to the glory of God. In his study of Irenaeus's theology, John Behr argues that two witnesses in particular informed the bishop of Lyon's theology of martyrdom: Ignatius and Blandina.[102]

Ignatius, the martyred bishop of Antioch, famously expressed his longing to be a grain of wheat ground by the wild beasts as an offering to God. His death threw light on the bond between Eucharist and martyrdom.[103] In the gospels, the institution of the Eucharist is closely related to the narrative of the passion of Jesus Christ. This link was proclaimed plainly by Paul: "For as often as you eat this bread and drink the cup, you proclaim the Lord's death until he comes"

(1 Cor. 11:26). The driving force of the drama of history is the love of God, a love made manifest in Jesus's sacrificial obedience.[104] In this drama, the Eucharist is not just a courage booster. Partaking of the body and blood of Christ unites the Christian to Christ's act of obedience unto death. In this union, the martyr is strengthened by Christ's own strength and prolongs Christ's own witness. The eschatological dimension of the Eucharist is also manifest in martyrdom, where the kingdom is open to the martyrs. This dimension can be seen in the biblical account of the death of Stephen, who has a vision of Jesus standing by the throne of God in a posture of welcome, ready to crown his witness's triumph (cf. Acts 7:55–56). Similar motifs are found in the accounts of the martyrdoms of Ignatius and Polycarp. The connection between Eucharist, eschatology, and martyrdom is especially applicable to the martyrdom of Ignatius and that of Romero. In their martyrdom, their grain of wheat is baked by the Spirit into bread for the life of the world—*vivens homo, vivens panis.*

The second exemplar in Irenaeus's theology of martyrdom was a slave girl martyred in Lyons. Irenaeus writes in *The Letter of the Churches of Vienne and Lyons* of a great persecution of Christians that took place in Gaul in 177.[105] Of the Christians arrested, some, seeing the kind of torture and death that awaited them, renounced the faith. The heroine in the story is Blandina. Her example of fidelity inspired the wavering will of the believers to remain true. According to the letter, "Blandina was suspended on a stake, and exposed to be devoured by the wild beasts who should attack her. And because she appeared as if hanging on a cross, and because of her earnest prayers, she inspired the combatants with great zeal. For they looked on her in her conflict, and beheld with their outward eyes, in the form of their sister, him who was crucified for them, that he might persuade those who believe in him, that everyone who suffers for the glory of Christ has fellowship always with the living God."[106]

The role of Blandina in the story is surprising. John Behr observes that "she is named, while her mistress is not, and as a young slave girl she is the epitome of weakness in the ancient world, and therefore also the vessel in which the power of God can be fully manifest."[107] Blandina's social and physical weakness would have habituated her to relying on power that was not her own, namely the power of the Holy Spirit. The identification of this woman from the margins as an exemplar of the *vivens homo* blazes the way for Romero's *ressourcement* of Irenaeus—*Gloria Dei, vivens pauper*. This theological vision is fully Irenaean; more than that, it is Christian. It reflects a biblical doctrine of election and a scriptural theology of history: "God chose what is foolish in the world to shame the wise" (1 Cor. 1:27); "Power is made perfect in weakness" (2 Cor. 12:9). Not only was she truly alive, but she gave life to others. Indeed this is a mark of life; it is life-giving— *vivens homo, vivificans homo*. When her companions looked on her, they grew stronger because they saw in the form of their sister the image of the crucified Christ, the God of the weak and the poor.

Like Blandina for Irenaeus, the poor for Romero are the least in the world, and for the same reason they are fitting vessels for God's power and presence. The weakness of the flesh of the poor, its vulnerability to hunger, thirst, bruising, piercing, and disappearance, softens it for the Spirit. Those who saw Blandina hanging on a stake "beheld with their outward eyes, in the form of their sister, him who was crucified for them."[108] These witnesses do not attain their vision of the crucified God-human by closing their eyes to the horror surrounding them but by looking at Blandina's suffering body "with their outward eyes." Likewise, the vision of the God of the poor can be attained only by looking in solidarity with eyes that have been opened by the Spirit to the need of the poor.

Like Irenaeus, Romero's theology of martyrdom identifies the martyr as the fulfilled human, the person fully alive. In Rutilio Grande, Romero saw an exemplar of the *vivens homo*. In what may well be wordplay on the martyred priest's name, Romero speaks of Father Rutilio as an exemplar of the greatness (*grandeza*) of the human. As Romero explains, "The greatness of the man is not found in moving to the city, nor is it in having titles, riches, money; the greatness of the man is found in being more of a man, more human" (*Homilías*, 2:320). Countering narratives that confuse greatness with progress and perhaps even "the American dream," Romero adds, "True development does not consist in having more but in being more, and Rutilio was what he began to be here." By pouring himself into the life of his parishes at Aguilares and El Paisnal, Rutilio became more human, more alive, more *grande*. Why was Grande martyred? Because he gave life to the poor. Romero was emphatic on this point in his address at Louvain. Not all priests were being persecuted. Only those who dedicated themselves to working among the poor and to denouncing the structures that kept them poor were targeted as subversive. In El Salvador, liberation and martyrdom are not simply juxtaposed, nor is the latter the consolation for the failures of the former: the two are meant to be complementary. In the case of El Salvador, liberation and martyrdom were linked together from early on. The martyrs were witnesses of liberation, and they were martyred for this reason. The *vivens homo* is the one who orients his or her life to the *vivens pauper*, the one who has heeded Paul VI's admonition that social conditions need to change from less human to more human ones.[109] For Romero, the martyrs witness to the true worth of life. Their witness can be summed up by a simple aphorism: "No tener más, sino ser más" (*Homilías*, 2:321).

"Not having more, but being more." The aphorism has its proximate roots in the Petrine ministry of Paul VI. At an address to the diplomatic corps on January 7, 1965, the pope spoke of the importance of holding together technical and moral development. "It is not enough that humanity grows in what it has, it needs to grow in what it is. And to return to the well-known expression of a contemporary philosopher, it is the 'supplement of soul' that the great body of humanity most needs at present."[110] The philosopher to whom Paul VI alludes is in all likelihood Henri Bergson. In *Two Sources of Morality*, Bergson writes of the need for a "supplément d'âme" to humanize the scientific progress achieved in modernity.[111] Without this supplement, the purpose of the universe, which Bergson describes as a "machine for making gods," will go unfulfilled.[112] The Bergsonian language is not repeated, but its personalist philosophy is found again later that year in *Gaudium et Spes* 35: "A man is more precious for what he is than for what he has." *Populorum Progressio* reprises these motifs. The achievement of greater justice and fraternity in the social sphere is more important than scientific advances. These advances are important. They provide, as it were, the raw materials that societies need to flourish, but they do not by themselves constitute human development. Paul VI interprets the contemporary longing for liberation as a desire to "do, know, and have more, in order to be more" (*Populorum Progressio* 5).[113]

Human nature is not static; diverse social conditions promote its progress or decline. As historical beings, human beings are not passive victims of their social circumstances; they have agency and responsibility to work toward the elimination of obstacles and advance toward their own fulfillment. "Each human can grow in humanity, in being worth more, in being more" (*Populorum Progressio* 15).[114] Individual responsibility does not eliminate the need for social accountability. Wealthy societies are charged to be on their guard against jealously seeking their own advantage without consideration to that of societies that are less prosperous. To selfishly pursue their good alone risks the most important values of any society, "sacrificing the will to be more to the desire to possess in greater abundance" (*Populorum Progressio* 49).[115] The addictive power of this desire was expressed with brutal honesty by the conquistador Bernardo de Vargas Machuca, whose motto was *A la espada y al compás, más y más y más y más* (By the sword and the compass, more and more and more and more).[116] Machuca's *más* makes him less, yet his nihilistic vision is at the root of the pedagogy of death that has been the legacy of Latin America. This vision contributes to the dystopic world terrifyingly described by Ivan Petrella and named with tragic irony Vita, a world where a tiny portion of humanity treats the vast majority as speed bumps on the road of their *dolce vita*.[117] The society that adopts Machuca's vision will find itself startled from its dreams by the hard words of the Lord: "Fool, this night your very soul will be demanded from you" (Luke 12:20).[118]

In Romero's Irenaean vision, the *vivens homo* is not one who has more but one who is more. "No tener más, sino ser más." The aphorism is repeated in Romero's homilies.[119] It could serve as the motto of Grande and the Salvadoran martyrs with one important addition: *dar más*. "No tener más, sino ser más, para dar más." Not having more but being more in order to give more. As we saw with Blandina, *vivens homo, vivificans homo*. This vision of the *vivens homo* as someone who gives to the *vivens pauper* informs the pedagogy of life that Romero hoped to inculcate in his archdiocese. The martyrs as *vivens homo* par excellence are the church's best pedagogues of life. This is one reason why the martyr can never be a figure of the past. The church that is faithful to the proclamation of the gospel will always have martyrs. In the words of Rino Fisichella, "In the martyr each one of us can see human coherence in its definitive transparency where the perfect identification of faith and life, verbal profession and daily action, is realized."[120] The correlation of life and martyrdom is performed in Archbishop Escobar Alas's decision to follow his pastoral letter on violence with one on martyrs.[121] The letter also presents the martyrs as those who have lived out their baptismal vocation to the full and can say with Rutilio Grande: "All life is Eucharist."[122] By water and Spirit they have become by grace what Jesus is by nature, beloved children in whom the Father is well pleased.[123]

One of the signs of our times is the desire for authenticity over authority and aesthetics over logic. Without denying the appeal of reasonable arguments, love is more credible, and greater love have none than the martyrs. They are the church's most eloquent preachers, perennial Chrysostoms. Fisichella states, "The history of the martyrs manifests with such lucidity that the death of each one of them, if on the one hand it stunned the spectators, on the other hand it shook their consciences to such a degree that they opened themselves to conversion and faith: *Sanguis martyrum, semen christianorum.*"[124] The witness of the martyrs is evidence that God's revelation still has the power to convert people today. The martyrs teach the church that the way to the kingdom is a mystagogical journey that follows the movement of Jesus in the gospels.[125] They also teach that the coming of the kingdom will evoke an ever-growing resistance from the profiteers of the present age. Romero's own martyrdom exemplifies the power and ambiguity of the witness of the martyrs.

Romero as Martyr

Jesuanic martyrs like Romero and Grande are the "introductory letter" to the book of the crucified peoples.[126] The power of Romero's martyrdom to point to their suffering depends to a significant extent on the truthfulness with which he is remembered. In the interest of this goal, it would behoove us to consider one of the most famous sayings associated with Romero: "If they kill me, I will rise again in the people of El Salvador."[127] The phrase has been cited many times and has become an interpretive slogan for Romero's theological vision. It was first published by José Calderón Salazar for the Mexican newspaper *Excelsior* on the day after Romero's death.

Despite the popularity that the phrase has enjoyed since its publication, there are serious questions regarding its authenticity.[128] The chronology of events as narrated by Calderón is difficult to square with what is known about Romero's schedule during those days. Moreover, the attitude toward death reported by the interview is at odds with that found in public and private statements of Romero. In public, Romero spoke with reserve about the possibility of being killed. Privately, he expressed fear about his death and experienced something akin to the *timor gehennalis* of Christ's agony in Gethsemane. The language attributed to Romero in the interview is at odds with that of his diaries, his sermons, and other records of his conversations. In fact, the language of the slogan resembles that of a statement written by Calderón in response to death threats that the Mexican journalist received in 1978.[129]

The theological vision voiced in the interview clashes in significant ways with the vision that he sought to cast during his time as archbishop. The ecclesiology of the phrase elides the distinction between the people of God and the people of El Salvador. This distinction was one that Romero emphasized as paramount before and after the alleged date of this interview. The church is the people of God. This means that it has its origin in God; it belongs to God and has its destiny in God. The people of El Salvador have a history that God desires to elevate into the history of salvation of which the church is the body. Confusing the people of God with the people of El Salvador would lead to either the idolatrization of the nation or the immanentization of the church. Neither alternative is ecclesiologically acceptable. It is precisely because the people of God are not identical to the people of El Salvador that the church receives a mission and has something unique to contribute to the national situation. The eschatology of the phrase resembles that of the leftist slogans carried on placards by members of the leftist popular organizations at the funeral of Romero. Many of these said something like "Romero is not dead. He lives in the fights of the people."[130] This is agonistic and wholly immanent eschatology. There is little sense here of the "not yet" horizon of hope or the palm of martyrdom or the joy of entering the kingdom. It resembles a doctrine of resurrection sung in the Credo of the Misa Nicaragüense.[131]

Vos estáis resucitando
en cada brazo que se alza
para defender al pueblo
del dominio explotador;
porque estáis vivo en el rancho,
en la fábrica, en la escuela,
creo en tu lucha sin tregua,
creo en tu resurrección.

You are resurrecting
in each arm that is raised
to defend the people
from oppressive exploitation
because you are alive in the ranch
in the factory, in the school,
I believe in your tireless struggle.
I believe in your resurrection.

As we saw in chapter 4, Romero was familiar with this Christology, but he accepted it only with caveats. He would never limit the presence of Christ to the places of struggle, nor would he limit the places of struggle to those represented by popular political organizations. Instead, he would want to find ways of illuminating the just claims of these groups by the light of the risen Christ and find ways of strengthening historical hopes by the power of the transcendent hope of the gospel. We will never know for sure whether Romero claimed that he would be raised in the Salvadoran people. Calderón never retracted the story, and its posthumous publication closed the door on any challenges by Romero. Whatever may be the case, even if this were authentic it would not be representative of his theological vision.

More characteristic of Romero's theological vision are the reflections he wrote down in his journal during what turned out to be his final spiritual exercises conducted in Planes de Renderos from February 25 to 29, 1980. By Calderón's chronology, this retreat happened over a week before the late-night interview. In his journal, Romero restated the principle that guided his pastoral ministry: "The primacy of the human over created things. Humans should have at their disposal the material things necessary for their integral salvation."[132] He reflected on the importance of his role as archbishop and his fears that personal vanity or vulnerability to ideology would frustrate his desire to "encounter Christ and participate obediently in God's saving plan."[133] Romero also meditated on his death. He felt the snare of his enemies drawing ever closer and was afraid. He feared for his friends because an attempt on his life might well strike others near him.[134] But he feared for himself too. "It is hard for me to accept a violent death," he wrote.[135] Father Azcue offered encouragement to his archbishop, and Romero received it. He writes: "Jesus helped the martyrs, and, if necessary, I will feel him very near when I surrender to him my last breath. But more valuable than the moment of death is surrendering to him one's whole life, to live for him."[136] Romero concludes his notes to the exercises with a prayer of consecration to God and rededication to the Sacred Heart of Jesus.

> Thus I consent my consecration to the Sacred Heart of Jesus, which was always my source of inspiration and Christian joy of my life. Thus I also place under his loving providence my entire life and accept with faith in him my death, no matter how hard it may be. I do not even want to give my death an intention as I would like for the peace of my country or the flowering of our church . . . because the Heart of Jesus will know how to give it the meaning he wants. Being happy and confident are enough for me, knowing with certainty that in him is my life and my death, that, in spite of my sins, I have placed trust in him and I will not be confounded,

and that others will continue the works of the church and the country with more wisdom and holiness.[137]

In contrast with Calderón's interview, Romero refuses to assign a particular meaning to his death. He entrusts all his hopes and fears to the sacred heart of Jesus. Almost twenty years earlier, during another set of spiritual exercises, Romero had confessed his longing to be known as "being the bishop of the heart of Jesus."[138] The consecration to the heart of Jesus meant for Romero not the end of struggle with death but a new phase in that struggle that would lead to the altar of *El Hospitalito* on March 24, 1980. Damian Zynda's summation of Romero's spirituality better captures the complexity of the martyred archbishop's theological vision than Calderón's famous interview.

> Oscar Romero possessed a longing for God that remained constant throughout his life—although its content and form shifted. How he understood that longing and the manner through which he encountered God, however, broadened, deepened, and widened as he grew in self-knowledge and matured in his relationship with God. Graced, yet wounded, he struggled against the temptation to deny his humanity and divinity. In his graced struggles, Romero was recreated and reoriented more fully toward God and concerns outside himself. His sustained struggles advanced him farther into the vision of God, and in the process, Romero revealed God's glory.[139]

THE HOPE OF GLORY

Romero returned to El Salvador from his trip to Louvain on February 6, 1980.[140] He landed at the new airport near La Libertad around 4:00 p.m. and was met by Father Urrutia along with other friends. On the drive to San Salvador, they discussed the latest events in the nation. Forty-five minutes later they arrived at the Divina Providencia hospital. The *Hospitalito*, a hospice center for cancer patients, was the place where Romero lived during his years as archbishop, but it was more than that. It was his home, his spiritual oasis. By praying and sharing the most ordinary aspects of his life along with some of his sickest parishioners and the Carmelite sisters who cared for them, Romero renewed his faith. When he arrived to the *Hospitalito* on that afternoon, he was met by the sisters, who were overjoyed to see him, and by a mountain of mail that had piled up in his absence. Romero recorded his impressions of this encounter: "How wonderful to return home, after some days of absence! However, the worries have begun."[141] In the weeks ahead, the worries grew, but Romero did not despair. The dominant note in his life was hope, and this note resounded with power in his final homily.

The Anniversary Mass for Sara Meardi de Pinto

It is worth pausing to ponder a curious fact. Óscar Romero was not killed while preaching one of his two-hour-long homilies to a packed cathedral and an international radio audience. He was killed while celebrating an intimate mass for the eternal rest of Sara Meardi de Pinto on the first anniversary of her death. Romero was targeted for assassination because he was a prophet; he got in the way. But he died as a priest fulfilling his pastoral duties. On account of this coincidence of dates, the martyrdom of Óscar Romero is now mysteriously yoked to the memory of Sara Meardi de Pinto.

Who was Sara Meardi de Pinto?[142] Sara Meardi belonged to an upper-class family. Her father, Mauricio Meardi, was at one point the largest coffee producer and wealthiest man in El Salvador. Sara grew up in a household where attending boarding school in Switzerland was a family tradition. When her grandson Jorge Francisco was born, the polyglot Sara sang nursery rhymes to him in German, French, and Italian. By contrast, Jorge Pinto, who married Sara in 1929, had a family background in journalism and showed greater affinity with the struggles of the poor masses than the conservative Meardi family. When the journalistic activities of Jorge Pinto Sr. landed him in jail in 1943, Sara took her son to visit his father daily. While languishing in jail, Jorge Sr. was seriously wounded during a firefight. The resulting injuries left him incapacitated, and Sara dedicated most of her energies to caring for her convalescing husband. His final words to his wife as he died in 1957 were "Sarita, never stop looking for the truth."[143] Later on, when the son followed in the footsteps of the father and was incarcerated for his antigovernment reporting, Sara visited him in jail and supported him through his hunger strikes.[144] On March 24, 1979, after months of health struggles, Sara Meardi de Pinto succumbed to a thrombosis and died. Regarding his mother's death, Jorge Jr. wrote in *El Independiente* that she "embraced our cause with love because our cause was based on love of country, love of the people, love of democracy, love of our friends and enemies, love of the dispossessed and love of those who possess everything. She, our mother, inspired all this in us and accompanies us on the path of sacrifices for peace and concord."[145] By her very life, Sara Meardi understood and taught that one cannot be a Christian while absolutizing riches.[146]

Romero knew the family of Doña Sarita well. He appreciated the work of *El Independiente* in printing stories that presented the truth about the persecution of the church. When Jorge Pinto became sick, Romero lifted this prayer concern in his Sunday homily (*Homilías*, 6:64–65). On more than one occasion, Romero had dinner at the home of the Pintos and even gave piggyback rides to Doña Sarita's grandson.[147]

At the anniversary mass of March 24, 1980, Jorge Pinto tells of seeing Romero kneeling in prayer, breviary in hand, as people arrived for the mass. The congregation that Monday afternoon included family members and friends of the Meardi and Pinto families, staff of *El Independiente*, and nuns and patients from the *Hospitalito*. In other words, the congregation resembled a snapshot of Salvadoran society.

The reading on which Romero based his homily came from John 12:23–26. In this pericope, Jesus compares his glorification to the fate of a grain of wheat that falls to the ground and, by dying, brings forth much fruit. The homily begins by presenting Doña Sarita as a witness to the true liberation that El Salvador needs. Romero praises her noble spirit and generosity. She oriented all her cultural formation and elegance to the cause of liberation. She was the grain of wheat that was fruitful in life and in death. In a jarring if by now characteristic move, Romero chooses a paragraph from *Gaudium et Spes* as Doña Sarita's encomium and exordium. Her witness confirms the hopes articulated by the council fathers at Vatican II. For understanding the weight of this reference to *Gaudium et Spes* it would be helpful to offer an interpretive framework. First, I will consider the place of paragraph 39 within the conciliar document. Then I will examine Romero's usage of this paragraph in his homilies.

Hopes and Hope in Gaudium et Spes *39*

Gaudium et Spes is a peculiar document with a complex history.[148] At one level, it complements the Dogmatic Constitution on the Church, *Lumen Gentium*. Whereas that document looked *ad intra* to the nature of the church, *Gaudium et Spes* was more focused *ad extra* on its mission. The document adopts an inductive methodology that correlates the signs of the times with theological resources. Each chapter begins by posing a contemporary problem and ends with a dense Christological solution.[149] *Gaudium et Spes* 39 is the theological coda concluding the chapter that reflects on the value of human activity. The questions that people are asking themselves regarding the purpose of human activity at the individual and social level find their answer in the coming kingdom of God. The transformation of all things in Christ might seem to make historical ends superfluous. If there is going to be a new earth, why waste time and energy worrying about this earth? The council fathers teach the opposite. The consummation of history shows the transcendent value of historical events.

> We do not know the time for the consummation of the earth and of humanity, nor do we know how all things will be transformed. As deformed by sin, the shape of this world will pass away; but we are taught that God is preparing a new dwelling place and a new earth where justice will abide, and whose blessedness will answer and surpass all the longings for peace which spring up in the human heart. Then, with death overcome, the sons of God will be raised up in Christ, and what was sown in weakness and corruption will be invested with incorruptibility. Enduring with charity and its fruits, all that creation which God made on man's account will be unchained from the bondage of vanity. Therefore, while we are warned that it profits a man nothing if he gain

the whole world and lose himself, the expectation of a new earth must not weaken but rather stimulate our concern for cultivating this one. For here grows the body of a new human family, a body which even now is able to give some kind of foreshadowing of the new age. Hence, while earthly progress must be carefully distinguished from the growth of Christ's kingdom, to the extent that the former can contribute to the better ordering of human society, it is of vital concern to the Kingdom of God. For after we have obeyed the Lord, and in His Spirit nurtured on earth the values of human dignity, brotherhood and freedom, and indeed all the good fruits of our nature and enterprise, we will find them again, but freed of stain, burnished and transfigured, when Christ hands over to the Father: "a kingdom eternal and universal, a kingdom of truth and life, of holiness and grace, of justice, love and peace." On this earth that Kingdom is already present in mystery. When the Lord returns it will be brought into full flower. (*Gaudium et Spes* 39)

Published versions of this passage include up to ten footnotes for the one paragraph, and some of these footnotes include multiple references. The biblical references all come from the New Testament, mostly from Paul.[150] In addition to these, there are references to Pius XI's *Quadragesimo Anno*, the preface for Christ the King, and even Irenaeus.[151] In agreement with Paul, the bishop of Lyon asserts that the figure of this world is passing away but that its substance and matter remain. God does not wipe the slate clean. The new creation is not out of nothing, *ex nihilo*. God renews the things that he made in his wisdom. The new creation comes from the old, *ex vetera*. Glimmers of the new creation already shine in the present age and strengthen hope for the transfiguration of all things in Christ. These rays also shed light on the relation between earthly progress and the growth of the kingdom of God. Without a proper vision of this relation, the object of hope is blurred and the journey of humanity toward God turns to either quietist alienation or Promethean activism.

Romero appeals to *Gaudium et Spes* 39 in three sermons prior to his martyrial homily. He uses the passage in his homily for Ascension Day 1978, titled "The Hour of Glorification." Commenting on the Ascension passage from Acts 1, Romero terms Christ the Lord of history. This is a common title in Romero's Christological book.[152] He attributes it to Vatican II. No doubt he has in mind *Gaudium et Spes* 41: "For though the same God is Savior and Creator, Lord of human history as well as of salvation history, in the divine arrangement itself, the rightful autonomy of the creature, and particularly of man is not withdrawn, but is rather re-established in its own dignity and strengthened in it." The history of salvation that is celebrated by the liturgical calendar and the history of the nation marked in the civic calendar are distinct but not divorced; they hold hands in the journey of the people of God through the history of El Salvador. The manner in which Romero lifts up the events of the week to the light of the gospel is possible only because Christ is the Lord of history. He is the alpha and the omega, the cornerstone and compass for all social movements. The Lord of history has the power to redeem history. Nothing is to be lost.[153] He can smooth the jagged edges and fit the apparently disconnected fragments together. In the offering of these to the Father, temporality is wondrously raised into eternity without being swept away. The Thomistic axiom regarding the relation of nature and grace in the economy of salvation can be adapted to this situation. Eternity does not destroy history but perfects it. God "uses the history of the peoples to inject his history of salvation" (*Homilías*, 3:472). The Lord of history is the Lord of eternity. In him, the eternal glory of God shines on the darkness of Salvadoran history and promises its definitive transfiguration. *Gaudium et Spes* 39 helps Romero highlight the convergence without confusion of temporal progress and the growth of the kingdom of God. Improving the infrastructure and investing in the social institutions of the country do not bring about the kingdom of God, but "the more a people progresses in a humanist way, the more it disposes itself to be the matter that God saves" (*Homilías*, 2:473). To speak in more overtly Irenaean terms, Christian social action habituates history to the presence and work of the Holy Spirit.

Romero's second reference to *Gaudium et Spes* 39 is found in a homily from November 19, 1978, titled "The Church, a Community Actively Waiting for the Return of Christ." In it, Romero speaks of salvation as a historical and communal event. For Romero, Christians live in the final phase of history, the day of the Lord, a day of certainty, doubt, and readiness. The tension between the certainty regarding the coming of his day and the uncertainty regarding the day of his coming is key to Christian spirituality. It is a tension that fuels expectation, hope. The relaxation of the tension contributes to spiritual sloth; the gospel promises become the opiate of the people. Instead of being ready, the church falls asleep at its post.[154] Romero reads *Gaudium et Spes* as a modern-day parable of the Wise Virgins that reminds the church to wait for the kingdom by using the things of this world to prepare the way (*Homilías*, 3:405). For Romero, *Gaudium et Spes* 39 renews God's promise for the transfiguration of all peoples while offering a timely warning to not get too comfortable on Tabor. "It is very nice to live off a piety of songs and prayers, spiritual meditations, and contemplation alone. That will come in the hour of heaven, where there will not be any injustices, where sin will not be a reality that Christians have to dethrone. . . . Now—Jesus said to the apostles who were contemplative on Tabor and did not want to leave ever— let us go down, there is work to do" (*Homilías*, 3:406).

The eschatological light of glory illumines the problems of earth so as to encourage the church in its work. Christians are called to reflect the eschatological life even in the midst of the earthly pilgrimage. *Gaudium et Spes* 39 encourages Christians to descend Tabor in order to promote social progress that contributes to the common good of all (not the few). Romero's church has started workshops for seamstresses and bakers so that people will progress materially in a manner that also promotes their spiritual development. Social progress cannot be confused with the kingdom of God, but it can assist it. For its part, things eternal serve as the compass that points to the true north of temporal progress and the ruler that measures where progress has fallen short. In spite of everything, Romero finds hope in his congregation. "What beautiful hope! Even when our preaching goes against the flow and it seems as if we are plowing in the sea, we know that the work we do now shall yield fruits of conversion and holiness" (*Homilías*, 3:408).

The third homily where Romero appeals to *Gaudium et Spes* 39 was preached on February 10, 1980, "God Calls Us to Build Our History with Him." The encounter of the human with the glory of God is a humbling one. Before the majesty of God, Peter falls to his knees, Isaiah professes his uncleanness, and Paul sees himself as an aborted one. The manner in which God cleanses Isaiah, raises Peter, and restores Paul's vision exemplifies how God wants to offer the project of true liberation to humankind. In El Salvador, three projects jockey for first place in defining and building the nation. The most radical plan of liberation is that of the kingdom of God. "No matter how bold an agrarian transformation or the nationalization of the banks, beyond these there is God offering the nationalization of the children of God, the liberation from sin" (*Homilías*, 6:256). The Christian is committed to building history according to God's design. *Gaudium et Spes* 39 then serves as a reminder not to confuse earthly progress with the coming of the kingdom. At the same time, the passage serves as a goad that pushes society to reflect more and more the kingdom of God. At a minimum, this calls for removing hindrances to the kingdom. "And the project of the kingdom of God is opposed to a situation in which the few have everything and the majority have nothing" (*Homilías*, 6:256).

In sum for Romero, *Gaudium et Spes* 39 preaches Christ as the Lord of history. He is the alpha, the omega, and also the way; the origin, summit, center, and goal of temporal existence.[155] Since Christ is the Lord of history, there is a Chalcedonian logic to history. Secular history and salvation history must be united without confusion and distinguished without separation. This logic carries over into hope, where one can distinguish between secular hopes and eschatological hope. On the one hand, when these hopes are collapsed, the proclamation of the Church is tempted by the monophysite heresy. The sacred swallows the secular. Christianity becomes a homogenizing historical force that robs earthly hopes of any legitimate autonomy or significance. One might say that this was the temptation that the church fought against during the Christendom era. On the other hand, when these hopes are separated, the church's message of hope appears to be of little relevance for the many aspirations and longings of contemporary society. This is the situation in which the church seems to find itself in postmodern societies, where the most common response to the proclamation of the gospel is an indifferent yawn.[156]

The dynamics of hope that Romero illustrates from *Gaudium et Spes* 39 receive a profound articulation by Thomas Aquinas that will help us understand Romero's usage. Aquinas speaks of hope as "a movement of the appetitive power ensuing from the apprehension of a future good, difficult but possible to obtain [*boni futuri ardui possibilis adipisci*]; namely, a stretching forth of the appetite to such a good."[157] Secular hopes differ from eschatological hopes with respect to their end. The future, arduous, possible good that is the object of secular hope is immanent and historical. Economic justice, racial equity, national security, political stability are all proper objects of secular hope. On account of the multiplicity of human historical ends, secular hopes are plural. By contrast, the object of eschatological hope is singular, transcendent, and eternal, namely God. It is not that human beings have two different ends, one historical and another eternal, that then need to be reconciled. Instead, human beings have one end, the vision of God in eternity, to which all historical ends and hopes are oriented. Dominic Doyle defines the unity in distinction of secular hopes and eschatological hope in terms of participation. "Gathered into the 'great hope,' secular hopes cannot be regarded as ultimately insignificant, in the sense of bearing no relation to God as the final end. To the contrary, insofar as they participate in the primary goal of hope, they are caught up in the movement to God as the ultimate end."[158] Hope is the virtue of the wayfarer, and eschatological hope, because it is already united to God, serves to purify and perfect secular hopes. The hope in the resurrection of the body empowers the courage to resist those who can kill the body but not the soul. Secular hopes for their part are intrinsic to human existence as historical and material beings; their perfection and elevation prepare persons for union with God.

In Romero's final homily, *Gaudium et Spes* 39 is more than an argument from authority: it is Sarita's sermon to those gathered to pray for her. She is an exemplar of the "great hope" that unites the longings of the Salvadoran people. She understood the restlessness that drove her husband and son to work for improving society by speaking the truth as journalists. Indeed, in her own way, she was their collaborator in the struggle for liberation. Her ecclesial word teaches the gathered assembly that working to ameliorate the situation of sin in which the country finds itself is not an optional endeavor from which some Christians may excuse themselves. Working for the betterment of society is not a matter of counsel. On the contrary, "It is a task that God blesses, God wants, and God demands from us" (*Homilías*, 6:456). The ideals that guide this task may well come from outside the church. Christianity does not have a monopoly on good ideas, ideals, or idealists. The uniqueness of the church and its contribution to these ideals comes from having people like Doña Sarita, people who have been schooled in eschatological hope: "We have to try to purify these ideals in Christianity. We have to dress them in hope of what lies beyond because this makes them stronger, because we have the assurance that all these ideals that we work for on earth, if we feed them with Christian hope, will never fail. We will find them purified in that kingdom where the reward is in proportion to what we have done on this earth" (*Homilías*, 6:457).

Doña Sarita did not write fiery editorials or publish explosive investigative reports, but she planted her own grain of wheat by setting aside her social privilege and standing by those in suffering. More than that, she herself entered into suffering, and from this crucible she prayed. Sarita prayed in life, and she prays in glory. Prayer may seem trivial, but it has the power to purify and strengthen the secular hopes that so many have for El Salvador. Eschatological hope sows seeds of eternity in history, and prayer is among the most eloquent expressions of hope.[159] The vision of God can transfigure the simplest of acts into signs of the kingdom. Everyone has at least a grain of wheat to contribute. The grain may be something as simple as an understanding smile or as radical as one's very life.

The Offering of Hope

The sermon ends with the expression of Romero's hope. He prays that the Eucharist may draw the people of God into communion with the life and death of Jesus for the sake of a harvest of peace and justice for the people of El Salvador. And since prayer is the interpreter of hope, Romero appropriately ends with an invitation to join in prayer.

> The holy mass, now, this Eucharist, is just such an act of faith. To Christian faith at this moment the host of wheat appears changed for the body of the Lord, who offered himself for the redemption of the world, and in this chalice the wine is transformed into the blood that was the price of salvation. May this body immolated and this blood sacrificed for humans nourish us also, so that we may give our body and our blood to suffering and to pain—like Christ, not for self, but to bring about harvests of justice and peace for our people. Let us join together, then, intimately in faith and hope at this moment of prayer for Doña Sarita and ourselves. (*Homilías*, 6:457–58)

The conjunction of Eucharist, martyrdom, and eschatology already explicit since Ignatius's letter to the Romans is performed at Romero's assassination. In the words of one of the sisters present, "It was as though the Lord had spoken to him: 'I don't want you just to offer me bread. Now you are the victim, you are my offering.' Monseñor fell immediately at the foot of the crucifix, offering up his priestly ministry just as he had done each day since his ordination."[160] Years earlier during his spiritual exercises Romero had the opportunity to reflect on his own mortality and recorded his meditations in his spiritual notebook. "I will die . . . fall. . . . I will be a dead leaf (the way)—humility. . . . The world will go on. . . . No one remembers those who have gone on. It is absurd to seek glory, a post. . . . *Sic transit gloria mundi.* The only thing that abides is love, having served God. The priest has so many opportunities. Death is the end of work. If death is feared, it is because there is something. . . . Why do I fear death? . . . What is definitive comes after death, which is like the graduation ceremony."[161]

According to Jesús Delgado, Romero found an answer to his questions in the words of Jesus from Revelation 3:20: "Listen! I am standing at the door, knocking; if you hear my voice and open the door, I will come in to you and eat with you, and you with me." As Delgado points out in his biography, Romero usually dined at 6:30 p.m.[162] He died at 6:25 p.m.

TO THE SALVADORAN TABOR AND BACK AGAIN

When Romero returned to El Salvador on February 16, 1979, from the meeting of bishops in Puebla, he met with an unusually hospitable reception from the airport authorities.[163] At least on this one occasion, the prophet was welcome in his home country. The airport manager personally cleared him through customs and made available the use of the diplomatic lounge, should the archbishop want to rest before heading out to the expectant crowds. Romero was appreciative of the gesture but declined. He longed to greet his friends, and besides he heard that there was going to be a mass celebrated at 7:30 p.m. in honor of his return. With little time to spare, Romero went straight to the cathedral, vested and processed into worship. In the homily, he expressed his gratitude for the gift of Puebla. The contact with fellow Latin American bishops and Pope John Paul II had enriched his heart. Nevertheless, he was glad to be back. "The most beautiful part of a trip, when one loves one's native land, is the return. I feel proud, satisfied, and deeply happy with you. It is a homecoming" (*Homilías*, 4:197).[164]

The strong sentiments that he felt for his congregation were mostly due to the bonds of prayer and witness that tied him to his archdiocese even while he was away. These sentiments were no doubt renewed by the applause that greeted his entrance to the cathedral and by the curious incident of the airport employee who, when unloading the archbishop's bag from the plane, was overheard saying, "There goes the truth." Romero admits: "The phrase fills me with optimism because in my suitcase I am not carrying contraband, nor am I packing lies, I bring the truth. I went to Puebla to learn more of the truth" (*Homilías*, 4:207).

In this book, we have traveled to the Salvadoran Tabor in order to learn more of Óscar Romero and his theological vision. There are many vistas that we did not see on our journey and some that we passed over too quickly. The fault in this case is not in Romero but in the guide. In any case, my hope is that in light of what we have seen, we can say with the unnamed baggage handler, "There goes the truth."[165]

After his homecoming from Puebla, Romero was asked if he would now need to change his preaching because of what he had learned there. Romero replied with a qualified negative. "There is no reason for the truth to change, the truth must always be said, perhaps with more nuance, but always acknowledging our limitations. The truth is the concrete word of a person who has his own style, his own way of being, but is no more than an instrument of God" (*Homilías*, 4:207–8).

Romero is not Christ, but he can be a window to Christ, or, as Todd Walatka calls him, an icon of the option for the poor. "His mission to serve and speak for the poor in El Salvador was driven by deep compassion and can be seen as one of the ways in which the Holy Spirit is speaking to our age."[166] Romero is a father of the Latin American church who has much to teach the church universal about homiletics, soteriology, Christology, ecclesiology, eschatology, and more. He is the *doctor transfigurado*, the voice of the voiceless, a pedagogue of life, a Salvadoran Irenaeus who preached the scandal of the Transfiguration: *Gloria Dei, vivens pauper*. But Romero is also a son of the church in El Salvador, and what he has to teach cannot be learned in abstraction from the people of God who raised him and whom he served. One of the meanings of the word *romero* is "pilgrim," and Óscar the pilgrim can be understood only within the communion of the pilgrim people of God in El Salvador. Without a sense of solidarity for the people for whom he lived and died (*sentir con la iglesia*), his teaching will be sidelined, perhaps by being relegated to the inspirational section of the bookstore. However, when Romero is seen not as a solitary saint or lonely pilgrim but as the first fruits of the rich theological fields of Latin America, then there is hope for new and greater harvest feasts. The grain of wheat that he was is a sign that Latin America can be a breadbasket for the church in its mission to the world.

Climbing the Salvadoran Tabor with Romero is an enlightening and enriching experience. It is good to be here! However, it would be a mistake to start building booths. Monseñor Romero's theological vision does not allow for settling down yet. He urges us to listen to Christ (*Ipsum audite!*) and return home carrying more of the truth of the *Divino Salvador del Mundo*. Miguel Cavada Díez and Guillermo Cuéllar's singing of this truth is an appropriate hymn to carry on the *Bajada* from the Salvadoran Tabor, rejoicing at the *Descubrimiento* of Romero's Christ and Christ's Romero, the pilgrim's Christ and Christ's pilgrim.

> Cristo mesoamericano
> Toma su cuerpo en tus manos
> Para ser un pueblo nuevo
> Con vida y dignidad.
> Cristo mesoamericano
> Bebe su sangre en tus labios
> Para ser un pueblo nuevo
> Con vida y dignidad.
>
> Cristo negro, Cristo maya,
> Cristo miskíto y chortí,
> Cristo lenca, Cristo nahua,
> Galileo y quiché.
> Cristo río y montaña,
> Cristo árbol, Cristo mar,
> Cristo puma y quetzal,
> Cristo selva por talar.
>
> Cristo pueblo maltratado.
> Cristo pascua y libertad.
> Cristo mucha muchedumbre,
> Que anhela resucitar.
> Cristo vida y esperanza;
> Cristo Verbo, Buena Nueva;
> Cristo voz de los profetas;
> Romero de la verdad.

Mesoamerican Christ
Take his body in your hands
To be a new people
With dignity and life.
Mesoamerican Christ
Drink his blood in your lips
To be a new people
With dignity and life.

Black Christ, Mayan Christ,
Mikito and Chorti Christ,
Lenca Christ, Nahuatl Christ,
Galilean and Kiché.
Christ the river and mountain,
Christ the tree, Christ the sea,
Christ the puma and quetzal,
Christ forest yet to be cut down.

Christ the mistreated people.
Christ Easter and liberty
Christ the great multitude
that longs to be resurrected.
Christ life and hope;
Christ the word, good news;
Christ, voice of the prophets;
Romero of truth.

Chapter 1. Introduction to a Scandal

1. José Luis Escobar Alas, ed., *Beatificación Monseñor Óscar Romero* (San Salvador: Archdiocese of San Salvador, 2015), xix. All translations from Spanish to English are my own.

2. Cf. Óscar Romero, *Homilías: Monseñor Óscar A. Romero*, ed. Miguel Cavada Diez, 6 vols. (San Salvador: UCA Editores, 2005–9), 3:331. Throughout, I use this edition for the homilies that Romero preached as archbishop. Subsequent citations are given parenthetically in the text. All translations from Spanish to English are my own. Romero speaks of the church as the mountain where the prophet Isaiah announces that the veil that covers the nations in ignominy will be removed.

3. Romero is citing from *III Conferencia General del Episcopado Latinoamericano* (also known as *Puebla*), paras. 32–39; hereafter cited in the text as *Puebla* with paragraph number(s). For the documents from the Latin American episcopal conferences (CELAM), I am using the version found in Consejo Episcopal Latinoamericano, ed., *Las cinco Conferencias Generales del Episcopado Latinoamericano* (Bogotá: San Pablo, 2014). All Spanish-English translations from these conference proceedings are my own.

4. Cf. ibid., 2:205–6. See also Karl Rahner, ed., *Sacramentum Mundi: An Encyclopedia of Theology*, vol. 6 (Montreal: Herder and Herder, 1970), 1–4; F. Compagnoni, G. Piana, and S. Privitera, eds., *Nuevo diccionario de teología moral* (Madrid: San Pablo, 1992), 579–84. The first are scandalized by anything. They make mountains out of molehills. The second are offended by virtues that they do not practice. Only the third react in an appropriate manner to the scandal of seeing someone fall.

5. Cf. Anna Peterson, *Martyrdom and the Politics of Religion: Progressive Catholicism in El Salvador's Civil War* (Albany: State University of New York Press, 1997), 24–42, 29.

6. Paul Lehmann, *The Transfiguration of Politics* (New York: Harper and Row, 1975). For Lehmann, Jesus's transfiguration points to both a

reconfiguration of law and power. It signals a refocusing toward people affected by systems of organization and governing thought and practice. The moment of Transfiguration in the Gospel of Matthew reasserts the humanizing work of Jesus's messianic presence.

7. James R. Brockman, *Oscar Romero: Bishop and Martyr* (Maryknoll, NY: Orbis Books, 1982); José Delgado Acevedo, *Óscar A. Romero: Biografía* (San Salvador: UCA Editores, 1990); Marie Dennis, Renny Golden, and Scott Wright, *Oscar Romero: Reflections on His Life and Writings* (Maryknoll, NY: Orbis Books, 2000); Jon Sobrino, *Archbishop Romero: Memories and Reflections* (Maryknoll, NY: Orbis Books, 1990); Ana María Pineda, *Romero and Grande: Companions on the Journey* (Hobe Sound, FL: Lectio, 2016); Martin Maier, *Óscar Romero: Mística y lucha por la justicia* (Barcelona: Editorial Herder, 2015); Santiago Mata, *Monseñor Romero: Pasión por la iglesia* (Madrid: Ediciones Palabra, 2015); Roberto Morozzo della Rocca, *Primero Dios: Vida de Monseñor Romero* (Buenos Aires: Edhasa, 2010); Scott Wright, *Oscar Romero and the Communion of Saints* (Maryknoll, NY: Orbis Books, 2009).

8. For a helpful summary of this debate, see Roberto Casas Andrés, *Dios pasó por El Salvador: La relevancia teológica de las tradiciones narrativas de los mártires salvadoreños* (Bilbao: Desclée De Brouwer, 2009), 179–85. Casas Andrés helpfully contrasts the two readings of Romero as the conversion theory and the evolutionary theory. The first theory was more common in the first decades following the assassination and was motivated more by a desire to keep alive the cause for which Romero died than by a desire for historiographical accuracy. The second theory has been more common in recent decades as the process of beatification took off and an attempt to discover the "historical" was undertaken. The first approach is characteristic of Sobrino's *Archbishop Romero* and María López Vigil's *Piezas para un retrato* (San Salvador: UCA Editores, 1990). The standard bearer for the second approach is Morozzo della Rocca, *Primero Dios*, 185–95.

9. These two titles are nicely conjoined by Carlos Omar Durán Vasquéz in his thesis "Óscar Romero: Hijo y padre de la iglesia: La eclesiología de sus homilías" (master's thesis, Pontificia Universidad Antonianum, 2015).

10. Casas Andrés, *Dios pasó*, 188–92.

11. *Orientación*, March 30, 1980, 4. *Orientación* was the weekly paper for the archdiocese of San Salvador.

12. Ibid.

13. Ibid., 3.

14. Ibid., 2.

15. Casas Andrés, *Dios pasó*, 192–98.

16. Escobar Alas, *Beatificación Monseñor Óscar Romero*, xviii.

17. Ibid., xx.

18. Rodolfo Cardenal, "Mons. Romero: 'Padre de los pobres.' Un beato muy incómodo," *Revista Latinoamericana de Teología* 95 (2015): 139–62.

19. Ibid., 154.

20. Ibid., 161.

21. Cf. Casas Andrés, *Dios pasó*, 210–12.

22. "'El Profeta,' Yolocamba-Ita," *Por el valle de las hamacas* (blog), March 24, 2014, https://lfnt.wordpress.com/2014/03/24/el-profeta-yolocamba-ita/.

23. Casas Andrés, *Dios pasó*.

24. Ibid., 177.

25. José Comblin, "The Holy Fathers of Latin America," in *Fathers of the Church in Latin America*, ed. Silvia Scatena, Jon Sobrino, and Luiz Carlos Susin (London: SCM Press, 2009), 13–23.

26. Elmar Klinger, "Fathers of the Universal Church in Latin America," in Scatena, Sobrino, and Susin, *Fathers of the Church*, 102.

27. Ana María Bidegain and Maria Clara Bingemer rightly note that "the classic patristic figure is a wise man, holy and well-versed in grammar, speaking from his *cathedra*, backed by the institutional authority of the Church, and in many cases locked as much in polemical argument against his fellow-theologians as against those he is attacking as heretics, as though it fell to him alone to define the ultimate criteria of catholicity." Ana María Bidegain and Maria Clara Bingemer, "Latin American Matristics: Beginnings of Recognition?," in Scatena, Sobrino, and Susin, *Fathers of the Church*, 89–90.

28. In spite of these difficulties, women like Sor Juana Inés de la Cruz are now being called Latin American church mothers on account of their contribution to church life and thought. Michelle Gonzalez, *Sor Juana: Beauty and Justice in the Americas* (Maryknoll, NY: Orbis Books, 2003), 197.

29. Cf. Comblin, "Holy Fathers," 14–15.

30. Henrique de Lima Vaz, "Igreja-reflexo vs. igreja-fonte," *Cadernos Brasileiros* 46 (1968): 17–22. His terminology of source-churches and reflection-churches has also been adopted by Alberto Methol Ferré, an Uruguayan philosopher whose historical analysis of Latin America left a deep impression on that of Pope Francis. Alberto Methol Ferré and Alver Metalli, *La América Latina del siglo XXI* (Buenos Aires: Edhasa, 2006).

31. For most of its history, Latin American Catholicism was strongly stamped by Tridentine Catholicism. This form of Catholicism placed high value on the sacred immanence of God. Material objects could be transparent veils to the divine presence. Relics and images played a very important

role in Tridentine piety in the Americas. The latter were brought over from Europe but were also manufactured locally from the beginning of the colonial era. Of course, the material locus of sacred immanence par excellence was the Eucharist. The theology of Trent reaffirmed the doctrine of transubstantiation, which in turn ratified local piety. Tridentine piety emphasized the importance of self-mortification. At the same time it was a communitarian piety that encouraged the building of rich worship spaces, pilgrimages to shrines, public processions on feast days, and the formation of *cofradías*, lay religious societies to assist the clergy in coordinating these efforts. See Brian Larkin, "Tridentine Catholicism in the New World," in *Cambridge History of Religions in Latin America*, ed. Virginia Garrard-Burnett, Paul Freston, and Stephen C. Dove (New York: Cambridge University Press, 2016), 107–32.

32. Alfonso García Rubio, "Em direção à V Conferência Geral do Episcopado da AL e do Caribe: Fidelidade ao legado de Medellín?," *Atualidade Teológica* 11, no. 25 (2007): 40.

33. Josep Ignasi Saranyana, *Teología en América Latina*, vol. 3, *El siglo de las teologías latinoamericanistas (1899–2001)* (Vervuert: Iberoamericana, 2002), 257–63.

34. Juan Carlos Scannone, "La teología de la liberación: Caracterización, corrientes, etapas," *Stromata* 38 (1982): 3–40.

35. Ibid., 20.

36. As interpreted by his compatriot Juan Carlos Scannone, "One of the fundamental differences in this current with respect to the other trends in contemporary Latin American theology is in its understanding of 'the people' as referring to the secular people but also as being employed analogously to 'the people of God.' Other Latin American theologies understand 'the people' as the oppressed classes, races, and cultures in dialectical opposition to the oppressors. On not a few occasions they transplanted this agonistic understanding of 'the people' to 'the popular church.' The Argentine version of liberation, for its part, without neglecting the fact of dependency and structural injustices, conceives of 'the people' first and foremost from a cultural-historical perspective. The people constitute a subject with a history (memory, conscience, and historical project). Its meaning draws close to that of the nation, understood not as a territory or state, but from a particular culture." Juan Carlos Scannone, "Perspectivas eclesiológicas de la 'teología del pueblo' en la Argentina," in *Ecclesia tertii millenii advenientis: Omaggio a P. Angel Antón, professore di ecclesiologia alla Pontificia Università Gregoriana nel suo 70° cumpleanno*, ed. E. Chica, S. Panizzolo, and H. Wagner (Casale Monferrato: PIEME, 1997), 690–91, quoted in Saranyana, *Teología en América Latina*, 329.

37. Cf. Juan Carlos Scannone, "Pope Francis and the Theology of the People," *Theological Studies* 77 (2016): 118–35. Given the genesis and foci of the *teología del pueblo*, it is not surprising to find that methodologically it privileges the use of cultural analysis over economic analysis, history over sociology, popular wisdom over Marxist theory. Perhaps for these same reasons, some have defined *teología del pueblo* over against liberation theology. Indeed, the very phrase *teología del pueblo* was coined by the Uruguayan liberation theologian Juan Luis Segundo by way of specifying the object of his critique. Regardless of how the relation of these two theologies is settled, what is clear is that the *teología del pueblo* deeply influenced two important persons for our story. First, it was a theology that deeply marked the formation of Jorge Bergoglio, now Pope Francis. His encyclical *Evangelii Gaudium* offers to the universal church many of the teachings of the *teología del pueblo*. Second, it was a theology promoted by Eduardo Pironio at the 1974 Synod of Bishops; that synod contributed to the formulation of Paul VI's encyclical *Evangelii Nuntiandi*, which in turn played an important role in Puebla. This second connection raises questions regarding the possible resonances (not necessarily dependence) between the *teología del pueblo* and Romero's theological vision.

38. Methol Ferré and Metalli, *América Latina*, 53.

39. Cf. ibid., 79.

40. García Rubio, "Em direção," 39–40.

41. Gabriel Flynn, "Introduction: The Twentieth-Century Renaissance in Catholic Theology," in *Ressourcement: A Movement for Renewal in Twentieth-Century Catholic Theology*, ed. Gabriel Flynn and Paul D. Murray (Oxford: Oxford University Press, 2012), 4.

42. Cf. ibid. According to Flynn, the Dominican theologian Yves Congar was resolute in his opposition to National Socialism. Recalling his years of imprisonment (1941–45), Congar states: "In captivity, I adopted a militant anti-Nazi attitude which had its own consequences and inconveniences. However, it admitted me to the fellowship of courageous men in an atmosphere of resistance which was a great tonic" (ibid., 13). The Jesuit Henri de Lubac was just as indomitable in his resistance to Nazism and lost close priestly friends to the Gestapo.

43. Roberto S. Goizueta, *Christ Our Companion: Toward a Theological Aesthetic of Liberation* (Maryknoll, NY: Orbis Books, 2009). Goizueta is right that "the faith of the people calls for a *ressourcement* from the margins, a retrieval of the wounded yet glorified body of Christ as the locus of theology" (98). A turn to Óscar Romero is one answer to this call. Romero, together with Ellacuría, transposes the social and historical categories of the "poor" and

the "victims" into an explicitly theological register as "el pueblo crucificado" (the crucified people). The poor are a privileged locus of encounter with Christ not on account of their own moral worth but by the power of the Spirit (38). In calling attention to the divorce between a symbol and the practices that generate and sustain the symbol, Goizueta lifts up the example of Romero as one that reconciles the estranged pair. "When one sees the image of Archbishop Oscar Romero worshipfully lifting the chalice heavenward during the Eucharistic consecration and, simultaneously, watches his chest explode from the force of an assassin's bullet, no theological explanations of the Eucharistic symbol are necessary" (74). Goizueta is surely right about the interpretation of Romero's martyrdom, even if his narration of it is more dependent on the depiction of it in the film *Romero* (starring Raúl Julia, directed by John Duigan, 1989) than on the actual event. "A Latino/a *ressourcement* would retrieve the sacramental understanding of the unity of symbol and referent as itself a dangerous memory that calls for and makes possible courageous protest" (99).

44. The phrase originates in Bernard of Clairvaux, who insisted that the path to wisdom ("consideración") begins and returns to knowledge of oneself: "Sapiens, si sibi sapiens erit; et bibet de fonte putei sui primus ipse." Bernard of Clairvaux, *On Considerations* 2.3, "Bibet de fonte sui primus ipse." Quoted in Étienne Gilson, *L'esprit de la philosophie médiévale* (Paris: Librairie Philosophique J. Vrin, 1969), 220n1. "Aux compagnons qui le pressaient de leur décrire ses extases, saint Bernard répondait, non seulement que de telles expériences ne sont pas communicables, mais que, dans la faible mesure où elles le sont, il est superflu de les communiquer, parce qu'elles sont individuelles de plein droit. Le Verbe ne visite jamais de la même manière deux âmes différentes." Étienne Gilson, *Théologie et histoire de la spiritualité* (Paris: Librarie Philosophique J. Vrin, 1943), 20.

45. Gustavo Gutiérrez, *We Drink from Our Own Wells: The Spiritual Journey of a People* (Maryknoll, NY: Orbis Books, 1984), 5. "At the root of every spirituality there is a particular experience that is had by concrete persons living at a particular time. The experience is both proper to them and yet communicable to others. . . . The great spiritualities in the life of the church continue to exist because they keep sending their followers back to the sources" (37).

46. M. González, *Sor Juana*, 153. She goes on to explain that "a Latin American *ressourcement* emerges in the spirit of the *ressourcement* movement in theologies from marginalized contexts. However the project of *ressourcement* is not merely historical retrieval; it is also critical engagement with the current situation in light of the lessons of the past" (154).

47. Óscar Romero, *La voz de los sin voz: La palabra viva de Monseñor Romero,* ed. Rodolfo Cardenal, Ignacio Martín-Baro, and Jon Sobrino (San Salvador: UCA Editores, 1980), 193; hereafter cited parenthetically in the text as *Voz.*

48. My narration is indebted to José Luis Moreno's thorough study of the reception of the Irenaean aphorism in "'Gloria Dei, vivens homo': Uso actual de la fórmula de Ireneo," in *XIV Simposio Internacional de Teología de la Universidad de Navarra,* ed. José María Casciaro (Navarra: Servicio de Publicaciones de la Universidad de Navarra, 1996), 215–31.

49. "The *doxa* of the gracious God who descends on the sanctuary of creation is, in essence, the man who has been conformed to God. *Gloria Dei vivens homo*: all Irenaeus' theology would have to be developed from this starting-point" (Hans Urs von Balthasar, *The Glory of the Lord,* vol. 1, *Seeing the Form* [San Francisco: Ignatius Press, 1982], 455). "Irenaeus stands as the founder of the theology of the Church with his stance which is at once markedly anti-Gnostic and pre-Alexandrian, that is to say, not as yet Platonizing. The emphasis lies on the glorious creation of God—*gloria Dei vivens homo* (the glory of God is a living man)—and on the miracle of the temporal order of salvation" (*The Glory of the Lord,* vol. 2, *Studies in Theological Style* [San Francisco: Ignatius Press, 1984], 17).

50. The 1968 "Letter to the Jesuits of Latin America" from the provincials of the Society of Jesus bemoans the social conditions of the continent and calls for the apostolate of the order to orient itself toward liberation from these. The provincials are aware that this reorientation will not be easy. "Somos conscientes de la profunda renovación que esto supone. Es necesaria cierta ruptura con algunas actitudes de nuestro pasado, para vincularnos nuevamente con nuestra tradición humanista: 'Gloria Dei, vivens homo,' la gloria de Dios es el hombre vivo (S. Ireneo)." "Reunión de los Provinciales Jesuitas de América Latina con el P. General, Pedro Arrupe, Río de Janeiro, Casa da Gávea: 6 al 14 de mayo de 1968," May 1968, Conferencia de Provinciales Jesuitas en América Latina y El Caribe, http://historico.cpalsj.org/wp-content/uploads/2013/06/Reunion-de-los-Provinciales-Jesuitas-de-AL-con-Arrupe.pdf.

51. All references from the documents produced by the conferences of the Council of Latin American Bishops (CELAM) are drawn from *Cinco Conferencias Generales.* The translations from Spanish to English are my own. As with Puebla (see note 4), I will cite the other conferences by the name of the place where the gathering took place followed by the document division numbers (e.g., "*Medellín* 1.2" for the conference at Medellín, with chapter and section numbers). At Medellín the phrase is not used directly. There

is an oblique reference to its themes when it speaks to the doctrinal foundations of the liturgy (9.3). "La liturgia, momento en que la iglesia es más perfectamente ella misma, realiza indisolublemente unidas la comunión con Dios y entre los hombres, y de tal modo que aquella es la razón de ésta. Si busca ante todo la alabanza de la gloria de la gracia, es consciente también de que todos los hombres necesitan de la gloria de Dios para ser verdaderamente hombres." The correlation of the glory of God and the full humanity of people alludes in turn to *Sacrosanctum Concilium* 10: "From the liturgy, therefore, and especially from the Eucharist, as from a font, grace is poured forth upon us; and the sanctification of men in Christ and the glorification of God, to which all other activities of the church are directed as toward their end, is achieved in the most efficacious possible way." Second Vatican Council, *Sacrosanctum Concilium*, December 4, 1963, www.vatican.va/archive /hist_councils/ii_vatican_council/documents/vat-ii_const_19631204 _sacrosanctum-concilium_en.html. At the conference in Puebla, one of the cognate statements of the phrase is cited directly and completely in John Paul II's inaugural discourse to the gathering of bishops on January 28, 1979. Expounding on the famous passage from *Gaudium et Spes* 22 ("Only in the mystery of the incarnate Word does the mystery of man take on light"), John Paul II says (*Puebla* 1.9), "La Iglesia posee, gracias al Evangelio, la verdad sobre el hombre. Esta se encuentra en una antropología que la Iglesia no cesa de profundizar y de comunicar. La afirmación primordial de esta antropología es la del hombre como imagen de Dios, irreductible a una simple parcela de la naturaleza, o a un 'elemento anónimo de la ciudad humana' [*Gaudium et Spes* 12.3 and 14.2]. En este sentido, escribía San Ireneo: 'La gloria del hombre es Dios, pero el receptáculo de toda acción de Dios, de su sabiduría, de su poder, es el hombre' [*Tratado contra las herejías* 3.20.2–3]." Second Vatican Council, *Gaudium et Spes*, December 7, 1965, www.vatican .va/archive/hist_councils/ii_vatican_council/documents/vat-ii_const _19651207_gaudium-et-spes_en.html.

52. At Santo Domingo the phrase is used to orient the bidirectional character of worship: "El culto cristiano debe expresar la doble vertiente de la obediencia al Padre (glorificación) y de la caridad con los hermanos (redención), pues la gloria de Dios es que el hombre viva. Con lo cual lejos de alienar a los hombres los libera y los hace hermanos" (Conclusiones 34). At Aparecida the formula appears in the context of the church's ministry among the sick. "La Iglesia ha hecho una opción por la vida. Esta nos proyecta necesariamente hacia las periferias más hondas de la existencia: el nacer y el morir, el niño y el anciano, el sano y el enfermo. San Ireneo nos dice que 'la gloria de Dios es el

hombre viviente,' aun el débil, el recién concebido, el gastado por los años y el enfermo. Cristo envió a sus apóstoles a predicar el Reino de Dios y a curar a los enfermos, verdaderas catedrales del encuentro con el Señor Jesús" (417).

53. "The expression, *God of life*, sums it all up perfectly—but on the condition we understand *life* as concrete human life and as fundamental logic or rationality. Otherwise the expression evaporates into an abstract, spiritualist theology. God is the God of life because the basic actual divine will is that all men and women have life and life in abundance (cf. John 10:10). The poor believe and hope in the God of life because this is the God who ensures concrete human life for all, especially for them. God is the God of life because God takes on human life as absolute truth, goodness, and beauty." Pablo Richard, "Theology in the Theology of Liberation," in *Mysterium Liberationis: Fundamental Concepts of Liberation Theology*, ed. Ignacio Ellacuría and Jon Sobrino (Maryknoll, NY: Orbis Books, 1993), 164.

54. Alex García-Rivera, *The Community of the Beautiful: A Theological Aesthetics* (Collegeville, MN: Liturgical Press, 1999), 11. The translation of the Irenaean saying is odd. García-Rivera quotes the Latin on the footnote, but the phrasing of the English appears to substitute Irenaeus's *gloria Dei* with von Balthasar's *Herrlichkeit*.

55. Miguel Díaz, "God," in *Hispanic American Religious Cultures*, vol. 2, ed. Miguel De La Torre (Santa Barbara, CA: ABC-CLIO, 2009): "Together with Irenaeus, the second-century theologian, Latino/a theology proclaims that the glory of God is the human being fully alive. Faced with homogenization and globalization—these are powerful social, cultural, and economic forces that strive to melt away and suppress particular expressions of human life—our challenge is to affirm the particular that glorifies God today. This struggle to affirm particularity in the midst of communal diversity is not foreign to God's life. If one understands *la lucha* in terms of creative and life-giving relations, then God's life is *lucha*. God's struggle involves the ongoing creative and life-giving relations of one divine person to another so that the divine community can eternally emerge *from* and be sustained *in* distinct familial relations (Mother/Father, Child, Spirit)" (643–44).

56. Nancy Pineda-Madrid, "Notes toward a Chicana Feminist Epistemology," in *A Reader in Latina Feminist Theology: Religion and Justice*, ed. María Pilar Aquino, Daisy L. Machado, and Jeanette Rodríguez (Austin: University of Texas Press, 2002), 241–66. Work on a Chicana feminist epistemology would develop a richer understanding of the meaning of humanization for Chicanas and in this way provide "greater insight into the meaning of *gloria Dei vivens homo* for Chicanas" (261). The expression does not literally mean

"The glory of God is the human person fully alive," as the author claims (266n53), but this is a common translation.

57. Cf. M. C. Steenberg, "Two-Natured Man: An Anthropology of Transfiguration," *Pro Ecclesia* 14, no. 4 (2005): 416; Édouard Divry, *La Transfiguration selon l'Orient et l'Occident: Grégoire Palamas-Thomas d'Aquin vers un dénouement oecuménique* (Paris: Pierre Téqui, 2009), 94–95.

58. The saying is found in Irenaeus, *Against Heresies* (*Adv. haer.*) 4.20.7, in *Ante-Nicene Fathers*, vol. 1, *The Apostolic Fathers, Justin Martyr, and Irenaeus*, ed. Alexander Roberts and James Donaldson (Peabody, MA: Hendrickson, 1994), 489–90.

59. John Behr, *Irenaeus of Lyons: Identifying Christianity* (Oxford: Oxford University Press, 2013), 209.

60. "Irenaeus imagines Christ's covenantal flesh as disrupting the substantialist hierarchy of cosmological and anthropological essences that marked Ptolemaeic-Gnostic thought. Irenaeus's goal was not simply to defeat the Gnostic argument. His larger goal was to rescue theological discourse from what in Gnostic hands it was becoming: a discourse of death, the death of embodied life." J. Kameron Carter, *Race: A Theological Account* (Oxford: Oxford University Press, 2008), 23.

61. Eric Osborn, *Irenaeus of Lyons* (Cambridge: Cambridge University Press, 2001), xi.

62. Thomas Greenan Mulheron, "La opción por los pobres en las homilías de Monseñor Romero y de San Juan Crisóstomo: Análisis de las convergencias y de las peculiaridades en los presupuestos teológicos y en las orientaciones morales" (PhD diss., Universidad Pontificia Comillas de Madrid, 2003). Greenan finds parallels between the two preaching bishops. They had similar characters. They were both controversial figures whose strong denunciation of the abuse of the poor led to their persecution and untimely deaths at the hands of the ruling powers of their time and place. The homilies of these two bishops belong to the patrimony of the universal church and merit careful study. Greenan's effort yields the following fruits. The preferential option for the poor preached by Romero is present too (though naturally without the technical phrase) in the preaching of the bishop of Constantinople. To what can the correlations between these two be attributed? Greenan floats a Jungian idea of recurring patterns in human psychology (122). But he does not place too much weight on this thesis. "Chiefly, then, what Romero and Chrysostom have in common is their compassionate humanity. Both felt in their very flesh the misery of the people sunken in poverty and were moved to speak and act on their behalf" (122). At base, Greenan suggests that the

correlation between the two is evidence of the perennial character of Christian tradition of which both are teachers. "Perhaps another way of saying this is to declare that the essential message of the gospel remains constant with the passing of centuries when the expositors of this message are in accord with the values of the kingdom" (5). Greenan also sees ecumenical significance in the comparison, since they represent wings of the church that have been divided for a millennium. The study of how both preached for the poor can become a bridge for an encounter of East and West in the service of the poor. Both Romero and Chrysostom are fathers of the poor. "The word *father* conveys a sense of security and trust, and Christians, in spite of Jesus' prohibition (Mt 23:8–11), speak of our *Fathers in faith*. A father is one who has daughters and sons and, with tenderness, educates and guides them toward maturity. In fact, Saint Paul attributed to himself the title *Father* (1 Cor 4:15)" (1344). Romero and Chrysostom are fathers in this sense. In life and beyond life, they have many children, and their teaching has guided and continues to guide many children of the church. They are fathers of the universal church, fathers of the church of the poor.

63. Claudia Marlene Rivera Navarrete, "La denuncia profética de la riqueza: Resonancia de la patrística en la teología latinoamericana de la liberación" (MA thesis, Universidad Centroamericana "José Simeón Cañas," 2015).

64. Margaret Pfeil, "*Gloria Dei, Vivens Pauper*: Romero's Theology of Transfiguration," *Sign of Peace* 4, no. 2 (Spring 2005): 6–9.

65. Damian Zynda, *Archbishop Oscar Romero: A Disciple Who Revealed the Glory of God* (Scranton, PA: University of Scranton Press, 2010).

66. Margaret Pfeil, "Oscar Romero's Theology of Transfiguration," *Theological Studies* 72 (2011): 87–115.

67. Evidence of the importance of this term can be found in the titles of popular collections of Romero's writings like *La voz de los sin voz*.

Chapter 2. Microphones of Christ

1. *Orientación*, August 3, 1986, 7. For whatever reason, this plan was not implemented.

2. Most scholarship on Romero is focused on the three years that he served as archbishop. It is as if the first sixty-two years of his life belonged to a private life and as if he began his public ministry only after Grande's baptism by blood. Of course, this is not the case. Romero had been serving

as a priest for thirty-two years before his installation as archbishop, and there is thus much more to his preaching of the gospel than the sermons preached between 1977 and 1980. We will consider a few of these sermons in future chapters as we study his homilies on the Transfiguration. Even for the three-year period of his archbishopric Romero preached many more sermons than those available in print. In other words, an examination of Romero's theology based on its preaching must reach beyond the cathedral sermons of San Salvador while acknowledging the incomplete documentation beyond these. With these caveats in place, it is possible to sketch out some broad contours of Romero's preaching practice.

3. The translations from Spanish are my own.

4. Herman Melville, *Moby Dick* (New York: Barnes and Noble Books, 1994), 33.

5. Bartolomé de las Casas, *Historia de las Indias*, ed. André Saint-Lu (Caracas: Biblioteca Ayacucho, 1986), vol. 3, chap. 4, pp. 13–14.

6. Ibid.

7. Bartolomé de las Casas was one of the people shaken and eventually won over by the preaching of the likes of Montesinos. His vision of Christ being crucified in the Indies a thousand times over led him to become the defender of the indigenous and eventually of the African. Cf. Isacio Pérez Fernández, O.P., *Fray Bartolomé de las Casas, O.P.: De defensor de los indios a defensor de los negros* (Salamanca: Editorial San Esteban, 1995). Bishops Antonio de Valdivieso and Juan del Valle were both disciples of Las Casas who preached and worked on behalf of the indigenous. Antonio de Valdivieso, the first bishop of Nicaragua, was the first bishop martyred in the Americas. He was stabbed to death in his house on the evening of February 26, 1550, by a group of mercenaries hired by the governor of Nicaragua to silence his demand for Indian reparations. See Enrique Dussel, *A History of the Church in Latin America: Colonialism to Liberation* (Grand Rapids, MI: William B. Eerdmans, 1981), 52–53; Juan Friede, *Vida y luchas de don Juan del Valle, primer obispo de Popayán y protector de indios* (Popayán, Colombia: Editorial Universidad, 1961). The episcopacy of Juan del Valle in Popayán, Colombia, was marked by constant friction with the encomenderos and the civil authorities. These frictions were caused above all by del Valle's denunciations of the abuse of the indigenous. The conflict climaxed in the aftermath of a synod convened by Del Valle in 1558. The synod not only defended the equality of the indigenous with the Spanish but made its deliberations available in Spanish rather than Latin so as to reach a wide audience.

8. Ordina E. Gonzáles and Justo González comment, "It is important to realize that these men—soldiers as well as clerics—were not hypocrites. They truly believed that they were serving God. . . . As he lay dying among his fellow conquistadores, Francisco Pizarro, the cruel conqueror of the Inca empire, drew a cross with his own blood so he could die contemplating the cross." Ordina E. González and Justo L. González, *Christianity in Latin America: A History* (New York: Cambridge University Press, 2008), 3.

9. Quoted in Luis Rivera-Pagán, *A Violent Evangelism: The Political and Religious Conquest of the Americas* (Louisville, KY: Westminster/John Knox Press, 1992), 29. The decree by the Borgia Pope Alexander VI traced a longitudinal line that divided evangelizing and civilizing Catholic endeavors between the Spanish and the Portuguese. The location of the line was renegotiated a year later by the Treatise of Tordesillas and accounts for why the only Portuguese colony in the Americas is Brazil.

10. Quoted in ibid., 147.

11. For more information on Pedro de Córdoba, see Miguel Ángel Medina, *Los dominicos y América: Doctrina cristiana para instrucción de los indios* (Salamanca: Editorial San Esteban, 1987). Pedro de Córdoba was the leader of the first Dominican community in Hispaniola and is credited with writing the sermon that Montesinos preached. In addition to being the first to preach to the indigenous and the first to write a sermon on behalf of the indigenous, he was also the first to draft a catechesis for the indigenous. Regarding Pedro de Alvarado, I will have more to say in the next chapter. For now, suffice it to say that his legacy is ambiguous, as he is credited with both planting the cross in what would become El Salvador and giving the first turn to the spiral of violence that continues to afflict the country.

12. In the words of Jon Sobrino, "When giving the homilies, Archbishop Romero was literally transfigured. The rather timid man who felt uncomfortable among the great ones of this world became in the pulpit the powerful orator uttering the courageous, liberating words that met his people's needs." Jon Sobrino, introduction to *A Prophetic Bishop Speaks to His People: The Complete Homilies of Archbishop Oscar Arnulfo Romero*, trans. Joseph V. Owens (Miami, FL: Convivium Press, 2015), 1:31.

13. Martin Maier, *Monseñor Romero: Maestro de espirtualidad* (San Salvador: UCA Editores, 2010), 27.

14. Roberto Morozzo della Rocca, *Oscar Romero: Prophet of Hope*, trans. Michael J. Miller (Boston: Pauline Books and Media, 2015), loc. 1917, Kindle.

15. Mariano Imperato, "Romero Predicador," in, Óscar Romero: *Un obispo entre guerra fría y revolución*, ed. Roberto Morozzo della Rocca (Madrid: Editorial San Pablo, 2012), loc. 1282–83, Kindle.

16. In an Easter sermon titled "Grace, the Divine Gift of Easter," Romero states: "I want to say to you, dear brothers and dear journalists who are here with us, that when you take the message of our homilies with you, do not fix your eyes only on the illumination that this message gives to the sad reality of our people, because then it does seem to be a merely political speech. What I want you to see above all is that the main thing in my message is the theology of the word of God, that what we come on our Sundays to church to reflect on is the revelation found in the divine word of the Lord, that this morning, the curiosity that someone has brought to see what the archbishop says about the killings of this week, that is not the main thing. We illumine these events but from the sublime theology of the transcendence of the word of God. For this reason, even if there were no descriptions of our realities, the word of God would always need to be reflected upon and this Word will serve as the foundation of our Christian life" (*Homilías*, 4:437).

17. On Saturday, January 26, 1980, Romero met with Fathers Ellacuría and Estrada. Together they reflected on how Romero's sermon of the previous week had been received and also spent time talking about the events of the week that would be featured in next morning's sermon.

18. See Morozzo della Rocca, *Primero Dios*, 344n128 and 346–47n149.

19. While preaching on the parable of the ten lepers who in their illness had organized a kind of leper cooperative, Romero remarks, "I live in a hospital and I truly feel close to the pain, to the groans of suffering at night, to the sadness of the one who arrives having to leave his family to be admitted in a hospital. Let us think of the long lines of sick people waiting at our hospitals in search of a little bit of health that they do not find. Let us think also of the sick family member, perhaps listening to me next to the radio. Oh that my word would bring you some consolation! We are thinking of you, dear sick brother" (*Homilías*, 1:385).

20. Miguel Cavada Diez, "Introducción general," in Romero, *Homilías*, 6:11.

21. Given the oral character of his preaching, the vast majority of Romero's sermons are accessible only through transcriptions of audio recordings of his sermons. Morozzo della Rocca considers these to be, overall, faithful to the preached sermons, but there are inaccuracies. In some cases, the source of the error is not clear. For example, consider the following selections from his final homily. Moments before he is shot, Romero invites the

congregation to prepare themselves for the act of faith that is the Eucharist. The version published in the collection *La voz de los sin voz* reads as "Con fe cristiana **parece** que en este momento **la voz de diatriba** se convierte en el cuerpo del Señor que se ofreció por la redención del mundo" (*Voz*, 295) and has been translated in *Voice of the Voiceless: The Four Pastoral Letters and Other Statements*, trans. Michael J. Walsh (Maryknoll, NY: Orbis Books, 2000), 193, as "To Christian faith at this moment the voice of diatribe appears changed for the body of the Lord, who offered himself for the redemption of the world." The version published in *Homilías* reads: "Con fe cristiana **sabemos** que, en este momento, **la hostia de trigo** se convierte en el cuerpo del Señor, que se ofreció por la redención del mundo" (*Homilías*, 6:457–58) and has been translated in *Voice of the Voiceless* as "With Christian faith we know that, at this moment, the host of wheat becomes the body of the Lord who offered himself for the redemption of the world" (193). The audio recording of Romero's sermon leaves no doubt that the second reading is the correct one. The fact that the mistaken words of the incorrect version are not even close in sound to the audio recording raises questions. Were the editors working from another, poorer recording? A set of notes with textual holes filled in from memory? It is interesting to note that this version of the text matches the transcription made by Jorge Pinto from the recording of the sermon that was made at his request. See Jorge Pinto, *El grito del más pequeño* (Mexico City: Impresos Continentales, 1985), 279. Regardless of the reason, the two versions color the final moments of Romero in starkly different hues. In the first case, *it seems* as if Romero believes that *the voice of diatribe*, the fight for social justice, is to be identified with the body of Christ, as if the class struggle were the source of salvation. Cf. Morozzo della Rocca, *Primero Dios*, 337n37. Such a message would echo the kind of politicized liberation theology he rejected. In the second case, Romero proclaims a basic Catholic doctrine of the Eucharist in support of a more integral liberation theology. The Eucharist knits the members of Christ more closely together and strengthens them to so as to offer themselves not to the class struggle but to suffering with Christ. The purpose of this suffering is the subject of the next-to-last sentence, where there is another textual difficulty. Both the *Voice* and *Homilías* versions read, "Que este cuerpo inmolado y esta carne sacrificada por los hombres nos alimente también a dar nuestro cuerpo y nuestra sangre al sufrimiento y al dolor, como Cristo: no para sí, sino para dar **conceptos** de justicia y de paz a nuestro pueblo" (May this body immolated and flesh sacrificed for humanity nourish us too so that we may give our body and blood to suffering and pain, like Christ, not for self, but to give concepts of peace and justice to our people). The English version solves the problem by means of a paraphrase: "May this body immolated and this blood sacrificed for humans nourish us also, so that we may give our body and our blood to suffering and to pain—like Christ, not for self, but to bring about justice and peace for our people" (*Voice of the Voiceless*, 193). The disputed term is *conceptos*. Some students of Romero's homilies claim that what Romero said was not *conceptos* but *cosechas*. In a message to Morozzo della Rocca, Carlos Colorado hints that these errors are due to the bias of the editors working at the UCA, who tend to present a more radicalized version of Romero than what the facts bear (cf. Morozzo della Rocca, *Primero Dios*, 337–38n37). Though there is some truth to this charge in the persistence of the conversion narrative that surrounds the beginning of Romero's time as archbishop and in the continued use of the discredited interview with Calderón that birthed the Salvadoran resurrection slogan, at least on this occasion the case is more ambiguous because the recording is unclear. However, in this example, unlike the previous one, the sound recording is inconclusive. Romero says something that sounds like *cosechos*, which is not a Spanish word. Certainly, the word harvest (*cosechas*) fits the context of the scripture readings and the Eucharist better. Romero is preaching about the grain of wheat falling to the ground, and it seems odd that he would interpret the offering of the Christian in an abstract and conceptual manner. What El Salvador needed most was not a new social theory but a harvest of justice and peace.

22. Jon Sobrino, "Introducción general," in *Homilías*, 1:21.

23. Miguel Cavada Diez, "Introducción general," in *Homilías*, 4:14.

24. There are forty-six sermons in volume 1, forty-four in volume 2, twenty-five in volume 3, thirty-one in volume 4, twenty-eight in volume 5, and nineteen in volume 6. Sermons of 1977 on the church are "The Paschal Church" (April 17, 1977), "The Mission of the Church" (May 8, 1977), "The Church before Pain and Violence" (May 11, 1977), "The Church Is Christ in Our History" (May 15, 1977), "What Is the Church" (May 29, 1977), "The Church, Communion of Humanity and God" (June 5, 1977), "The Church of the Archdiocese" (July 24, 1977), "The Church, Body of Christ in History" (August 6, 1977), "The Service of the Virgin and the Church" (August 15, 1977), "Characteristics of Our Church" (August 21, 1977), "The Church of the Covenant of God and True Poverty" (August 28, 1977), "The Church of the Holy Spirit and the Church of the Cross" (September 4, 1977), "The Church of True Independence, the Church of True Liberty" (September 11, 1977), "The Church, Continuation of the Incarnation of Christ" (September 24, 1977), "Saint Michael Archangel and the

Struggle of the Church" (September 29, 1977), "The Church, Community of Faith" (October 2, 1977), "The Church of Integral Promotion" (October 9, 1977), "The Church in Prayer, the Missionary Church" (October 16, 1977), "The Missionary Church" (October 23, 1977), "The Eschatological Church" (November 6, 1977), "The Eschatological Sense of the Church" (November 13, 1977), "Christ, Manifestation of God and Humanity; The Church, Manifestation of Christ" (December 25, 1977), "The Church of Hope" (November 27, 1977), "The Church of Salvation" (December 11, 1977), "The Church in Latin America" (December 12, 1977), and "The Church, Hierarchical Ensemble to Transmit the Life of Christ" (December 19, 1977). Sermons of 1978 on the church: "The Church, Certain Seed of Unity for the Human Race" (January 22, 1978), "The Church of the Beatitudes" (January 29, 1978), "The Church Whose Weakness Rests on Christ" (February 5, 1978), "The Church, Spiritual Israel" (February 19, 1978), "The Resurrected One Lives in His Church" (April 2, 1978), "The Church, the Return of Christ in the Spirit" (April 23, 1978), "Pentecost, Birthday of the Church" (May 14, 1978), "The Missionary, Spiritual, and Social Dynamism of the Kingdom of God in the Church" (August 20, 1978), "The Pope, Lieutenant of Christ in the Church" (August 27, 1978), "The Church, a Community That Is Prophetic, Sacramental, and Loving" (September 10, 1978), "The Church, Community of Love" (September 17, 1978), "The Church of John Paul" (October 1, 1978), "The Church, Vineyard of the Lord" (October 8, 1978), "The Church, Communion of Life, Charity, and Truth, for the Salvation of the World" (October 29, 1978), "The Church, Holy but in Need of Purification" (November 5, 1978), "The Church, Spouse of Christ" (November 12, 1978), and "The Church, a Community Actively Waiting for the Return of Christ" (November 19, 1978). Sermons of 1979 on the church: "Christ, an Ever New Word of the Church" (February 18, 1979), "Christ, the Groom of the Church" (February 25, 1979), "Grace, the Divine Gift of Easter Which the Church Distributes among Humanity" (May 13, 1979), "The Mission of the Church in the Midst of the National Crisis" (August 6, 1979, October 21, 1979), and "In the Church the Priestly Liberation of Christ Is Prolonged" (November 4, 1979). Sermons of 1980 on the church: "The Church, a Service of Personal, Communal, and Transcendent Liberation" (March 23, 1980).

25. Cf. Sobrino, "Introducción general," in *Homilías*, 1:17.

26. *Homilías*, 2:248: "See then how picturesque and, at the same time, how effective is the church as teacher of the spiritual life. The liturgical year comes to be hence something like a course, a great university established

around the world so that all human beings, according to Vatican II, when they celebrate the mysteries of salvation are immersed in its redemptive grace. It is not the remembrance of the past, it is the present mystery that saved the world until the consummation of the ages. Each liturgical year makes present the mystery of Christ that unfolds especially in our Sunday mass."

27. *Homilías*, 2:26. Romero supports this sacramental reading of the liturgical calendar with an appeal to *Sacrosanctum Concilium* 102: "Within the cycle of a year [the church] unfolds the whole mystery of Christ, from the Incarnation and Birth until the Ascension, the day of Pentecost, and the expectation of blessed hope and of the coming of the Lord. Recalling thus the mysteries of redemption, the church opens to the faithful the riches of her Lord's powers and merits, so that these are in some way made present for all time, and the faithful are enabled to lay hold upon them and become filled with saving grace."

28. So for example, the Advent sermon on John the Baptist, entitled "The Word Became Flesh and Dwelt among Us," which will be referenced later in this chapter, is divided into three points: "Christ is the word of God that became human," "The Church is the prolongation of the mystery of the incarnation of Christ," and "God became human so that humans can become God." As this example shows, there is a movement from point to point. In this case the movement follows the pattern of exitus-reditus, descent and ascent, of the Incarnation. In other cases, the order may follow that of an ecclesial document. In all cases, these three points are intended to open the scriptures read in the mass. In most cases, as in the sermon that we will study later in this chapter, the lectionary texts are woven through the three points, though one text may be dominant in a particular point. Sometimes, each of the points is paired to one of the lectionary texts. For example, Romero's final Transfiguration sermon preached on March 2, 1980, "Lent, God's Plan for the Transfiguration of All Peoples," is divided into three points: "The transfigured Christ, fullness and goal of the history of Israel," "In the transfigured Christ, God offers a plan of integral liberation for all peoples," and "The transfigured Christ is the anticipated presence of the definitive liberation" (*Homilías*, 5:340). The first point is paired with the reading from Genesis 15:5–12, 17–18, which tells of the day when God made a covenant with Abram. The second point is paired with Luke's account of the Transfiguration (Luke 9:28–36). The third point is paired with the epistle lesson from Philippians 3:17–4:1, where Paul tells his readers that their citizenship is in heaven.

29. I will explain Romero's interpretation of the signs of the times more fully in chapter 5 when considering Romero's ecclesiology.

30. *Homilías*, 3:400: "Salvation is a historic event, not of the past, but of the present history of each people, each person, each community. And this is important that we keep in mind, that if we focus directly every week on historical events, it is not out of a desire for moving away from the gospel and the mind of the church, but so that we will look for the salvation that God is working out among the Salvadorans, incarnate in their own history, in our historic events."

31. Sobrino, "Introducción general," in *Homilías*, 1:13.

32. "This is the splendor of Christian service: 'To serve is to reign.' When I call myself your deacon, your servant, I am not being obsequious in order to gain your applause. In no way have I sought it. You have given it to me spontaneously. It does not puff me up because I know that it is simply the expression of a people who identify themselves with the one who is addressing the word to them and seeking to serve them, precisely, where they feel most deeply.* I insist that it is not opportunism; it is more. Forgive me for saying this to you. I am not so interested in your friendship [*simpatía*] as in God's. I am not so interested in ruling over your hearts, in which thanks be to God, I feel so cherished that I am almost the king of this community, as I am in feeling above all, like royalty in the presence of God. To serve him is to rule, and the more humbly I serve him in the people, the more I will reign*" (*Homilías*, 5:350–51). Each asterisk mark denotes a spontaneous burst of applause from the congregation.

33. Cf. Cavada Diez, "Introducción general," in *Homilías*, 6:11.

34. "Yo quisiera que lo principal de mi predicación lo recogieran como una catequesis, como una predicación de la palabra de Dios. Naturalmente que hay gente que sólo está esperando aspectos políticos, polémicos y creen que toda mi predicación es política y es polémica, y que estoy subvirtiendo con mi predicación. El objetivo principal de mi predicación es el anuncio de este misterio" (*Homilías*, 4:415).

35. Cf. Michael E. Connors, C.S.C., "Romero: A Homiletic Saint for Our Times," in *Archbishop Romero and Spiritual Leadership in the Modern World* (Lanham, MD: Lexington Books, 2015), 93–97. Connors states that "Romero mystagogically linked his preaching with the liturgy, and in so doing he mystagogically linked Catholic Social Teaching with the liturgy" (96). On Connors's reading, Romero can help bridge the gap between ethics and spirituality, the *lex vivendi* and the *lex orandi*, by promoting a more mystagogical approach to preaching. This seems right to me, but his suggestion that Romero attained

these homiletical insights by in some way moving beyond the tradition of the church fathers and the council fathers seems stuck in a static reading of tradition as "archival" (96) and "mechanically deductive" (94). Connors says that while Romero "loved and honored the texts of Scripture, and loved and honored the tradition from the early Fathers to the Fathers of the Second Vatican Council, he intuitively arrived at the understanding that a new day demands a new word" (96). The contrast is overdrawn. If anything, Romero's own claims of undying fidelity to the magisterium and the pope show that being deeply traditional and radically open to the movement of the Spirit are not to be seen as radically opposed commitments.

36. Quoted in *Homilías*, 6:227.

37. For instance, Paul VI's apostolic exhortation *Evangelii Nuntiandi* is the source of the structure of a sermon Romero preached at Rutilio Grande's funeral on March 14, 1977 (*Homilías*, 1:31–36). For Paul VI, the church contributes to the cause of liberation people who are inspired by faith, led by the social doctrine of the church, and motivated by love. These three traits of the agents of liberation become concrete and personal in Rutilio Grande. In preaching, "The magisterium should not be exposed in *concepts*, but should rather be used to illumine and change *reality*." Sobrino, "Introducción general," in *Homilías*, 1:25, emphasis in original.

38. In Romero's preaching he refers to the church sometimes as the microphone of God and sometimes as the microphone of Christ. The lack of rigor could be condemned as sloppy, but both are figures of speech, and Romero is not a Scholastic theologian but a preacher. In any case, the relation in distinction and the distinction in relation between Word and voice is something that Romero is attentive to. The church is the microphone of God because it is the body of Christ. The church is the microphone of Christ because it is not Christ. It bears the Word in its heart and body, but it is not the Word.

39. The Latin American bishops said at Puebla in 1979, "The poor merit preferential attention, regardless of the personal or moral situation in which they find themselves. Made in God's image and likeness to be his children, this image is obscured and mocked. This is why God takes their defense and loves them. It is thus that the poor become the first addressees of mission and their evangelization is par excellence the sign and proof of the mission of Jesus" (*Puebla* 1141).

40. Is this not often the case today? How many student advisees are neglecting a call to serve the church for NGOs and nonprofits? Why? In some cases, there is a reductive understanding of liberation that neglects the

transcendental nature of the human. In other cases, young people do not see the church as a prolongation of the homily of Christ but as another gospel. Too often the church does not sound like a microphone of Christ but like the megaphone of a polarized culture.

41. The bishops at Puebla spoke of the need of the church to be attentive both to the cry of the poor and to the cry of youth. In youth, the church finds "a restlessness that questions everything; a risk-taking spirit that leads it to commitments and radical situations; a creative capacity with new answers to the world in change that it aspires to improve constantly as a sign of hope. Their most spontaneous and strongest personal aspiration is freedom, being emancipated from external tutelage. They are signs of joy and happiness. They are very sensitive to social problems. They demand authenticity and simplicity and reject with rebelliousness a society permeated by hypocrisy and distorted values" (*Puebla* 1168). The church needs to learn to trust the youth. What's more, "Since youth are a truly animating force of the social body and especially of the ecclesial body, the church makes a preferential option for them according to its evangelizing mission to the continent" (*Puebla* 1186).

42. Imperato, "Romero Predicador," loc. 1300–1302, Kindle.

43. Connors, "Romero," 97. Connors helpfully highlights the way in which preaching is an incarnational event for Romero. Romero's goal is not the transmission of "notional truths" but an encounter with the one who is Truth in person, Christ by the power of the Spirit. Romero allows the Word to invade his flesh and invites the congregation to let themselves be transfigured by this Word.

44. "The cry of liberation of this people is an outcry that rises to God and that nothing and no one can stop. Those who fall in the struggle—as long as it is out of genuine love for the people and in search of true liberation—we should consider as present among us, not only because they remain present in the memories of those who continue their struggles, but also because the transcendences of our faith teaches us that human life does not end with the destruction of the body. We hope, rather, that by divine mercy, it is after death that we human beings will attain the full and absolute liberation" (*Homilías*, 5:243).

45. "It has been shown, once more, that violence does not construct, especially the violence of a hard [political] Right that instrumentalizes the repressive violence of the armed forces to violate, for profit, the sacred human rights of freedom of expression and organization that the people already knows how to defend" (*Homilías*, 5:244).

46. "True revolution does not kill other human beings, because life belongs to God alone. True revolution does not consist in painting on walls and crying loudly in the streets. True revolution consists in developing political projects that better structure a just people of brothers and sisters" (*Homilías*, 5:245).

47. Another significant piece of homiletical catechism is the sermon he preached on July 16, 1978, "The Sowing of the Word of the Kingdom" (*Homilías*, 3:91–109).

48. John Drury, *Painting the Word: Christian Pictures and Their Meaning* (New Haven, CT: Yale University Press, 1999). A triptych, even when it was made for private devotion, had some of the centralized order of public worship and seemed to expect a celebration of the mass. A diptych is a more decidedly private thing. Made for private (often lay) use, it usually had a portrait of its owner at prayer on one side and an image of the heavenly being to whom the prayer is offered on the other. So its content was the relation between the two, the infinite dialogue of prayer made visible in its sustained tension (12–13).

49. Ibid., 11.

50. Cf. *Homilías*, 5:205.

51. The composition of new creeds was commonplace at the time. In fact, at the end of his Ascension Day sermon on May 22, 1977, Romero invites his congregation on this occasion to recite, not "our creed" (the Nicene), but a version produced by the archdiocese. "The church believes in God the Creator, in Jesus Christ the Redeemer, and in the Holy Spirit the Sanctifier. The church believes that the world is called to be subject to Jesus Christ through the gradual installation of the kingdom of God. The church believes in the communion of saints and in the love that unites human beings. The church believes in the human, called to be a child of God, and she believes in the kingdom of God as the progressive change of the world of sin into a world of love and justice that begins already in this world and attains its fulfillment in eternity" (*Homilías*, 1:97–98). The profession of this creed commits the church to resist both Marxism and capitalism as materialisms.

52. Morozzo della Rocca, *Oscar Romero: Prophet*, loc. 1404–7, Kindle.

53. Morozzo della Rocca, *Primero Dios*, 17, and *Oscar Romero: Prophet*, loc. 925, Kindle.

54. At times, the government attempted to block the transmission of Romero's sermons by broadcasting classical music on the same frequency. Thomas Greenan Mulheron, "Opción por los pobres," 7. For instance, the chorus "See the Conquering Hero Comes" from Handel's *Judas Maccabaeus*

can be heard playing in the background of Romero's preaching on March 18, 1979. The use of a piece of music from an oratorio that tells the story of a popular Jewish revolt against a ruling elite with foreign connections is fascinating. Either the regime loved irony or they were tone deaf to the dramatic resonances.

55. Mark Lewis Taylor, "Subalternity and Advocacy as Kairos for Theology," in *Opting for the Margins: Postmodernity and Liberation in Christian Theology*, ed. Joerg Rieger (Oxford Scholarship Online, January 2005), n.p.

56. The voices of Montesinos and Las Casas cried out on behalf of the indigenous. They cried because they heard Christ's voice in the moans and clamors of the indigenous. The witness of these friars was important and not to be easily dismissed by applying the allegedly more enlightened standards of the present day. However, as effective as these preachers were at shaking the conscience of the Spanish, they were less successful in empowering the indigenous to speak for themselves. The manner in which these defenders of the poor made their case has garnered the opprobrium of contemporary academics who see these figures as simply another face of empire. The critique is not altogether without merit, yet Taylor correctly identifies in many academic circles "a kind of sophisticated awareness of the complexity in speaking or advocating about the worlds of the poor, which leads many to abstain from the attempt altogether" (ibid., 34).

57. Taylor suggests a way beyond the impasse. First, the advocate should be honest with a clear-sighted awareness of the risk of objectification inherent in advocacy. The journey of advocacy is a *via negativa* potholed with self-contradictions. Second, advocates need to be attentive to the voices of the subaltern close to home. The resistance to exploitation in the advocate's own social location renders the advocacy for those in other locations more authentic and more resistant to fetishizing. Third, the liberation of the advocate must in some way be at stake in the advocacy. Taylor presents this criterion as a check against the benevolent paternalism that characterizes colonial and neocolonial assistance.

58. Romero carefully and consistently distinguishes between the "people of God" as a theological reality and the people of El Salvador as a social reality. The two groups are related and share many common needs and dreams, but they are distinct. We will consider this point further when we study Romero's ecclesiology in chapter 5.

59. Cf. *Puebla* 1145: "Acercándonos al pobre para acompañarlo y servirlo, hacemos lo que Cristo nos enseñó, al hacerse hermano nuestro, pobre como nosotros. Por eso el servicio a los pobres es la medida privilegiada

aunque no excluyente, de nuestro seguimiento de Cristo. El mejor servicio al hermano es la evangelización que lo dispone a realizarse como hijo de Dios, lo libera de las injusticias y lo promueve integralmente."

60. The manner in which Romero speaks of this ministry is telling. For instance, in a homily preached on August 28, 1977, he remembers the murder by machete of three catechists and says, "*We* want to be united with this family in their pain and *we* want to be the voice of those who have no voice in order to cry against so many abuses of human rights" (*Homilías*, 1:281, emphasis added). The subject who speaks for the poor is the church, an ecclesial, not royal, "we." Significantly, the ecclesial grounding of Romero's representative ministry is recognized by those he is representing. Romero reads from a letter that he received from the families of Victor Rivas and Julio Ayala, two men who were disappeared by the police on April 24, 1977. In this letter, the relatives of these *desaparecidos* spoke to Romero in words that shook him to the core: "The voice of the church is for us the voice of justice, the voice of those of us who are not heard" (*Homilías*, 2:207, January 15, 1978).

61. Cf. *Homilías*, 6:42.

62. Augustine, sermon 288, "On the Birthday of John the Baptist," in *The Works of St. Augustine: A Translation for the 21st Century*, vol. 3/8, *Sermons 273–305A*, ed. John E. Rotelle, trans. Edmund Hill (Hyde Park, NY: New City Press, 1994), 112.

63. Ibid., 115; Tim Denecker and Gert Partoens, "*De uoce et uerbo*: Augustine's Exegesis of John 1:1–3 and 23 in Sermons 288 and 293a auct (Dolbeau 3)," *Annali di Storia dell'Esegesi* 31 (2014): 108. According to the bishop of Hippo, a word while remaining in the mind can be voiced in many ways. "In an analogous way, Christ the Word abided with the Father (John 1:1–3) while many and diverse heralds were sent ahead, and inversely, Christ, the Word that took on the flesh (John 1:14), only came into the world after having been announced by many and diverse preceding heralds."

64. Romero admits that "I feel this immense responsibility, brothers and sisters, that each time that I preach, I am no more than a humble channel, like the microphone that is transmitting, amplifying my voice. I am the microphone, nothing more, to bring to your ears that which God wants to say to you" (*Homilías*, 1:488).

65. Taylor, "Subalternity and Advocacy." Taylor describes "delirium" phenomenologically: "What is this delirium? We can begin to understand it by noting that when an entitled advocate seeks practices and thinking that are both for them (the subaltern) and for him-/ herself (the entitled advocate), as

I suggested above in the third mode of authentic advocacy, then the voice of the subordinate other is, in a sense, no longer simply outside of the advocate. This other is also in us, as well as outside us" (37). Why is this important? "It subverts the secure status of the entitled advocate without doing away with the basic awareness of the relevance of a distinction between worlds of elites and worlds of the subordinated. The delirium is an important aspect of subaltern studies where a dance of relinquishment occurs—a relinquishment of objectification and assimilation that fosters rupture and reorientation so that the subaltern may find voice. I say 'may find voice,' because in the dance of this delirium, even though we have a better chance through it of rising above the problem of subaltern speechlessness, there is no guarantee that we will do so" (39).

66. Barbara Reid, O.P., "Romero the Preacher," in *Archbishop Romero: Martyr and Prophet for the New Millennium*, ed. Robert Pelton, C.S.C. (Scranton, PA: University of Scranton Press, 2006), 17–32. What I do not find in Romero is much of Nathan the prophet. I have been struck by the contrast in homiletical approaches in many mainline churches in the United States compared to that most common in Latin America. Nathan the prophet was sent by God to condemn David's adultery with Bathsheba and the cover-up that led to the murder of her husband Uriah. The story is well known. Nathan tells David a parable about two men, one rich, one poor, and a little lamb. By telling a parable, Nathan leads David to pass judgment on himself. A more direct approach, a straightforward denunciation might have been useless against the king and might have led to the compounding of sins by adding Nathan's exile or murder to the list. In the United States, students learn to preach like Nathan the prophet. The Nathan approach is inductive, subtle. It works by misdirection and guile. In Latin America, the approach is like that of John the Baptist. He is direct and hard. He denounces his listeners as a brood of vipers. He warns of axes poised to strike at the root of the tree. He promises the coming of one who is even more fearsome than he, bringing fire. Like Nathan, John the Baptist also preaches against his king for murder and adultery. But the results are very different. Herod does not repent. The only judgment Herod passes is against John the Baptist, who is put to death. Both approaches are biblical. Both are speaking truth to power, but in different ways and with different risks. There is more John the Baptist in Romero than Nathan.

67. Ibid., 17. Less on the mark, I think, is Reid's characterization and contrast of Romero's preaching before and after the assassination of Rutilio Grande on March 12, 1977. On the basis of no textual evidence but simply

the common (and somewhat misleading) conversion narrative of Romero's life, she says, "My guess is that before that date he was a didactic preacher, one who expounded on the meaning of the Scriptures as text, a preacher who explained the Church's teaching as an enforcer" (18). Romero became a prophetic preacher in response to the death of Grande. This reading of Romero has been challenged by recent biographers like Roberto Morozzo della Rocca and by Romero himself (cf. Morozzo della Rocca, *Primero Dios*, 185–95). It also flies in the face of Reid's helpful reminder of the variety of prophetic callings in scripture.

68. Cf. *Teología en Conjunto: A Collaborative Hispanic Protestant Approach*, ed. José David Rodríguez and Loida I. Martell Otero (Louisville, KY: Westminster John Knox Press, 1997). The concept of *en conjunto* carries methodological weight. It is intended to express the theologizing of a group of people who are both diverse in culture and conjoined in purpose. Theology done *en conjunto* aspires to model a collaboration among scholars that is rarely found and even less frequently rewarded by the academy. Justo González also refers to this methodological solidarity as *Fuenteovejuna* theology in remembrance of a play by Lope de Vega, where the people of the town of Fuenteovejuna maintain their solidarity in the face of police attempts to divide the community. Cf. Justo González, *Mañana: Christian Theology from a Hispanic Perspective* (Nashville, TN: Abingdon Press, 1990), 28–30.

69. It is crucial to note that the "I" in Montesino's preaching is not individualistic. The sermon was drafted in *conjunto* by the community of Dominicans in La Española under the leadership of Pedro de Córdoba. All the friars signed their names on the manuscript. Montesinos was chosen to deliver the message because of his oratorical gifts in sermon delivery, but he spoke on behalf of the entire religious community. The "voice" that is crying out is an ecclesial one.

70. Quoted in *Medellín* 14.2.

71. Earlier I said that one of the limitations of the first preachers in the Americas was that even as they preached on behalf of the indigenous they were less successful in empowering them to speak in their own voices. Extending Romero's use of Augustine to these early voices of the voiceless, we can say that Montesinos heard the voice of the indigenous; he heard their cry and this was already a miracle. However, the friar did not hear the words in the cry. For this reason, he did not question the necessity of being also the words of the voiceless and voice of the wordless. After all, as Augustine said: "A word has full value, even without a voice; a voice is worthless without a word" (sermon 288, 3). In the case of Las Casas, he did hear echoes of the

Word in the voices of the indigenous, but these were mostly the moans of the crucified rather than the words of the good teacher.

72. Romero does not limit either revelation or salvation to the people of God. He states: "Salvation is not exclusive to the Bible or the church. God has a thousand more ways. He can even use the natural religions to bring, through inspired humans, the message of salvation to many who were not baptized and who will no doubt enjoy a place in heaven, perhaps even higher than that of many of the baptized because they were faithful in listening to the voice of the Spirit speaking through those people" (*Homilías*, 5:83).

73. It is not only the poor that are voiceless. Romero speaks of the suffering, the victims of abuse, and the socially marginalized as voiceless (cf. *Homilías*, 1:230). Even so, it is for the poor campesinos that Romero most often speaks. Romero might be criticized for not speaking for those who have been rendered voiceless because of their gender (the feminist critique) or their race (the black liberationist critique). The critique may have merit, but its weight needs to be balanced by two considerations. First, the focus on the poor is not meant to neglect other forms of exclusion. Second, the focus on the poor campesino is the way in which Romero contextualized the reading of the signs of the times offered by the bishops at the council in Medellín and their missiological preferential option for the poor. We will return to these matters in chapter 5 when discussing Romero's understanding of the preferential option for the poor.

74. Pope Francis, *Evangelii Gaudium* 198, 2015, https://w2.vatican.va /content/francesco/en/apost_exhortations/documents/papa-francesco _esortazione-ap_20131124_evangelii-gaudium.html. Incidentally, this exhortation could be read as homiletical guide for a new evangelization that is very much in the spirit of Romero.

75. Cf. *Homilías*, 5:40. Romero explains this call by drawing on the thought of John Paul II in *Redemptor Hominis*, in particular paragraphs 13 and 14. Paragraph 13 speaks to the uniqueness, concreteness, and transcendence of every human being, who, among all creatures on earth, God has willed for himself. Paragraph 14 develops this thought further by speaking to how this divine will is historically enacted. Even before birth, even before conception, each one of us has a history, each one can say, "I exist in the mind of God as a project, which if realized, will make of me a saint, because a saint is nothing less than the fulfillment of a life according to God's thought" (*Homilías*, 5:37). Our personal history begins before birth and ends after death as we face judgment and either sink to hell for misusing our freedom or are raised to heaven.

76. Quoted in Jon Sobrino, *Witnesses to the Kingdom: The Martyrs of El Salvador and the Crucified Peoples* (Maryknoll, NY: Orbis Books, 2003), 40.

77. Quoted in ibid., 45–46.

78. Maier, *Oscar Romero*, 84.

79. Quoted in José Pacífico Berra Zarinelli, "Monseñor Romero: Su significado para la eclesiología" (MA thesis, Universidad Centroamericana "Jose Simeon Cañas," 1990), 70.

Chapter 3. The Transfiguration of El Salvador

1. Robert Brenneman, *Homies and Hermanos: God and Gangs in Central America* (New York: Oxford University Press, 2012), loc. 208–10, Kindle. Brenneman notes that "most gang members are told when they join one of Central America's transnational gang cells, that their new commitment must last hasta la morgue—that is, 'all the way to the morgue.' And many Central Americans, both gang members and onlookers, have concluded that the morgue rule is true, believing that 'once a gang member, always a gang member.'"

2. Justo González, "From All Four of Earth's Faraway Corners," in *Mil voces para celebrar: Himnario metodista* (Nashville, TN: United Methodist Publishing House, 1996), 378.

3. *Fiestas Agostinas: Año de gracia jubilar 2000*, ed. Modesto López Portillo (San Salvador: Imprenta Criterio, 2000), 15.

4. Jesús Delgado Acevedo, *Historia de la iglesia en El Salvador* (San Salvador: Dirección de Publicaciones e Impresos, 2011), 33.

5. Santiago Barbarena proposes that the name was suggested by the Latin title that the feast has in liturgical books, namely, *Transfiguratio Divini nostri Salvatoris*. The problem with this explanation is that it lacks any documentary evidence. Delgado Acevedo, *Historia de la iglesia*, 33.

6. Delgado quotes from the final prayer for the Christmas mass: "Oh, omnipotent God, grant, we pray, that the savior of the world who has been born to us grant us immortality at the end, since he himself makes us be born to divinity in this world" (ibid., 276n61).

7. Cf. ibid., 274–75n52.

8. Cited by Carlos Gregorio López, *Mármoles, clarines y bronces: Fiestas cívico-religiosas en El Salvador, siglos XIX y XX* (San Salvador: Editorial Universidad Don Bosco, 2011), 3. López admits that the serendipitous finding of this text challenged his own historiography of the origins and development

of national celebrations. Nationalist discourse in El Salvador began earlier and was less anticlerical than most historians thought.

9. Jose T. Alferrez, ed., *Anuario de la Provincial Eclesiástica de El Salvador* (San Salvador: Curia Metropolitana, 1941), 17.

10. Pope Pius XII, "Radiomensaje de su santidad Pío XII al I Congreso Eucarístico Nacional de El Salvador," November 26, 1942, https://w2 .vatican.va/content/pius-xii/es/speeches/1942/documents/hf_p-xii_spe _19421126_eucaristico-salvador.html#_edn*.

11. The abiding relevance of Romero's analysis is made clear by the fact that Archbishop Escobar appeals to it in his own pastoral letter as a faithful prolongation of Medellín and an example of the kind of rigorous reflection that must be conducted to grapple with the current situation. Arguably Ignacio Ellacuría's essay "Violencia y cruz" (in *Escritos teológicos*, vol. 3 [San Salvador: UCA Editores, 2001], 427–82) informed the content of the pastoral letter more than Romero, but since he is not beatified the letter does not invoke his assistance, and the shape of the letter owes more to the martyred archbishop than to the martyred professor.

12. José Luis Escobar Alas, *Veo en la ciudad violencia y discordia: Carta pastoral* (San Salvador: Arzobispado de San Salvador, 2016), para. 20.

13. Bartolomé de las Casas, *A Short Account of the Destruction of the Indies* (New York: Penguin Group, 1992), 63–64.

14. Escobar Alas, *Veo en la ciudad*, para. 24.

15. Ibid., 26.

16. Escobar cites from Pope Francis's *Evangelii Gaudium* 53: "The excluded are not the 'exploited' but the outcast, the 'leftovers'" (para. 50). Indeed, large portions of this pastoral letter may be read as an application of *Evangelii Gaudium* to El Salvador.

17. Ibid., 53.

18. Escobar Alas, *Veo en la ciudad*, para. 60.

19. Ibid., 33.

20. Nancy Pineda-Madrid, *Suffering and Salvation in Ciudad Juarez* (Minneapolis, MN: Fortress Press, 2011), 69.

21. Ibid.

22. Gustavo Gutiérrez, "Notes for a Theology of Liberation," *Theological Studies* 31, no. 22 (1970): 243–61. The Peruvian founding father of liberation theology, Gustavo Gutiérrez, observes that in Latin America terms like *economic development* and *social progress* have been given a quasi-mystical status. These have been intended to stir hope but have ultimately increased frustration because they do not get to the root of the problem. If the problem is

underdevelopment, then the solution is development. However, if the real problem is oppression, then the remedy is liberation. Two master themes help unite liberation and salvation. The first of these is the unity of Creation and salvation. The Creator is the Redeemer. Creation is God's first saving act, and the history of Israel is a prolongation of this act. The second theme uniting salvation and liberation is that of the eschatological promises. The prophetic announcements of universal peace and the new heavens and new earth are accompanied by denunciations of socially unjust conditions and the expectation that these must be overcome.

23. Elsa Tamez, *The Amnesty of Grace: Justification by Faith from a Latin American Perspective* (Nashville, TN: Abingdon Press, 1993). Elsa Tamez acknowledges problems with the transmitted Protestant doctrine. The historical experience of the church in Latin America, particularly the Protestant Church, raises new questions. The new reformers do not only ask like Martin Luther, "Where do we find a merciful God?" but also "How can we bring about a just world? How can we be merciful? How do you preach justification to someone who experiences permanent marginalization? How does one uphold the Reformation slogans of *sola gratia, sola fide* without devaluing the importance of human action in society?" The Latin American experience then leads to a new reading of justification by faith in Paul that links the lack of knowledge of God with the absence of justice. In light of this understanding of the human predicament, justification entails the gift of inclusion of those who have been socially marginalized and are now counted as members of the people of God.

24. Jon Sobrino, *No Salvation outside the Poor: Prophetic-Utopian Essays* (Maryknoll, NY: Orbis Books, 2008). Cyprian of Carthage, in the context of the Novatian schism, stated that *extra ecclesiam nulla salus*, "outside the church there is no salvation." The Jesuit Jon Sobrino in the context of economic class schisms reformulates the saying as *extra pauperes nulla salus*, "outside the poor there is no salvation." He understands that this adaptation of Cyprian is challenging. It is a scandal to the successful who identify wealth with salvation and is a stumbling block to the pious who see the poor as lazy. Nevertheless, the formula is urgently needed because of the growing inequality between the poor and the rich. There is need for a new understanding of salvation that starts from the fact that Christ became poor. The transcendent God became trans-descendent and con-descendent. The poor are God's chosen bearers of salvation not because they are strong but because they are weak and rejected. By virtue of who they are, they denounce a world

of selfish abundance and call it to repent, turn, and be saved by siding with them in transforming society.

25. The inclusion of the Methodist Tamez on this list may seem unwarranted. Clearly Romero could not have read her work, yet a few facts justify her inclusion. First, one of Tamez's books, *La hora de la vida: Lecturas bíblicas* (San José, Costa Rica: DIE, 1978), is found in Romero's personal library. Ownership does not necessarily suggest familiarity, but, second, Tamez's thinking is representative of a line of socially engaged Protestant theology of which Romero knew and approved.

26. See the entry "Transfiguration" by G. H. Guyot in *New Catholic Encyclopedia*, 2nd ed., vol. 14 (Washington, DC: Thomson Gale, 2003), 155.

27. Romero is aware of the more primitive (at least in the West) observance (cf. *Homilías*, 2:276). In the East, the origins of the feast are also unclear. As John Baggley states, "It is possible that the Feast may derive from the dedication of three basilicas on Mount Tabor, the 'high mountain' where, according to tradition, the Transfiguration occurred." See John Baggley, *Festival Icons for the Christian Year* (Crestwood, NY: St. Vladimir's Press, 2000), 58.

28. On all years, the Old Testament lesson comes from Dan. 7:9–10, 13–14, where Daniel has a vision of the Son of Man. The epistle lesson comes from 2 Pet. 1:16–19, where the writer recalls the revelation of the transfigured Jesus. On year A, the gospel lesson comes from Matt. 17:1–9; on year B from Mark 9:1–9; and on year C from Luke 9:28b–36. Romero preached patronal feast sermons at the cathedral on 1976 (B), 1977 (C), 1978 (A), and 1979 (B).

29. *Semanario Chaparrastique*, no. 1632, August 9, 1946, 1. The *Semanario Chaparrastique* was the weekly newspaper of the diocese of San Miguel. I accessed it through the archdiocese's website dedicated to Romero's canonization cause: www.romeroes.com/monsenor-romero-su-pensamiento /prensa-escrita/semanario-chaparrastique.

30. Ibid.

31. Ibid.

32. It was published in parts in the *Semanario Chaparrastique* from August 16 to September 6, 1963, in response to requests from the readership of the weekly paper. See *Semanario Chaparrastique*, no. 2910, August 16, 1963, 6.

33. Ibid.

34. Romero cites from a message from Pius XII to the first ambassador of El Salvador to the Holy See. Pius XII states: El Salvador "bears in its

name the highest religious vocation and in its history the indelible print of the most deeply rooted Catholicism. If we wish to leave aside the somewhat nebulous times of the mythic Votan or the prehistoric times of the heroic Quetzalcoatl, none can deny that your chronicles open with Pedro de Alvarado, who in 1524 placed his conquests under the protection of the most blessed Trinity and in 1528 gave the name of San Salvador to your capital." See Pope Pius XII, *Discurso del Santo Padre Pío XII al Señor Héctor Escobar Serrano, primer embajador de la República de El Salvador ante la Santa Sede*, March 25, 1952, https://w2.vatican.va/content/pius-xii/es/speeches/1952 /documents/hf_p-xii_spe_19520325_ambassador-el-salvador.html.

35. The reference is Pius XII's charge to the Salvadoran ambassador to the Holy See, Héctor Escobar Serrano, on March 25, 1962. Ibid.

36. *Semanario Chaparrastique*, no. 2910, August 16, 1963, 6.

37. Ibid.

38. See Pope Paul VI, "Radiomensaje de Su Santidad Pablo VI al Congreso Eucarístico de El Salvador," April 19, 1964, https://w2.vatican.va /content/paul-vi/es/messages/pont-messages/documents/hf_p-vi_mess _19640419_eucaristico-el-salvador.html.

39. *Semanario Chaparrastique*, no. 2911, August 23, 1963, 6. Aquinas explains: "That the glory of his soul did not overflow into his body from the first moment of Christ's conception was due to a certain divine dispensation, that, as stated above (3:14:1 ad 2), he might fulfil the mysteries of our redemption in a passible body" (*Summa theologica* [hereafter *ST*] 3.45.2, trans. Fathers of the English Dominican Province, *The Summa Theologica of St. Thomas Aquinas* (Allen, TX: Christian Classics, 1948).

40. The term *claritas* in Thomas refers to a quality of transparency and brightness. The clarity of the Transfiguration is an anticipation of the clarity of glory. The light of Tabor differs from the light of glory in its transience. The nature of the body is not changed definitively but only temporarily. As Thomas explains, in the Resurrection clarity becomes an immanent quality of the body, but at the Transfiguration it is only "a transient passion [*per modum passionis transeuntis*], as when the air is lit up by the sun" (*ST* 3.45.2).

41. See Pope Leo I's sermon 51 on the Transfiguration preached on the vigil of the Second Sunday of Lent, trans. Charles Lett Feltoe, in *Nicene and Post-Nicene Fathers*, 2nd ser., vol. 12, ed. Philip Schaff and Henry Wace (Buffalo, NY: Christian Literature Publishing, 1895), rev. and ed. for New Advent by Kevin Knight, www.newadvent.org/fathers/360351.htm.

42. *Semanario Chaparrastique*, no. 2911, 6. Romero draws on Pope Leo I, sermon 51, sec. 6 (I am translating Romero's version): "'This is my son,'

who was born from me and is with me from before all ages, the one who is with me, one single divinity, one single power, one single eternity. 'This is my son,' not adopted as all humans may be through sanctifying grace, but my son by nature, the one who is born eternally from my very essence, equal to me in everything. 'This is my son' by whom all things were made and without whom nothing was made, because everything that I do, in the same way, inseparably, he does with me. Our unity is never divided, and I who beget him being different from him who is begotten, you should not think of him as something different from me. 'This is my son,' who does not pretend to be like me as usurper, but rather remaining in the form of my own glory, only out of need of redeeming the human race, in accord with me, he inclined the unchanging divinity to take the form of a servant. 'In him I am well pleased' because 'in him' is my entire divine nature, all truth and perfection from which spring all good things. 'In him' is the fountain of all beauty, all truth, and perfection from which spring all beauties, truths, and perfections. 'Listen to him' because he is God and in him are truth and life. He is my virtue and wisdom, the key to all my revelations." This passage is one of Romero's lengthiest citations from the church fathers. Doubtless, the rhetorical power of the prose in conjunction with its theological density attracted Romero to the great apologist for Chalcedon.

43. *Semanario Chaparrastique*, no. 2911, 6.

44. Ibid. See *ST* 3.45.3: "Christ wished to be transfigured in order to show men his glory, and to arouse men to a desire of it, as stated above (Article 1). Now men are brought to the glory of eternal beatitude by Christ—not only those who lived after him, but also those who preceded him; therefore, when he was approaching his passion, both 'the multitude that followed' and that 'which went before, cried, saying: "Hosanna,"' as related in Matthew 21:9, beseeching him, as it were, to save them. Consequently it was fitting that witnesses should be present from among those who preceded him—namely, Moses and Elias—and from those who followed after him—namely, Peter, James, and John—that 'in the mouth of two or three witnesses' this word might stand."

45. On Romero's work against the Masons, see René Antonio Chanta Martínez, "Antimasonería y antiliberalismo en el pensamiento de Oscar Arnulfo Romero, 1962–1965," *REHMLAC* 3, no. 1 (2011): 121–41. Chanta notes that as director of the weekly *Chaparrastique* Romero wrote harsh editorials against Masonry. The reasons for Romero's attack stem from a historiography that blamed Masons for a secularization of the state that drove a wedge between El Salvador and Rome in 1872, ending the concordat that

had existed between the two since 1862. Romero's attack was also driven by fears that Masons were currently infiltrating the highest posts in government and education. As such, historically and in actuality, Masonry represented a threat to the Catholic culture of El Salvador. Chanta argues that Romero's concerns were very much in harmony with official Roman Catholic warnings and prescriptions regarding the Masons, to which by the middle of the last century were added a similar cluster of concerns regarding communism. In the author's judgment, the interpretation offered by Romero of the Masons' role in the history of El Salvador, even if oversimplified, was on the whole in accord with the actual situation. In addition to his study of Romero's anti-Masonic polemic, Chanta makes a strong and timely appeal for greater study of the years of Romero's life before he became archbishop. Indeed, his study of this little-known chapter of Romero's history can open fresh vistas that allow for better understanding the first Salvadoran raised to the altars. For instance, Chanta points out that in Romero's first anti-Masonic writing, which dates to September 7, 1962, Romero blames the collusion of liberalism and Masonry for the vastly unequal distribution of wealth in El Salvador. Chanta states that "this editorial is, in my judgment, very significant in the trajectory of Romero, since he is already denouncing the unjust distribution of wealth and social inequality before the celebration of the Second Vatican Council and the gatherings of the Latin American episcopate in Medellin and Puebla" (127n12).

46. *Semanario Chaparrastique*, no. 2913, September 6, 1963, 3.

47. Óscar Romero, "El Divino Salvador," sermon, August 20, 1976, published in seven parts in the diocesan paper *Diario de Oriente*, August 20 and 27 and October 1, 8, 15, 22, and 29, 1976, www.romeroes.com/monsenor -romero-su-pensamiento/prensa-escrita/diario-de-oriente?start=60.

48. Ibid., pt. 1 in *Diario de Oriente*, no. 30999, August 20, 1976, 2.

49. Ibid., pt. 3 in *Diario de Oriente*, no. 31005, October 1, 1976, 3.

50. Ibid. In support of this assertion, Romero turns to Paul VI's *Evangelii Nuntiandi*, the apostolic exhortation that followed the 1974 synod of bishops on the topic of evangelization in the modern world. This gathering, which included among its officials both Eduardo Pironio and Karol Wojtyła, "reemphasized the essential missionary character of the church and the duty of each member to bear witness to Christ in the world." Dennis Sadowski, "Evangelization at the Margins Drives USCCB Convocation Planning," Catholic News Service, March 6, 2017, http://www.catholicnews.com /services/englishnews/2017/evangelization-at-the-margins-drives-usccb -convocation-planning.cfm.

51. Pope Paul VI, *Evangelii Nuntiandi* 36, December 8, 1975, http://w2 .vatican.va/content/paul-vi/en/apost_exhortations/documents/hf_p-vi _exh_19751208_evangelii-nuntiandi.html.

52. Pope Paul VI, *Lumen Gentium* 1, November 21, 1964, www.vatican .va/archive/hist_councils/ii_vatican_council/documents/vat-ii_const _19641121_lumen-gentium_en.html.

53. Romero, "Divino Salvador," pt. 6 in *Diario de Oriente*, no. 31008, October 22, 1976, 3.

54. Ibid., pt. 7 in *Diario de Oriente*, no. 31009, October 29, 1976, 3.

55. Romero's first pastoral letter as archbishop had been released on Easter Sunday, April 10, 1977. It was titled, appropriately, "The Easter Church." As bishop of Santiago de María, Romero had issued a pastoral letter on Pentecost, May 18, 1975. Its title was "The Holy Spirit in the Church."

56. Dan. 7 or 2 Pet. 1.

57. Óscar Romero, *Mons. Óscar A. Romero: Su diario* (San Salvador: Imprenta Criterio, 2000), November 21, 1979, 312; henceforth referred to as *Diario*.

58. Romero reads the section of the letter that states: "What does the Church ask of you today? She tells you in one of the major documents of this council. She asks of you only liberty, the liberty to believe and to preach her faith, the freedom to love her God and serve Him, the freedom to live and to bring to men her message of life. Do not fear her. She is made after the image of her Master, whose mysterious action does not interfere with your prerogatives but heals everything human of its fatal weakness, transfigures it and fills it with hope, truth and beauty." Pope Paul VI, *Address to the Rulers*, December 8, 1965, http://w2.vatican.va/content/paul-vi/en/speeches /1965/documents/hf_p-vi_spe_19651208_epilogo-concilio-governanti .html.

59. The readings for 1978 (Year A) were Matt. 17:1–9; Gen. 12:1–4; 2 Tim. 1:8–10; for 1979 (Year B), Mark 9:1–9; Gen. 22:1–2, 9a, 15–18; Rom. 8:31b–34; for 1980 (Year C), Luke 9:28–36; Gen. 15:5–12, 17–18; Phil. 3:17–4:1.

60. November 27, 1977; February 19, 1978; September 24, 1978; December 3, 1978; October 21, 1979; December 3, 1979; March 9, 1980.

61. Cf. *Sacrosanctum Concilium* 109.

62. Margaret Pfeil, "Oscar Romero's Theology of Transfiguration," *Theological Studies* 72 (2011): 91.

63. Arthur Michael Ramsey, *The Glory of God and the Transfiguration of Christ* (Eugene, OR: Wipf and Stock, 1949), 144.

64. Baggley, *Festival Icons*, 58.

65. Pfeil, "Oscar Romero's Theology," 89.

66. Sobrino, *Archbishop Romero*, 4.

67. Jon Sobrino, *Christology at the Crossroads* (Maryknoll, NY: Orbis Books, 1978), xi.

68. Sobrino purported to offer a Christology that was ecclesial, historical, and Trinitarian. By *historical*, Sobrino meant to focus attention on the Jesus of history rather than the Christ of faith. The exegetical challenges facing the recovery of the historical Jesus are daunting but must be faced if Christian faith is to be founded not on abstractions, myths, or dogmas but on the man who lived and was killed in Palestine, the man that the disciples knew and preached. For Sobrino, the historical focus entailed approaching the gospels with historical categories. Greater emphasis was to be given to what Jesus did than to what he said, for his history is first praxis before it is doctrine. When it comes to doctrine, greater emphasis was to be given to the message of the kingdom of God than to the messenger. Sobrino contended that this emphasis faithfully replicated Jesus's own, for he preached much more about the kingdom than about himself. What emerges from Sobrino's study of the historical Jesus is that this person, far from being some idealized human being whose death mysteriously reconciles us to God, was the cause of conflict and that it was for this reason that he was killed. By *Trinitarian*, Sobrino did not mean to lead his readers to Chalcedon but to a deeper reflection of how following Jesus in his humanity was integral to Christology. "Christology is possible only if the Father continues to be the ultimate horizon of reality, the Son continues to be the definitive example of how human beings can correspond to the Father, and life according to the Spirit of Jesus continues to be the authentic Christian way of acting that makes us and daughters in and through the Son" (xxiv–v).

69. Sobrino recalled the events in the following terms: "I did not attend the Mass that August 6, but a few hours after its conclusion a fellow priest brought me a tape of the homily. I turned on the recorder and chills went up my spine. Bishop Romero's first point was a criticism of the christologies being developed in El Salvador—'rationalistic, revolutionary, hate-filled christologies.' Bishop Romero began his homily with a virulent criticism of my own christology." Sobrino, *Archbishop Romero*, 4.

70. Morozzo della Rocca notes that the copy in Romero's library is unopened, but this is not conclusive (*Primero Dios*, 162n146). It is certainly the case that the book is long and that it would have taken precious time from his episcopal ministry to work his way through its complex arguments.

In any case, as Morozzo della Rocca admits, Romero would have been familiar with the Basque Jesuit, having heard him lecture on the topic of "Jesus
Christ and the Kingdom of God" at the seminary San José de la Montaña in
1974.

71. Pfeil, "Oscar Romero's Theology," 92–93.

72. Romero states: "Now, since the sixties, a new concern has arisen in
theology to want to study this Christology more deeply. And there are two
currents: one current called Christology from above and the other Christology from below. From above I understand as the consideration of the
God who becomes human and by Christology from below, the human who
in Christ became God." The definition for the second one sounds almost
adoptionist. Surely, this is not Romero's intent, but is in fact a strong current
against which Christologies from below like Sobrino's must swim.

73. Cf. Pope John Paul II, *Address to the Third General Conference of the Latin
American Episcopate, Puebla, Mexico*, January 28, 1979, https://w2.vatican.va
/content/john-paul-ii/en/speeches/1979/january/documents/hf_jp-ii
_spe_19790128_messico-puebla-episc-latam.html.

74. Pope Leo I, sermon 51, sec. 2. For the Latin text, I consulted http://
frcoulter.com/leo/latin/tractatus51.html.

75. Ibid., sec. 5.

76. Secretaria Arzobispal, San Salvador, July 1947. Confident that the
Divine Savior is also the Divine Pilot, the people of El Salvador are exhorted
to cry out to him, "Lord, save us for we perish" and to reverently lift their
eyes and heart to the beloved Son. If they do, then their souls will be transfigured by sacramental grace and they will confirm the faith that was handed
to them by their fathers.

77. Cited in Josef Pieper's *In Tune with the World: A Theory of Festivity*
(South Bend, IN: St. Augustine's Press, 1999), 23. A festival is more than
a good time. The Thomist philosopher Josef Pieper describes a festival as a
phenomenon of wealth, not of material wealth, but of existential wealth. A
festival praises the Creator and celebrates the creation despite the inscruta-
bility of the first and the contradictions of the second. It is an affirmation
that in spite of everything that is going on it is good to be alive. Festivals are
not for the stingy. Festivals are not for the naysayers. Festivals are for those
who, in spite of everything, hope.

78. *Orientación*, July 30, 1978, 7.

79. Ibid.

80. According to Canty, "Perhaps what is most striking at first glance is
the prominence of 'fittingness' in these questions. Fittingness was scarcely

mentioned in the *Scriptum*, but here it plays an important role in three of the questions. Also, although the question on clarity is present in all of the investigations during this period, and the question of the 'witnesses' is also important, Thomas is singular in devoting a separate question to the Father's voice. Indeed the proportion between the examination of Christ's transfiguration per se and the examination of the 'circumstances' is highly unusual in the Summa. Most of the theological investigations of the transfiguration during the middle of the thirteenth century concentrate on Christ's transfiguration and conclude the study with a brief question or two on the circumstantial details. In the *Summa theologiae*, however, Thomas gives almost equal space to the transfiguration and to the circumstantial details." Aaron Canty, *Light and Glory: The Transfiguration of Christ in Early Franciscan and Dominican Theology* (Washington, DC: Catholic University of America Press, 2011), 225.

81. Charles R. Pinches, *A Gathering of Memories: Family, Nation, and Church in a Forgetful World* (Grand Rapids, MI: Brazos Press, 2006), 116.

82. Ibid., 114.

83. Ibid., 117.

84. Given this focus on history, it is interesting that Romero does not stop to reflect on the significance of the timing of the event itself. In the tradition there is considerable discussion over how to interpret the opening of the account: "six days later" according to Matthew 17:1 and Mark 9:2 and "about eight days after" according to Luke 9:23. Origen gives these numbers an eschatological interpretation. However this theme does not appear in the less allegorizing Leo and Aquinas. Cf. Kenneth Stevenson, "From Hilary of Poitiers to Peter of Blois: A Transfiguration Journey of Biblical Interpretation," *Scottish Journal of Theology* 61, no. 3 (2008): 291.

85. Even as he was throwing open the windows of the church to the world, John XXIII understood that the light of Christ can become a sign of contradiction. "Christ, always radiant in the center of history and life. People are either with him and his Church, and in this case enjoy light, goodness, order, and peace. Or they are without him or against him, and deliberately against his Church. Then they become sources of confusion, cause harshness in human relations, and persistent dangers of fratricidal wars." Pope John XXIII, *Solemne Apertura del Concilio Vaticano II: Discurso de Su Santidad Juan XXIII*, October 11, 1962, https://w2.vatican.va/content/john-xxiii /es/speeches/1962/documents/hf_j-xxiii_spe_19621011_opening-council .html. Romero cites from these opening remarks to Vatican II in his 1963 Transfiguration homily. *Semanario Chaparrastique*, no. 2913, 3.

86. *Orientación*, July 30, 1977, 5.

87. Pfeil, "Oscar Romero's Theology," 90.

88. Ibid., 97.

89. Ibid.

90. *Orientación*, July 30, 1978, 7.

91. In a letter to Cardinal Baggio, Romero compares his actions to those of Ambrose of Milan, who barred Emperor Theodosius from the church as penance for a massacre he authorized. Romero explains that he was open to dialogue with the president, but "in order to not be manipulated into investing with religious legitimacy an authority that had until now been so removed from the common good, I believed that my duty was, as I have written, to condition that dialogue to facts and not only to words of goodwill" (Morozzo della Rocca, *Primero Dios*, 181).

92. Pfeil, "Oscar Romero's Theology," 112.

93. *Orientación*, August 1, 1976, 3.

94. The quotation comes from Irenaeus, *Against the Heresies* 3.20.2, ed. Roberts and Donaldson, 450. John Paul II references this text in his inaugural address at Puebla (*Puebla* 1.9, p. 228).

95. Las Casas, *Historia de las Indias*, vol. 3, pt. 4, 13–14***.

96. Theologians certainly are allowed to dream, and Pineda-Madrid finds the thought of Shawn Copeland moving in the right direction. "The history of human suffering and oppression, of failure and progress, are transformed only in light of the supernatural. If human activity is not an abstraction but a concrete reality that embraces the billions of human beings who ever have lived, are living, or will live, and if each and every human person is a part of the whole of interpersonal relationships that constitute human history, then we, too—each one of us—shall be transformed" (quoted in Pineda-Madrid, *Suffering and Salvation,* 93). In Romero's language the longed-for transformation is called transfiguration, a vision of the transfigured Christ and his creation that is seen inchoately even in this life.

97. Ignacio Ellacuría, "Cruz y violencia," in *Escritos teológicos*, 3:427–82. Earlier versions of this essay were published in 1969 and 1973. Hence Romero could have read the essay. In any case, he would have been exposed to Ellacuría's thoughts on this subject through their personal contact.

98. Ellacuría's essay offers the intellectual moorings for José Escobar Alas's 2016 pastoral letter on violence (*Veo en la ciudad,* cf. paras. 5, 37, 64, 74).

99. Ellacuría, "Cruz y violencia," 445.

100. Ibid.

101. Ibid., 446.

102. Claudia Marlene Rivera Navarrete pointed out this lacuna in a lecture in San Salvador on March 13, 2017. Violence is a symptom, but of what? She found Escobar Alas's analysis of violence in his first pastoral letter a step forward in diagnosing the problem. In her judgment, the basic disease is social exclusion, which is grounded on inequality. In other words, violence is a symptom of blindness to the equal dignity of all persons as creatures made in the image of God. Cf. Rivera Navarrete, "Denuncia profética." Drawing on Jon Sobrino's analysis, Rivera Navarrete presents the consequences of the *mysterium iniquitatis* in stark terms. "Dehumanization is the consequence of the idolatrization of wealth. The consequence is serious because the rich person loses the humanity that grace conferred on her from birth being created as the living image of God. Then, the dehumanization is extended to the poor one, who, according to the aforementioned definition, is denied a name, freedom, and thus existence. The poor are not human; they do not exist; they have no face because they have been rendered invisible" (68).

103. Ellacuría is well aware of the difficulty that Christians have in reading these psalms. "An apparently flabby conception of Christianity and the human, which at bottom falls into tolerance for the unjust oppressor, has rendered us incapable of understanding texts and attitudes that are so strong, so primitive, if you will, that they scandalize the 'civilized' Christians" ("Cruz y violencia," 451).

104. Ibid., 454.

105. Ibid., 458.

106. Óscar Romero, "A propósito de Managua y del sufrimiento: ¿Por qué Dios lo permite?," *Diario de Oriente*, no. 30835, January 5, 1973, 4.

107. As important as it is for Christians to keep this distinction in mind as a bulwark against the atheistic solution to the problem of pain, Romero wisely does not seek to solve the problem. Indeed, he believes that "the complete understanding of the problem would be a sign of the limitation of God and of the capacity of the human mind to encompass the Most High." Instead of a solution, Romero reminds his readers of the old saying "God writes straight on crooked lines" (ibid.).

108. "This is the mark of an underdeveloped civilization! Not standing the light of reason found in some writings!" (*Homilías*, 1:165).

109. In his homily from November 11, 1979, "The Three Christian Forces That Will Forge the Liberation of Our People," Romero avers: "We must not deify progress as if life were impossible without it. We have to keep in mind that the first thing is God, and next to God, the human. If progress leads away from God or leads away from and mutilates and runs over the

human, it is not true progress. Only the one who is poor in spirit will know how to place God and the human above all else. This is the key to civilization. It is not in having grand buildings or great airfields or great roads, if these are only for a privileged minority and not for the people with whose blood all these were built" (*Homilías*, 5:521–22).

110. "Peace can write the finest pages of history, inscribing them not only with the magnificence of power and glory but also with the greater magnificence of human virtue, people's goodness, collective prosperity, and true civilization: the civilization of love." Pope Paul VI, *If You Want Peace, Defend Life*, December 8, 1976, https://w2.vatican.va/content/paul-vi/en/messages /peace/documents/hf_p-vi_mes_19761208_x-world-day-for-peace.html.

111. Cf. also *Homilías*, 5:518.

112. John Paul II, *Message to the Peoples of Latin America*, 8, quoted in Romero, *Homilías*, 4:457.

113. Works of beneficence cannot patch up a fundamentally unjust social situation. In the words of the Second Vatican Council, it is imperative "that the demands of justice be satisfied lest the giving of what is due in justice be represented as the offering of a charitable gift" (Pope Paul VI, *Apostolicam Actuositatem* 8, November 18, 1965, www.vatican.va/archive/hist_councils /ii_vatican_council/documents/vat-ii_decree_19651118_apostolicam -actuositatem_en.html). The Spanish version from which Romero draws is more direct: "No se brinde como ofrenda de caridad lo que ya se debe por título de justicia" (*Homilías*, 5:519; cf. 4:374); "Do not give as charitable offering that which is already owed by right of justice."

114. Quoted in *Homilías*, 4:465, 4:442, 3:430, 1:185.

115. Óscar Romero, *The Violence of Love*, ed. James R. Brockman (Maryknoll, NY: Orbis Books, 2004).

116. Pierre Rousselot, *The Problem of Love in the Middle Ages: A Historical Contribution*, trans. Alan Vincelette (Milwaukee, WI: Marquette University Press, 2001).

117. A characteristic text from Aquinas that supports Rousselot's argument is *ST* 1-2.109.3: "Now to love God above all things is natural to man and to every nature, not only rational but irrational, and even to inanimate nature according to the manner of love that can belong to each creature."

118. For a more textually developed example, one can read from Gilbert of Holyand's commentary on the Song of Songs. "Sharp and effective and truly violent is that affection, good Jesus, which moves and wins your affection! Strong and violent is the force of charity that reaches and penetrates the very affections of God and like an arrow transfixes one's vital organs.

What wonder if the kingdom of heaven suffers violence? The Lord Himself bears the wound of violent love. But see by what shafts He is wounded. You have wounded, he says, my heart with one of your eyes and with one hair of your neck. Do not hesitate, O Bride, to aim such weapons at your Spouse. Use devout glances as your darts" (quoted in Rousselot, *Problem of Love*, 174).

119. The two concepts of love should not be set up as incompatible or mutually exclusive. Rousselot's own work shows that people like Bernard of Clairvaux can be brought forward as representatives for both schools.

120. Cf. Pfeil, "Oscar Romero's Theology," 97.

121. Escobar Alas, *Veo en la ciudad*, para. 10.

122. Cf. ibid., para. 74.

123. Cf. ibid., para. 163.

Chapter 4. The Face of the Divino Salvador

1. López Portillo, *Fiestas Agostinas*, 6. "The imperial image, traditional and of noble expression, looks to the undeniable past of the tradition that was received by faith and cannot be changed."

2. Ibid.

3. Ibid., 6.

4. Las Casas, *Historia de las Indias*, vol. 1, chap. 2, p. 26.

5. John A. Mackay, *El otro Cristo español: Un estudio de la historia espiritual de España e Hispanoamérica* (Mexico City: Centro de Comunicación Cultural CUPSA, 1993).

6. Mackay describes him as "a Christ who is known in life as a child and in death as a corpse, whose helpless childhood and tragic fate are presided over by the Virgin Mother; a Christ who became human out of eschatological interests and whose reality resides permanently in a magic host that dispenses immortality; a Virgin Mother who, having not tasted death, became the Queen of Life. That is the Christ and that is the Virgin that came to America! He as the Lord of death and of the life to come; she as the Sovereign Lady of the present life" (ibid., 121).

7. Cf. ibid., 147.

8. Ibid., 23.

9. He is concerned about the manner in which Mary eclipses her son. The threshold of a church in Cuzco reads: "Come to Mary all you who are weary and overburdened, and she will give you rest." The substitution of

Mary for Jesus in this citation of Matthew 11:28 would surely startle Protestant and Catholic sensibilities.

10. George Casalis, "Jesus: Neither Abject Lord nor Heavenly Monarch," in *Faces of Jesus: Latin American Christologies*, ed. José Míguez Bonino (Maryknoll, NY: Orbis Books 1977), 72–76.

11. Cf. Ricardo Rojas, *El Cristo invisible* (Buenos Aires: La Facultad, 1928). Rojas writes of this Jesus: "We have an Indian Christ, and this brings me consolation, since in the three Magi who worshipped Jesus in Bethlehem, only the races of the continents known then were represented. That court lacked a copper-skinned king, the Inca of America" (87). Needless to say, the encounter between the copper-skinned Inca king and the King of Kings was no joyful epiphany.

12. Loida Martell-Otero, "*Encuentro con el Jesús sato*: An *Evangélica Soterology,*" in *Jesus in the Hispanic Community: Images of Christ from Theology to Popular Religion*, ed. Harold J. Recinos and Hugo Magallanes (Louisville, KY: Westminster John Knox Press, 2009), 74–91. "I believe that *sata* is an appropriate term because it is a specifically cultural term that aids in the articulation of a contextual Christology from a Puerto Rican perspective. I also believe it connotes the existential conjunction of *mestizaje* and periphery. It expresses the experience of being peripheralized—stereotyped, rejected, and insulted by the hegemonic centers of society. It underscores the experience of being relegated to the bottom rung of society precisely as one who is perceived to be nonhuman, impure, and of no intrinsic value—*sobraja*. To use *sato/a* as a Christological term is to raise the specter of the theological scandal of the Incarnation. No one wants to be called *sato/a*" (77).

13. José Míguez Bonino, "Who Is Jesus Christ in Latin America Today?" in Míguez Bonino, *Faces of Jesus*, 3.

14. Ibid., 6.

15. Ibid., 4.

16. Lisa Sowle Cahill, "Christ and Kingdom: The Identity of Jesus and Christian Politics," in *Hope and Solidarity: Jon Sobrino's Challenge to Christian Theology*, ed. Stephen J. Pope (Maryknoll, NY: Orbis Books, 2008). "Ratzinger claims that Jesus was recognized as divine already during his lifetime, a claim that can be regarded as highly debatable without in any way rejecting the confession of Christ as divine and human. To make his argument, Ratzinger takes Gospel accounts, based on the experience of the resurrection, as historical records of events in the life of Jesus (e.g., the Transfiguration). He does this in the name of taking history seriously and avoiding 'Gnosticism.' As one reviewer puts it, Ratzinger 'parts company with the critical majority

in treating even this floridly mythological episode [the Transfiguration] as a historical event no more problematical for open-minded historians than Jesus' birth in Palestine.' Ratzinger fails to differentiate between aspects of the Gospels that are more and less likely to reflect historical events, having dismissed the relevance of historical research. Historical facts are posited on the basis of special revelation— after all, a gnostic move?" (loc. 6184–92, Kindle). See also Thomas W. Martin, "What Makes Glory Glorious? Reading Luke's Account of the Transfiguration over against Triumphalism," *Journal for the Study of the New Testament* 29, no. 1 (2006): 3–26. Martin argues that most readers of the story of the Transfiguration have fallen into Peter's trap and projected a glory onto Jesus that was not his own, a glory that he in fact wanted to reject. The glory of God is to be found in the amorphous cloud and not in the delusions of the grandeur of Old Testament theophanies.

17. Speaking of how Jesus's contemporaries encountered and experienced him, Luis Pedraja writes, "While they may have thought of him as an extraordinary human being, a prophet, or a miracle worker, it is doubtful that he had a halo *or glowed in the dark*" (590, emphasis added). To be sure, Pedraja is not denying the Transfiguration, and his point is basically correct. However, that he could make this casual remark at the beginning of an essay on Christology is one more example of the insignificant place that the Transfiguration has occupied in the Latino/a theological imagination. Luis Pedraja, "Christology," in De La Torre, *Hispanic American Religious Cultures*, 2:489–98.

18. The transfiguration of Saint Seraphim of Sarov makes this point powerfully. His disciple Motovilov tells the story of how the saint's figure was changed as they conversed about the presence of the Holy Spirit in the believer. "Father Seraphim took me very firmly by the shoulders and said: 'We are both in the Spirit of God now, my son. Why don't you look at me?' I replied: 'I cannot look, Father, because your eyes are flashing like lightning. Your face has become brighter than the sun, and my eyes ache with pain.' Father Seraphim said: 'Don't be alarmed, your Godliness! Now you yourself have become as bright as I am. You are now in the fullness of the Spirit of God yourself; otherwise you would not be able to see me as I am.'" *The Spiritual Instructions of Saint Seraphim of Sarov*, ed. Franklin Jones (Los Angeles: Dawn Horse Press, 1991), 51–52.

19. Cf. *Homilías*, 5:222.

20. Cf. *Homilías*, 5:163.

21. As Romero explains in his Pentecost sermon of 1979, "The sign is like a language, and thus, as happens with one who does not understand a

language can perceive the signs, but does not know what these are saying, so it is with the one who receives the signs, the sacraments, without a catechesis. . . . The signs are an unknown language, and hence we have not given the sense of our baptism, of our confirmation, of all the sacraments" (*Homilías*, 4:498).

22. *Evangelii Nuntiandi* 30.

23. Cf. *Homilías*, 5:221.

24. Cf. Isa. 40:5. The NRSV translation of *basar* as people is accurate for this reason but at the same time unintentionally hides this connection.

25. The word *encarnación* has richer cultural resonances in Spanish than in English. Luis Pedraja explains: "Although both *incarnation* and *encarnación* come from the same Latin root, the closest cognates in English are words such as *carnal, carnage, carnival, carrion*, or *carnivore*. Unfortunately, these words often carry negative connotations. However, in Spanish, unlike English, the words associated with the Incarnation are not necessarily negative. For instance, in Mexico, the Spanish word *carnal* can mean 'brother,' 'close friend,' or 'family,' indicating that person is of the same flesh." Luis Pedraja, *Jesus Is My Uncle* (Nashville, TN: Abingdon Press, 1999), 75.

26. Cf. Homilies of October 15, 1978, and December 23, 1978.

27. Cf. Dorothy Lee, "Transfiguration and the Gospel of John," in *In Many and Diverse Ways: In Honor of Jacques Dupuis*, ed. Daniel Kendall, S.J., and Gerald O'Collins (Maryknoll, NY: Orbis Books, 2003), 158–69.

28. Cf. Jesús Delgado Acevedo, "Las fiestas en honor al Divino Salvador y el origen del nombre '*La bajada*' con que se conoce la procesión del 5 de agosto," *Orientación*, August 4, 2002, 5–11.

29. Quoted in ibid., 9.

30. López, *Mármoles, clarines y bronces*, 47.

31. Quoted in Delgado Acevedo, "Fiestas," 10.

32. *Orientación*, July 31, 1977, 5.

33. *Orientación*, August 14, 1977, 3.

34. Ibid.

35. Ignacio Ellacuría, "Liturgia y liberación," in *Escritos teológicos*, 4:31. For Ellacuría, the liturgy can serve true Christian liberation only when the liturgy is itself liberated from certain dangers. First, the liturgy has been too otherworldly. In preparing and anticipating the life to come, the liturgy has tended to overlook this life. Second, the liturgy has emphasized the *ex opere operato* character of the sacraments to the detriment of the life of faith. The *ex opere operato* highlights the objective and universal mediation of grace in the sacraments to the detriment of its subjective and particular reception.

Historically, the liturgy has contributed to the oppression of people in Latin America and not to their liberation. If the new liturgy does not seriously make the liberation of the people of Latin America in their concrete historic circumstance, it risks becoming an instrument of alienation once more. The way out of the pitfalls of these historically oppressive liturgical forms lies in the sublimation (not elimination) of its otherworldliness and *ex opere operato*. It is not a liturgical revolution that is needed but a meatier incarnation. The liturgy of the mass needs to be reread. The penitential liturgy with which the mass begins should interpret the active character of sin as oppression and the passive character of sin as the lack of freedom. The liturgy of the Word should feed the congregation with the biblical witness to liberation rather than with the servings from other non-Christian tables. Most important (and perhaps most surprising) of all, the liturgy of the Eucharist needs to be sacrificial. The sacrificial dimension of the Eucharist vaccinates Christian liberation against progressivism, a check against too excessive a focus on the formation of new social structures without attending to the new people needed for those needed changes. However, there is a danger here of falling back to an *ex opere operato* individualist sacramentalism that does not see the connection between dying with Christ at the mass and dying with his people on the streets. The authorized liturgical texts and acts are not helpful. There is need for new texts and forms that empower the congregation to feel what it means to have co-died, been co-buried, and co-risen with Christ. "The mass lived thus, in its three phases (penitential, prophetic and sapiential) with its culmination in the communion of all the people, is the fruit of the sacrifice itself and shows us how much the liturgy can offer to what Christian liberation should be: a redemptive liberation" (40).

36. Saranyana, *Teología en América Latina*, 3:353–55.

37. Ibid., 358–59. See also Bernardo Guerrero Jiménez, "Religión y canción de protesta en América Latina: Un ensayo de interpretación," *Revista Ciencias Sociales* 4 (1994): 55–64. Godoy's song tells the story of the birth of Christ in a Nicaraguan context. This Christ is born in the mountains of Segovia, where, not coincidentally, César Augusto Sandino was born, and, not surprisingly, this child dreams of growing up to be a guerrilla fighter. Yupanqui's song has a more melancholic tone, as he tells of a gaucho poet who is persecuted for his couplets. This "payador" has seen much poverty in the land, but no God. In fact, God, if he is present at all, is only found at the dining table of the boss. Initially, these songs of protests kept their distance from Christianity and the church except when they were the object of the protest. But over time, a greater openness and a

closer approach to both developed, as seen in the development of the *misas campesinas*.

38. Romero alludes to the song "Yo tengo fe" by Palito Ortega in several homilies (*Homilías*, 1:169, 2:73, 5:280). This song expresses confidence in the power of love to overcome all adversities. He also mentions the song "Por la calzada de Emaús" from the *Misa panamericana* (*Homilías*, 2:398).

39. José María Vigil and Ángel Torredas, *Misas centroamericanas: Transcripción y comentario teológico* (Managua: Centro Ecuménico Antonio Valdivieso, 1988), 12.

40. Cf. *Homilías*, 6:284.

41. The line may also be translated as "without being ashamed of that [lottery] ticket."

42. Montserrat Galí Boadella draws attention to the renovations that took place at the Cathedral of Cuernavaca, led by its bishop, Sergio Méndez Arceo, in the early 1950s. These included the turning around of the altar to face the people, the removal of nineteenth-century ornamentation, the restoration of sixteenth-century murals, the use of the vernacular, and the promotion of the *Misa panamericana*. This mass was sung every Sunday at 11:00. Its use of popular Mexican rhythms accompanied by mariachi music was an important point of reference for future Latin American masses. Some of these masses, like the Argentine *Misa criolla* (1964) of Ariel Ramírez, required such a high degree of musical sophistication to perform that they quickly became concert hall pieces. For these masses to become truly popular, they would need to forsake orchestras and soloists for a simpler musical style suitable for the growing base ecclesial communities (cf. Saranyana, *Teología en América Latina*, 3:356–57).

43. Vigil and Torredas, *Misas centroamericanas*, 5. Vigil also notes what he terms "Teilhardian" themes in some of the lyrics, as when in the offertory the people sing, "All of nature longs for liberty." Of course, this is simply an echo of Paul's language in Romans 8:19–23, but Vigil may be right in pointing out a connection between liberation and Teilhard's vision of the Christification of the universe. On Romero's explicit appeal to Teilhard de Chardin, see Romero, "A propósito de Managua," 4.

44. Vigil and Torredas, *Misas centroamericanas*, 5.

45. Vigil and Torredas comment: "These songs shatter the abstract universalism of those who pretend to hide social contradictions by covering both oppressor and oppressed under the cloak of a fictitious Eucharistic fellowship" (ibid., 10).

46. Ibid.

47. The creed, set to marimbas, sings traditional doctrines like the divinity of Christ and the virginity of Mary, but its main emphasis is Christ the liberator who comes to make things right in a creation that is beautiful but "mutilated by the criminal ax." Christ's most cherished titles are "worker," "architect," "bricklayer," and "mechanic." This is a Christ who lives among his people on the factory floor, at the ranch, in the school. In this creed, the surest sign of resurrection is the ceaseless struggle (*lucha sin tregua*) to defend the people from oppression.

48. Cf. *Homilías*, 2:146, 147, 456; 4:68, 70, 74, 75, 94, 484; 5:342.

49. Cf. *Homilías*, 4:75. In the words of *Gaudium et Spes* 22, "For, since Christ died for all men, and since the ultimate vocation of man is in fact one, and divine, we ought to believe that the Holy Spirit in a manner known only to God offers to every man the possibility of being associated with this paschal mystery." Romero underscores the universality of the call in a sermon where he speaks to the question of predestination. After instructing his listeners about the Reformation debates (albeit not very accurately) and Trent's intervention, Romero turns to Christ for a solution to the problem. In this connection, Romero brings up *Gaudium et Spes* 22, which states that the mystery of being human is revealed in Christ. What freedom means can be understood only by identifying oneself with Christ. "No one knows their vocation without knowing Christ" (*Homilías*, 3:136). Does this mean that only Christians know what it really means to be human? Not at all. There are sinners in the church and saints without. Romero recalls how during his time studying at Rome, Mahatma Gandhi visited the eternal city "clad in sheets and accompanied by a little goat" and met with Pope Pius XI (*Homilías*, 3:137). Reflecting on the visit, the pope said, "We have met a pagan saint!" Romero's lesson from that encounter is that "there are saints in paganism, perhaps holier than in the Catholic Church, because Christ, who is the revelation of humanity, can be known." In other words, *Gaudium et Spes* 22 is a warrant for a universal call to holiness because this is the truest human vocation.

50. Saranyana, *Teología en América Latina*, 3:363.

51. Vigil and Torredas, *Misas centroamericanas*, 23.

52. Saranyana, *Teología en América Latina*, 3:364. Vigil and Torredas state that the "people" who are the subject of this mass are "the Salvadoran people, the poor people" and that the most important characteristic of this "poor people" is that they have become conscientized, self-aware (*Misas centroamericanas*, 21). Whether this is what the composer meant or not, Óscar Romero would surely have disagreed with this reading. What makes the poor

the poor people of God is first and foremost their baptism, which they are now living, as Vigil and Torredas suggest, in an awakened state. Moreover, Romero would have disagreed with Vigil and Torredas's utilitarian analysis of the mass, which seems to value it first as "a pedagogic and conscienticizing instrument" (23).

53. I accessed the lyrics at "Cristo mesoamericano," *Iglesia Descalza* (blog), September 1, 2009, http://iglesiadescalza.blogspot.com/2009/09/cristo-mesoamericano.html.

54. Cf. Romero's homilies from October 1, 1978; December 17 and 24, 1978; April 8, 1979; December 23 and 24, 1979; and March 1, 1980.

55. The most poignant sign of Moltmann's popularity is the copy of his book *The Crucified God* that is stained with the blood of one of the Jesuits martyred at the University of Central America in San Salvador on November 16, 1989.

56. Sobrino, *Christology at the Crossroads*, 217–29.

57. Sobrino states that "the Christian belief in God as a Trinity takes on a new and dynamic meaning in the light of the cross. God is a trinitarian 'process' on the way toward its ultimate fulfillment (1 Cor. 15:28), but it takes all history into itself. In this process God participates in, and lets himself be affected by, history through the Son; and history is taken into God in the Spirit. What is manifest on the cross is the internal structure of God himself" (ibid., 226).

58. Antonio Agnelli, *Il Cristo di Romero: La teologia que ha nutrito il Martire d'America* (Bologna: Editrice Missionaria Italiana, 2010), 79–89. On Agnelli's reading of Moltmann, Golgotha reveals how the crucified God walks the kenotic path of the Incarnation to its most radical and surprising conclusion: the Father abandons the Son, and both persons experience the agony of this separation. Agnelli sums up the theological challenge of Moltmann's theology of the cross thus: "Hence we must not speak only of the suffering of God, but in a very clear way of *suffering in God*" (85, emphasis in original).

59. *Homilías*, 2:358, emphasis added.

60. *Homilías*, 4:356, emphasis added.

61. According to Aquinas, Christ suffered physically, emotionally, and spiritually (*ST* 3.46.7), but without losing the joy of the vision of God (*ST* 3.46.8). On this topic, see Thomas J. White, "Jesus' Cry on the Cross and His Beatific Vision," *Nova et Vetera* 5, no. 3 (2007): 555–82.

62. Jon Sobrino states, "Others, such as Tertullian, Ambrose (and Thomas Aquinas), admit that Jesus suffered abandonment by God in his human psychology, but say this did not cause him anguish or despair." Jon

Sobrino, *Jesus the Liberator: A Historical-Theological View* (Maryknoll, NY: Orbis Books, 1993), 237–38. Sobrino reads Mark's account of the Crucifixion as the most authentic one by which all other biblical and postbiblical accounts must be measured. This evangelist captures the tragedy of Jesus's death and the radical discontinuity of his divine abandonment better than any other. Sobrino states that "whereas, for Jesus, the 'infinite distance' of God as mystery was always accompanied by the 'absolute closeness' of God as Father, this vanishes on the cross: there is no closeness of God, no experience of God as a kind Father. The accounts give no sign that Jesus heard any word from the Father in answer to his questions" (239). Applying the Markan standard, Sobrino finds that both Luke and John "soften Jesus' end" in order to avoid the scandalous discontinuity between Jesus's life and death revealed at the cross (237). The airbrushing of the Crucifixion only gained in popularity over the centuries. Sobrino finds in the writings of the fathers and the Scholastics not the faithful development of doctrine from scripture but the understandable if mistaken reading of scripture through extrabiblical doctrinal lenses. Despite his dim outlook on the history of biblical interpretation of Jesus's cry of abandonment and his confidence on recent historical approaches to the Gospel of Mark, Sobrino admits that "it is difficult, if not impossible to know what Jesus' real relationship to his God was as he died" (239).

63. Thomas White's judgment on this matter seems to me worth pondering. Noting that the words in Mark 15:34 are a citation from Psalm 22:1, which ends on a note of hope, he suggests it is possible that Jesus's lament was also a prophetic statement of hope. Sobrino rejects this line of inquiry as speculative and an example of yet another way in which Christians have tried to soften the hard, antitriumphalist message of Mark's account (*Jesus the Liberator*, 237). "What is certain," White states, "is that the references to the psalms present in Christ's last words in all four Gospels were interpreted in messianic fashion in the earliest Church. The entire early Christian community seems to have believed that Christ in fact died in prayer and that his citation of the psalms had prophetic overtones. If this is the case, however, it becomes absurd to presume the existence of an experience of radical disillusionment, despair, or accusation underlying Christ's last words. On the contrary, the early Christian interpretation of Christ's last words may simply be the best historical understanding of what Jesus intended them to signify. Therefore, even from the perspective of 'historical reason alone,' the interpretation of biblical faith remains an open possibility. Yet, theologically speaking, if it need not be seen as an act of abandoning God through

hopelessness, Christ's cry to God must be considered as a cry of hope to God for deliverance" (Thomas J. White, "Jesus' Cry," 561–62).

64. Agnelli, *Cristo di Romero*, 87.

65. Michael J. Dodds, "Thomas Aquinas, Human Suffering, and the Unchanging God of Love," *Theological Studies* 52 (1991): 334.

66. The identification of God with human suffering is the fruit of love. Following Aquinas, Dodd argues that the union effected by love can become so close that even the language of compassion breaks down. Cf. *ST* 2-2.30.1.ad2: "Since pity [*misericordia*] is sympathy [*compassion*] for another's distress, it is directed, properly speaking, towards another, and not to oneself, except figuratively. . . . Accordingly just as, properly speaking, a man does not pity himself, but suffers in himself, as when we suffer cruel treatment in ourselves, so too, in the case of those who are so closely united to us, as to be part of ourselves, such as our children or our parents, we do not pity their distress, but suffer as for our own sores." It is not simply that I feel sympathy or compassion for someone, that I suffer with someone. It is that their suffering moves me to also suffer and act to alleviate their suffering. This is the love of the Good Samaritan for the man left for dead on the side of the road. There is a real connection between these two that has been forged by love, but love can make for a closer union still. Parents do not feel compassion for their children's distress but suffer as for their own wounds.

67. The other example that Dodd offers is that of Bartolomé de las Casas, whose famous declaration of seeing Christ scourged a thousand times in the Indies became popularized by Gustavo Gutiérrez. Interestingly, the reference to Las Casas raises a question that Dodd does not address but is crucial to guiding the mission of the church. How is it that Christ loves as "something of himself" those who are not yet members of his mystical body, the church? Dodd states that "if Christ has identified himself with the poor and the suffering, then the first work of the Church is not so much to bring Christ to the poor, but rather to find him there" ("Thomas Aquinas," 342). This was indeed true for Las Casas, who saw Christ as the head of the indigenous in a certain respect. The love of Christ for the indigenous already incorporated them to his mystical body even if imperfectly. For Romero, something similar can be said because Christ's love overflows the boundaries of the visible church. Nevertheless, the fact that Dodd does not answer all the questions that could be posed or even required by his study is not fatal to his reflection because at the end of this incomplete exploration he rightly returns to mystery.

68. Sobrino, *Jesus the Liberator*, 233–53.

69. Ibid., 244, 245.

70. Ibid.

71. Ibid.

72. Ibid., 245.

73. Cf. homily from May 30, 1978. The poem is found in Alfredo Espino, *Jícaras tristes* (San Salvador: Consejo Natural para la Cultura y el Arte, 1996), 65.

74. In J. R. R. Tolkien's *The Lord of the Rings*, there is a scene of transfiguration that expresses well the hope that fuels Romero's vision. In their quest to destroy the magical ring of power, Sam and Frodo must enter the stronghold of Sauron, a Satan-like creature who seeks to cover the world in darkness: "Near the borders of Sauron's land, Sam and Frodo arrived at a crossroads connecting the formerly magnificent cities of the realm. By the light of the setting sun, Frodo and Sam saw the ruin which the hand of the enemy had wrought on what once was a beautiful land and on the noble civilization which its denizens had built. The statue of an ancient king that stood watch on the crossroads was now desecrated. Its head had been cut off and replaced with a roughly made, grinning head of Sauron. The fading sunlight shone on Sam's face. Suddenly, caught by the level beams, Frodo saw the old king's head: it was lying rolled away by the roadside. 'Look, Sam!' he cried, startled into speech. 'Look! The king has got a crown again!' The eyes were hollow and the carven beard was broken, but about the high stern forehead there was a coronal of silver and gold. A trailing plant with flowers like small white stars had bound itself across the brows as if in reverence for the fallen king, and in the crevices of his stony hair yellow stonecrop gleamed. 'They cannot conquer for ever!' said Frodo. And then suddenly the brief glimpse was gone. The Sun dipped and vanished, and as if at the shuttering of a lamp, black night fell" (J. R. R. Tolkien, *The Lord of the Rings: One Volume* [New York: Houghton Mifflin Harcourt, 2002], 702). Tolkien was famously antagonistic to allegory, but he was a practicing Catholic whose imagination was formed by the world of the Bible and the sacred liturgy. The brief glimpse that Frodo has of the crowned king is prophetic. It is a vision of what will come to pass: the king will return. The prophetic vision generates in turn a prophetic cry: "They cannot conquer for ever." The vision is brief. It soon fades into darkness, but the glimpse is enough to sustain them on their journey. Beauty has the power to transform reality. Another scene from *Lord of the Rings* highlights the limits of evil. Once Sam and Frodo enter the land of Mordor, their path darkens

and the perils mount. The quest seems doomed to fail, but they plod on to its conclusion. Wearied from the journey, they lie down to rest, but Sam keeps watch. "The land seemed full of creaking and cracking and sly noises, but there was no sound of voice or of foot. Far above the Ephel Dúath in the West the night-sky was still dim and pale. There, peeping among the cloud-wrack above a dark tor high up in the mountains, Sam saw a white star twinkle for a while. The beauty of it smote his heart, as he looked up out of the forsaken land, and hope returned to him. For like a shaft, clear and cold, the thought pierced him that in the end the Shadow was only a small and passing thing: there was light and high beauty for ever beyond its reach. His song in the Tower had been defiance rather than hope; for then he was thinking of himself. Now, for a moment, his own fate, and even his master's, ceased to trouble him. He crawled back into the brambles and laid himself by Frodo's side, and putting away all fear he cast himself into a deep untroubled sleep" (922).

75. *Orientación,* July 29, 1978, 7.

76. Attributed to L. M. Argumedo. In Archdiocese of San Salvador, *Solemnidades patronales de El Divino Salvador del Mundo,* program guide, 1966, 13.

77. The following verse, though often omitted, strengthens the resemblance. *Salva, Señor, al pueblo que te invoca* (Save, Lord, the people who invoke you), / *En tu inmensa bondad siempre confiado* (in your immense goodness always trusting); / *Tu bendición no apartes de su lado* (Do not withdraw your blessing from our side); *Acuérdate que somos tu heredad* (Remember that we are your inheritance).

78. Archdiocese of San Salvador, *Solemnidades patronales de El Divino Salvador del Mundo,* program guide, 1954, and program guide, 1966, 12.

79. This hymn, by Moseñor Rafael F. Claros, is in the *Solemnidades patronales de El Divino Salvador del Mundo,* program guide, 1968, 13.

80. On Romero's anti-Masonic writings, see Chanta Martínez, "Antimasonería y antiliberalismo."

81. Pfeil, "Oscar Romero's Theology," 87.

82. Ibid., 115.

83. Ibid., 88.

84. Nurya Martínez-Gayol, "'Todo como sintiere ser a mayor gloria de Dios N. Señor': Posibles conflictos en la determinación de la 'mayor gloria de Dios,'" *Estudios Eclesiásticos* 79 (2004): 413–31. Martínez-Gayol emphasizes the importance of discernment for the proper interpretation of Ignatius's saying. Greater conformity to the poor Christ may in a concrete circumstance not be what conduces to the greater glory of God. The "universal

good," as Ignatius understood it, was more divine than the particular good. If the good of saving souls is advanced by a person entering a university to study theology or by accepting a high ecclesiastical post, then that is the path of greater glory to God, even if it means becoming less conformed to Christ in his poverty for a season. Hence the question arises of a possible conflict between the three vectors of the movement toward the greater glory of God. The free and unconditional surrender to the divine will in all things is what gives the Ignatian saying its definitive sense (cf. 415).

85. Santiago Arzubialde, "El significado de la fórmula 'A mayor gloria de Dios' en el texto de las Constituciones de la Compañía de Jesús," *Estudios Eclesiásticos* 76 (2001): 593–630.

86. Cf. ibid., 610.

87. Romero finds a beautiful synthesis of these epiphanies in a prayer from the breviary for Epiphany: "Today the church has joined her heavenly spouse, because in the Jordan Christ purified its sins. The Magi rushed with gifts to these royal nuptials and with the water made wine, the guests rejoice" (*Homilías*, 4:142).

88. Romero typically calls the Transfiguration a theophany, but he also terms it an epiphany. Cf. *Homilías*, 4:271.

89. Douglass Sullivan-González, *The Black Christ of Esquipulas: Religion and Identity in Guatemala* (Lincoln: University of Nebraska Press, 2016), loc. 1480, Kindle.

90. The parish priest Nicolás de Paz wrote the first devotionals to what he referred to as the "Cristo Crucificado de Esquipulas" in 1723. The first prayer guides written for the devout instructed them to look at "the black Face with perfection, the brown Body with texture, in the middle of such shades, sometimes black, others brown" (ibid., loc. 951–52, Kindle).

91. Ibid., loc. 961, Kindle.

92. The clergy had their own complex cluster of concerns. There was a felt need to defend the conformity of the color of the image to the orthodoxy standards set by Trent. Father Miguel Muñoz explains in an 1845 letter to Archbishop García-Peláez that "black is ugly and frightening for us, and thus, the color white is equally so for nations of dark colors. The Ethiopians paint Judas and the demons a horrible white and they paint the saints black. Thus it is that neither blackness nor whiteness nor green in the images induces error nor is contrary to the worship of the Catholic Church" (quoted in ibid., loc. 1873–75, Kindle). Father Juan Paz Solórzano rejected claims that the statue had become black from the smoke of burning candles. Far less was it black because Jesus was black. "He is not; his dark color imitates

the reality of dead blood as it should appear" (quoted in ibid., loc. 280–81, Kindle).

93. Anne Cary Maudslay speaks of hearing pilgrims singing hymns to "the black Christ of Esquipulas" (quoted in ibid., loc. 2222, Kindle). Nine years later, after visiting the sanctuary in 1907, Juan Tomás Butler derides the image in a Protestant paper. "The whole world knows and ought to know that Jesus was not a black, but a Jew" (quoted in ibid., loc. 2379, Kindle). Carlos Secords unmasks this Christ as the "black and repulsive image of Nimrod, the chief of the old apostasy against God" and urges his readers to throw off their idols and abandon Rome (quoted in ibid., loc. 2370–71, Kindle).

94. Ibid., loc. 286–90, Kindle.

95. Romero explains Christ's vacillation as a mark of his humanity. "Observe his self-preservation instinct. Chris is not an insensitive being. Christ is a man of flesh and bone, of nerves and muscles like us. A man who feels what someone feels when the National Guard takes him somewhere to be tortured. It was there that Christ lifted his face drenched in tears to the one who could deliver him and prayed that his Father's will should be done" (*Homilías*, 4:338).

96. Ramón Cué, *Mi Cristo roto* (Buenos Aires: Editorial Guadalupe, 1999), 24.

97. *Homilías*, 1:97; *Homilías*, 3:216.

98. Cf. *Homilías*, 1:97.

99. "In the symbol of the host downtrodden in Aguilares, let us see the face of Christ on the cross. That beautiful poem, the *Cristo roto*, describes to us the momentous hour in which all the sins of humanity passed through the face of Christ crucified: the adulterers, the thieves, those who trample the dignity of human beings, all sinners. And in this hour of the nation, how many hate and lie! And we too sin, perhaps, many times! We are all sinners. Behold, it is my face, your face, the faces of those who persecute and slander us, are passing, as in a movie film, on the divine face of Christ, who dies, agonizes, and says: "My body and blood, which are given for the forgiveness of all these sins, wait for you there." And we gather in that consecrated host all the pain of that Christ, all the love for sinners, all his feelings that are very different from those who offend him" (*Homilías*, 1:135). Romero's reference points to the end of the book, when the priest has been reflecting on the meaning of the broken Christ's missing face (Cué, *Mi Cristo roto*, 139).

100. "As that poem of the *Cristo roto* says, kneel each night before the Crucified One and kiss his foot, not with a romantic kiss, but with a committed

kiss, to tell him that you are willing to love him even if it means dying like him, crucified. Tell him that you want to kiss his foot, even if that Christ that you kiss is perhaps your worst enemy and you have to forgive him" (*Homilía*, 3:216). Romero is alluding to the point in the play when the priest has just made his peace with the broken Christ that he brought to his home (Cué, *Mi Cristo roto*, 35).

101. Pedraja, *Jesus Is My Uncle*, 55. Pedraja's formulation draws on the Latino experience of feeling embraced by God amid a society built on exclusion and also on the reflections of Eberhard Jüngel. See Jüngel's *God the Mystery of the World: On the Foundation of the Theology of the Crucified God in the Dispute between Theism and Atheism*, trans. Darrell L. Guder (Grand Rapids, MI: Eerdmans, 1983). Jüngel states that "God is love precisely in that he loves his Son in his identity with man, that is, with the scandalously murdered man Jesus. Love here is not directed toward a loveworthy Thou. . . . Rather, it makes what is totally unloveworthy into something worthy of love" (329). It seems to me that Jüngel potentially sets up an unhelpful contrast between love as receptive and love as creative. The unlovable sinner is still a creature in the image of God and as such lovable. To be sure, its image has been defaced by sin. God's love ennobles and beautifies the image that the creature already bears.

102. Fyodor Dostoyevsky, *The Idiot* (New York: Penguin Books, 1955), 366.

103. *Homilías*, 5:269, 282.

104. *Homilías*, 1:372: "I, the persecuted church, am the face of Christ. Do not be ashamed of being my child."

105. Cf. Agnelli, *Cristo di Romero*, 35, 37.

106. Cf. ibid., 99.

Chapter 5. The Transfigured People of God

1. Evelyn Galindo, "Apuntes de la deshumanización: La Vía crucis del pueblo salvadoreño," *Legacies of War in El Salvador* (blog), December 24, 2012, http://postwarelsalvador.blogspot.com/2012/12/apuntes-de-la -deshumanizacion-la-via.html.

2. Felipe Guamán Poma de Ayala, *Nueva Crónica y buen gobierno* (Alicante: Biblioteca Virtual Miguel de Cervantes, 2012), drawing 272, www.kb .dk/permalink/2006/poma/info/en/frontpage.htm.

3. Las Casas, *Historia de las Indias*, vol. 3, chap. 138, p. 510.

4. In setting out this objective, the Conference at Medellín had historical antecedents in Latin America. The Council of Trent (1545–63) was convened for the purpose of offering a Catholic version of ecclesial reform that would distinguish it from that of the Protestant reformers. The work of the council is too multifaceted to treat here. Larkin draws attention to the manner in which the council, while moderating some excesses, largely reaffirmed the forms of popular piety that drew the Reformer's scorn in the first place. A few Latin American prelates were present at the council, and certainly important Spanish figures like Melchor Cano, who engaged both Continental and American questions, made important contributions to the deliberations. But overall, this was a council of Europeans and for Europeans. Even so, Trent's teachings were binding for all Catholics, and they made their way to Spanish America. For instance, the Third Council of Lima met from 1582 to 1583 to translate the teachings of the Council of Trent to Latin America. The proceedings of the council were dominated not by debates about faith and works but by missionary questions. José de Acosta was the chief theologian at this council. It promoted a common catechism with three levels (the *Doctrina cristiana*, the *Catecismo breve para los rudos y ocupados*, and the *Catecismo mayor para los que son más capaces*) and stated that these should be translated also into Quechua and Aymara. The council also promoted the formation of schools for the indigenous (in their own language) and seminaries for the Spanish (the indigenous were excluded from ordination at the time). The council also produced a guide for confessors of the indigenous. In addition to using the Ten Commandments as a moral mirror, which was the custom in *Confesionarios*, the manual offered specific questions that could be asked of the indigenous that would suit their station in life (caciques, witches, etc.). With the exception of its prohibition of indigenous ordinations, the success of this council is confirmed by the fact that its instructions were not superseded until the Concilio Plenario Lationoamericano of 1899. Cf. Saranyana, *Teología en América Latina*, 1:170–79.

5. This methodology was first developed among young Catholic workers. As applied at Medellín, the method begins with seeing the pertinent facts: "There are in existence many studies of the Latin American people. The misery that besets large masses of human beings in all of our countries is described in all of these studies. That misery, as a collective fact, expresses itself as injustice that cries to the heavens" (*Medellín* 1.1). This act of seeing that is assisted by sociological historical methods is followed by a judgment of what is seen from a doctrinal basis: "The Latin American church has a message for all men on this continent who 'hunger and thirst after justice.'...

For our authentic liberation, all of us need a profound conversion so that 'the kingdom of justice, love and peace' might come to us" (*Medellín* 1.1). After seeing the reality and judging it theologically comes a need to act in a pastoral manner. This action may involve calls for social change, political reform, and conscientization in the spirit of Paulo Freire. The bishops said: "The Latin American church encourages the formation of national communities that reflect a global organization, where all of the peoples but more especially the lower classes have, by means of territorial and functional structures, an active and receptive, creative and decisive participation in the construction of a new society" (*Medellín* 1.7).

6. Roberto Goizueta, "Knowing the God of the Poor," in Rieger, *Opting for the Margins*, n.p.

7. Ibid., 153.

8. Rohan M. Curnow, "Which Preferential Option for the Poor? A History of the Doctrine's Bifurcation," *Modern Theology* 31, no. 1 (2015): 27–59.

9. "For the Roman Magisterium, the means of combating erroneous understandings of the Option remain the same: Christology and Christian anthropology are at the root of any genuine Option for the Poor. Liberation theologians would concur with such an argument, but would then relate Christology and anthropology to the hermeneutics of history." Ibid., 54.

10. Elsa Tamez, "Poverty, the Poor, and the Option for the Poor: A Biblical Perspective," in *The Option for the Poor in Christian Theology*, ed. Daniel Groody (Notre Dame, IN: University of Notre Dame Press, 2007), 50. Tamez mentions examples of how institutions that have contributed to the economic captivity of Latin America, like the International Monetary Fund, have felt free to adopt the language without making any real changes to their policies.

11. Stephen Pope, "Proper and Improper Partiality and the Preferential Option for the Poor," *Theological Studies* 54 (1993): 242–71.

12. A poor person simply by virtue of being poor does not have special insight into economic theory or into strategies for sustainable growth or for funding universal health care. One can think of the midwife who rejoices in the gift of life in the newborn or the astrophysicist who marvels at the anthropic principle evident in the natural order of the universe. Cf. ibid., 60.

13. Ibid. Pope suggests a helpful distinction between care and love. Divine partiality is shown in how God cares for his creatures' temporal well-being. In this case, the care is proportional to the degree of need a person has. Divine partiality is also shown in how God loves his creatures and provides for their eternal well-being. In this case, God glorifies those who have

responded positively to his grace. These two, divine care and divine love, are not separated in God. God cares for his creatures because he loves them. He feeds the hungry with good things and also offers the bread of heaven. Moreover, the former is ordained to the latter, and the latter informs the former. Care goes astray when it is separated from love, for then it becomes either a patronizing display of noblesse oblige or a job. "The patronizing misuse of the distinction between love and care is resisted by acknowledging that since all human beings are needy, we are all, in different ways and at different times, objects of the care of one another" (258). In sum, following Aquinas, God cares in proportion to need and loves in proportion to grace. The proportion here is not one of intensity. When it comes to love's proportion to grace, the "more" refers to the degree of union willed by God. When it comes to care's proportion to need, the "more" refers to . . . what? It is hard to say. Certainly not in that their material needs are always met first. In tasking the church with privileging the poor in its prayers and care? In the severity of the judgment with which God will hold accountable the ones responsible (the theme of divine reversal)? In the degree of Christ's divine identification with their suffering?

14. Cf. Jan G. J. Van den Eijden, *Poverty on the Way to God: Thomas Aquinas on Evangelical Poverty* (Leuven: Thomas Institut te Utrecht, 1994). Van den Eijden offers a Thomistic explanation for the poverty of Jesus that enriches the theological basis for the preferential option. First, there are missional reasons for Jesus's poverty. He became poor so as to be freed from social cares that would impede his practice of preaching. By being poor Jesus sought to avoid suspicions that his teaching was for sale. The voluntary embrace of poverty clears obstacles and stumbling blocks for the propagation of the gospel. This poverty may be termed evangelical; the gospel is offered free of charge. There are what might be termed sacramental reasons. Jesus becomes poor in order to facilitate the exchange of spiritual goods with humanity. The key text is 2 Corinthians 8:9: "For you know the generous act of our Lord Jesus Christ, that though he was rich, yet for your sakes he became poor, so that by his poverty you might become rich." This text was traditionally limited in its interpretation to the Incarnation. The poverty of Christ was identified with the "natural poverty" of human nature and hence with the kenosis entailed in assuming human nature. Aquinas extends this poverty to include Christ's entire manner of life—natural, social, and economic poverty. The most visible expression of the poverty of Christ was the Crucifixion, where his body hung naked from a cross. His embrace of material poverty was a preparation and prefiguration of his complete self-offering on

the cross. In the wondrous exchange of 2 Corinthians 8:9, Christ's poverty makes us rich in two ways. By way of an example, Jesus shows us how poverty can free us for intimacy with God. By means of a sacrament, the poverty of Jesus is for us and for our salvation. As a sacramental reality, its meaning is to a significant extent veiled within the mystery of the life of Christ. Like the sacraments, it has a visible material dimension, external poverty, and an interior spiritual dimension, the total offering to God. In sum, the poverty of Christ makes visible the love of God for humanity.

15. *De locis theologicis* 1.1: "quibus idonea possit argumenta depromere, sive conclusiones suas theologus probare cupit, seu refutare contrarias." Melchor Cano, *De locis theologicis*, ed. Juan Belda Plans (Madrid: Biblioteca de Autores Cristianos, 2006).

16. "The theologians and theology of liberation (TL) have retaken the old formula of Melchor Cano and speak of the poor as *lugar teológico*. They refer specifically to the poor of Latin America, whose manifestation as a historic force and whose entrance into the church will lead to the awakening of the human conscience of the person and the rebirth of the true church." Olegario González de Cardedal, "Problemas de fondo y método en la cristología a partir del Vaticano II," *Salmantinencis* 32 (1985): 363–400.

17. John S. Pobee, "Europe as Locus Theologicus," *Ecumenical Review* 45, no. 2 (1993): 194–201. For Pobee, the phrase serves to gesture to the audience for whom theology must be relevant. Valerie Torres, "*La Familia* as *Locus Theologicus* and Religious Education in *lo Cotidiano*," *Religious Education* 105, no. 4 (2010): 444–61. Torres does not explain the significance of the term beyond a quote from Roberto Goizueta that includes the phrase (447). Gemma Tulud Cruz, "Migration as *Locus Theologicus*," *Colloquium* 46, no. 1: (2014): 87–100. Torres appears to consider the phrase as so self-explanatory that it appears only in the title. The same is true of Bert Roebben in "The Vulnerability of the Postmodern Educator as *Locus Theologicus*: A Study in Practical Theology," *Religious Education* 96, no. 2 (2001): 175–92. Bertha Sofía Pitalúa Quiñonez, "Género y comunicación como lugares teológicos de la revelación: ¿Cómo comunicar a Dios en una sociedad llena de discriminaciones?," *Reflexiones Teológicas* 12 (2014): 131–56. In distinction to the other authors just mentioned, Pitalúa does offer a rationale for utilizing the term *lugares teológicos* by linking it with the context in which God acts and reveals himself. Judith Gruber, "Rethinking God in the Interspace: Interculturality as a *Locus Theologicus*," *Svensk Missionstidskrift* 100, no. 3 (2012): 247–61. A *locus theologicus* is "a theological resource, which guides and informs our way of knowing and conceptualising God" (260). In all these cases, the use

of the phrase is at best underdefined. More attuned to the historic uses of the phrase is Geoffrey Wainwright's "Der Gottesdienst als Locus Theologicus," *Kerygma und Dogma* 28, no. 4 (December 1982): 248–58. Wainwright rightly distinguishes between the Protestant use of the phrase by Melancthon to identify theological themes and the Catholic use by Cano, which names theological sources. Worship can be considered a *locus theologicus* in both ways, as source and content of theology.

18. Juan Carlos Scannone, "Cuestiones actuales de epistemología teológica: Aportes a la teología de la liberación," *Stromata* 46 (1990): 317–18.

19. José Ortega y Gasset offers a metaphor that may be helpful: "To see an object we have to, in a certain way, adapt our visual apparatus. If our visual adaptation is inadequate we will not see the object or see it poorly. Let the reader imagine that we are looking at a garden through the glass of a window. Our eyes will adapt so that the ray of vision penetrates the glass without stopping at it and goes through to grasp the flowers and the leaves. Since the goal of the vision is the garden and to it is the visual ray cast, we will not see the glass. Our vision will go through it without perceiving it. The purer the glass, the less we will see it. But then, by means of an effort, we can detach ourselves from the garden and, retracting our visual ray, fix it on the glass. Then, the garden disappears before our eyes and we see only confused masses of color of it that appear to be fixed to the glass. Therefore, seeing the garden and seeing the glass are two incompatible operations; the one excludes the other and require different visual adaptations" (*La deshumanización del arte y otros ensayos de estética* [Madrid: Alianza Editorial, 1996], 17). Ortega y Gasset applies this metaphor to the aesthetic experience. Seeing a work of art, as a work of art, requires an aesthetic adaptation. The pictured and the picture are two different objects. We live with the former; we contemplate the latter. Perceiving the work of art means pulling back from the reality represented to the act of representation. The metaphor can be applied to the distinction between the *loci theologici* and the *loci hermeneutici*. All *loci theologici* are seen through *loci hermeneutici*. Prior to the modern era, all attention was focused on the *loci theologici*. The patristic and Scholastic theologians knew full well that they were seeing these through the glass darkly of *loci hermeneutici*. All theology was done *sub conditione creaturae* and *sub conditione peccati*. In fact the difficulty of human knowledge attaining God was modeled in negative theology and in discourses about the simplicity of God. What few in the premodern era were interested in was in writing about particular *loci hermeneutici*. They were interested in describing what they could see of the garden of theology, not in describing the stains and cracks on the glass

through which they were seeing this garden. As Ortega y Gasset explains, seeing the glass and seeing the garden are two different and incompatible operations. The danger in the classical view was forgetfulness of the glass. The danger in the modern view is confusing the cracks, stains, and blurred images on the glass for the garden.

20. "A *lugar hermenéutico* can become a proper *lugar teológico* thanks to a process of discernment that discovers the imprint of a weighty witness of the Word of God in a historically concrete situation" (177). Carlos Schickendantz, "Autoridad teológica de los acontecimientos históricos: Perplejidades sobre un lugar teológico," *Revista Teología* 115 (2015): 157–83.

21. Ignacio Ellacuría, "Los pobres, 'lugar teológico' en América Latina," *Misión Abierta* 4/5 (1981): 225–40.

22. In the case of Gustavo Gutiérrez, fellow liberationists like Leonardo Boff claim that he embraced the epistemological inversion of locus as formal rather than material object. Of course, this inversion is one that Boff strongly advocated. However, even opponents of Gutiérrez like Jorge Costadoat absolve the Peruvian theologian of this charge. "In its most radical presentations, then, reality is not judged in light of faith, but faith in the light of reality. There has been a Copernican inversion in the way of constructing theology. The manner of understanding theological science has changed to such a degree that one can seriously doubt whether one is dealing with theological science strictly speaking or with something else, a kind of philosophy of history, or, perhaps more accurately, a secularized version of a theology of history." Saranyana, *Teología en América Latina*, 3:302.

23. See Clodovis Boff's critique in "Teologia da libertação e volta ao fundamento," *Revista Eclesiástica Brasileira* 268 (2007): 1001–22. Boff returns to the foundations of liberation theology in light of the gathering of CELAM in Aparecida in 2007. He begins by exposing what he terms "the fatal flaw" of liberation theology—the ambiguity of the epistemological location of the poor. He exempts the "founding fathers" of liberation theology like Gustavo Gutiérrez from his critique. Boff is addressing not the best of liberation theology but the most common of liberation theology, the liberation theology that is actually practiced on the ground by those who self-identify as liberation theologians like Jon Sobrino. It is interesting that Boff does not name other "liberation theologians" or explain how Sobrino is a particularly prominent exemplar of the "fatal flaw" that needs to be examined. Nor does Boff name other "founding fathers" or elaborate on why Gutiérrez receives a pass. In any case, Boff points to the careless manner in which Sobrino speaks of the poor as giving theology its "fundamental direction"

and its "most decisive location." Boff's chief concern with liberation theology regards the priority of God and faith vis-à-vis the poor. Liberation theologians insist that "faith in the revealed God" is the first principle of liberation theology. The problem is that de facto the theology does not actually begin from this first principle. The articles of faith are regarded as theological statements that are dutifully confessed but fail to do any real work in the theology. An epistemological inversion appears to be taking place where the poor substitute for God as the operative first principle of theology. The study of the perfections of God, the divine excellency of his names, cedes ground to the study of human urgencies. Boff sees in this shift the unfolding logic of modernity that displaces God to make room for the human. In Europe, the anthropocentric turn of modernity reoriented theology from *Ad majorem Dei gloriam* to *Ad majorem hominis gloriam, etiam Deus*. In Latin America the turn took a more concrete but equally problematic direction: *Ad majorem pauperis gloriam, etiam Deus*.

24. Cf. González de Cardedal, "Problemas de fondo," 399.

25. For a brief sketch of his life, see Laura Moreno, "Su vida, testimonio de amor y fidelidad a Dios," *Teología: Revista de la Facultad de Teología de la Pontificia Universidad Católica Argentina* 53, no. 79 (2002): 43–98.

26. In *El Apóstol*, Romero published a synopsis of Pironio's farewell speech to his diocese when he was called to join the Vatican curia. In that speech, Pironio offered a description of the tasks of the bishop that resonated strongly with Romero's own. "A bishop is not a technician, an administrator, or a boss. The bishop is, essentially, a pastor, a father, a brother, and a friend, who blazes a trail with human beings, sowing hope in their way, sharing their pain and joys, committing them to peace in justice and love, teaching them to be brothers and leading them to integral and joyful salvation in Jesus Christ" ("La voz del pastor," *Apóstol* 17 [1976]: 3).

27. The issue of August 1, 1978, carried a piece by Pironio entitled "The Joy of Hope," which is an excerpt from "The Renewal of the Religious Life and the Hope of the Young," published in *Joyful in Hope*. Pironio's "Meditation for Difficult Times" also found its way into *Orientación* on July 29, 1979. The original is found in Eduardo Pironio, *Alegres en la esperanza* (Madrid: Ediciones Paulinas, 1979), in English, *Joyful in Hope* (Slough: Society of Saint Paul, 1980), 155–82. Incidentally, a copy of this book is found in Romero's personal library at his house in the *Hospitalito*.

28. Eduardo Pironio, *Escritos pastorales* (Madrid: Biblioteca de Autores Cristianos, 1973), 205–27.

29. Ibid., 206.

30. Ibid., 211.

31. See *Diario,* June 26, 1978; May 9, 1979; January 30, 1980.

32. Pironio, "Reflexión teológica."

33. In his homily of July 24, 1977, Romero affirms Pironio's analysis of sin in its personal and social dimensions as described in Pironio, "Reflexión teológica," 91–92.

34. To speak of liberation is not to introduce a new word into theological speech or to tread on merely profane realities. On the contrary, the theme is as old as the people of Israel and as eschatological as the paschal mystery of Christ. In Pironio's time the term *liberation* was used by many, even if in different ways. In some circles, the term was feared and considered a front for heterodoxy. In others, the term was blown out of theological proportion. The theme of liberation, Pironio states, "does not exhaust the essence of Christianity. To want to reduce everything to 'liberation' limits the Christian message, cuts short the horizon of theology, and diminishes apostolic activity." Pironio, "Reflexión teológica," 67.

35. Pironio appeals to Paul's exhortation in Ephesians 4:24: in order to transform society it is imperative to clothe oneself with the new humanity that has been created in the likeness of God "in justice and true holiness." Therefore, "if the Christian aspires to become a prophet and a worker for liberation (which is demanded by his or her apostolic vocation), he or she should begin by being poor and crucified, a true friend of God and universal brother and sister to all humankind." Ibid., 68.

36. Ibid., 206.

37. Ibid., 205.

38. Óscar Romero, "Cuadernos espirituales: Mons. Óscar Arnulfo Romero, 1966–1980," unpublished transcriptions, Biblioteca de Teologia Juan Ramon Moreno, San Salvador, entry for June 9, 1970.

39. The question that animates Jesuits like Rutilio Grande is "What must I do for Christ?" (*Homilías* 2.323). Romero recounts with pride how the Jesuits expelled from El Salvador learned to be authentically Christian while serving in Central America, "for Ignatius of Loyola teaches that one learns not only in the spiritual retreat, but living here, where Christ is suffering flesh, here where Christ is a thing, where Christ is a cross one carries, not meditating in the chapel next to a *via crucis,* but living in the people; it is Christ with the cross on the way to Calvary" (*Homilías* 2.323).

40. Rady Roldán Figueroa, "The Mystical Theology of Luis de la Puente," in *A Companion to Jesuit Mysticism,* ed. Robert A. Maryks (Leiden: Brill, 2017), 61.

41. A synopsis of his life and works can be read in *Diccionario histórico de la Compañía de Jesús: Biográfico-temático*, vol. 3, ed. Charles E. O'Neill and Joaquín Ma. Domínguez (Madrid: Universidad Pontificia Comillas, 2001), 2244–45. According to Jesús Delgado Acevedo, Romero continued to draw on de la Puente throughout his mature years of ministry. See Jesús Delgado Acevedo, "La cultura de monseñor Romero," in Morozzo della Rocca, *Óscar Romero: Un obispo*, loc. 744–46, Kindle.

42. Zynda, *Archbishop Óscar Romero*, 6–8.

43. The fiftieth anniversary of Pius XI encyclical *Mens Nostra*, which encouraged the use of the Spiritual Exercises of Ignatius "not only among the clergy both secular and regular, but also among the multitudes of the Catholic laity" (Pope Pius XI, *Mens Nostra: Encyclical of Pope Pius XI on the Promotion of the Spiritual Exercises* 11, December 20, 1929, https://w2.vatican.va/content/pius-xi/en/encyclicals/documents/hf_p-xi_enc_19291220_mens-nostra.html), coincided with the gathering of CELAM in Puebla in 1979. Father Enrique Nuñez Hurtado, a Jesuit, set himself the task of conducting interviews of those present regarding the significance of the Spiritual Exercises, as he put it, "in, from and for Latin America." He designed a questionnaire and approached as many as were willing. The result was a set of twenty short and varied reflections on the challenges of walking the Ignatian way in the midst of the social whirlwinds sweeping Latin America. Among the interviewees were Clodovis Boff, Virgilio Elizondo, Jon Sobrino, and Óscar Romero. Enrique Nuñez Hurtado, *Ejercicios espirituales en, desde y para América Latina: Retos, intuiciones, contenidos* (Torreón, Mexico: Casa Iñigo, 1980).

44. Óscar Romero, interview in Hurtado, *Ejercicios espirituales*, 102.

45. Ibid., 104.

46. Ibid., 102.

47. Ibid., 103. In this section I draw on Edgardo Colón-Emeric, "Para un verdadero sentir en la iglesia: Lecciones sobre la educación teológica hoy en América Latina," *Cuadernos de Teología* 32 (2013): 156–74.

48. Óscar Romero in Hurtado, *Ejercicios espirituales*, 105.

49. San Ignacio de Loyola, *Obras de San Ignacio de Loyola* (Madrid: Biblioteca de Autores Cristianos, 1997), 302.

50. Pedro de Leturia explains that the rules for *sentir con la iglesia* are the "mature fruit of the purification and of the appropriation of the true gospel" (*Estudios Ignacianos*, vol. 2, *Ejercicios espirituales* [Rome: Institutum Historico, 1957], 153).

51. Joaquín Salaverri, "Motivación histórica y significación teológica del ignaciano 'sentir con la iglesia,'" *Estudios Eclesiásticos* 31 (1957): 146.

52. Cf. Leturia, *Estudios Ignacianos*, 2:154ss. The first set covers rules 1–9, the second rules 10–12, the third rules 13–18. Among these rules that Ignatius proposes in order to *sentir con la iglesia* there are two whose language lends itself to an easy but incorrect interpretation. The first: "After all judgment, we must have souls bound and ready to obey in all the things the true bride of Christ our Lord, which is our holy mother the hierarchical church." The second: "We must always be ready to accept the principle that the white that I see is black, if the hierarchical church so determines it to be; believing that between Christ our Lord, the husband, and the church, his bride, there is the same spirit that governs and rules for the health of our souls; because by the same Spirit and our Lord, who gave the ten commandments, is our holy mother church governed and ruled" (Loyola, *Obras*, 302, 303). The interpretation of these maxims as rules that require blind obedience to hierarchical authority is understandable but nevertheless incorrect. In the first place, one must have in mind the historical context that gives a place to this rule. The polemic between Catholic and Protestant, or, to be more specific, between Erasmus and Luther, renewed old debates between the Skeptics and the Stoics about the veracity of our perceptions. The terms of the debate receive their classical formulation in the question of Cicero: How can one say with certainty that something is white when what happens is that what is black feigns to be white? (cf. Marjorie O'Rourke Boyle, "Angels Black and White: Loyola's Spiritual Discernment in Historical Perspective," *Theological Studies* 44, no. 2 [1983]: 256). In the context of the renewal of this old debate, the rules for *sentir con la iglesia* entrust the determination of opinions to the judgment of the church. In the second place, Saint Ignatius does not speak of *sentir con la iglesia (sentire cum ecclesia)* but rather of a true *sentir en la iglesia (sentire vere in ecclesia militante)*. That is to say, the posture of obedience is born in the bosom of the church. It is not the obedience of a vassal toward a feudal lord. Rather, it is the result of discerning how the church fights with steadfastness in the world. Cf. Yves Congar, *True and False Reform in the Church* (Collegeville, MN: Liturgical Press, 2011), 236–37.

53. Leturia, *Estudios Ignacianos*, 2:162.

54. Ignatius proposes the Scholastics (Lombard, Bonaventure, and Aquinas) as guides for speculative theology, and the Patristics (Jerome, Augustine, Gregory the Great, etc.) as guides for practical theology, although one could argue that Ignatius prioritizes Scholasticism as the interpreter of the patristic tradition. With respect to the saints, Ignatius proposes caution before enthusiasm in canonizing the living as models of holiness. It is interesting

that Ignatius does not present himself either as an exemplary theologian or as a model of holiness and even puts the brakes on any popular process of canonization. Any testimony of holiness must be evaluated with caution and obedience to the hierarchy.

55. Cf. Boyle, "Angels Black and White," 254.

56. Leturia affirms that "the anti-Catholic error has always wavered, according to the times, between negation or exaggeration of one of these two extremes: either to reduce it all to God, to the supernatural, and to grace, denying and minimizing man, nature, and freedom; or to divinize man, nature, and the autonomous will, to the point of annulling divinity." Leturia, *Estudios Ignacianos*, 2:173–74.

57. Romero, "Aggiornamento," *El Chaparrastique*, no. 2981, January 15, 1965, 1.

58. Mata, *Monseñor Óscar Romero: Pasión por la iglesia* (Madrid: Ediciones Palabra, 2015), loc. 1612–14, Kindle.

59. Pope Paul VI, *Ecclesiam Suam* 36, August 6, 1964, http://w2.vatican .va/content/paul-vi/en/encyclicals/documents/hf_p-vi_enc_06081964 _ecclesiam.html.

60. Óscar Romero, "Dos palabras peligrosas," *Orientación*, no. 1257 (February 13, 1972), 3.

61. Ibid.

62. Romero, "Cuadernos espirituales," June 8, 1970; emphasis in original.

63. Delgado Acevedo states: "A este tema Romero dedica 200 fichas, de las cuales destaco los siguientes títulos: Cartas du Pere Croiset: Sobre las apariciones del Sagrado Corazón de Jesús; Doble aspecto de la devoción al Sagrado Corazón; La esencia del cristianismo: Jesús amor; Historia de la devoción al Sagrado Corazón; Escritos de santa Margarita María de Alacoque." In Morozzo della Rocca, *Óscar Romero: Un obispo*, loc. 604–6, Kindle.

64. Romero, "Cuadernos espirituales," June 8, 1970.

65. Ibid.

66. Ibid.

67. Ibid.

68. "Quidquid recipitur ad modum recipientis recipitur." *ST* 1.75.5.

69. Karl Rahner discerns the sign of the times to be atheism, so his interpretation of the Spiritual Exercises has its focus in the "Contemplation in Order to Reach Love," with the object of "encountering God in all things." Hans Urs von Balthasar discerns the modern problem as the

tension between pairings of authority and autonomy, freedom and obedience, and in consequence his theology dwells extensively on the call of the King. J. Matthew Ashley, "Ignacio Ellacuría and the Spiritual Exercises of Ignatius Loyola," *Theological Studies* 61, no. 1 (2000): 21.

70. Ignacio Ellacuría, "A Latin American Reading of the Spiritual Exercises of Saint Ignatius," *Spiritus* 10, no. 2 (2010): 205–42n8. The Spiritual Exercises for Ellacuría offer Latin America two gifts: a theological experience that discerns the presence of God in the midst of history and also a contextual space that exposes the historicity of ideologies. Cf. J. Matthew Ashley, "A Contemplative under the Standard of Christ: Ignacio Ellacuría's Interpretation of Ignatius of Loyola's Spiritual Exercises," *Spiritus* 10, no. 2 (2010): 192–204.

71. Isidro González Modroño explains it in these terms: "*Sentir con la iglesia* implies, in the first place, participation in the evangelical sensibility before the signs of the times, although one questions the literalness of the answers of the tradition of the church, needful today of a new hermeneutic." Quoted in Darío Mollá, "El 'sentido verdadero' en el servicio de la iglesia según la Congregación General 34 de la Compañía de Jesús," *Estudios Eclesiásticos* 71 (1996): 47.

72. Douglas Marcouiller and Jon Sobrino, *El sentir con la iglesia de Monseñor Romero* (San Salvador: Centro Monseñor Romero, 2004), 21.

73. Ibid.

74. "The changes in the world are for the church today a sign of the times in which the church recognizes itself. [The church] feels that it is God himself who compels her through the newness of the world and that she must be aware of the newness of the world in order to respond to the word of God and adapt its activity in and for the world" (*Voz*, 72).

75. In his diary, Romero recalls that Doctor Jiménez visited him to ask for a greater show of support from the archbishop for the political work of the Christian Democrats on the ruling junta in addressing the national crisis. Romero agreed but insisted on continuing to give voice to the people's demands and to call for an end to the government's use of repressive force. It is interesting that in the homily where Romero spoke of this encounter he almost flipped the conversation on its head. Doctor Jiménez seems to have wanted a more, not less, politically partisan mass. See *Diario*, February 11, 1980.

76. Pope Paul VI, *Angelus Domini*, August 6, 1978, http://w2.vatican.va /content/paul-vi/it/angelus/1978/documents/hf_p-vi_ang_19780806 .html.

77. I will attribute the content of the letter to Romero, even if it could equally be credited to Rivera y Damas, because the final product was approved by the archbishop and he is the subject of the present study.

78. Cf. *Homilías*, 6:32: "I want to insist, dear brothers, on a distinction that in our time needs to be made very clear. It is not the same thing to say 'the people' as to say 'the people of God.' What is the difference? 'The people' is everyone who lives in the homeland [*patria*]. All those are the Salvadoran people, including those who do not believe, those who are indifferent. All those, believers and unbelievers, are the people. But when we say 'the people of God,' we intend to speak of the Christian community, among the Salvadorans; those who have received the message of Christ, who have been converted, and who, to make their conversion manifest, have been baptized and are preparing—as John the Baptist said—'a perfect people for the coming of the Lord.' Hence, the people of God are a selection. We do not say this with pride or conceit because, perhaps, we are not the people of God when we have not been converted in truth. Furthermore, the people of God are those who, even outside the borders of the church, have not known Christ but have placed their hope and trust in God."

79. Pope Pius XI, "Radiomensaje de Su Santidad Pío XI al I Congreso Eucarístico Nacional de El Salvador," November 26, 1942, https://w2 .vatican.va/content/pius-xii/es/speeches/1942/documents/hf_p-xii_spe _19421126_eucaristico-salvador.html.

80. Cf. "The Pope, Christ's Lieutenant in the Church" (*Homilías*, 3:193–210); "The Church of John Paul" (*Homilías*, 3:283–300); "The Reply of God to the Present World" (*Homilías*, 3:301–6). See also Romero's use in a homily (*Homilías*, 5:367–70) of a letter that John Paul I addressed to G. K. Chesterton regarding the story "The Ball and the Cross." In sum, Romero felt a strong bond of kinship with the simple catechist whose Petrine ministry was tragically short.

81. The sermon of July 15, 1979, "Christ Has Entrusted Us a Prophetic Mission," states unambiguously that the church is being persecuted "because of its *preferential option for the poor*, because it tries to become incarnate in the affairs of the poor and say to all the people, the rulers, the rich, the powerful, if you do not become poor, if you do not become interested in the poverty of our people as if they were your very family, you will not rescue the society" (*Homilías*, 5:110). The *preferential option* challenges the rich and poor too. The spiritual poverty entailed by the option is the remedy for empowering the poor to resist the lure of the consumerist society (cf. *Puebla* 1156). This spiritual poverty has an evangelical dimension. As Romero says, "How

wise was the Lord Jesus Christ in telling the apostles to go evangelize in the person of a poor pilgrim! Today's church needs to convert itself to this commandment of Christ. It is no longer the time for the grand vestments, the grand useless buildings, the grand ceremonies of our church. All this, perhaps in another time, had its purpose, and we need to continue to give it purpose for the sake of evangelization and service. But now, above all, the church wants to present itself as poor among the poor and poor among the rich so as to evangelize poor and rich" (*Homilías*, 5:111). See also the homily "The Poverty of the Beatitudes" of February 17, 1980. This sermon is the last sermon before the beginning of Lent. Consequently, Romero offers his congregation a preview of the costly pilgrimage on which they are to embark, even as he reminds them of the hope for which they will undergo penitence and privation. Easter and Pentecost offer hope of the renewal that the country and the world desperately need. "Let us not cry only structure changes because new structures are useless if there are not new persons who lead and live these structures so needed by the country" (*Homilías*, 6:275).

82. "Now as you excel in everything—in faith, in speech, in knowledge, in utmost eagerness, and in our love for you—so we want you to excel also in this generous undertaking. I do not say this as a command, but I am testing the genuineness of your love against the earnestness of others. For you know the generous act of our Lord Jesus Christ, that though he was rich, yet for your sakes he became poor, so that by his poverty you might become rich. I do not mean that there should be relief for others and pressure on you, but it is a question of a fair balance between your present abundance and their need, so that their abundance may be for your need, in order that there may be a fair balance. As it is written, 'The one who had much did not have too much, and the one who had little did not have too little.'"

83. Cf. *Puebla* 1166–1205.

84. Las Casas, *Historia de las Indias*, vol. 3, chap. 138, p. 510.

85. Cf. *Homilías*, 2:355: "If Christ is the representative of the entire people in his agonies, in his humiliation, in his limbs pierced by nails on a cross, we must discover the suffering of our people. It is our tortured people, our crucified, spit-upon, humiliated people whom Jesus Christ our Lord represents in order to give our very difficult situation a sense of redemption."

86. The phrase is derived from Zephaniah 2:3: "Seek the LORD, all you humble of the land, who do his commands; seek righteousness, seek humility; perhaps you may be hidden on the day of the LORD's wrath." The phrase "humble of the land" can also be translated as the "poor of the land."

87. Romero understands that the Magnificat may be called insurrectional. His commentary on Mary's song is telling: "He has brought down the powerful from their thrones *when these have become an obstacle for the tranquility of the people*" (*Homilías*, 5:282).

88. Romero alludes here to a popular song by Carlos Mejía Godoy, "You Are the God of the Poor," from the Nicaraguan mass that we discussed in the previous chapter.

89. Pironio quoted in *Homilías*, 5:111.

90. Regarding the option as a vaccine against communism was the opinion that one of the people surveyed in preparation for the fourth pastoral letter stated and that Romero noted with approval (cf. *Homilías*, 5:193). Seeing the option as a cure for division is something that Romero learned from Puebla (*Puebla* 1140). Since the preferential option is Christ's own, then the weakness of solidarity with the poor is evidence of a tenuous relation with Christ (cf. *Homilías*, 5:327).

91. Romero sent Mother Teresa a telegram on the occasion of her reception of the Nobel Prize that he read in his homily of October 21, 1979 (cf. *Homilías*, 5:456).

92. A frequent charge that Romero fended off (*Homilías*, 5:479, 509; *Homilias*, 6:75).

93. Mata, *Monseñor Romero*, loc. 2141–42, Kindle. According to Ricardo Urioste, Romero's act of identification with the church entailed three things. "In the first place, it meant a continuous nearness by means of constant and fervent prayer. [Romero] confessed that he found in God the strength to go on. In the second place, it meant love and service to others without considering the consequences, including offering his life on the altar of God for the people that he loved and defended to the point of death. Third, it meant for him filial fidelity to the teachings coming from the church" (loc. 2142–45, Kindle). Urioste fleshes out his interpretation of Romero's episcopal motto in "Monseñor Romero y su 'sentir con la iglesia,'" *La espiritualidad de Monseñor Romero: Sentir con la iglesia*, ed. Jon Sobrino (San Salvador: Fundación Monseñor Romero, 2015), 59–81.

94. See respectively *Homilías*, 1:337; *Homilías*, 3:283–300.

95. See *Homilías*, 6:378, and *Homilías*, 6:268–69, respectively.

96. See also *Homilías*, 4:426, 319; 5:381, 259.

97. *Diario*, November 11, 1979: "No hay más que una Iglesia, ésta que Cristo predica, la Iglesia que debe de darse con todo el corazón, porque aquel que se llama católico y está adorando sus riquezas y no quiere desprenderse

de ellas no es ni cristiano; no ha comprendido el llamamiento del Señor, no es Iglesia. El rico que está de rodillas ante su dinero aunque vaya a misa y aunque haga actos piadosos si no se ha desprendido en el corazón del ídolo dinero, es un idólatra, no es un cristiano. No hay más que una Iglesia, la que adora al verdadero Dios y la que le sabe dar a las cosas su valor relativo."

98. Romero's thoughts turned to ecumenism during the week of prayer for Christian unity. He wrote editorials in *Chaparrastique* to mark this occasion in 1951, 1965, and 1966.

99. Óscar Romero, "Ecumenismo," *Chaparrastique*, no. 2982 (January 21, 1965): 1.

100. In several homilies Romero uses the story of a Protestant's conversion to Catholicism to illustrate the importance of Catholic sacramental belief and practice. "Hay una página bella de un protestante que se hizo católico y dice en su diario íntimo: 'Yo no era católico por los sacramentos, yo pensé que eso era invención de los hombres y que estorbaba mis relaciones directas con Cristo. Quería creer en Cristo sin la Iglesia, pero cuando comprendí que los sacramentos son acciones de Cristo, le doy gracias a Dios de que haya una Iglesia que realice en nombre de Cristo, la redención de Cristo. Así hay que mirar los sacramentos'" (*Diario*, December 3, 1978; see also March 5, 1978).

101. Óscar Romero, "Ecumenismo, sinceridad y prudencia," *Chaparrastique*, no. 3032 (January 21, 1966): 1.

102. Óscar Romero, "La palabra del Arzobispo," *Orientación*, no. 4051 (January 29, 1978): 2. According to Romero, Catholics are to eschew approaches that downplay the importance of truth and cover up doctrinal differences behind the veil of a false irenicism. Moreover, they are to be careful that when they pray with non-Catholics they do so in a manner that is not naive to the risks of misinterpretation. Armed with sincerity and prudence, "Catholics and non-Catholics should advance without fear" (2).

103. Ibid.

104. Romero blames an overly intellectual concept of the faith on the Catholic-Protestant polemics of the sixteenth century. Against Luther's one-sided emphasis on the subjective dimension of the faith, the Council of Trent responded with a one-sided emphasis on the objective dimension of the faith. Luther emphasized the act of faith as trust, Catholicism, the content of the faith as truth. The result was the separation of faith from ethics. Romero mentions Luther's famous and easily misunderstood aphorism of *Pecca fortiter* as paradigmatic of this divorce. However, the effects of the divorce are not limited to the Protestant churches. Catholics too have suffered from an overly dogmatic presentation of the gospel. One of the great

gifts of Vatican II was overcoming this tension. In a sense, for Romero, Vatican II accomplished what Luther tried but failed to do. The council offered a holistic, biblical account of faith. "It is not only the acceptance of truths, it is the acceptance of the will of God. It is not only the surrender of my mind to the truths of God. It is the surrender of my mind and heart to what God wants" (*Homilías*, 1:369). It is important to note that Romero admits that his knowledge of Luther is secondhand. Nonetheless, Luther's dialectical approach, his addition of "sola" to "fide," runs against the grain of Romero's holistic gospel.

105. Brother Roger attended the third meeting of CELAM at Puebla in 1979. The invitation to attend as an observer was extended by Eduardo Pironio. The presence of Brother Roger received mixed responses. The secretary of CELAM at the time, Alfonso López Trujillo, barred his participation at the Eucharist with the rest of the attendants. However, Brother Roger did receive the opportunity to address the assembly in plenary. Cf. Sabine Laplane, *Frère Roger, de Taizé: Avec presque rien. . . .* (Paris: Éditions du Cerf, 2015), loc. 6567–80, Kindle. While attending Puebla, the abbot of Taizé met Romero, and the two became good friends (*Diario*, February 7, 1979). Plans were made for a future visit to El Salvador. Romero was particularly excited by the prospects that such a visit held for the seminarians on account of Brother Roger's charism for working with youth (*Diario*, November 14, 1980).

106. Cf. *Homilías*, 1:440.

107. See his word to the Protestants in his homily of October 23, 1977 (*Homilías*, 1:417–18).

108. See the homily of November 18, 1979 (*Homilías*, 5:543–68).

109. See Medardo Ernesto Gómez, *Teología de la vida* (Managua: Ediciones Nicarao, 1992), 107–11.

110. Cf. Marcouiller and Sobrino, *Sentir con la iglesia*, 21.

111. Margaret Eletta Guider, "Sentir con la Iglesia: Archbishop Romero, an Ecclesial Mystic," in *Archbishop Romero: Martyr and Prophet for the New Millennium*, ed. Robert Pelton (Scranton, PA: University of Scranton Press, 2006), 85.

Chapter 6. The Vision of God

1. Óscar Romero, "En la Tierra Prometida," *El Chaparrastique*, no. 2132, October 5, 1956, 1.

2. Ibid.

3. Ibid.

4. Ibid.

5. Ibid.

6. Óscar Romero, "Una semana santa en Jerusalén," *El Chaparrastique*, no. 2158, April 12, 1957, 1, 4.

7. *Diario*, January 28, 1980.

8. *Diario*, January 29, 1980.

9. *Diario*, January 30, 1980. The conversation with Pironio was very encouraging. Pironio told Romero that the reports that were reaching the Vatican about the church's action in El Salvador were positive. The cardinal also offered Romero a scripture verse for meditation from Matthew 10:28— "Do not fear those who kill the body but cannot kill the soul." Romero recalled how Pironio applied this text to Romero's experience in El Salvador: "If those who kill the body are terrible, how much more terrible are those who machine-gun the spirit, slandering, defaming, destroying a person, and he thought that this was precisely my martyrdom, even within the church, and that I should take heart." These words prepared Romero for his conversation with the pope, which though largely positive, still required Romero's justification of his leadership.

10. Cf. Rodrigo Polanco, "*Gloria enim Dei vivens homo, vita autem hominis visio Dei*: Reflexiones sobre el *homo vivens* en el pensamiento de San Ireneo," *Anales de la Facultad de Teología* 61 (2010): 159–91. "Gloria del Padre equivale a recibir la vida y la salvación como don del Padre. Participar de la gloria es participar de la vida e incorrupción de Dios, es participar de lo mismo que es Dios. Y esto es la comunión con Dios que le hace falta al hombre para vivir de acuerdo al plan de Dios. La gloria que Dios otorga como participación en su luz (= gloria, naturaleza) es la que salva al hombre en un camino continuo de servicio a Dios" (172).

11. Irenaeus, *Against the Heresies* 4.20.7, ed. Roberts and Donaldson, 489–90; emphasis added.

12. The Latin text comes from Irénée de Lyon, *Contre les hérésies* 4, ed. Adelin Rousseau, Sources Chrétiennes 100 (Paris: Editions du Cerf, 1965), 648.

13. J. Moreno, "'Gloria Dei, vivens homo.'"

14. Antonio Orbe, "Gloria Dei vivens homo: Análisis de Ireneo, *adv. haer.* IV, 20, 1–7," *Gregorianum* 73, no. 2 (1992): 263.

15. Rafael Amo Usanos, "La carne habituada aportar vida," *Estudios Eclesiásticos* 83 (2008): 425–55.

16. Ibid., 439.

17. On Irenaeus's reading, Isaiah 42:5 promises the coinherence of these two vital principles because the God who made heaven and earth is the God "who gives breath [πνοή] to the people upon it and spirit [πνεῦμα] to those who walk in it." Paul speaks of the Spirit as the gift of the last Adam (cf. 1 Cor. 15:45). See also Isaiah 57:16, "For I will not continually accuse, nor will I always be angry; for then the spirits [πνεῦμα] would grow faint before me, even the souls [πνοή] that I have made."

18. Irenaeus offers an analogy. "But as the engrafted wild olive does not certainly lose the substance of its wood, but changes the quality of its fruit, and receives another name, being now not a wild olive, but a fruit-bearing olive, and is called so; so also, when man is grafted in by faith and receives the Spirit of God, he certainly does not lose the substance of flesh, but changes the quality of the fruit [brought forth] of his works, and receives another name, showing that he has become changed for the better, being now not [mere] flesh and blood, but a spiritual man, and is called such" (*Adv. Haer.* 5.10.2, ed. Roberts and Donaldson, 536).

19. "All human history prior to the encounter with the incarnate Son was intended for growth into the reception of that experience. All human history since is intended for the accustomization of humanity to the life offered in the incarnate Christ—an accustomization that is the working in humanity of the Holy Spirit, who will bring to perfection at the eschaton that which man experiences in token even now." M. C. Steenberg, *Of God and Man: Theology as Anthropology from Irenaeus to Athanasius* (London: Bloomsbury T&T Clark, 2009), 52.

20. "Christ's transfiguration is, for Irenaeus, the manifestation into the world of God's being, his presence, the 'face' which was, under the first covenant, unapproachable to men." Steenberg, "Two-Natured Man," 416.

21. Rafael Amo Usanos, "Carne," 455.

22. Irenaeus, *Against Heresies* 4.20.7, ed. Roberts and Donaldson, 490.

23. T. H. White's depiction of the character of Merlyn in *The Once and Future King* illustrates the confusions and humor that can result from living in this manner. As he explains to young Arthur, "Now ordinary people are born forwards in time . . . and nearly everything in the world goes forward too. This makes it quite easy for the ordinary people to live. . . . But I unfortunately was born at the wrong end of time, and I have to live backwards from in front, while surrounded by a whole lot of people living forwards from behind" (*The Once and Future King* [New York: Ace Books, 1987], 35). One might say that the Christian too was born again at the wrong end of time. Christians live backwards, from the end. When ordinary people look at the end of the

cosmos, they see a world with an expiration date, a universe bound to decay: suns become red giants, red giants become black holes. When Christians look to the end, they see things that look like the beginning: Jerusalem, Adam and Eve, the Garden of Eden, Creation. According to Merlyn, "Some people call it having the second sight." Irenaeus calls this "seeing prophetically."

24. Cf. Delgado Acevedo, "Cultura de Monseñor Romero," loc. 742–43, Kindle.

25. See chapter 1 for the discussion of the transmission history of the Irenaean dictum.

26. Romero, "Cuadernos espirituales," July 14, 1975. Pironio's reflections in Guatemala reprise a series of Lenten meditations that he gave at the Vatican the previous year. These were later published in *Queremos ver a Jesús* (Madrid: BAC, 1980).

27. Romero, "Cuadernos espirituales," 190.

28. Ibid., 191; emphasis added.

29. Ibid., 194.

30. Ibid.

31. Sobrino, *Archbishop Romero*, 15.

32. Ibid.

33. Ibid., 16.

34. Cf. Delgado Acevedo, "Cultura de Monseñor Romero," loc. 742–43, Kindle.

35. Sobrino, *Archbishop Romero*, 16.

36. *Diario*, January 11, 1980.

37. Cf. Todd Walatka, *Von Balthasar and the Option for the Poor: Theodramatics in the Light of Liberation Theology* (Washington, DC: Catholic University Press, 2017), 16n36.

38. In his diaries, Romero speaks a number of times of his collaborations with Ellacuría and Sobrino. But nowhere does he cite them except in this speech.

39. Cf. *Medellín*, Justicia 1; *Puebla* 29.

40. Cf. *Lumen Gentium* 8.

41. Another echo of Ellacuría is heard in this address when Romero describes the persecution of the church as "bearing the destiny of the poor" (188). Romero does not cite Ellacuría, but the phrasing resembles the theologian's reflections on the responsibility that the Christian has to engage the world.

42. See, for instance, the now classic work on this topic, A. N. Williams, *The Ground of Union: Deification in Aquinas and Palamas* (New York: Oxford

University Press, 1999). See also A. J. Ollerton, *"Quasi Deificari:* Deification in the Theology of John Calvin," *Westminster Theological Journal* 73 (2011): 237–54; Kelly Steve McCormick, "Theosis in Chrysostom and Wesley: An Eastern Paradigm on Faith and Love," *Wesleyan Theological Journal* 26, no. 1: 38–103; Luc-Thomas Somme, *Thomas d'Aquin la divinisation dans le Christ* (Geneva: Editions Ad Solem, 1998); Carl E. Braaten and Robert J. Jenson, *Union with Christ: The New Finnish Interpretation of Luther* (Grand Rapids, MI: William B. Eerdmans, 1998); Daria Spezzano, *The Glory of God's Grace: Deification According to St. Thomas Aquinas* (Ave Maria, FL: Sapientia Press, 2015).

43. Romero seeks to lead his people in finding the truth in "the joy of a conscience divinized by God" (*Homilías,* 3:316). The holistic liberation preached by the church is not limited to the inward renewal of the individual. The church "promotes, divinizes" the culture of a people (*Homilías,* 1:388).

44. See *Homilías,* 2:531: "United to my sacrifice present at this altar, this people is divinized and now leave the cathedral to keep working, to keep struggling, to keep suffering, but always united to the eternal priest who remains present in the Eucharist so that we know how to encounter him the next Sunday too."

45. Escobar Alas, *Veo en la ciudad,* para. 163.

46. See for instance, his homily for January 1, 1978. In this sermon Romero offers a brief but wonderful reflection on the Christological import of the Marian title of *Theotókos* (*Homilías,* 2:180–82). The doxological term served as a bulwark against heresies in the fourth century and also as the wellspring for two Christological currents in the twentieth century—Christology from above and Christology from below. The former current he associates with the Incarnation; the second, with divinization. The language of Romero in this homily is not as precise as one would expect to find in a treatise on Christology. The manner in which he speaks of Mary as mother of God is open to misunderstanding. He says "She was not only mother of a man who became God, but mother of a God who became incarnate in her very bowels" (*Homilías,* 2:180). It would be a mistake to read Romero's Christological reflections as being open to adoptionist Christologies. Romero insists that both natures are united in one divine person. "What Christ does as God, we can say God does. But also what Christ does as human, since he is united to God, we say that God does. This is why the council says that God became human, and since then we humans feel that our nature has been elevated in him" (*Homilías,* 2:181). Incidentally, the editors of *Homilías* attribute this reference to *Ad Gentes* 3, but Romero's words are more reminiscent of *Gaudium et Spes* 22.

47. The promise of becoming "partakers of the divine nature" (2 Pet. 1:4) is found in several homilies but only within quotation from *Dei Verbum* 2 (*Homilías*, 3:159, 5:81) or John Paul I (*Homilías*, 5:369). The acclamation "You are gods" from Psalm 86:2, which is also quoted by Jesus (John 10:34), does not appear in his homilies.

48. Cf. *Homilías*, 1:144.

49. Jon Sobrino writes, "The most important element for understanding the logic of salvation in this biblical tradition of Jesus of Nazareth is the theologal grounding. The Most High, in order to be the God of salvation, has come down to our history, and he has done so in a twofold manner: he has come down to the human level and, within the human, to what is humanly weak. To express it more precisely, *transcendence* has become *transdescendence*, benevolent closeness, and thus has become *con-descendence*, affectionate embrace. The same is expressed in the Christological language of the first centuries: *salus quoniam caro*. Christ is salvation because he is flesh, *sarx*. That is the new logic" (*No Salvation*, 55).

50. *Homilías*, 4:485. See also *Homilías*, 6:284: "This is the commitment of being Christian: Following Christ in his incarnation. And if Christ is the majestic God who becomes a humble human to the point of dying on the cross as a slave and he lives with the poor, so must it be with our Christian faith. The Christian who wants to live without making a commitment to be in solidarity with the poor is not worthy of being called a Christian."

51. The vaccine against *conformismo* can be as practical as organizing sewing classes that encourage people to wait *actively* for their salvation. "And I have always told you on these occasions, that the church does not promote sewing classes or workshops, etc., only to help people to progress materially. It wants to place in the heart a true wisdom, a spirit, a mysticism to tell the people that progress must not be confused with the kingdom of God but it helps the kingdom of God" (*Homilías*, 3:410).

52. *Diario*, February 4, 1980.

53. Alejandro [Alex] García-Rivera, *A Wounded Innocence: Sketches for a Theology of Art* (Collegeville, MN: Liturgical Press, 2003), 4.

54. Richard Viladesau, "*Theosis* and Beauty," *Theology Today* 65 (2008): 189.

55. Ibid.

56. Quoted in James B. Nickoloff, "Gustavo Gutiérrez Meets Giuseppe Verdi: The Beauty of Liberation and the Liberation of Beauty," *Religion and the Arts* 17 (2013): 204. While living in Lima during the 1980s Nickoloff frequented Gustavo Gutierrez's parish. Nickoloff tells of Gutierrez's

practice of playing classical music through the chapel speakers half an hour before the beginning of mass. The juxtaposition of the "father of liberation theology," playing elite Western music for a congregation of mostly poor, uneducated *limeños* was jarring. Here was a man who spoke eloquently about the need for the gospel to take on flesh in Peru, a man who took pride in the power of Andean music to erect a bulwark against colonization. "How then could this apostle of indigenization seem to be promoting art from an alien, even oppressive source?" When Nickoloff found enough courage to ask Father Gustavo the question, the Peruvian priest replied, "Don't you think the poor have a right to Beethoven?" (204). The answer was enigmatic and led Nickoloff to reflect on the relation of beauty and justice, Gutierrez and Beethoven, liberation and opera, Arguedas and *Aida*.

57. Rubem Alves, "From Liberation Theologian to Poet: A Plea That the Church Move from Ethics to Aesthetics, from Doing to Beauty," *Church and Society* 83 (1993): 23. Like Augustine, Alves came to this realization late in life. In Alves one finds an example of a postliberation theologian. The Brazilian Presbyterian who had been among the pioneers of liberation theology became disillusioned with the direction of that movement and began to head along a different, lonely path. In his own words, "The Rubem Alves of the theology of liberation, the one who spoke about action, changed. I became different. I believe God has strange ways of doing things. I decided to accept the risk of playing the role of the jester" (20). Alves does not explain why he changed. Instead he focuses on the how. He turned from doing to beauty, from ethics to aesthetics, from theologian to poet. Alves draws on the Augustinian distinction between *uti* and *frui* to explain the significance of the shift. The order of utility pertains to instrumentality, to efficacious action, to doing. The order of fruition pertains to what gives pleasure, enjoyment, and happiness. Liberation theologians have largely operated in the order of utility and neglected that of fruition. What is useless is treated as not important or even as a problem. But the problem is that "happiness has to do with things that are totally useless" (23). A Mozart sonata is useless. Michelangelo's *Pietà* is useless. Even paradise is useless. Humans are drawn to these things because they are beautiful, and this is Alves's point. People on the margins want bread, they want justice, they want all kinds of useful things. But "the poor also want beauty" (23). Alves rereads Satan's testing of Jesus along these lines: "Satan told Jesus that he should be a practical being, he should become a baker. And Jesus said, 'No, I would rather be a poet'" (23). Liberation theologians became obsessed with doing things, but only beauty can change the world. The visions of horror, suffering, and injustice

that surround us belong to reality but do not have the power to change that reality. There is a kind of political action that is motivated by outrage, but "then there is another type of political action that is like that of Michelangelo and the Pietà" (24). As in the story of Sleeping Beauty, only the kiss of true love will awaken the dead to life.

58. M. González, *Sor Juana*, 156. This is one of the reasons why she engages in a *ressourcement* from the margins of Sor Juana Inés de la Cruz, whose lyrical works unite beauty and justice.

59. Goizueta, *Christ Our Companion*, 116.

60. Ibid., 119.

61. Viladesau, "*Theosis* and Beauty," 183.

62. Matthew Whelan, "The Land of the Savior: Óscar Romero and the Reform of Agriculture" (PhD diss., Duke Divinity School, 2016), 75.

63. Whelan states that "Romero thinks the greatest injustice afflicting El Salvador is profoundly personal, occurring in the enclosure of the self and its possessions from the claims of others. It is an injustice that ultimately implicates everyone and wounds the capacity for communion. The roots of such injustice necessarily ramify outward, entangling and warping structures, institutions, and landscapes" (ibid., 484n534).

64. Romero himself had little personal experience with Eastern Orthodoxy. As he notes, the Orthodox branch did not spread much in Latin America (*Homilías*, 2:238). However, Romero expressed appreciation for the depth of their theological perspective (*Homilías*, 4:142).

65. Willis Jenkins, *Ecologies of Grace: Environmental Ethics and Christian Theology* (New York: Oxford University Press, 2008), 207–25.

66. Ibid., 208.

67. Ibid., 225.

68. Cf. Sergei Bulgakov, "The Exceeding Glory," in *Sergius Bulgakov: A Bulgakov Anthology*, ed. Nicolas Zernov and James Paine (Eugene, OR: Wipf and Stock, 1976), 188–91.

69. Cf. ibid., 190.

70. Cf. ibid., 191.

71. Jenkins states this longing in evocative terms appropriated from Bulgakov: "Creation thirsts for the Son of God, groans for the daughters and sons of humanity. Through its liturgical cultivation, the church slakes and liberates creation, sustaining and glorifying creatures within its glorification of God" (*Ecologies of Grace*, 214).

72. Ibid., 218.

73. Cf. *Homilías*, 1:297–98.

74. Ibid.

75. Pope Paul VI, *Address during the Last General Meeting of the Second Vatican Council*, December 7, 1965, https://w2.vatican.va/content/paul-vi/en/speeches/1965/documents/hf_p-vi_spe_19651207_epilogo-concilio.html; *Homilías*, 1:180. The version that Romero uses may come from either the Latin or a non-official Spanish translation. It differs from the English in a couple of ways. First, the Spanish version that Romero uses says that the face of Christ needs to be recognized in the face of each human being, "especialmente si se ha hecho transparente por sus lágrimas y por sus dolores." This version more closely follows the Latin (maxime si lacrimis ac doloribus effectus est translucidus) and presents a more suggestive metaphor for how suffering makes someone transparent to Jesus. Second, the Spanish version removes a grammatical ambiguity in English. Tears wash the face of the sufferer, not the viewer. Romero in his preaching expands on both of these points, namely the purifying power of suffering and the need for washing of both the sufferer and the companion.

76. Cf. Walatka, *Von Balthasar*, 155. Walatka's brilliant study of von Balthasar in conversation with Latin American theology is worth considering at greater length than I can afford here. According to Walatka, the poor make an ethical, social, and political claim on all vocations. Every Christian is called to orthodoxy, orthopraxis, and orthopathy (cf. 151). "Each and every person is called to incarnate the mercy of God toward the weak and suffering, and this first demands the development of a disposition of sympathy." The cultivation of this disposition is the result of being, as Sobrino insists, "honest with reality" (cf. Walatka, *Von Balthasar*, 155). This disposition of sympathy is fundamental but insufficient by itself. Mercy calls for effectively alleviating someone's suffering. The Good Samaritan was not simply moved to compassion; he did something about the pitiful situation. Even here, acting compassionately is not the final goal. "Mercy must go beyond temporary aid and strike at the structural causes of suffering and oppression" (156–57). At the same time, mercy calls for acting in situations when the causes of suffering may not be overcome or even ameliorated. Mercy is what moves Christians to care for what the world considers hopeless cases that are drains on resources like the terminally ill patients at the *Hospitalito*. Von Balthasar would say that it is in such circumstances that the uniqueness of Christian mercy is most clearly seen in distinction from Promethean social improvement projects.

77. *Diario*, May 14, 1979.

78. Romero does not explicitly apply the language of epiphany or theophany to the poor. He does speak on numerous occasions of seeing

Christ in the poor. Martin of Tours is celebrated as one who had the happy privilege of seeing Christ in the poor (*Homilías*, 5:529, 6:278). In this sense it is closely related to epiphany (cf. *Homilías*, 2:144).

79. García-Rivera, *Wounded Innocence*, 92.

80. Cf. García-Rivera, *Community of the Beautiful*, 92.

81. *Diario*, May 19, 1979. Romero visited the parish of Colón on May 19, 1979. He met with the parish priest and a group of Sisters of the Sacred Heart in a hacienda where a group of members of the parish worked. He found a congregation that was cold, unwelcoming, and depressed. He attributed their mood to the degrading conditions that they experienced. The owner of this hacienda was something of a despot, and Romero promised himself not to accept similar invitations in the future.

82. *Diario*, March 8, 1980.

83. Ibid.

84. *Diario*, August 26, 1979.

85. Romero noted the death of Felipe de Jesús Chacón in his homily of August 27, 1978, *Homilías*, 3:206.

86. *Diario*, August 26, 1979. Romero names this martyred catechist in several homilies: September 11, 1977 (*Homilías*, 1:306); August 20, 1978 (*Homilías*, 3:177); August 27, 1978 (*Homilías*, 3:206); August 26, 1979 (*Homilías*, 5:261); September 2, 1979 (*Homilías*, 5:284). He compares Felipe to Saint Bartholomew, who tradition tells was flayed for announcing the gospel.

87. Cf. Óscar Romero, *La iglesia, cuerpo de Cristo en la historia: Segunda carta pastoral* (San Salvador: n.p., 1977), 175. See also Armando Márquez Ochoa, *Martirologio de Monseñor Romero: Testimonio y catequesis de la Iglesia salvadoreña* (La Libertad, El Salvador: CEBES, 2005); Walter Guerra, ed., *Testigos de la fe en El Salvador: Nuestros sacerdotes y seminaristas diocesanos mártires 1977–1993* (San Salvador: n.p., 1993).

88. José Ignacio González Faus, "El mártir testigo del amor," *Revista Latinoamericana de Teología* 48 (2002): 38.

89. Rino Fisichella, "Martirio," in *Diccionario de teología fundamental*, ed. René Latourelle, Rino Fisichella, and Salvador Pié-Ninot (Madrid: San Pablo, 1992), 859.

90. Casas Andrés, *Dios pasó*, 368.

91. Sobrino, *Witnesses to the Kingdom*, 101.

92. Sobrino interprets the theological task as a three-dimensional matrix of knowing and doing. First, there is what Ellacuría calls *hacerse cargo de la realidad*. He terms this the pre-Socratic movement, a "having to face reality directly, in a sort of intellectual loneliness, without being able to cite anyone

as an absolute authority" (*Witnesses to the Kingdom*, 105). This step starts from an encounter with reality, a grabbing of reality (or being grabbed by reality) that is unmediated by prior conceptual categories. This kind of encounter is necessary in order to perceive the signs of the times. Sobrino contrasts the role that reality plays in biblical hermeneutics in the Northern Hemisphere to that in Latin America. In the North, reality is an obstacle that must be hurdled in order to understand the meaning of the text. In the South, it is an aid to the text. The second dimension is what Ellacuría calls *cargar con la realidad*. This is the Aristotelian or analytical movement of conceptualization, a taking responsibility for reality by bringing philosophical systems to bear in order to be intellectually honest to this reality. Third, there is what Ellacuría calls *encargarse de la realidad*. This is the Socratic movement of engaging with the reality that has been grasped and studied in order to transform it. El Salvador highlights the relation of the cross to the kingdom of God. "Not every kingdom leads to the cross, and not every cross stems from the kingdom" (*Witnesses to the Kingdom*, 110). The unmasking of the antikingdom at the cross reveals something of the kingdom by way of contrast. One may quibble with Sobrino about the extent to which a preconceptual encounter with reality is possible or the sharpness with which he draws the contrast between the role of context in Northern versus Southern theologies. Nevertheless, his application of Ellacuría's methodology to hagiology is suggestive; Sobrino paves the way for enriching the concept of holiness and giving concreteness to what heroic degrees of the theological virtues of faith, hope, and love entail in a Latin American reality.

93. A sacrament is an oasis, a wellspring of life that God carves out in the desert of human existence. "Baptism, confirmation, penitence, Communion are signs that God has come to the world and to the human, who is by nature a desert, so as to produce flowers of eternity. The sacraments give the human vegetation, fertility, fecundity" (*Homilías*, 2:60).

94. Cf. Fisichella, "Martirio," 859. In the Old Testament, the prophets suffer persecution and sometimes death for proclaiming the word of God. The examples of Jeremiah, Zachariah, Elijah, and the suffering servant are noteworthy. Of particular significance for the development of a theology of martyrdom were the persecutions that the Jews underwent in the Maccabean era. The story of the torture and execution of a mother and her seven sons told in 2 Maccabees offered a narrative template for future martyrologies.

95. Sobrino, *Witnesses to the Kingdom*, 123. Reflecting on the question of martyrdom in El Salvador, Sobrino expands on Romero's theology of martyrdom. Sobrino speaks of three categories of martyrdom. First, there are the

active martyrs, "those who have struggled directly against oppression, and who have freely and consciously lost their lives because of it" (*Witnesses to the Kingdom*, 109). One thinks of people like Grande, Romero, the Maryknoll sisters, and Ellacuría. Second, there are the fallen martyrs, those "who were not defenseless but lost their lives for defending the people in accordance with their conscience" (109). Sobrino terms this a *quaestio disputata*. How is one to honor people like Camilo Torres? Finally, there are the anonymous martyrs, "the immense majority of the poor, who died innocent, defenseless, unjustly, in their day-to-day poverty or in great massacres" (109). They die from diseases that opt for the poor, like cholera, and from massacres in El Mozote. How should they be remembered? Like the Holy Innocents? Sobrino states that "these poor do not even qualify to be declared martyrs, mainly because they never have a chance to accept martyrdom freely, but neither can they cultivate the so-called conventional heroic virtues required for sainthood, because of the socioeconomic conditions in which they live." Yet these martyrs are heroic in their own way. "For most of them it consists of work, the struggle to survive, and the hope that life is possible" (109). Sobrino speaks of this kind of quotidian holiness in the midst of poverty as "primary sainthood" (110).

96. Aquinas writes: "The good of one's country is paramount among human goods: yet the Divine good, which is the proper cause of martyrdom, is of more account than human good. Nevertheless, since human good may become Divine, for instance when it is referred to God, it follows that any human good in so far as it is referred to God, may be the cause of martyrdom" (*ST* 2-2.124.5.ad3).

97. On Christian courage being more characterized by active resistance than aggression, see *ST* 2-2.124.2.ad3. Not all courage is virtuous, since "the praise awarded to fortitude depends somewhat on justice. Hence Ambrose says (De Offic. i) that 'fortitude without justice is an occasion of injustice; since the stronger a man is the more ready is he to oppress the weaker'" (*ST* 2-2.123.12.ad3).

98. Hans Urs von Balthasar, "Martirio y misión," in *Puntos centrales de la fe* (Madrid: BAC, 1985), 366.

99. José Luis Escobar Alas, *Ustedes también darán testimonio porque han estado conmigo desde el principio: II carta pastoral* (San Salvador: Arzobispado de San Salvador, 2017), para. 77.

100. "They are men and women who have preached, precisely, this adaptation to poverty. They are truly men and women who have gone to the dangerous borders where . . . they can point to someone and that someone

turns up dead, like Christ. These are the ones that I call truly just. And if they have stains, who does not have them?" (*Homilías*, 5:354).

101. The manner in which Romero speaks of flawed martyrs prompts Roberto Casas Andrés to call for a revision of traditional understandings of sanctity. This revision is necessary in order to be faithful to signs of the times today, which call for a more direct engagement of the church in the political sphere. The "persons who incorporate the political processes of liberation with generosity and radical obedience" are political saints. They feed the hope of the church and the poor. Casas speaks of another revision to the understanding of sanctity to which the martyrs of El Salvador call. Sanctity needs to be reinterpreted in a way that is less individualistic and less focused on heroic exemplars. Casas Andrés explains that "the crucified people possess a genre of holiness in which what is seen is more the passivity of redemptive suffering than the attitude of active struggle against unjust structures" (*Dios pasó*, 337). Following Jon Sobrino, this kind of sanctity can be called "primordial sanctity" or better yet, "primary sanctity" (Casas Andrés, *Dios pasó*, 338). This is the sanctity of those who lack the means to cultivate heroic virtues because of socially unjust structures that render practices like contemplation an impossible luxury. For these "sinful saints" survival itself is a heroic struggle. By daily refusing to give up, they affirm the goodness of life even under the condition of structural sin. These two kinds of sanctity need each other. "Without witnesses, primordial sanctity would not demonstrate the fullness of salvation to which it points. And without crucified peoples, the holiness of the witnesses would be nothing more than mere show which does not lead us to go deeper into the reality but to draw apart from it" (339).

102. Behr, *Irenaeus of Lyons*, 198–203.

103. Servais Pinckaers, *The Spirituality of Martyrdom . . . to the Limits of Love* (Washington, DC: Catholic University of America Press, 2016), 74–77.

104. Cultic language is woven into the narratives of the martyrologies of Ignatius of Antioch and Polycarp of Smyrna. It is even present in Paul's writings (cf. Phil. 2:15, 2 Tim. 4:6). This connection of martyrdom to the cultic language of sacrifice, a sacrifice that finds its maximal expression in the Eucharist, underscores the uniqueness of the Christian martyr. In the words of von Balthasar, what is distinctive and peculiar of the Christian martyr is "'being crucified with Christ.' . . . The Christian does not die for an idea, however sublime, like human dignity, liberty, solidarity with the oppressed (even though this is all in play and included). The Christian dies for someone and for someone who previously died for him." Von Balthasar, "Martirio y misión," 366.

105. Cf. Behr, *Irenaeus of Lyons*, 14. The author of the letter, of which only fragments are preserved in Eusebius's *Church History* 4.1, is not certain, but Behr considers it likely to be Irenaeus.

106. Eusebius, *Church History* 5.1.41, trans. Arthur Cushman McGiffert, in *Nicene and Post-Nicene Fathers*, 2nd ser., vol. 1, ed. Philip Schaff and Henry Wace (Buffalo, NY: Christian Literature Publishing, 1890), rev. and ed. for New Advent by Kevin Knight, www.newadvent.org/fathers/250105.htm.

107. Behr, *Irenaeus of Lyons*, 201.

108. Eusebius, *Church History* 5.1.41.

109. Pope Paul VI, *Populorum Progressio: Encyclical on the Development of Peoples* 21, March 26, 1967, http://w2.vatican.va/content/paul-vi/en/encyclicals /documents/hf_p-vi_enc_26031967_populorum.html: "What are less than human conditions? The material poverty of those who lack the bare necessities of life, and the moral poverty of those who are crushed under the weight of their own self-love; oppressive political structures resulting from the abuse of ownership or the improper exercise of power, from the exploitation of the worker or unjust transactions. What are truly human conditions? The rise from poverty to the acquisition of life's necessities; the elimination of social ills; broadening the horizons of knowledge; acquiring refinement and culture. From there one can go on to acquire a growing awareness of other people's dignity, a taste for the spirit of poverty, an active interest in the common good, and a desire for peace. Then man can acknowledge the highest values and God Himself, their author and end. Finally and above all, there is faith— God's gift to men of good will—and our loving unity in Christ, who calls all men to share God's life as sons of the living God, the Father of all men." Romero references this passage in his homilies of July 17, 1977 (*Homilías*, 1:206) and of January 15, 1978 (*Homilías*, 2:212–13). The passage is repeated in the address that Romero gave on February 14, 1978, when he was awarded a doctorate *honoris causae* from Georgetown University (in Óscar Romero, *Homilías y discursos, 1977–1980* (Milan: KKIEN, 2015), e-book, loc. 10544, Kindle, and in the homily of August 5, 1979, *Homilías*, 5:180).

110. Pope Paul VI, *Discurso a los miembros del cuerpo diplomático acreditado ante la Santa Sede*, January 7, 1965, http://w2.vatican.va/content/paul-vi/es /speeches/1965/documents/hf_p-vi_spe_19650107_diplomatic-corps. html. Paul VI states: "Allí es, en efecto, donde hay que buscar la solución de uno de los mayores problemas de nuestra época: no basta que el hombre se crezca en lo que posee, ha de crecer en lo que él es. Y para volver a tomar la expresión harto conocida de un filósofo contemporáneo, es un

'suplemento de alma' lo que el gran cuerpo de la humanidad más necesita en este momento."

111. Henri Bergson, *Les deux sources de la morale et de la religion* (1948; electronic ed., Chicoutimi: Jean-Marie Tremblay, 2003), www.uqac.uquebec.ca /zone30/Classiques_des_sciences_sociales/index.html, 166.

112. Ibid., 170.

113. I am translating from the Spanish version of the encyclical because it is the version that would have been used by Romero and because the Spanish follows more closely Romero's terminology than the Latin version. The Spanish reads, "hacer, conocer y tener más para ser más." The Latin reads, "ut magis operentur, discant, possideant, ut ideo pluris valeant."

114. The Spanish reads, "Cada hombre puede crecer en humanidad, valer más, ser más." The Latin reads, "Quivis homo potest humanitate crescere, plus plusque valere, seipsum perficere."

115. The Spanish reads, "sacrificando la voluntad de ser más al deseo de poseer en mayor abundancia." The Latin reads, "si voluntatem magis rectiusque excellendi postponunt voluntati plus possidendi."

116. Matthew Restall, *Seven Myths of the Conquest* (New York: Oxford University Press, 2003), 99.

117. See Ivan Petrella, *Beyond Liberation Theology: A Polemic* (London: SCM Press, 2008). Vita is an actual community started by born-again drug dealer Ze das Drogas as a shelter in southern Brazil where people like him could turn their lives around. It ended up becoming a dumping ground for social undesirables, ex-humans. Petrella finds in Vita a metaphor for the world spawned by globalization. It illustrates that "zones of social abandonment are spurred by an idolatrous logic in which the value of life is determined by the ability to contribute to the market as a producer or consumer" (20). Incidentally, for Petrella, the Irenaean saying represents a holistic anthropology that rejects the socially consequential Greek dualism of body and soul (cf. 15). In other words, the Irenaean vision that Romero retrieves and revises is one of the antidotes to Vita.

118. John Paul II affirms this emphasis on human value and perfectibility in his inaugural discourse in Puebla, where he alludes to *Gaudium et Spes* 35 and states, "In order to reach a life worthy of the human, it is not possible to limit oneself to have more, one must aspire to be more." Juan Pablo II, *Discurso inaugural* 3.4, in *Puebla*, p. 233.

119. *Homilías*, 5:400: In the family, parents are entrusted to form children "que no pongan su afán en el tener más, sino en ser más." *Homilías*, 5:495:

Denouncing the idolatry of wealth, Romero states: "No vale el hombre por lo que tiene, sino por lo que es."

120. Fisichella, "Martirio," 858.

121. The first letter, *Veo en la ciudad violencia y discordia*, was released on March 24, 2016. The second one, *Ustedes también darán testimonio porque han estado conmigo desde el principio*, was released on March 12, 2017. The year 2017 marks the centenary of the birth of Romero, the fortieth anniversary of the death of Grande, and the twenty-fifth anniversary of the signing of the peace accords (also the quincentennial of the Reformation).

122. Quoted in Escobar Alas, *Veo en la ciudad*, para. 165.

123. Escobar Alas presents Jesus as the perfect martyr, the fullness of martyrdom. First, Jesus is the image of the committed baptized believer. "An image that should serve us in undertaking a serious examination of conscience in order to verify if we are being faithful to our baptismal commitment or not" (*Ustedes también darán testimonio*, para. 313). The martyrs call on all Christians to live their baptism in a radically committed manner so as to denounce and resist the idols. They are to imitate Padre Navarro, who, like the character in Romero's story of the Bedouin, dies while declaring, "This way, not that way"—"Not by violence, not by vengeance, not by selfishness, not by individualism, not by avarice, not by unjust distribution of wealth, not by monopolization, but by love, by solidarity, by forgiveness, by justice, by truth, by peace, by the way of God" (para. 320)—in other words, not by the way of the idols of death but by the way of the witnesses of the kingdom even unto death, by the way of the committed baptized believer, the way of the martyrs, the way of Jesus Christ. Second, Jesus is the image of the bread of heaven offered at the Eucharist. His self-offering calls on Christians to concelebrate by offering themselves together with him not only in the Divine Liturgy but in daily living. Again, there is an invitation here for self-examination. "Let us ask ourselves if, after participating in the Eucharist, we give ourselves in service to others, especially to the poor, the sick, the marginalized, the excluded, the widows, the orphans. Or do we leave church turned into—in the words of Father Rutilio—fireworks that burst in smoke and sound high in the sky but make no sound or smoke on earth where we should accomplish our mission" (para. 321). If Jesus is the martyr par excellence, Mary is the proto-confessor. She too experienced persecution because of Jesus, as the flight to Egypt makes clear. She endured suffering in seeing her son being put to death. Through it all, she kept the faith.

124. Fisichella, "Martirio," 864.

125. As Sobrino states: "Jesus walks from Galilee to Jerusalem—a journey that is not only geographic, but anthropological and theologal; and he moves from proclaiming the kingdom of God (liberation) to accepting the cross (martyrdom)" (*Witnesses to the Kingdom*, 117).

126. Ibid., 330.

127. I am indebted to Roberto Morozzo della Rocca's treatment of this question in *Primero Dios*: 307–10.

128. There is no record of an existing relationship between Romero and Calderón, and it seems unlikely that Romero would have spoken by phone late at night in the grandiloquent language reported by Calderón. Cf. Morozzo della Rocca, *Primero Dios*, 308–9.

129. Ibid., 310.

130. Ibid., 309.

131. Vigil and Torredas, *Misas centroamericanas*, 13.

132. Romero, "Cuadernos espirituales," February 25, 1980.

133. Ibid.

134. Ibid.

135. Ibid.

136. Ibid.

137. Ibid.

138. Ibid., June 8, 1970.

139. Zynda, *Archbishop Oscar Romero*, 146.

140. *Diario*, February 6, 1980.

141. Ibid.

142. Pinto, *Grito del más pequeño*, 20–26.

143. Ibid., 115.

144. Ibid., 77.

145. Ibid., 240.

146. Ibid., 309. Another interesting note: Sara Meardi attended frequently the parish at Apopa, where she had a residence. This is the parish dedicated to Catherine of Alexandria, where Romero preached a festal sermon in 1977.

147. Pinto, *Grito del más pequeño*, 264.

148. The title itself stands out as an amalgam of previously uncorrelated terms. It is a constitution, suggesting an unchanging doctrinal deposit, and it is pastoral, gesturing in the direction of change and adaptation. Distinctive to this document is its intended audience. Its interlocutors are not simply Catholics or even Christians but all human beings. Cf. Schickendantz, "Autoridad teológica," 157–83.

149. The approach proved controversial. It was seen by some as eschewing proclamation to the world for the sake of conversation with it. The contrast is sometimes framed as adopting a more Thomistic approach where grace perfects nature instead of a more Augustinian one where the City of God and the Earthly City are in constant conflict. The former highlights the Incarnation; the latter, the cross. According to Edward Hahnenberg, "Proponents of 'correlational theology' emphasize the need to dialogue. They see theology as a mutually enlightening and mutually critical conversation between one's religious tradition and the contemporary situation." By contrast, "Proponents of 'kerygmatic theology' (from the Greek kerygma, meaning 'proclamation') seek instead to proclaim the faith in its totality and beauty. They are not as concerned with dialogue. Truth, they believe, speaks for itself." In brief, "The first approach presumes a positive evaluation of the world, created good by a loving God; the second is more conscious of the corruption brought by sin." Edward P. Hahnenberg, *A Concise Guide to the Documents of Vatican II* (Cincinnati, OH: St. Anthony Messenger Press, 2007), loc. 1519–23, Kindle.

150. Acts 1:7; 1 Cor. 7:31; 2 Cor. 5:1–2; 2 Pet. 3:13; 1 Cor. 2:9; Rev. 21:4–5; 1 Cor. 15:42; 1 Cor. 15:53; 1 Cor. 13:8; 1 Cor. 3:14; Rom. 8:19–21; Luke 9:25.

151. The passage from Irenaeus comes from *Against the Heresies* 5.36, ed. Roberts and Donaldson, 566): "For since there are real men, so must there also be a real establishment [*plantationem*], that they vanish not away among non-existent things, but progress among those which have an actual existence. For neither is the substance nor the essence of the creation annihilated (for faithful and true is He who has established it), but the fashion of the world passes away; 1 Corinthians 7:31 that is, those things among which transgression has occurred, since man has grown old in them. . . . But when this [present] fashion [of things] passes away, and man has been renewed, and flourishes in an incorruptible state, so as to preclude the possibility of becoming old, [then] there shall be the new heaven and the new earth, in which the new man shall remain [continually], always holding fresh converse with God."

152. Cf. homilies of August 7, 1977; August 28, 1977; September 18, 1977; December 24, 1977; December 31, 1977; April 16, 1978; May 7, 1978; August 27, 1978; November 26, 1978; December 17, 1978; August 26, 1979; December 9, 1979.

153. Cf. his homily from November 26, 1978: "Do you not think that it will be a very beautiful glory that I, a creature of this kingdom of creation,

may be just an atom in that kingdom that Christ will surrender to the Father and that will never perish? Who is alone in history? Who is an atom lost in the distance? All has been foreseen. Even the littlest child, even the campesino coffee harvester who finds no appreciation from his brothers, even the smallest will find his place in that kingdom that Christ will offer to the Father and that will be all in all without exceptions. Who will be great in the kingdom of heaven? The one who has filled himself most of Christ."

154. Romero tells an anecdote from Aloysius Gonzaga, S.J. (d. 1591), to highlight the importance of readiness. "What would you do if you knew that today was the Day of Judgment? Go to church to praise. Go to church to confess. Stay in the playground playing because I know that I am doing the will of God and that is how the Lord receives me. Be where you have to be. . . . Be at your post."

155. Gabino Uríbarri, S.J., "'Cosmovisión de la esperanza': La actualidad del servicio de la iglesia a la esperanza de la humanidad según *Gaudium et Spes*," *Estudios Eclesiásticos* 81 (2006): 435–56.

156. The question of hope facing the church today is asked not against the backdrop of atheistic Marxism but against postmodern indifference. In this context, it is incumbent for Christians to offer reasons for hope, a hope that looks to the eschatological fulfillment of all things in glory without abandoning hope for partial instantiations on earth. William Brownsberger, "Hope and the Hopeless: The Contemporary Addressee of *Gaudium et Spes*," *New Blackfriars* 89, no. 1019 (2008): 60–76. "The wedge driven between nature and grace, by Christian theology itself, created the prongs of a decision for the Christian: since he could not manage to reconcile supernature, on the one hand, and his own thoughts, awarenesses and activities in the world, on the other, he would opt for the one or the other. He would retreat from the world, closed in on himself, or else actively pursue a very secular and worldly cultivation" (64). "The rapid decline in the Gospel's ability to awaken interest coincides in some measure with the recrudescence of domesticated Christianity. Christianity withers wherever it would leech life from an alien body" (67). Among the most conspicuous examples of this withering are indifference and distraction, the result of which is boredom. "Distraction is aimed at shielding persons from anxiety, which is concentrated in the thought of death, but the unintended outcome of distraction is less than positive: it produces a deadening and banalization of human hope" (61). Increasingly there are more and more opportunities for fleeing the troubles of the world. "Consumer culture distracts man from considering ultimate questions and, what is perhaps more, it is born of and in turn nurtures a lateralizing of desire

and élan. Today horizontal transcendence replaces vertical transcendence" (71). In our time, distraction is the chief allay of boredom and the nemesis of serious engagement with the world.

157. *ST* 1–2.40.2.

158. Dominic Doyle, "*Spe Salvi* on Eschatological and Secular Hope: A Thomistic Critique of an Augustinian Encyclical," *Theological Studies* 71 (2010): 369.

159. Cf. *ST* 2-2.17.4; *ST* 2-2.83.1.

160. Dennis, Golden, and Wright, *Oscar Romero*, 99.

161. Romero, "Cuadernos espirituales," November 27, 1970.

162. Delgado Acevedo, Óscar A. Romero, 205.

163. *Diario*, February 16, 1979.

164. Romero voices a similar sentiment when returning from a trip to Rome in May 1979 (*Homilías*, 3:433).

165. In a private conversation with Jon Sobrino at the UCA on April 22, 2016, he summed up the powerful attraction (and repulsion) of Romero's ministry in similar terms: "He spoke the truth."

166. Cf. Walatka, *Von Balthasar*, 166. In his book, Walatka applies Balthasar's missiological anthropology to the Salvadoran martyrs. Accordinging to Walatka, "For Balthasar, saints are like icons of Christ, whose lives re-present and draw others into the truth and beauty of God. The Christological depth of the concrete life of the saint indicates something of God's mercy, judgment, and, ultimately, love of the world " (162). Romero is one such icon. "Romero's life not only shed light on certain aspects of God's Word, it also reveals the full dimensions of the drama of salvation. Romero's life and death unveils, as perhaps nothing else does, the conflictual nature of drama, historical opposition to the Kingdom of life, and the important place of oppression within theodramatics" (168).

Two useful Web resources on Romero are www.romeroes.com (Spanish language; most comprehensive site for writings by Romero) and www.romero trust.org.uk (most comprehensive site for primary and secondary literature by and on Romero in English).

Agnelli, Antonio. *Il Cristo di Romero: La teologia que ha nutrito il Martire d'America.* Bologna: Editrice Missionaria Italiana, 2010.

Alberigo, Giuseppe. *A Brief History of Vatican II.* Maryknoll, NY: Orbis Books, 2006.

———. *The Reception of Vatican II.* Washington, DC: Catholic University of America Press, 1987.

Alberigo, Giuseppe, and Joseph A. Komonchak, eds. *History of the Second Vatican Council.* 5 vols. New York: Orbis Books, 1997.

Albornoz Olivares, Luis Mauricio. "La salvación como visión de Dios: Aproximación en clave profética al concepto de salvación en san Ireneo de Lyon." *Veritas* 24 (2011): 165–85.

Alferrez, Jose T., ed. *Anuario de la Provincial Eclesiástica de El Salvador.* San Salvador: Curia Metropolitana, 1941.

Alves, Rubem. "From Liberation Theologian to Poet: A Plea That the Church Move from Ethics to Aesthetics, from Doing to Beauty." *Church and Society* 83 (1993): 20–24.

Aquinas, Thomas. *The Summa Theologica of St. Thomas Aquinas.* Translated by the Fathers of the English Dominican Province. Allen, TX: Christian Classics, 1948.

Arzubialde, Santiago. "El significado de la fórmula 'A mayor gloria de Dios' en el texto de las Constituciones de la Compañía de Jesús." *Estudios Eclesiásticos* 76 (2001): 593–630.

Ashley, J. Matthew. "A Contemplative under the Standard of Christ: Ignacio Ellacuría's Interpretation of Ignatius of Loyola's Spiritual Exercises." *Spiritus* 10, no. 2 (2010): 192–204.

————. "Ignacio Ellacuría and the Spiritual Exercises of Ignatius Loyola." *Theological Studies* 61, no. 1 (2000): 16–39.

Ashley, J. Matthew, Kevin Burke, S.J., and Rodolfo Cardenal, S.J. *A Grammar of Justice: The Legacy of Ignacio Ellacuría Today*. Maryknoll, NY: Orbis Books, 2014.

Augustine. *The Works of St. Augustine: A Translation for the 21st Century*. Vol. 3/8. *Sermons 273–305A*. Edited by John E. Rotelle. Translated by Edmund Hill. Hyde Park, NY: New City Press, 1994.

Baggley, John. *Festival Icons for the Christian Year*. Crestwood, NY: St. Vladimir's Press, 2000.

Behr, John. *Irenaeus of Lyons: Identifying Christianity*. Oxford: Oxford University Press, 2013.

Bergson, Henri. *Les deux sources de la morale et de la religion*. 1948. Electronic ed., Chicoutimi: Jean-Marie Tremblay, 2003. www.uqac.uquebec.ca/zone 30/Classiques_des_sciences_sociales/index.html.

Berra Zarinelli, José Pacífico. "Monseñor Romero: Su significado para la eclesiología." Master's thesis, Universidad Centroamericana "José Simeón Cañas," 1990.

Beyer, Gerald. "The Meaning of Solidarity in Catholic Social Teaching." *Political Theology* 15, no. 1 (2014): 7–25.

Bidegain, Ana María, and Maria Clara Bingemer. "Latin American Matristics: Beginnings of Recognition?" In Scatena, Sobrino, and Susin, *Fathers of the Church*, 89–100.

Binford, Leigh. *El Mozote: Vidas y memorias*. San Salvador: UCA Editores, 2011.

Bingemer, Maria Clara. *Latin American Theologies: Roots and Branch*. Maryknoll, NY: Orbis Books, 2016.

Boff, Clodovis. "Teologia da libertação e volta ao fundamento." *Revista Eclesiástica Brasileira* 268 (2007): 1001–22.

Boff, Leonardo. *Church: Charism and Power*. Eugene, OR: Wipf and Stock, 2011.

Boyle, Marjorie O'Rourke. "Angels Black and White: Loyola's Spiritual Discernment in Historical Perspective." *Theological Studies* 44, no. 2 (1983): 241–57.

Braaten, Carl E., and Robert J. Jenson. *Union with Christ: The New Finnish Interpretation of Luther*. Grand Rapids, MI: William B. Eerdmans, 1998.

Brenneman, Robert. *Homies and Hermanos: God and Gangs in Central America*. New York: Oxford University Press, 2012.

Brockman, James R. *Oscar Romero: Bishop and Martyr.* Maryknoll, NY: Orbis Books, 1982.

Brownsberger, William. "Hope and the Hopeless: The Contemporary Addressee of *Gaudium et Spes.*" *New Blackfriars* 89, no. 1019 (2008): 60–76.

Bulgakov, Sergei. "The Exceeding Glory." In *Sergius Bulgakov: A Bulgakov Anthology*, edited by Nicolas Zernov and James Paine, 188–91. Eugene, OR: Wipf and Stock, 1976.

Burke, Kevin F., S.J. *The Ground beneath the Cross: The Theology of Ignacio Ellacuría.* Washington, DC: Georgetown University Press, 2000.

Cahill, Lisa Sowle. "Christ and Kingdom: The Identity of Jesus and Christian Politics." In *Hope and Solidarity: Jon Sobrino's Challenge to Christian Theology*, edited by Stephen J. Pope, 242–53. Maryknoll, NY: Orbis Books, 2008.

Cano, Melchor. *De locis theologicis.* Edited by Juan Belda Plans. Madrid: Biblioteca de Autores Cristianos, 2006.

Canty, Aaron. *Light and Glory: The Transfiguration of Christ in Early Franciscan and Dominican Theology.* Washington, DC: Catholic University of America Press, 2011.

Cardenal, Rodolfo. *Historia de una esperanza: Vida de Rutilio Grande.* San Salvador: UCA Editores, 2015.

———. *Manual de historia de Centroamérica.* San Salvador: UCA Editores, 2016.

———. "Mons. Romero: 'Padre de los pobres.' Un beato muy incómodo." *Revista Latinoamericana de Teología* 95 (2015): 139–62.

Carter, J. Kameron. *Race: A Theological Account.* Oxford: Oxford University Press, 2008.

Casalis, George. "Jesus: Neither Abject Lord nor Heavenly Monarch." In Míguez Bonino, *Faces of Jesus*, 72–76.

Casas Andrés, Roberto. *Dios pasó por El Salvador: La relevancia teológica de las tradiciones narrativas de los mártires salvadoreños.* Bilbao: Desclée De Brouwer, 2009.

Cavada Diez, Miguel. "Introducción general." In Romero, *Homilías*, vol. 4.

———. "Introducción general." In Romero, *Homilías*, vol. 6.

Cavanaugh, William. "Dying for the Eucharist or Being Killed by It?" *Theology Today* 58, no. 2 (2001): 177–89.

———. "The World in a Wafer: A Geography of the Eucharist as Resistance to Globalization." *Modern Theology* 15, no. 2 (1999): 181–96.

Chanta Martínez, René Antonio. "Antimasonería y antiliberalismo en el pensamiento de Oscar Arnulfo Romero, 1962–1965." *REHMLAC* 3, no. 1 (2011): 121–41.

Chasteen, John Charles. *Born in Blood and Fire: A Concise History of Latin America.* New York: W. W. Norton, 2011.

Ching, Erik. *Authoritarian El Salvador: Politics and the Origins of the Military Regimes, 1880–1940.* Notre Dame, IN: University of Notre Dame Press, 2014.

Clarke, Kevin. *Love Must Win Out.* Collegeville, MN: Liturgical Press, 2014.

Cohen, Will. "Why Ecclesial Structures at the Regional Level Matter: Communion as Mutual Inclusion." *Theological Studies* 75 (2014): 308–30.

Colón-Emeric, Edgardo. "Para un verdadero sentir en la iglesia: Lecciones sobre la educación teológica hoy en América Latina." *Cuadernos de Teología* 32 (2013): 156–74.

Comblin, José. "The Holy Fathers of Latin America." In Scatena, Sobrino, and Susin, *Fathers of the Church,* 13–23.

Compagnoni, F., G. Piana, and S. Privitera, eds. *Nuevo diccionario de teología moral.* Madrid: San Pablo, 1992.

Congar, Yves. *True and False Reform in the Church.* Collegeville, MN: Liturgical Press, 2011.

Connors, Michael E., C.S.C. "Romero: A Homiletic Saint for Our Times." In *Archbishop Romero and Spiritual Leadership in the Modern World,* 93–97. Lanham, MD: Lexington Books, 2015.

Consejo Episcopal Latinoamericano, ed. *Las cinco Conferencias Generales del Episcopado Latinoamericano.* Bogotá: Ediciones Paulinas, 2014.

Crawford, Nathan. "Forming a Community of Resistance: Oscar Romero and Joerg Rieger in Conversation." *American Theological Inquiry* 8, no. 1 (2015): 21–31.

Cué, Ramón. *Mi Cristo roto.* Buenos Aires: Editorial Guadalupe, 1999.

Cunningham, Lawrence. "Saints and Martyrs: Some Contemporary Considerations." *Theological Studies* 60, no. 3 (1999): 529–37.

Curnow, Rohan M. "Which Preferential Option for the Poor? A History of the Doctrine's Bifurcation." *Modern Theology* 31, no. 1 (2015): 27–59.

Danner, Mark. *The Massacre at El Mozote.* New York: Vintage Books, 1994.

De La Torre, Miguel, ed. *Hispanic American Religious Cultures.* 2 vols. Santa Barbara, CA: ABC-CLIO, 2009.

Delgado Acevedo, Jesús. "La cultura de monseñor Romero." In Morozzo della Rocca, *Óscar Romero: Un obispo.*

———. "Las fiestas en honor al Divino Salvador y el origen del nombre

'*La bajada*' con que se conoce la procesión del 5 de agosto." *Orientación*, August 4, 2002, 5–11.

———. *Historia de la Iglesia en El Salvador*. San Salvador: Dirección de Publicaciones e Impresos, 2011.

———. Óscar A. Romero: Biografía. San Salvador: UCA Editores, 1990.

Denecker, Tim, and Gert Partoens. "*De Uoce et Uerbo*: Augustine's Exegesis of John 1:1–3 and 23 in Sermons 288 and 293a auct (Dolbeau 3)." *Annali di Storia dell'Esegesi* 31 (2014): 95–118.

Dennis, Marie, Renny Golden, and Scott Wright. *Oscar Romero: Reflections on His Life and Writings*. Maryknoll, NY: Orbis Books, 2000.

Díaz, Miguel. "God." In De La Torre, *Hispanic American Religious Cultures*, 2:637–46.

Díaz Araya, Alberto, Luis Galdames Rosas, and Wilson Muñoz Henríquez. "Santos patronos en los andes: Imagen, símbolo y ritual en las fiestas religiosas del mundo andino colonial (siglos XVI–XVII)." *Alpha: Revista de Artes, Letras y Filosofía* 35 (2012): 23–39.

Divry, Édouard. *La Transfiguration selon l'Orient et l'Occident: Grégoire Palamas-Thomas d'Aquin vers un dénouement oecuménique*. Paris: Pierre Téqui, 2009.

Dodds, Michael J. "Thomas Aquinas, Human Suffering, and the Unchanging God of Love." *Theological Studies* 52 (1991): 330–44.

Donovan, Mary Ann. "Alive to the Glory of God: A Key Insight in St. Irenaeus." *Theological Studies* 49 (1988): 283–97.

Dorr, Donald. *Option for the Poor: A Hundred Years of Catholic Social Teaching*. Maryknoll, NY: Orbis Books, 1992.

Dostoyevsky, Fyodor. *The Idiot*. New York: Penguin Books, 1955.

Doyle, Dominic. "*Spe Salvi* on Eschatological and Secular Hope: A Thomistic Critique of an Augustinian Encyclical." *Theological Studies* 71 (2010): 350–79.

Drury, John. *Painting the Word: Christian Pictures and Their Meaning*. New Haven, CT: Yale University Press, 1999.

Durán Vasquez, Carlos Omar. "Óscar Romero, hijo y padre de la Iglesia: La eclesiología de sus homilías." Master's thesis, Pontificia Universidad Antonianum, 2015.

Dussel, Enrique. *A History of the Church in Latin America: Colonialism to Liberation*. Grand Rapids, MI: Eerdmans, 1982.

Ellacuría, Ignacio. "Cruz y violencia." In *Escritos teológicos*, 3:427–82.

———, ed. *Escritos teológicos*. 4 vols. San Salvador: UCA Editores, 2001.

———. "A Latin American Reading of the Spiritual Exercises of Saint Ignatius." *Spiritus* 10, no. 2 (2010): 205–42.

————. "Liturgia y liberación." In *Escritos teológicos*, 4:29–40.

————. "Los pobres, 'lugar teológico' en América Latina." *Misión Abierta* 4/5 (1981): 225–40.

Ellacuría, Ignacio, and Jon Sobrino, eds. *Mysterium Liberationis: Fundamental Concepts of Liberation Theology*. Maryknoll, NY: Orbis Books, 1993.

Escobar Alas, José Luis, ed. *Beatificación Monseñor Óscar Romero*. San Salvador: Archdiocese of San Salvador, 2015.

————. *Ustedes también darán testimonio porque han estado conmigo desde el principio: II carta pastoral*. San Salvador: Arzobispado de San Salvador, 2017.

————. *Veo en la ciudad violencia y discordia: Carta pastoral*. San Salvador: Arzobispado de San Salvador, 2016.

Espín, Orlando O. *The Wiley Companion to Latino/a Theology*. Malden, MA: John Wiley and Sons, 2015.

Espino, Alfredo. *Jícaras tristes*. San Salvador: Consejo Natural para la Cultura y el Arte, 1996.

Eusebius. *Church History*. Translated by Arthur Cushman McGiffert. In *Nicene and Post-Nicene Fathers*, 2nd ser., vol. 1, edited by Philip Schaff and Henry Wace. Buffalo, NY: Christian Literature Publishing, 1890. Revised and edited for New Advent by Kevin Knight. www.newadvent org/fathers/250105.htm.

Faggioli, Massimo. *Vatican II: The Battle for Meaning*. New York: Paulist Press, 2012.

Fisichella, Rino. "Martirio." In *Diccionario de teología fundamental*, edited by René Latourelle, Rino Fisichella, and Salvador Pié-Ninot, 858–71. Madrid: San Pablo, 1992.

Fleisher, Barbara J. "The Ignatian Vision for Higher Education: Practical Theology." *Religious Education* 88, no. 2 (1993): 255–72.

Flynn, Gabriel. "Introduction: The Twentieth-Century Renaissance in Catholic Theology." In *Ressourcement: A Movement for Renewal in Twentieth-Century Catholic Theology*, edited by Gabriel Flynn and Paul D. Murray, 1–21. Oxford: Oxford University Press, 2012.

Friede, Juan. *Vida y luchas de don Juan del Valle, primer obispo de Popayán y protector de indios*. Popayán, Colombia: Editorial Universidad, 1961.

Galeano, Eduardo. *Open Veins of Latin America: Five Centuries of the Pillage of a Continent*. New York: Monthly Review Press, 1997.

Galilea, Segundo. *Tentación y discernimiento*. Madrid: Narcea, 1991.

Galindo, Evelyn. "Apuntes de la deshumanización: La Vía crucis del pueblo salvadoreño." *Legacies of War in El Salvador* (blog), December 24, 2012.

http://postwarelsalvador.blogspot.com/2012/12/apuntes-de-la -deshumanizacion-la-via.html.

García Mateo, R. "San Ignacio de Loyola y san Pablo." *Gregorianum* 78, no. 3 (1997): 523–44.

García-Rivera, Alex. *The Community of the Beautiful: A Theological Aesthetics.* Collegeville, MN: Liturgical Press, 1999.

———. *A Wounded Innocence: Sketches for a Theology of Art.* Collegeville, MN: Liturgical Press, 2003.

García Rubio, Alfonso. "Em direção à V Conferência Geral do Episcopado da AL e do Caribe: Fidelidade ao legado de Medellín?" *Atualidade Teológica* 11, no. 25 (2007): 9–42.

Garrard-Burnett, Virginia, Paul Freston, and Stephen C. Dove, eds. *Cambridge History of Religions in Latin America.* New York: Cambridge University Press, 2016.

Gelin, Albert. *Les pauvres de Yahvé.* Paris: Éditions du Cerf, 1953.

Germillon, Joseph, ed. *The Church and Culture since Vatican II: The Experience of North and Latin America.* Notre Dame, IN: University of Notre Dame Press, 1985.

Gilson, Etienne. *L'esprit de la philosophie médiévale.* Paris: Librairie Philosophique J. Vrin, 1969.

———. *Théologie et histoire de la spiritualité.* Paris: Librarie Philosophique J. Vrin, 1943.

Goizueta, Roberto S. *Caminemos con Jesús: Toward a Hispanic/Latino Theology of Accompaniment.* Maryknoll, NY: Orbis Books, 1995.

———. *Christ Our Companion: Toward a Theological Aesthetic of Liberation.* Maryknoll, NY: Orbis Books, 2009.

———. "Knowing the God of the Poor." In Rieger, *Opting for the Margins,* n.p.

Gómez, Medardo Ernesto. *And the Word Became History.* Minneapolis, MN: Augsburg Press, 1992.

———. *Teología de la vida.* Managua: Ediciones Nicarao, 1992.

Gonzáles, Orlinda E., and Justo González. *Christianity in Latin America: A History.* New York: Cambridge University Press, 2007.

González, Álvaro Artiga. "Los cristianos y la política en el pensamiento de Mons. Romero." *Revista Latinoamericana de Teología* 97 (2016): 25–54.

González, Justo. "From All Four of Earth's Faraway Corners." In *Mil voces para celebrar: Himnario metodista,* 378. Nashville, TN: United Methodist Publishing House, 1996.

————. *Mañana: Christian Theology from a Hispanic Perspective.* Nashville, TN: Abingdon Press, 1990.

González, Michelle. *Sor Juana: Beauty and Justice in the Americas.* Maryknoll, NY: Orbis Books, 2003.

González-Andrieu, Cecilia. *Bridge to Wonder: Art as a Gospel of Beauty.* Waco, TX: Baylor University Press, 2012.

González de Cardedal, Olegario. "Problemas de fondo y método en la cristología a partir del Vaticano II." *Salmantinencis* 32 (1985): 363–400.

González Faus, José Ignacio. "El mártir testigo del amor." *Revista Latinoamericana de Teología* 48 (2002): 33–46.

Grande, Rutilio. *Homilies and Writings.* Collegeville, MN: Liturgical Press, 2015.

————. *El pensamiento teológico-pastoral de las homilías de Monseñor Romero.* San Salvador: Publicaciones del Arzobispado de San Salvador, 1998.

Grenni, Héctor. "El Salvador en tiempos de Monseñor Romero: El camino hacia la guerra civil (1978–1980)." *Americanía* 3 (2016): 187–214.

Groody, Daniel, ed. *The Option for the Poor in Christian Theology.* Notre Dame, IN: University of Notre Dame Press, 2007.

Gruber, Judith. "Rethinking God in the Interspace: Interculturality as a *Locus Theologicus.*" *Svensk Missionstidskrift* 100, no. 3 (2012): 247–61.

Guerra, Walter, ed. *Testigos de la fe en El Salvador: Nuestros sacerdotes y seminaristas diocesanos mártires, 1977–1993.* San Salvador: n.p., 1993.

Guerrero Jiménez, Bernardo. "Religión y canción de protesta en América Latina: Un ensayo de interpretación." *Revista Ciencias Sociales* 4 (1994): 55–64.

Guider, Margaret Eletta. "Sentir con la Iglesia: Archbishop Romero, an Ecclesial Mystic." In *Archbishop Romero: Martyr and Prophet for the New Millennium,* edited by Robert Pelton. Scranton, PA: University of Scranton Press, 2006.

Gutiérrez, Gustavo. "Notes for a Theology of Liberation." *Theological Studies* 31, no. 22 (1970): 243–61.

————. *We Drink from Our Own Wells: The Spiritual Journey of a People.* Maryknoll, NY: Orbis Books, 1984.

Guyot, G. H. "Transfiguration." In *New Catholic Encyclopedia,* 2nd ed., 14:155. Washington, DC: Thomson Gale, 2003.

Hahnenberg, Edward P. *A Concise Guide to the Documents of Vatican II.* Cincinnati, OH: St. Anthony Messenger Press, 2007.

Hennelly, Alfred, ed. *Liberation Theology: A Documentary History.* Maryknoll, NY: Orbis Books, 1990.

Hill, Rowena. "Poured Out for You: Liturgy and Justice in the Life of Archbishop Oscar Romero." *Worship* 74, no. 5 (2000): 414–32.

Imperato, Mariano. "Romero Predicador." In Morozzo della Rocca, *Óscar Romero: Un obispo.*

Irenaeus. *Against Heresies.* In *Ante-Nicene Fathers,* vol. 1, *The Apostolic Fathers, Justin Martyr, and Irenaeus,* edited by Alexander Roberts, and James Donaldson. Peabody, MA: Hendrickson, 1994.

——— [Irenée de Lyon]. *Contre les hérésies* 4. Edited by Adelin Rousseau. Sources Chrétiennes 100 Paris: Editions du Cerf, 1965.

Jenkins, Willis. *Ecologies of Grace: Environmental Ethics and Christian Theology.* New York: Oxford University Press, 2008.

Jüngel, Eberhard. *God the Mystery of the World: On the Foundation of the Theology of the Crucified God in the Dispute between Theism and Atheism.* Translated by Darrell L. Guder. Grand Rapids, MI: Eerdmans, 1983.

Kelley, Geffrey B. "Bonhoeffer and Romero: Prophets of Justice for the Oppressed." *Union Seminary Quarterly Review* 46, no. 1 (1992): 85–105.

Klaiber, Jeffrey. *Church, Dictatorships, and Democracy in Latin America.* Maryknoll, NY: Orbis Books, 1998.

Klinger, Elmar. "Fathers of the Universal Church in Latin America." In Scatena, Sobrino, and Susin, *Fathers of the Church,* 101–10.

Kloppenburg, Buenaventura. "Las tentaciones de la teología de la liberación." *Mensaje Iberoamericano* 100 (1974): 4–9.

Konyndyk DeYoung, Rebecca. "Courage as a Christian Virtue." *Journal of Spiritual Formation and Care* 6, no. 2 (2013): 301–12.

Krier Mich, Marvin. *The Challenge and Spirituality of Catholic Social Teaching.* Maryknoll, NY: Orbis Books, 2011.

Laplane, Sabine. *Frère Roger, de Taizé: Avec presque rien. . . .* Paris: Éditions du Cerf, 2015.

Lara-Braud, Jorge. "Monseñor Romero: Model Pastor for the Hispanic Diaspora." *Apuntes* 1, no. 3 (1981): 15–21.

Larkin, Brian. "Tridentine Catholicism in the New World." In *Cambridge History of Religions in Latin America,* edited by Virginia Garrard-Burnett, Paul Freston, and Stephen C. Dove, 107–32. New York: Cambridge University Press, 2016.

Las Casas, Bartolomé de. *Historia de las Indias.* Edited by André Saint-Lu. 3 vols. Caracas, Venezuela: Biblioteca Ayacucho, 1986.

———. *A Short Account of the Destruction of the Indies.* New York: Penguin Group, 1992.

La Soujeoule, Benoît-Dominique de, O.P. *Introduction to the Mystery of the Church.* Washington, DC: Catholic University of America Press, 2014.

Lassalle-Klein, Robert. *Blood and Ink: Ignacio Ellacuria, Jon Sobrino, and the Jesuit Martyrs of the University of Central America.* Maryknoll, NY: Orbis Books, 2014.

Leclerq, Jean. "The Liturgical Roots of the Devotion to the Sacred Heart." *Worship* 34 (1960): 551–66.

Lee, Dorothy. "Transfiguration and the Gospel of John." In *In Many and Diverse Ways: In Honor of Jacques Dupuis,* edited by Daniel Kendall, S.J., and Gerald O'Collins, 158–69. Maryknoll, NY: Orbis Books, 2003.

Lee, Michael E. *Bearing the Weight of Salvation: The Soteriology of Ignacio Ellacuría.* New York: Herder and Herder Book, 2009.

Legorreta Zepeda, José de Jesús. *Cambio e identidad de la Iglesia en América Latina: Itinerario de comunión de Medellín a Aparecida.* Mexico City: Universidad Iberoamericana, 2014.

Lehmann, Paul. *The Transfiguration of Politics.* New York: Harper and Row, 1975.

Leturia, Pedro. *Estudios Ignacianos.* Vol. 2. *Ejercicios espirituales.* Rome: Institutum Historico, 1957.

Lima Vaz, Henrique de. "Igreja-reflexo vs. igreja-fonte." *Cadernos Brasileiros* 46 (1968): 17–22.

López, Carlos Gregorio. *Mármoles, clarines y bronces: Fiestas cívico-religiosas en El Salvador, siglos XIX y XX.* San Salvador: Editorial Universidad Don Bosco, 2011.

López García, José Tomás. *Dos defensores de los esclavos en el siglo XVII.* Marcaibo: Biblioteca Corpozulia, 1981.

López Portillo, Modesto, ed. *Fiestas Agostinas: Año de gracia jubilar 2000.* San Salvador: Imprenta Criterio, 2000.

López Trujillo, Alfonso. *De Medellín a Puebla.* Madrid: Biblioteca de Autores Cristianos, 1980.

López Vigil, María. *Piezas para un retrato.* San Salvador: UCA Editores, 1990.

Loyola, San Ignacio de. *Obras de San Ignacio de Loyola.* Madrid: Biblioteca de Autores Cristianos, 1997.

Lynch, John. *New Worlds: A Religious History of Latin America.* New Haven, CT: Yale University Press, 2012.

Mackay, John A. *El otro Cristo español: Un estudio de la historia espiritual de España e Hispanoamérica.* (Mexico City: Centro de Comunicación Cultural CUPSA, 1993.

Maier, Martin. "Los conflictos eclesiásticos del Arzobispo Óscar Romero." *Selecciones de Teología* 175 (2005): 223–34.

———. *Monseñor Romero: Maestro de espiritualidad.* San Salvador: UCA Editores, 2010.

———. *Óscar Romero: Mística y lucha por la justicia.* Barcelona: Editorial Herder, 2015.

Mang, Pum Za. "Oscar Romero: Champion of the Oppressed." *Asia Journal of Theology* 27, no. 2 (2013): 275–98.

Manwaring, Max G., and Court Prisk, eds. *El Salvador at War: An Oral History of Conflict from the 1979 Insurrection to the Present.* Washington, DC: National Defense University Press, 1988.

Marcouiller, Douglas. "Archbishop with an Attitude: Oscar Romero's *Sentir con la Iglesia.*" *Studies in the Spirituality of the Jesuits* 35 (2003): 1–52.

Marcouiller, Douglas, and Jon Sobrino. *El sentir con la iglesia de Monseñor Romero.* San Salvador: Centro Monseñor Romero, 2004.

Márquez Ochoa, Armando. *Martirologio de Monseñor Romero: Testimonio y catequesis de la Iglesia salvadoreña.* La Libertad, El Salvador: CEBES, 2005.

Martell-Otero, Loida. "*Encuentro con el Jesús sato*: An *Evangélica Soter*-ology." In *Jesus in the Hispanic Community: Images of Christ from Theology to Popular Religion*, edited by Harold J. Recinos and Hugo Magallanes, 74–91. Louisville, KY: Westminster John Knox Press, 2009.

Martin, Thomas W. "What Makes Glory Glorious? Reading Luke's Account of the Transfiguration over against Triumphalism." *Journal for the Study of the New Testament* 29, no. 1 (2006): 3–26.

Martínez-Gayol, Nurya. "'Todo como sintiere ser a mayor gloria de Dios N. Señor': Posibles conflictos en la determinación de la 'mayor gloria de Dios.'" *Estudios Eclesiásticos* 79 (2004): 413–31.

Mata, Santiago. *Monseñor Óscar Romero: Pasión por la iglesia.* Madrid: Ediciones Palabra, 2015.

Matz, Brian. *Patristics and Catholic Social Thought: Hermeneutical Models for a Dialogue.* Notre Dame, IN: University of Notre Dame Press, 2014.

McCormick, Kelly Steve. "Theosis in Chrysostom and Wesley: An Eastern Paradigm on Faith and Love." *Wesleyan Theological Journal* 26, no. 1: 38–103.

Medina, Miguel Ángel. *Los dominicos y América: Doctrina cristiana para instrucción de los indios.* Salamanca: Editorial San Esteban, 1987.

Meissner, Diethelm. *Die "Kirche der Armen" in El Salvador.* Neuendettelsau: Erlangen Verlag für Mission und Ökumene, 2004.

Melville, Herman. *Moby Dick.* New York: Barnes and Noble Books, 1994.

Methol Ferré, Alberto, and Alver Metalli. *La América Latina del siglo XXI.* Buenos Aires: Edhasa, 2006.

Míguez Bonino, José, ed. *Faces of Jesus: Latin American Christologies.* Maryknoll, NY: Orbis Books, 1977.

———. "Who Is Jesus Christ in Latin America Today?" In Míguez Bonino, *Faces of Jesus,* 2–6.

Mollá, Darío. "El 'sentido verdadero' en el servicio de la iglesia según la Congregación General 34 de la Compañía de Jesús." *Estudios Eclesiásticos* 71 (1996): 31–48.

Moodie, Ellen. *El Salvador in the Aftermath of Peace: Crime, Uncertainty, and the Transition to Democracy.* Philadelphia: University of Pennsylvania Press, 2010.

Moreno, José Luis. "'Gloria Dei, vivens homo': Uso actual de la fórmula de Ireneo." In *Esperanza del hombre y revelación bíblica: XIV Simposio Internacional de Teología de la Universidad de Navarra,* edited by José María Casciaro, 215–31. Pamplona: Servicio de publicaciones de la Universidad de Navarra, 1996.

Moreno, Laura. "Su vida, testimonio de amor y fidelidad a Dios." *Teología: Revista de la Facultad de Teología de la Pontificia Universidad Católica Argentina* 53, no. 79 (2002): 43–98.

Morozzo della Rocca, Roberto. *Óscar Romero: La biografía.* San Salvador: UCA Editores, 2015.

———. *Oscar Romero: Prophet of Hope.* Translated by Michael J. Miller. Boston: Pauline Books and Media, 2015.

———, ed. *Óscar Romero: Un obispo entre guerra fría y revolución.* Kindle ed. Madrid: Editorial San Pablo, 2012.

———. *Primero Dios: Vida de Monseñor Romero.* Buenos Aires: Edhasa, 2010.

Mulheron, Thomas Greenan. "La opción por los pobres en las homilías de Monseñor Romero y de San Juan Crisóstomo: Análisis de las convergencias y de las peculiaridades en los presupuestos teológicos y en las orientaciones morales." PhD diss., Universidad Pontificia Comillas de Madrid, 2003.

Nickoloff, James B. "Gustavo Gutierrez Meets Giuseppe Verdi: The Beauty of Liberation and the Liberation of Beauty." *Religion and the Arts* 17 (2013): 203–21.

Nuñez Hurtado, Enrique. *Ejercicios espirituales en, desde y para América Latina: Retos, intuiciones, contenidos.* Torreón, Mexico: Casa Iñigo, 1980.

O'Brien, John. *Theology and the Option for the Poor.* Collegeville, MD: Liturgical Press, 1992.

Ollerton, A. J. *"Quasi Deificari*: Deification in the Theology of John Calvin." *Westminster Theological Journal* 73 (2011): 237–54.

O'Neill, Charles E., and Joaquín Ma Domínguez, eds. *Diccionario histórico de la Compañía de Jesús: Biográfico-temático.* Vol. 3. Madrid: Universidad Pontificia Comillas, 2001.

Orbe, Antonio. "Gloria Dei vivens homo: Análisis de Ireneo, *adv. haer.* IV, 20, 1–7." *Gregorianum* 73, no. 2 (1992): 205–68.

Ortega y Gasset, José. *La deshumanización del arte y otros ensayos de estética.* Madrid: Alianza Editorial, 1996.

Osborn, Eric. *Irenaeus of Lyons.* Cambridge: Cambridge University Press, 2001.

Pedraja, Luis. "Christology." In De La Torre, *Hispanic American Religious Cultures*, 2:589–98.

———. *Jesus Is My Uncle.* Nashville, TN: Abingdon Press, 1999.

Pelton, Robert. *Archbishop Romero: Martyr and Prophet for the New Millennium.* Scranton, PA: University of Scranton Press, 2006.

Pérez Fernández, Isacio, O.P. *Fray Bartolomé de las Casas, O.P.: De defensor de los indios a defensor de los negros.* Salamanca: Editorial San Esteban, 1995.

Peterson, Anna L. *Martyrdom and the Politics of Religion: Progressive Catholicism in El Salvador's Civil War.* Albany: State University of New York Press, 1997.

Petrella, Ivan. *Beyond Liberation Theology: A Polemic.* London: SCM Press, 2008.

Pfeil, Margaret. *"Gloria Dei, Vivens Pauper*: Romero's Theology of Transfiguration." *Sign of Peace* 4, no. 2 (Spring 2005): 6–9.

———. "Oscar Romero's Theology of Transfiguration." *Theological Studies* 72 (2011): 87–115.

Pieper, Josef. *In Tune with the World: A Theory of Festivity.* South Bend, IN: St. Augustine's Press, 1999.

Pinches, Charles R. *A Gathering of Memories: Family, Nation, and Church in a Forgetful World.* Grand Rapids, MI: Brazos Press, 2006.

Pinckaers, Servais. *The Spirituality of Martyrdom . . . to the Limits of Love.* Washington, DC: Catholic University of America Press, 2016.

Pineda, Ana María. *Romero and Grande: Companions on the Journey.* Hobe Sound, FL: Lectio, 2016.

Pineda-Madrid, Nancy. "Notes toward a Chicana Feminist Epistemology." In *A Reader in Latina Feminist Theology: Religion and Justice*, edited by María Pilar Aquino, Daisy L. Machado, and Jeanette Rodríguez, 241–66. Austin: University of Texas Press, 2002.

———. *Suffering and Salvation in Ciudad Juarez.* Minneapolis, MN: Fortress Press, 2011.

Pinto, Jorge. *El grito del más pequeño*. México: Impresos Continentales, 1985.

Pironio, Eduardo. *Alegres en la esperanza*. Madrid: Ediciones Paulinas, 1979.

———. *Escritos pastorales*. Madrid: Biblioteca de Autores Cristianos, 1972.

———. *Joyful in Hope*. Slough: Society of Saint Paul, 1980.

———. *Queremos ver a Jesús*. Madrid: BAC, 1980.

———. "La voz del pastor." *Apóstol* 17 (1976): 3.

Pitalúa Quiñonez, Bertha Sofía. "Género y comunicación como lugares teológicos de la revelación: Cómo comunicar a Dios en una sociedad llena de discriminaciones?" *Reflexiones Teológicas* 12 (2014): 131–56.

Pobee, John S. "Europe as Locus Theologicus." *Ecumenical Review* 45, no. 2 (1993): 194–201.

Polanco, Rodrigo. "*Gloria enim Dei vivens homo, vita autem hominis visio Dei*: Reflexiones sobre el *homo vivens* en el pensamiento de San Ireneo." *Anales de la Facultad de Teología* 61 (2010): 159–91.

Poma de Ayala, Felipe Guamán. *Nueva Crónica y buen gobierno*. Alicante: Biblioteca Virtual Miguel de Cervantes, 2012.

Pope, Stephen J., ed. *Hope and Solidarity: Jon Sobrino's Challenge to Christian Theology*. Maryknoll, NY: Orbis Books, 2008.

———. "Proper and Improper Partiality and the Preferential Option for the Poor." *Theological Studies* 54 (1993): 242–71.

Pope Francis. *Evangelii Gaudium*. 2015. https://w2.vatican.va/content /francesco/en/apost_exhortations/documents/papa-francesco _esortazione-ap_20131124_evangelii-gaudium.html.

Pope John XXIII. *Solemne Apertura del Concilio Vaticano II: Discurso de Su Santidad Juan XXIII*. October 11, 1962. https://w2.vatican.va/content /john-xxiii/es/speeches/1962/documents/hf_j-xxiii_spe_19621011 _opening-council.html.

Pope John Paul II. *Address to the Third General Conference of the Latin American Episcopate*. January 28, 1979. https://w2.vatican.va/content/john-paul -ii/en/speeches/1979/january/documents/hf_jp-ii_spe_19790128 _messico-puebla-episc-latam.html.

Pope Leo I. Sermo 51. In *Sancti Leonis Magni Tractatus*. http://frcoulter.com /leo/latin/tractatus51.html.

———. Sermon 51. Translated by Charles Lett Feltoe. In *Nicene and Post-Nicene Fathers*, 2nd ser., vol. 12, edited by Philip Schaff and Henry Wace. Buffalo, NY: Christian Literature Publishing, 1895. Revised and edited for New Advent by Kevin Knight. www.newadvent.org/fathers /360351.htm.

Pope Paul VI. *Address during the Last General Meeting of the Second Vatican Council.* December 7, 1965. https://w2.vatican.va/content/paul-vi/en /speeches/1965/documents/hf_p-vi_spe_19651207_epilogo -concilio.html.

———. *Address to the Rulers.* December 8, 1965. http://w2.vatican.va /content/paul-vi/en/speeches/1965/documents/hf_p-vi_spe _19651208_epilogo-concilio-governanti.html.

———. *Angelus Domini.* August 6, 1978. http://w2.vatican.va/content /paul-vi/it/angelus/1978/documents/hf_p-vi_ang_19780806.html.

———. *Discurso a los miembros del cuerpo diplomático acreditado ante la Santa Sede.* January 7, 1965. http://w2.vatican.va/content/paul-vi/es/speeches /1965/documents/hf_p-vi_spe_19650107_diplomatic-corps.html.

———. *Ecclesiam Suam.* August 6, 1964. http://w2.vatican.va/content/paul -vi/en/encyclicals/documents/hf_p-vi_enc_06081964_ecclesiam .html.

———. *Evangelii Nuntiandi.* December 8, 1975. http://w2.vatican.va /content/paul-vi/en/apost_exhortations/documents/hf_p-vi_exh _19751208_evangelii-nuntiandi.html.

———. *If You Want Peace, Defend Life.* December 8, 1976. https://w2 .vatican.va/content/paul-vi/en/messages/peace/documents/hf_p-vi _mes_19761208_x-world-day-for-peace.html.

———. *Lumen Gentium.* November 21, 1964. www.vatican.va/archive/hist _councils/ii_vatican_council/documents/vat-ii_const_19641121 _lumen-gentium_en.html.

———. *Populorum Progressio: Encyclical on the Development of Peoples.* March 26, 1967. http://w2.vatican.va/content/paul-vi/en/encyclicals/documents /hf_p-vi_enc_26031967_populorum.html.

———. "Radiomensaje de Su Santidad Pablo VI al Congreso Eucarístico de El Salvador." April 19, 1964. https://w2.vatican.va/content/paul-vi /es/messages/pont-messages/documents/hf_p-vi_mess_19640419 _eucaristico-el-salvador.html.

Pope Pius XI. *Mens Nostra: Encyclical of Pope Pius XI on the Promotion of the Spiritual Exercises.* December 20, 1929. https://w2.vatican.va/content/pius -xi/en/encyclicals/documents/hf_p-xi_enc_19291220_mens-nostra .html.

———. "Radiomensaje de Su Santidad Pío XI al I Congreso Eucarístico Nacional de El Salvador." November 26, 1942. https://w2.vatican.va /content/pius-xii/es/speeches/1942/documents/hf_p-xii_spe _19421126_eucaristico-salvador.html.

Pope Pius XII. *Discurso del Santo Padre Pio XII al Señor Hector Escobar Serrano, primer embajador de la República de El Salvador ante la Santa Sede.* March 25, 1952. https://w2.vatican.va/content/pius-xii/es/speeches/1952/documents/hf_p-xii_spe_19520325_ambassador-el-salvador.html.

Purrer Delgado, Ulrike. *Diplomacia pastoral: La Iglesia y Arturo Rivera y Damas en el proceso de paz salvadoreño.* San Salvador: UCA Editores, 2015.

Ragon, Pierre. "Los santos patronos de las ciudades del México central (Siglos XVI y XVII)." *Historia Mexicana* 52, no. 2 (2002): 361–89.

Rahner, Karl. "Una orden antigua en una nueva época: La Compañía de Jesús y su devoción al corazón de Cristo." *Estudios Eclesiásticos* 59 (1984): 131–38.

———. ed. *Sacramentum Mundi: An Encyclopedia of Theology.* Vol. 6. Montreal: Herder and Herder, 1970.

Ramsey, Arthur Michael. *The Glory of God and the Transfiguration of Christ.* Eugene, OR: Wipf and Stock, 1949.

Recinos, Harold J., and Hugo Magallanes, eds. *Jesus in the Hispanic Community: Images of Christ from Theology to Popular Religion.* Louisville, KY: Westminster John Knox Press, 2009.

Reid, Barbara, O.P. "Romero the Preacher." In *Archbishop Romero: Martyr and Prophet for the New Millennium,* edited by Robert Pelton, C.S.C., 17–32. Scranton, PA: University of Scranton Press, 2006.

Restall, Matthew. *Seven Myths of the Conquest.* New York: Oxford University Press, 2003.

"Reunión de los Provinciales Jesuitas de América Latina con el P. General, Pedro Arrupe, Río de Janeiro, Casa da Gávea: 6 al 14 de mayo de 1968." May 1968. Conferencia de Provinciales Jesuitas en América Latina y El Caribe. http://his gtorico.cpalsj.org/wp-content/uploads/2013/06/Reunion-de-los-Provinciales-Jesuitas-de-AL-con-Arrupe.pdf.

Richard, Pablo. "Theology in the Theology of Liberation." In *Mysterium Liberationis: Fundamental Concepts of Liberation Theology,* ed. Ignacio Ellacuría and Jon Sabrino, 150–67. Maryknoll, NY: Orbis Books, 1993.

Rieger, Joerg, ed. *Opting for the Margins: Postmodernity and Liberation in Christian Theology.* Oxford Scholarship Online, 2005.

Rivera Navarrete, Claudia Marlene. "La denuncia profética de la riqueza: Resonancia de la patrística en la teología latinoamericana de la liberación." MA thesis, Universidad Centroamericana "José Simeón Cañas," 2015.

Rivera-Pagán, Luis N. "Completing the Afflictions of Christ: Archbishop Oscar Arnulfo Romero." *Apuntes* 28, no. 2 (2008): 65–78.

————. *A Violent Evangelism: The Political and Religious Conquest of the Americas.* Louisville, KY: Westminster/John Knox Press, 1992.

Rodríguez, Jeannette, and Ted Fortier. *Cultural Memory: Resistance, Faith, and Identity.* Austin: University of Texas Press, 2007.

Rodríguez, José David, and Loida I. Martell Otero, eds. *Teología en Conjunto: A Collaborative Hispanic Protestant Approach.* Louisville, KY: Westminster John Knox Press, 1997.

Roebben, Bert. "The Vulnerability of the Postmodern Educator as Locus Theologicus: A Study in Practical Theology." *Religious Education* 96, no. 2 (2001): 175–92.

Rojas, Ricardo. *El Cristo invisible.* Buenos Aires: La Facultad, 1928.

Roldán Figueroa, Rady. "The Mystical Theology of Luis de la Puente." In *A Companion to Jesuit Mysticism,* edited by Robert A. Maryks, 54–81. Leiden, Netherlands: Brill, 2017.

Romero, Óscar. *The Church Cannot Remain Silent: Unpublished Letters, 1977–1980.* Maryknoll, NY: Orbis Books, 2016.

————. "El Divino Salvador." Sermon, August 20, 1976. Published in seven parts in *Diario de Oriente,* August 20 and 27 and October 1, 8, 15, 22, and 29, 1976. www.romeroes.com/monsenor-romero-su-pensamiento /prensa-escrita/diario-de-oriente?start=60.

————. "Dos palabras peligrosas." *Orientación,* no. 1257 (February 13, 1972): 3.

————. "Ecumenismo." *Chaparrastique,* no. 2982 (January 21, 1965): 1.

————. "Ecumenismo, sinceridad y prudencia." *Chaparrastique,* no. 3032 (January 21, 1966): 1.

————. "En la Tierra Prometida." *Chaparrastique,* no. 2132, October 5, 1956, 1.

————. "The Gospel of Justice." Interview by Jorge Lara Braud. *Christianity and Crisis* 40, no. 8 (1980): 124–31.

————. *Homilías: Monseñor Óscar A. Romero.* Edited by Miguel Cavada Diez. 6 vols. San Salvador: UCA Editores, 2005–9.

————. *Homilías y discursos, 1977–1980.* Milan: KKIEN, 2015. E-book.

————. *La Iglesia, cuerpo de Cristo en la historia: Segunda carta pastoral.* San Salvador: n.p., 1977.

————. Interview by Enrique Nuñez Hurtado. In *Ejercicios espirituales en, desde y para America Latina: Retos, intuiciones, contenidos,* by Enrique Nuñez Hurtado, 101–5. Torreón, Mexico: Casa Iñigo, 1980.

————. *Mons. Óscar A. Romero: Su diario.* San Salvador: Imprenta Criterio, 2000.

———. "La palabra del Arzobispo." *Orientación*, no. 4051 (January 29, 1978): 2.

———. *A Prophetic Bishop Speaks to His People: The Complete Homilies of Archbishop Oscar Arnulfo Romero*. Vol. 1. Translated by Joseph V. Owens. Miami, FL: Convivium Press, 2015.

———. "A propósito de Managua y del sufrimiento: ¿Por qué Dios lo permite?" *Diario de Oriente*, no. 30835, January 5, 1973, 4.

———. "Una semana santa en Jerusalén." *El Chaparrastique*, no. 2158, April 12, 1957, 1, 4.

———. *The Violence of Love*. Edited by James R. Brockman. Maryknoll, NY: Orbis Books, 2004.

———. *Voice of the Voiceless: The Four Pastoral Letters and Other Statements*. Translated by Michael J. Walsh. Maryknoll, NY: Orbis Books, 1985.

———. *La voz de los sin voz: La palabra viva de Monseñor Romero*. Edited by Rodolfo Cardenal, Ignacio Martín-Baro, and Jon Sobrino. San Salvador: UCA Editores, 1980.

Rousselot, Pierre. *The Problem of Love in the Middle Ages: A Historical Contribution*. Translated by Alan Vincelette. Milwaukee, WI: Marquette University Press, 2001.

Salaverri, Joaquín. "Motivación histórica y significación teológica del ignaciano 'sentir con la Iglesia.'" *Estudios Eclesiásticos* 31 (1957): 139–71.

Santiago, Daniel. *The Harvest of Justice: The Church of El Salvador Ten Years after Romero*. New York: Paulist Press, 1993.

Saranyana, Josep Ignasi, ed. *Teología en América Latina*. 3 vols. Vervuert: Iberoamericana, 1999–2002.

Scannone, Juan Carlos. "Cuestiones actuales de epistemología teológica: Aportes a la teología de la liberación." *Stromata* 46 (1990): 293–336.

———. "Perspectivas eclesiológicas de la 'teología del pueblo' en la Argentina." In *Ecclesia tertii millenii advenientis: Omaggio a P. Angel Antón, professore di ecclesiologia alla Pontificia Università Gregoriana nel suo 70° cumpleanno*, edited by E. Chica, S. Panizzolo, and H. Wagner. Casale Monferrato: PIEME, 1997.

———. "Pope Francis and the Theology of the People." *Theological Studies* 77 (2016): 118–35.

———. "La teología de la liberación: Caracterización, corrientes, etapas." *Stromata* 38 (1982): 3–40.

Scatena, Silvia, Jon Sobrino, and Luiz Carlos Susin, eds. *Fathers of the Church in Latin America*. London: SCM Press, 2009.

Schickendantz, Carlos. "Autoridad teológica de los acontecimientos históricos: Perplejidades sobre un lugar teológico." *Revista Teología* 115 (2015): 157–83.

Second Vatican Council. *Gaudium et Spes*. December 7, 1965. www.vatican.va/archive/hist_councils/ii_vatican_council/documents/vat-ii_const_19651207_gaudium-et-spes_en.html.

—————. *Sacrosanctum Concilium*. December 4, 1963. www.vatican.va/archive/hist_councils/ii_vatican_council/documents/vat-ii_const_19631204_sacrosanctum-concilium_en.html.

Segovia, Fernando. "Memorial Service for Monseñor Oscar Arnulfo Romero." *Apuntes* 34, no. 2 (2014): 38–51.

Seraphim of Sarov. *The Spiritual Instructions of Saint Seraphim of Sarov*. Edited by Franklin Jones. Los Angeles: Dawn Horse Press, 1991.

Shortell, Timothy. "Radicalization of Religious Discourse in El Salvador: The Case of Oscar A. Romero." *Sociology of Religion* 62 (2001): 87–103.

Silveira, María del Pilar. "La mujer en el pensamiento de Mons. Romero: Reflexión desde lo femenino en el 30 aniversario de su martirio." *Iter: Revista de Teología* 52 (2010): 257–72.

Snow Fletcher, LeAnn. "The De-domestication of the Cross: The El Salvadoran Experience." *Living Pulpit* 16, no. 2 (2007): 22–24.

Sobrino, Jon. *Archbishop Romero: Memories and Reflections*. Maryknoll, NY: Orbis Books, 1990.

—————. *Christology at the Crossroads*. Maryknoll, NY: Orbis Books, 1978.

—————, ed. *La espiritualidad de Monseñor Romero: Sentir con la Iglesia*. San Salvador: Fundación Monseñor Romero, 2015.

—————. "Introducción general." In Romero, *Homilías*, vol. 1.

—————. Introduction to *A Prophetic Bishop Speaks to His People: The Complete Homilies of Archbishop Oscar Arnulfo Romero*, vol. 1., translated by Joseph V. Owens. Miami, FL: Convivium Press, 2015.

—————. *Jesus the Liberator: A Historical-Theological View*. Maryknoll, NY: Orbis Books, 1993.

—————. *No Salvation Outside the Poor: Prophetic-Utopian Essays*. Maryknoll, NY: Orbis Books, 2008.

—————. *Witnesses to the Kingdom: The Martyrs of El Salvador and the Crucified Peoples*. Maryknoll, NY: Orbis Books, 2003.

Somme, Luc-Thomas. *Thomas d'Aquin la divinisation dans le Christ*. Geneva: Editions Ad Solem, 1998.

Spezzano, Daria. *The Glory of God's Grace: Deification According to St. Thomas Aquinas.* Ave Maria, FL: Sapientia Press, 2015.

Steenberg, Matthew C. *Of God and Man: Theology as Anthropology from Irenaeus to Athanasius.* London: Bloomsbury T&T Clark, 2009.

―――. "Two-Natured Man: An Anthropology of Transfiguration." *Pro Ecclesia* 14, no. 4 (2005): 413–32.

Steenberg, Matthew C., and M. C. Steenberg. *Irenaeus on Creation: The Cosmic Christ and the Saga of Redemption.* Leiden: Brill, 2008.

Stevenson, Kenneth. "From Hilary of Poitiers to Peter of Blois: A Transfiguration Journey of Biblical Interpretation." *Scottish Journal of Theology* 61, no. 3 (2008): 288–306.

Sullivan-Gonzalez, Douglass. *The Black Christ of Esquipulas: Religion and Identity in Guatemala.* Kindle ed. Lincoln: University of Nebraska Press, 2016.

Swanson, Todd. "A Civil Art: The Persuasive Moral Voice of Oscar Romero." *Journal of Religious Ethics* 29, no. 1 (2001): 127–44.

Tamez, Elsa. *The Amnesty of Grace: Justification by Faith from a Latin American Perspective.* Nashville, TN: Abingdon Press, 1993.

―――. *La hora de la vida: Lecturas bíblicas.* San José, Costa Rica: DIE, 1978.

―――. "Poverty, the Poor, and the Option for the Poor: A Biblical Perspective." In *The Option for the Poor in Christian Theology,* edited by Daniel Groody, 41–54. Notre Dame, IN: University of Notre Dame Press, 2007.

Taylor, Mark Lewis. "Subalternity and Advocacy as Kairos for Theology." In Rieger, *Opting for the Margins,* n.p.

Tojeira, José María. *El martirio ayer y hoy: Testimonio radical de fe y justicia.* San Salvador: UCA Editores, 2005.

Tolkien, J. R. R. *The Lord of the Rings: One Volume.* New York: Houghton Mifflin Harcourt, 2002.

Torres, Valerie. "*La Familia* as *Locus Theologicus* and Religious Education in *lo Cotidiano.*" *Religious Education* 105, no. 4 (2010): 444–61.

Tulud Cruz, Gemma. "Migration as *Locus Theologicus.*" *Colloquium* 46, no. 1 (2014): 87–100.

Uríbarri, Gabino, S.J. "El corazón de Jesús: Manantial que sacia la sed. Apuntes para una renovación de la teología del sagrado corazón." *Estudios Eclesiásticos* 84 (2009): 387–417.

―――. "'Cosmovisión de la esperanza': La actualidad del servicio de la Iglesia a la esperanza de la humanidad según *Gaudium et Spes.*" *Estudios Eclesiásticos* 81 (2006): 435–56.

Urioste, Ricardo. "Monseñor Romero y su 'sentir con la Iglesia.'" In *La espiritualidad de Monseñor Romero: Sentir con la Iglesia*, edited by Jon Sobrino, 59–81. San Salvador: Fundación Monseñor Romero, 2015.

Usanos, Rafael Amo. "La carne habituada a portar vida." *Estudios Eclesiásticos* 83 (2008): 425–55.

Valiente, O. Ernesto. *Liberation through Reconciliation: Jon Sobrino's Christological Spirituality*. New York: Fordham University Press, 2016.

Van den Eijden, Jan G. J. *Poverty on the Way to God: Thomas Aquinas on Evangelical Poverty*. Leuven: Thomas Institut te Utrecht, 1994.

Vigil, José María, and Ángel Torrellas. *Misas centroamericanas: Transcripción y comentario teológico*. Managua: Centro Ecuménico Antonio Valdivieso, 1988.

Viladesau, Richard. "*Theosis* and Beauty." *Theology Today* 65 (2008): 180–90.

von Balthasar, Hans Urs. *The Glory of the Lord*. Vol. 1. *Seeing the Form*. San Francisco: Ignatius Press, 1982.

———. *The Glory of the Lord*. Vol. 2. *Studies in Theological Style*. San Francisco: Ignatius Press, 1984.

———. "Martirio y misión." In *Puntos centrales de la fe*. Madrid: BAC, 1985.

———. *The Scandal of the Incarnation: Irenaeus against the Heresies*. San Francisco: Ignatius Press, 1990.

Wainwright, Geoffrey. "Der Gottesdienst als Locus Theologicus." *Kerygma und Dogma* 28, no. 4 (December 1982): 248–58.

Walatka, Todd. *Von Balthasar and the Option for the Poor: Theodramatics in the Light of Liberation Theology*. Washington, DC: Catholic University Press, 2017.

Ward, Thomas W. *Gangsters without Borders: An Ethnography of a Salvadoran Street Gang*. New York: Oxford University Press, 2013.

Whelan, Matthew P. "The Land of the Savior: Óscar Romero and the Reform of Agriculture." PhD diss., Duke University, 2016.

White, T. H. *The Once and Future King*. New York: Ace Books, 1987.

White, Thomas J. "Jesus' Cry on the Cross and His Beatific Vision." *Nova et Vetera* 5, no. 3 (2007): 555–82.

Williams, A. N. *The Ground of Union: Deification in Aquinas and Palamas*. New York: Oxford University Press, 1999.

Williams, Rowan. "A Saint for the Whole People of God: Oscar Romero and the Ecumenical Future." Lecture given at St. Chad's RC Cathedral, Birmingham, December 12, 2014. Archbishop Romero Trust. www.romerotrust.org.uk/sites/default/files/The%20Archbishop%20Romero%20Trust%20Annual%20Lecture%202014.pdf.

———. "Sentir con la Iglesia." Sermon preached at a service to mark the thirtieth anniversary of the martyrdom of Archbishop Oscar Romero, given at Westminster Abbey in March 2010. Archbishop Romero Trust. www.romerotrust.org.uk/sites/default/files/Rowan%20Williams%202010.pdf.

Wright, Scott. *Oscar Romero and the Communion of Saints.* Maryknoll, NY: Orbis Books, 2009.

———. *Promised Land: Death and Life in El Salvador.* Maryknoll, NY: Orbis Books, 1994.

Zechmeister, Martha. "Mons. Romero: Mártir por la dignidad humana." *Revista Latinoamericana de Teología* 97 (2016): 55–64.

Zynda, Damian. *Archbishop Oscar Romero: A Disciple Who Revealed the Glory of God.* Scranton, PA: University of Scranton Press, 2010.

EDGARDO COLÓN-EMERIC

is director of the Center for Reconciliation

at Duke Divinity School.